T0365129

HOW TO LIVE THE GOOD LIFE:

A USER'S GUIDE FOR *MODERN HUMANS*

HOW TO LIVE THE GOOD LIFE:

A USER'S GUIDE FOR *MODERN HUMANS*

ARTHUR JACKSON

*A theory-based, empirically-driven guide to making choices
that are in one's long-term best interest...*

*To live the Good Life it is essential to understand human nature...
understanding human nature has been the eternal puzzle...*

HOW TO LIVE THE GOOD LIFE:
A USER'S GUIDE FOR MODERN HUMANS

Copyright © 2019 Arthur Jackson.

*All rights reserved. No part of this book may be used or reproduced by any means,
graphic, electronic, or mechanical, including photocopying, recording, taping or by
any information storage retrieval system without the written permission of the author
except in the case of brief quotations embodied in critical articles and reviews.*

iUniverse books may be ordered through booksellers or by contacting:

*iUniverse
1663 Liberty Drive
Bloomington, IN 47403
www.iuniverse.com
1-800-Authors (1-800-288-4677)*

*Because of the dynamic nature of the Internet, any web addresses or links contained in
this book may have changed since publication and may no longer be valid. The views
expressed in this work are solely those of the author and do not necessarily reflect the
views of the publisher, and the publisher hereby disclaims any responsibility for them.*

*Any people depicted in stock imagery provided by Getty Images are models,
and such images are being used for illustrative purposes only.
Certain stock imagery © Getty Images.*

*ISBN: 978-1-5320-7141-6 (sc)
ISBN: 978-1-5320-7142-3 (e)*

Library of Congress Control Number: 2019903326

Print information available on the last page.

iUniverse rev. date: 04/01/2019

CONTENTS

IN MEMORY OF BARUCH DE SPINOZA

Baruch de Spinoza – Dutch philosopher born in 1632 in a Sephardic Portuguese family of wealth. Excommunicated in 1656. One of the world's first thinkers to realize that meaning of life is part of the natural realm and subject to scientific consideration.

He used the term *conatus* – maintaining life with well-being which I interpret as "meaning of life." In my mind he opened the critical door joining science and religion which unfortunately was immediately slammed shut primarily due to the dominant power of religion in that time, and still is kept closed now primarily by those in the domain of science.

I originally had ignored Spinoza for all the wrong reasons and as a result had to make this critical discovery myself. *Meaning of life* is the concept that ties everything together. Without it the puzzle remains as myriads of disconnected pieces.

Spinoza got to the right answer first and deserves the homage of any who are now ready to reopen the door and move into the wonderful future of humanity this makes possible.

Arthur M. Jackson

APPRECIATION – PAST, PRESENT, AND FUTURE☺ 4

The author is deeply appreciative to all the people who through their questions and answers stimulated the desire to write this book which is seen as supporting the final steps in moving the human vision from focusing on the supernatural to focusing on the natural.

Especial appreciation to <u>Fred March</u> for his support in understanding exactly what I was attempting to achieve. <u>Gene Hudson</u> was of special importance in taking the ragged product of this effort and moving it many steps toward being more interesting and readable. He spent numerous difficult hours wading through my thick prose and working to get me to lighten up. <u>Shari Webber</u> carefully read and provided feedback and suggestions to help improve the clarity and focus. <u>Bob Stephens</u> has been a fountain of encouragement over many years. His support and comments have nudged me to plow on when most of my brain said, "give it up!" And for providing the final push I would like to thank <u>Richard and Barbara Lau</u> who produced the window of opportunity giving me the motivation to take the impossible step of actually producing hard copies – rough as they have been -- for distribution. To <u>Hilton and Flora Brown</u> special thanks are due for providing a place and being parts of a group to examine in-depth, over time the product of all this effort. To <u>Sue Fera</u> for leading me by the hand to move into a new realm, bringing computer automation into manuscript formatting, and reducing the hours of drudgery necessary to format and deal with the index and such. To <u>Jennifer Bardi</u> and <u>Fred Edwords</u> for helping me obtain the great cover for this new edition of my book. And last but not least many thanks to <u>Adrienne Juliano</u> for her careful reviewing and editing to produce the current edition, but even more importantly the validation that I'm not the only one who thinks what I have done is important. Of course the final product is totally my responsibility.

To you the reader I also give heartfelt thanks. Without you this would still only be a fantasy darting around in my brain. I solicit your input, suggestions, criticism, corrections large and small, and support. Also, I solicit your help and advice not only to improve what I have done, but for ideas to see how to open this window wider and share it with the world.

Forward by Frederic March
Past President of the Albuquerque Chapter of
The American Humanist Association

There are many books, secular and religious that instruct us on how to live the good life. But Arthur Jackson stands apart in grounding his approach on a system of philosophical wisdom informed by personal experience and a scientific view of human nature. The book avoids proverb-like simplicity in favor of a systematic treatment for intellectually curious minds seeking an in-depth understanding of potential pathways to an improved human condition through Humanism grounded on two books by psychoanalyst Erich Fromm:

1. PSYCHOANALYSIS AND RELIGION
2. AN INQUIRY INTO THE PSYCHOLOGY OF ETHICS

Life is not a selfish pursuit. Rather, the good life is achieved by adapting our minds to the tasks of helping humanity as a whole. Hence this book is grounded on a solid foundation of cognitive science.

And for Jackson, achieving the good life is not a selfish pursuit. Rather, the good life is achieved by adapting our minds to the tasks of helping humanity as a whole. His approach begins with a focus on religion that discards its old foundation of willful spirits as causal agents in favor of a new foundation of human nature revealed by science. It is not possible to convey the book's richness and system without an overview, however brief and inadequate, of its carefully constructed architecture.

Chapter 1: Humanity's Goal defines targets for humanity as a whole, pursuit of which can help each of us find our personal paths to the good life. The chapter's Table 1 is a brilliant stroke. It lists ten categories societal *Wisdom Potential* areas as they were manifested in our tribal ancestors as well as modern tribal societies, and contrasts each one with it respective "wisdom potential."

Chapter 2: Science of Religion and Ethics: presents a challenging new approach to the classical problem of "meaning" in our lives by applying a "science of religion and ethics. " This is a philosophical pursuit informed by "the practical application of wisdom," that introduces Jackson's system. The following chapters explore its various aspects.

Chapter 3: How to Live the Good Life describes a "science of religion and ethics" in some detail as a pathway to improving human communities at all scales including our global civilization.

Chapter 4: Humans as the Ultimate Reference System focuses on ways to replace "folk religions" by new institutions that "help real people with their real problems...to dramatically improve the quality of each person's life." With this in mind he reminds us *"humans are the ultimate reference system"* because that is the way that nature has configured their minds.

Chapter 5: Religious and Moral Behavior focuses on *"using a person's wisdom potential to achieve a sustainable feeling of well-being.* "Jackson presents 11 principles of "the Way to Wisdom" as a foundation for moral character development and as a strategy for transforming human society for the better.

Chapter 6: The Enlightened Person explores the nature of a person whose life is informed by the wisdom principles in the previous chapter to achieve attitudes capable of cultivating "a sustainable feeling of well-being."

Chapter 7: The Enlightened Community describes the kind of society we can achieve when its members are largely "enlightened persons."

Chapters 8-18 explore in some depth the meanings of each of the 11 wisdom principles defined in Chapter 5.

Chapter 19: Organizing an Enlightened Community; Chapter 20: Other Support Organizations: and Chapter 21: Spreading Meaning – A New Foundation for Civilization. These chapters focus on ways to actually achieve a global civilization grounded on enlightened communities.

How to Live the Good Life is a highly original and well thought out approach to human well-being that seems to recognize that many people today are already implementing some of those principles and strategies. I believe that the United Nations Declaration of Human Rights and its Millennium Development Goal embody important parts of Jackson's 10 Wisdom Potential Areas from Chapter 1; and the 11 Wisdom Principles at the heart of his book. The founding documents of the American Republic also seem to reflect some of this wisdom, but have lost considerable ground in the political turmoil of recent years.

The Economist scored 167 nations for their quality of democracy. Only thirty were "full democracies." The top ten included five Scandinavian countries plus Luxembourg, Holland, Switzerland. New Zealand and Australia. The U.S. ranked 18th I would love to see someone from a progressive think tank publish a study of how these top 10 plus the United States stack up against Jackson's criteria for enlightened nations. For those that want to go deeper into Jackson's approach he offers a series of 39 essays in a Volume II whose chapter titles appear in Volume I. The actual content is available at a website provided in the book.

In summary, I highly recommend this book to people who are serious about exploring sound philosophical and scientific principles at the heart of the American Humanist Association.

INTRODUCTION

HOW TO LIVE THE GOOD LIFE
(Also see Appendix A)

> *There is only one Good, Knowledge.*
> *There is only one Evil, Ignorance.*
>
> *Socrates*

How to Live the Good Life is a theory-based, empirical, experiment-driven effort to provide guidance to any sufficiently interested person in making moral choices; that is, those choices that are in their long-term best interest. It has as its organizing principle *"the meaning of human life"* (operationally defined). A primary premice of this approach is that "human beings are the ultimate reference system." This ties science into the meaning-of-human-life issue and makes clear that the purpose of science is not to understand the universe as it actually exists, but rather to integrate knowledge (i.e., improve our ability to predict) and work to ensure that all knowledge is used to help increasing numbers of people to improve their quality of life.

The aim of this book is the synthesis of all knowledge into one congruent, naturalistic system in which everything fits together and flows from one fact to another without artificial bridges or connections. The goal of this synthesis is to clarify how all human beings can achieve a meaningful life that must be based on their human nature. The search is for real meaning and worthwhile living based on knowledge and understanding. It attributes the current conditions of fruitless, nonproductive, useless human suffering, affliction, and anguish in the form of starvation, poverty, disease, depression, and so on to our collective ignorance. Knowledge is seen as providing the means for each individual to achieve their full positive potential.

A Brief Overview of this book is provided in Appendix A. You may find it helpful to read the overview before continuing.

How to Live the Good Life *interprets the "meaning of life" for the members of each species as being the perpetuation of their species. To do that individual members of the species are programmed to take nourishment, reproduce, and die. However, since the survival of the human species depends on changing memes (words, concepts, ideas; i.e., beliefs) even more than on changing genes, meaning of life for human beings involves their beliefs (memes) not just their genes. In order to achieve their full positive potential it is necessary that a person recognize that a sustainable feeling that their life has meaning comes out of their efforts to maintain and develop the human species. The beliefs that sustain this feeling can only be determined empirically (by studying people and societies). A given belief must be measured in terms of its effects on all of humanity and over generations, not merely in terms of some small segment of a particular person's life.*

To understand How to Live the Good Life: A User's Guide for Modern Humans *it needs to be read from front to back. If it is skimmed for general evaluation, or dipped into randomly the reader should recognize essential understanding will be lacking. Each idea depends on those that have already been presented. In order to develop the ideas presented here it has been necessary to redefine or give a different spin to essentially every significant concept in Western thought. Unless this is recognized and the new meanings utilized the reader is likely to miss the point of this effort by assuming the ideas being presented are ones they are familiar with.*

There will be some who question the wisdom of redefining these words. They would agree with the Ordinary Language Philosophers who say one should not use a word except as it is commonly understood. I follow a path closer to that of Bertrand Russell who had a goal to make words into accurate instruments of thought. My understanding of words is that they are tools for communication -- whether in one's own brain, or with others -- of either things existing in the world or in human minds.

When someone first gets the glimmer of a concept that is then expressed by a word or collection of words, it is normal that the person's grasp of the issue is fragmentary and misfocused. Possibly they are unaware of things that are crucial if they are to develop an accurate definition. As more is learned the definition must be altered to include this added knowledge. This is an essential process in the advancement of thought. A word's meaning must evolve as experience and thought evolve otherwise there is a force to maintain the status quo as well as outmoded ideas and behavior. It is my belief that the words providing the key ideas supporting our culture have severe deficiencies. Examples of such words are: religion, reality, science, meaning of life, good life, utopia, Enlightenment, psychology, sociology, anthropology, good mental health, human nature, good/evil, symbolic language, freedom, soul, God, and so on. Unless these weaknesses are corrected our thinking is severely retarded. **_As E.O. Wilson wisely points out, "The first step to wisdom, as the Chinese say, is getting things by their right name."_** [1] **_So far no society has gotten the key things by their right name._**

In keeping with the foregoing goal fanatical efforts are used here to avoid sexist language since the envisioned community demands the full participation of all members of the society. Therefore, no words are assigned either male or female gender just because this is customarily done. All unspecified individuals are assumed to be female as likely as male. Rather than using many he/she pronouns, "they" is frequently used in an effort to expand the modern practice permitting this option.

Although this book got its start in the mid-50s as a short essay for a college ethics class, it was only recently that I realized I have been struggling all these years to create a naturalistic *science of religion* incorporating a *science of ethics*. Before that I thought religion required the supernatural based on authority and/or custom. And I took ethics to be a collection of ideas having essentially no value in helping people select better over worse choices. Partially that was because I had become convinced that all behavior has an ethical dimension, and it, therefore, didn't seem useful to talk about religion and ethics/morals. However, I changed my mind about discarding ethics/morals as an area of discussion after reading Frans De Waal's book, *Good Natured,* forced me to recognize the value of ethics/morals -- that I use interchangeably. [2] (Also, see Volume II, Chapter 18-A, "Ethics, Morality, and Science," where De Waal's book is analyzed in some depth.) [3]

De Waal's writing convinced me that I had made a mistake. I now realize that when properly analyzed ethics is crucial in guiding human choices. And it is a key part of a naturalistic religion that must be the foundation on which everything important to human beings rests. A *science of religion and ethics* would not only guide all human behavior, it would lead to a more accurate definition of science itself. However, many people have been convinced that the foregoing thinking is based on erroneous ideas. One source of such thinking was the British philosopher G. E. Moore who in his 1903 book *Principia Ethica* named this the "naturalistic fallacy." [4] This conclusion results from a failure to recognize that we live in an empirical universe governed by "if-then," rather than one governed by Platonic ideals. Therefore, this position has prematurely been discarded as an option for these individuals. Though Moore has implied that there can be no *science of religion and ethics* because of the "naturalistic fallacy," he was clearly wrong. As a philosopher he thought of "ought" as a Platonic ideal – like the idea of a perfect circle. If religion and ethics/morals are defined empirically as dealing with beliefs that move a person toward or away from achieving their full positive potential, then these terms become meaningful within the naturalistic framework of science.

At the same time beliefs become subject to scientific study and we can determine with varying degrees of certainty if a particular belief moves us toward or away from achieving our full positive potential. This determination may not be easy or even 100% accurate for a specific belief, but it should be at least as accurate as indicating that a given medicine, vaccine, or food will promote the health or well-being of a particular person.

Since ethics and morality have been at the heart of philosophy and religion for thousands of years, clearly they are important. And, due to the long history during which these terms have been used, and because of their fundamental role in current thought they now seem to me to not only be worth salvaging, but to provide the mechanism for turning the soft sciences into hard sciences and in fact providing the foundation upon which all science rests.

***How to Live the Good Life: A User's Guide for* Modern Humans** currently consists of two volumes. VOLUME I -- presented here -- discusses the basic ideas [in Chapter Two] that lay the foundation for a *science of religion and ethics*. When key terms are introduced prior to Chapter Two they will be briefly defined so the reader need not guess what they might mean. Also, they are defined in the Glossary.

VOLUME II [5] provides additional supportive evidence, information, ideas, and so on for the material provided in the following pages.

The view presented here is that the human condition can best be improved by expanding science to include naturalistic religions that provide an organizing principle able to connect all knowledge into one congruent whole, available for use by all people. When any group is able to work to achieve the foregoing, I call this state "utopia." For me utopia is not a static, perfect state. Rather, it is the state that exists when a group is working collectively to improve the human condition.

To accomplish the foregoing a *science of religion and ethics* is required to plainly set forth the specifications necessary in order for human beings to achieve their full positive potential. For me all of this boils down to clarifying how people can experience more joy and experience it now and all of their tomorrows.

Because a *science of religion and ethics* would be concerned with all knowledge, anything written about it can be true only in the sense that any scientific principle is true -- that it leads to better understanding, new insights, more successful prediction, and so on.

The reader must view this book in that light. If they are looking for Truth in the Platonist sense, they will not find it here. The ideas presented are not seen as invariant truths, but rather as theories, hypotheses, or possibilities. If further thought or research shows them to be untenable or untrue, they must be discarded.

On the other hand this is a science focused on helping people to make the best choices possible in their life. It speaks for joy in living and focused action. More than that, it demands action. A *science of religion and ethics* is meant to change the world; to replace inadequate societies with better ones. The aim is to determine what is good and lasting in life and how such may be attained. The foregoing is a scientific pursuit and must be pursued scientifically. From the perspective of a *science of religion and ethics,* faith-based and authority-based societies can never be wholly adequate for any of their members. More humane and honest communities must be achieved. Herein lies a framework that, I hope, will help the reader join with others in building better communities, and make clear what "better" means.

Throughout history religions have been set up to tell people what to believe, what to do, as well as the how, what, where, when, and why of it all based on an authoritative if not authoritarian foundation. A *science of religion and ethics*, however, is a theory-based system dependent on empirical findings. It requires that participants become agents for change in whatever ways are necessary to allow them and an ever-increasing number of people to benefit from its ideas, recommendations, and practices. If readers would like to see a *science of religion and ethics* developed, they could do this by helping to establish organizations to work with other interested people to turn the vision presented here into reality.

Unless this book sparks a dialogue, action, and focused effort, it has failed in its purpose. To participate in a *science of religion and ethics* discussion group contact the author (arthur@arthurmjackson.com).

PREFACE

The aim of this book is to use the science paradigm to promote the establishment of a *science of religion and ethics* and encourage the development of Wisdom Groups that would function in a way analogous to hospitals and engineering companies; that is, they would use available, relevant scientific findings to help people live the Good Life and in the process expand scientific knowledge. Both of these are attempts to help people achieve maximum personal freedom and to use it well. These efforts are simply an expansion of the first and second goals of wisdom. The first goal of wisdom: Escape the bondage produced by the accident of one's birth. The second goal of wisdom is: Avoid replacing restrictions imposed by birth with different ones that dictate equally irrational limits on the ability to think and act.

Normally a person automatically accepts the religion and values of the family into which they have been born without much thought or examination. I was unable to follow that pattern. As a result I have labored since early youth to find alternative answers for the meaning of life. The ideas presented here developed out of those efforts to find answers that would guide my life that I could believe in enthusiastically without embarrassment, or being mentally shackled.

Common wisdom tells us that in catastrophe lies opportunity. I've been very fortunate because my early life afforded such opportunity. I grew up in a single-parent, dysfunctional family, without a father, in poverty, with almost no social ties, moving at least once a year, and some years as many as seven times. Collectively, all these things provided me something that was priceless. They set me free for my own wisdom quest, receptive to ideas from all cultures and all of history, and ultimately, they have led to the publication of this book.

My life's quest has been to fit all relevant ideas into one congruent whole. My conviction is that I have found a way to do this. Unfortunately, this approach -- which I take to be the only one that will work -- involves ideas considered taboo by most members of current societies -- those with a scientific bent as well as those more in tune with the humanities, not to mention a broad spectrum of nonacademics.

I claim to have laid the basis for a *science of religion and ethics* utilizing as an organizing principle *"meaning of human life."* I believe through good fortune -- being in the right places at the right time -- I have been able to ask many of the right questions. And, though I certainly haven't found the final answers, I hope that what I have assembled provides insights that will allow others to better focus on developing the answers humanity needs in order to get through the difficult years ahead and blaze a path toward a future in which each person is a self-fulfilled participant in a worldwide utopian society with a clear vision of what it takes to sustain this lovely planet with sufficient biodiversity to keep it an awesome place for human living.

I was raised in a Christian family with a single-parent mother, a younger brother, and an older sister by a previous marriage. We moved a great deal since Mother as the sole breadwinner had to play every angle to provide the necessities of life with limited advantages to draw from. Although for brief periods we lived near family, mostly we grew up pretty much independent of strong social ties. Outside sources of values, guidance, rules, standards, and requirements -- schools, churches, newspapers, movies, and related sources of input -- were disembodied forces even when enthusiastically embraced. As a result rarely was there clear guidance in setting personal goals, assessing abilities and weaknesses, evaluating motivations, and such. I rarely if ever consciously accepted anything just because it was the custom, or because it was supported by authority. Unless something made sense to me based on my own experience and understanding the best I could do was to reserve judgment until I gathered more data. That was the background for my interactions with religion.

Our family was Protestant (nonpracticing); however after I reached school age my mother encouraged us kids to attend Sunday School. I did so intermittently over the next several years even though I never liked it. Even when kind acts were done such as providing Christmas presents to our poor family, my primary feeling was shame rather than appreciation. The thing that finally led to my separation from church attendance at around the age of ten was my recognition of the implications of the ongoing message: "Only we are saved. All others are damned to Hell."

For me rather than being a reason to be with the "saved" this was rather a reason to opt out of a group with such a cruel God. Part of what made this possible were the effects of our frequent moves as I was growing up. I had attended various Protestant churches of different denominations. They all told the same story: "Only we are saved." It was the recognition that although they couldn't all be right, they all could be wrong that caused me to stop going to Sunday School. But for reasons I can't explain I wanted to learn what was right and what was wrong. I assume that this was part of a basic human drive for social connection, which each person plays out in a way appropriate to her or his particular circumstances.

I spent the next ten years or so of my life wading through religious ideas in an attempt to clarify this point. During this time I discovered science and was immediately attracted by its approach. This became an ever-expanding source of study and interest for me, which eventually led to my becoming a science teacher for six years. But since in my community science was suspect and religion was not, I continued to explore religion. As I searched for answers I alternated among the options available to me from examining various religions; agnosticism; atheism; being overwhelmed by confusion, fear, conflicting messages; being "turned off;" feeling ready to try again; going through such issues in a big spiral moving slowly toward clarity which happened when I found humanism, the American Humanist Association, and the International Humanist and Ethical Union.

I started off accepting without even realizing it, the core Christian assumptions: God created the universe, Jesus was God, people have immortal souls that go to Heaven or Hell depending on how they live, the Bible was written by God, and much, much more. Slowly, I began to identify more and more of these things that had been accepted with no conscious thought. As I learned that these things were not rational, logical, universally accepted, or useful for me, I tentatively doubted most of my culture's religious beliefs as I worked to determine to what extent I had been misled. This was not done consciously as part of a master plan, but rather feebly, haltingly, and with uncertainty. I searched and searched for a rational position. I did not necessarily expect to have every question answered. But I did want some assurance that my beliefs would have a better foundation than the accident of being born into my particular culture. I searched and listened to everyone I could find who had relevant things to say about religion. But their positions were always inadequate.

I began with tentative doubt. As my search to find a combination of reason and Christianity met with continued failure, my doubt became less and less tentative. In this first stage of doubt I was ashamed because I doubted and largely kept my doubt to myself. I could see that there were many things wrong with the supernatural view, but I still believed enough of the associated ideas to have a shaky foundation from which to look for an alternative belief system.

Eventually, I realized that it cannot be proven whether God exists or does not exist. More important, I realized that it does not matter whether or not She exists. Her [1] existence or lack thereof has nothing to do with humanity. Those who most profoundly and most deeply study God recognize that God is the Great Silence [2]. Any messages from God turn out to only be echoes from within the suggestible person's own brain. Our only connection with God is through other people, or a "feeling" in our brain. Either way it's our own thinking that guides us. We decide whether or not to be guided by our priest, family, friends, customs, and such. So the fact of God would be irrelevant since there is no way of knowing God's will, what God has in mind for us. Anyone who says they know God's will has a great deal to prove.

In addition it became clear to me that even if God's footprints could be clearly seen, the existence of God would not ensure human beings meaning per se. Given God, people might still be the accidental products of other God directed goals, or have been produced for other reasons, and such. So, in what way does God's existence provide people meaning? This is what the system presenting a worldview that makes up a given church has always tried to answer. In a universal sense, they have always failed because the results were not successful -- as measured by objective evidence -- even within the society of origin. When "missionaried" out of that society, they were even less successful, and frequently horrendous.

Christianity has destroyed numerous people and societies and needs to bear the responsibility for those deeds (along with the praise for its message of love and efforts that have led to the recognition of the importance of the person). Folk religions [3] in critical ways will always fail because their strength is in their appeal to the "tribal" genetic propensities -- belief in magic and the power of wishing, us vs. them, dominance/submission, territorial imperative. ("Tribal" propensities are discussed in Chapter One.) Focusing on, and promoting these propensities prevent the development of the parts of the mind essential for the long-term survival of our species, and the development of our "Symbolic Species," [4] or "wisdom" potential. For all these reasons I conclude that worldviews based on the God concept will always promote instability within the species.

We can only know what we are and not what God is. I saw that it is important not that we inquire into the nature of God, but that we inquire into the nature of human beings. When I discarded all supernatural explanations, I accepted a path not a position. This was the quest for Wisdom -- the spiritual quest.

I am not interested in destroying any person's religion. Rather, I want to build an approach based on wisdom that will make life better for everyone. The ultimate refutation of folk religions consists of providing an alternative that each person accepts eagerly because they realize it is truly what they have wanted all the time. An inability to accomplish the foregoing of course by default tends toward maintaining current folk religions and the present state of the world, and places a big question mark on the relevance of the ideas presented here.

Part of that current state of the world includes the threat of world calamity that could actually wipe out our species. Another part of that current state of the world is the existence of starvation, disease, poverty, corruption, ignorance, exploitation, suppression, abuse, crime, war, and all those atrocities perpetrated by Adolf Hitler, Stalin, the Ku Klux Klan, and all the other tyrants -- petty and not so petty -- throughout human history. All of these problems are in a fundamental way tied into the inherent, unfixable problems within folk religions that would be effectively addressed by a *science of religion and ethics*.

Folk religions have diverted human thinking from the real to the fanciful because they focus on confusing terms like Good vs. Evil which are Platonist ideals rather than on terms like *knowledge vs. ignorance* which are empirical concepts that include things that exist in the real world. Folk religions often say that the vicious actions by many people show that there is Evil in the universe. But for a *science of religion and ethics* the problem is not Good vs. Evil. That is where folk religions have misled us from the very beginning. The problem is between *knowledge and ignorance. Knowledge* provides us the potential to find Wisdom. I define *wisdom* as that aspect of *knowledge* which when applied to a person's life increases the probability that they will achieve their goals and that those goals will include achieving their full positive potential.

Today, we can move farther in the direction of becoming our best self than people of previous ages only because of the knowledge and experience past generations have provided us. <u>However, only an Enlightened Community has the required goals, structures and priorities for using resources to provide the necessary assistance each person needs</u> to achieve a sustainable feeling of well-being.

No person can become an Enlightened Person only through their raw "genetic" propensities. Part of what stops us is the trauma of our own childhood. We all have been subjected to so many destructive influences that most of us need therapeutic counseling and support to work through these barriers. Part of these influences is cultural -- all the errors, distortions, lies, and so on we have been exposed to, and that have influenced our thinking. These are too many, and too deeply imbedded in our being to get rid of by doing a little reading. People don't transcend their upbringing with four years of college education in which they study scores of books, many of them among the best yet written and spend countless hours of bull sessions with fellow classmates exploring the deepest questions they can ask. Even if this book were correct in every detail -- and it is not -- it could not permit someone to immediately metamorphose into an Enlightened Person, or achieve their full positive potential. It is my belief that a person can only become an Enlightened Person through active participation in an appropriately structured organization -- a Wisdom Group, and related organizations. Without the necessary organizations any progress will be too piecemeal and disorganized to initiate rapid, yet stabilizing changes.

The goal of this book is twofold: 1) to lay the basis for a *science of religion and ethics* and 2) to encourage the growth of organizations to help people apply the findings of a *science of religion and ethics*. My primary concern is not for what will ultimately happen, but to do a better job in handling the pain and suffering, the waste of lives that occurs today. My intent is to bring about conditions with as little delay as possible, which will ensure that all people achieve a joyful life based on knowledge, and contribute in the best ways possible to maintaining and developing the human species.

It is my fondest hope that this book will help many churches, synagogues, mosques, temples, and groups from every folk religion to see more clearly their mission and become part of the Wisdom Network to apply the findings of a *science of religion and ethics*. This would allow religion to move out of its enmeshment in separate cultural groups dependent on mysticism, obscurantism, custom, and authority. This would permit humanity to move toward a universality that will include all people based on cooperation, the methods of science, and study utilizing the relevant experiences drawn from as many people and societies as possible. Structures would be developed that are based on universal principles and therefore work for the cooperative benefit of all people. And these structures would exist in every society thereby helping each person to develop their full positive potential. However, this will not be achieved easily, and part of the reason is discussed later in connection with religious fundamentalists.

However, it needs to be recognized that folk religions have done as well as could reasonably be expected considering the time in which they developed. Historically, they have, in fact, gotten us through our difficult "childhood" of the past 50,000 years or so since our language ability evolved to a critical point. Since that time I believe humanity has been in the process of creating itself [5] out of the genetic elements of our evolutionary past. This has happened very fast because cultural evolution is so much faster than genetic evolution. Up to the evolution of the modern language ability human beings had "meaning of life" as a natural aspect of their existence in the same way as do the ants, bees, termites, and every other living thing. When human beings achieved their current language ability people gained the potential to evaluate their own existence and become "self determining and intentional creatures. [6] At that point we became capable of asking the question, what is the meaning of life? Why choose life rather than death?

And, that is the question each person today still needs to answer regardless of what she or he believes or what they doubt. They still need to get through this life -- or, choose not to. Since human beings are social animals, human warmth and affection are critical to this endeavor. The Wisdom Quest involves people working together and grounding their efforts on the methods of science. I have spent my life looking for others to work with in pursuit of the foregoing goal.

I realize in retrospect that when I studied ethics in college I had expected to find the answers about how to live the good life. I assumed these answers would be provided by those many learned people who had gone before. Instead, I found that not only had philosophers not blazed a clear path toward the good life that everyone could follow, they tended to focus their intellectual talents on every issue but the one I saw as being most important: meaning of human life.

As I began to understand the foregoing points, I decided then to tackle the problem myself and develop a science of philosophy to help myself and anyone else who was interested in finding the meaning of life through understanding the natural world. I have pursued that path ever since. However, I have recently recognized that what I actually have created is a *science of religion and ethics*. But this came about only after I recognized the relationship between folk religions, philosophy, science, and a *science of religion and ethics*. I now believe the key to this understanding is as follows: Folk religions are based on nonfalsifiable assumptions -- their claims are not testable, and they are not subject to experimental justification, nor refutation. In addition they cannot be questioned because this violates their traditions and their appeal to authority. Philosophy also is based on nonverifiable assumptions. However, the claims of philosophy can be examined, questioned, and recombined in new ways. Therefore, this is a fertile area of exploration. When assumptions are generated that are falsifiable they move out of philosophy into the realm of science. Basically this is the way that philosophy gave birth to the sciences, one by one, as it provided the testable assumptions on which each field of science rests. This is why there can be no Science of Philosophy. A *science of religion and ethics* requires an understanding of human nature in ways that were not possible until the development of evolutionary psychology and an evolutionary understanding of symbolic language. Further, it is based on an organizing principle or concept, which lays the basis for testable assumptions. Wisdom Groups would need to develop structures to use that knowledge to help build Enlightened Communities made up of Enlightened Persons. In other words, utopias.

If we are to make the final breakthrough and achieve our unique potential as goal-directed individuals it is essential to develop Wisdom Groups, based on a *science of religion and ethics*. A *science of religion and ethics* is not only the right answer; it is the obvious answer. But who will set up the Wisdom Groups? Who will lead us toward development of the Enlightened Community? Will you? Vital tasks need to be done. Any interested person can help. I hope you will join me in taking this step toward building a utopia to support humanity's progress toward the light at the end of the tunnel.

PROLOGUE

COMBINING SCIENCE AND RELIGION

Humanity is in desperate need of a new paradigm, and since I have spent most of my life struggling with this issue for my own life I think I have something constructive to offer. I present the following as essential assumptions or definitions in this new paradigm.

1. Science is the search for congruency; that is, the uniformity of nature.
2. Humanity itself is our ultimate reference system.
3. A New Foundation for Civilization is needed:

   a. The **Old foundation** – Spirit causality (i.e., God/supernatural), or reason (i.e., assumptions the truth of which are taken to be self-evident) – conflicts with current assumptions about knowledge.
   d. b. The **New foundation** – Human nature (i.e., empirical study based on an understanding of human evolution) – is what is recommended in this book.

This new paradigm is explored in detail in this book. My basic assumption is that there is only the natural world – that can be studied, experienced, and understood. However, that natural world is so much beyond our regular experiences that our common understanding of it is always limited and frequently inaccurate; therefore, true, self-evident assumptions have not been found up to this point, and I predict they never will be.

At the core of my new paradigm is the recognition that human nature lies totally in the natural world and has been imposed on us by our evolutionary history through our genetic propensities. Therefore all aspects of this matter are open to scientific study.

The essence of our being is the fact that we are social animals.

The most relevant of our genetic propensities imposed on us by our evolutionary history is our ability to use symbolic language. This put our species on a path toward what I call the "light at the end of the tunnel." This is the state in which human beings have reached dynamic stability based on memes (see Glossary). The tunnel is the metaphor for the path humanity has pursued since *Homo sapiens sapiens* evolved symbolic language and became *Modern Humans* some 50,000 to 100,000 years ago, and individuals lost their direct dependence on genes for their behavior; that is, their instincts.

Our genetic propensities that evolved from earlier instincts are imposed on us by our evolutionary past and provide the motivations that make us who we are. And who we are is the question for which the answer has been our concern since we became *Modern Humans*. Only in recent decades has the answer begun to become clear: Our species must achieve dynamic stability through memes rather than through genes as is done by all other species. Clarifying this matter lies at the core of my book.

At the heart of who we are is our nature shaped by our hunter-gatherer experiences over millions of years. The secret of living the Good Life is buried in that experience.

As I lay out in these writings, when we fully accept what our nature is we are then well on our way to living the Good Life. I take meaning of life as the concept that will guide everything else.

I believe that religion lies at the core of what we need to understand. To ignore it or misinterpret it is to flirt with disaster. Its essence exists totally in the natural domain and understanding it is crucial to relevant conversations about the future of humanity. The naturalistic components of religion are open to scientific study and understanding. Its supernatural components are only the gaudy wrapping that most people – including Richard Dawkins, Daniel Dennett, and Christopher Hutchins – apparently mistake as its essence. However, the supernatural is merely an element of spirit causality that has been with us for a long time. The supernatural is just a product of how brains work. So it, too, is open to scientific understanding! Religion's role in a society is to provide the binding force to help people work together in ways that benefit all, and provides a meaning for their life. When a particular formulation of the ideas for doing this fails, the society is in trouble, as is ours. Any who fail to recognize this point and to act appropriately to it are contributing to the chaos.

It is widely recognized that U.S. religious structures are not doing a satisfactory job. And I would venture to say that they never have. However, finding alternatives is what we don't know, what nobody knows in the essential way. My claim is that I am providing a blueprint to take us from chaos to order. I can't claim my blueprint is perfect. If it were it would already be producing the needed results. But I'm willing to claim that it points in the right direction and has the potential to change the world in the right way.

I hope that you, the reader, will be interested in supporting this approach. If you are, please contact me.

From the beginning of *Modern Human* history, communities have depended on the social structure known as religion to preserve the group. Religion's responsibility was to produce the stories and behaviors that would foster the survival of the group. When it failed, the group faltered and either disappeared or adopted a new religion more appropriate to the times.

Perhaps the best-known example of the foregoing is the Protestant Reformation when geographical groups of Roman Catholics became what were called Protestants because they were protesting the elitism and corruption of the Roman Catholic Church. The time when groups of Jews and gentiles became Christians and later when Roman "pagans" became Christians are other instances of this. A different kind of example is provided by ancient Egypt when, over time, the state religion stagnated producing loss of cohesion, vigor, and purpose, and eventual collapse of the culture.

Religion up to this time has been based on supernatural beliefs. A *science of religion and ethics* proposes that the core of this process relies on a genetic "tribal" propensity that encourages belief in magic and the power of wishing. This propensity plays out in myriad ways depending on the cultural specifics of the group. My best guess is that this propensity is based on what is called *hope* in human beings. It exists as the reward part of the flight or fight response in contrast to fear that is the punishment component. Of course this physiological state has been shaped by evolution for its value in increasing the likelihood of survival of the individual and thereby the survival of our species.

A breakthrough in human progress began when the ancient Greeks developed philosophy as a rational, alternative way to explain the elements of human life and the world in general. Philosophy tapped into humanity's "wisdom" potential made possible by symbolic language. In the realm of philosophy unlike in religion ideas could be questioned and new answers adopted. This leap forward began in Greece because its ruling aristocracy had an unusual combination of values including leisure time, education based on rhetoric, and independence from oppressive social control.

Over the course of time philosophy itself separated into two parts: 1) traditional speculative philosophy based on rational thinking, and 2) natural philosophy based on a more rigorous empirical study of the world from a naturalistic perspective independent of the gods and other supernatural entities.

In the 1840s natural philosophy became science and the differences between naturalistic science and supernatural religions became increasingly more obvious. At the same time the understanding of how things function increasingly moved out of the realm of religion into the realm of science. Astrology became astronomy. Alchemy became chemistry. Geology, biology, and the other early sciences were formalized. In addition practical applications of science became increasingly important as this knowledge began to be used to support commerce and community.

There were many factors that helped produce these changes. Underlying this process was an empirical attitude that captured the imagination of many Western intellectuals. This led to a widespread interest in studying the things of the world to understand how they actually behaved. The findings and tools of the craftsperson were valued and utilized rather than being shrugged off as vulgar and irrelevant as had been done by the elitist Greeks. An additional motivation came in the response by reasonable people to the fanatical, repressive, cruel, exploitive mystical explanations Christianity then provided. Some changes were favored because societies in Western Europe existed as small, independent groups within a larger shared culture. This permitted people oppressed in one place to find shelter elsewhere that promoted cross-pollination of ideas that increased the speed of the search to find how the world functioned. This knowledge about the things of the world slowly accumulated over time and was recognized by some thoughtful people as conflicting with the dogmatic answers provided by their religions.

However, in spite of the widespread recognition of the critical value of science in solving problems and answering questions, one domain was excluded from examination using the scientific method. This was the realm of meaning and values that remained firmly within the grip of supernatural religion. Philosophers said, and scientists agreed, that science was restricted to clarifying how things happen. Meaning and values were taken to require something outside the natural realm. Why do human beings exist? To serve God. Why does a tree exist? To serve humanity. And so on. However, meaning, through no coincidence, also gives rise to a person's motivations and the goals for their life. It was almost universally accepted that only religion could assign meaning to things. Only religion could define the meaning of human life and provide the values for making moral choices. Science was considered impotent to do such things.

But with the arrival of Charles Darwin and his theory of evolution by natural selection, the beginning of the final stage of movement from supernatural answers to naturalistic answers had begun. Progress since then has been very rapid. Over the past several decades all fields of knowledge, but especially evolutionary psychology have been developing the evidence that will make possible not only the recognition that meaning and values need to be defined from a naturalistic perspective, but how to do it. The primary tool for replacing the supernatural model of religion with a naturalistic one must be the understanding of religion and values from a naturalistic perspective based on human nature.

When our understanding of the currently available evidence provided by science reaches a critical level, the triumph of naturalistic science over supernatural religion will be complete. When this step is taken the possibility will then exist for each person to understand the meaning of their life in a way that will help them achieve their full positive potential. It is the goal of a *science of religion and ethics* to provide step-by-step answers to help people increase their odds of achieving the foregoing. So in that sense a *science of religion and ethics* provides the framework within which the propensity of humans to believe in magic and the power of wishing will be altered so it can be interpreted within a naturalistic understanding of life. This is an essential component of the new stability that humanity has been struggling toward since the evolution of symbolic language -- to understand human nature in the context of our ability to use symbolic language.

Science has been the key ingredient in this effort to move from instability to stability. The essence of the science paradigm is observation, hypothesis, experimentation, and testing results against predictions. This has provided the most reliable tool humanity has discovered so far to correct errors and improve the ability to predict. And it is this resource that must now be brought to bear on the most important issue that any person and our species in toto must confront – the meaning of our life. This includes how to maintain and develop our species. These are not separate questions, but part of the same thing. This book will address the foregoing in detail. The answers will differ from what is commonly accepted, but of course that is exactly what is needed!

CHAPTER 1

HUMANITY'S GOAL CAN NOW BE SEEN

All meaningful knowledge is for the sake of action,
And all meaningful action is for the sake of
friendship....John Macmurray

Ethnicity is a form of collective conceit....Roderick
MacLeisch [1].

The goal for each species (i.e., the requirements necessary to maintain the species) is to perpetuate itself and to change over time so it can continue to survive in a chaotic universe. As a result each individual member of the species is genetically programmed to eat, reproduce, and die. This is the way it was in the beginning and this is the way it has always been except for one species, *Modern Humans* [2] who evolved out of *Homo sapiens sapiens* [3].

When the modern language ability evolved some 50,000 to 100,000 years ago [4] a chain of events was initiated that led to a new paradigm for our species. *Modern Humans* with the ability to use symbolic communication, invented memes [5], that then replaced genes as the primary agents for dealing with change. These concepts act as tools that allow the species to very rapidly adapt to changes. This is because the evolution of memes is controlled by Lamarckian [6] – that is, they are altered by experience in the environment and immediately passed on in the altered form -- rather than Darwinian evolution based on random mutation of genes from which beneficial mutations are selected for over long time spans [7]. As a result of the foregoing human beings were able to expand into most niches and geographies on earth.

TRIBAL PROPENSITIES AND WISDOM POTENTIAL

This change from evolution by genes to memes significantly changes humanity's goal. However, up to the current time the unique goal of human life has been misperceived especially by those who have devoted their lives to understanding it; that is, priests, ministers, rabbis, imams, and the like. Although language provided us a "wisdom" potential (ability to use memes), primarily up to now we have been controlled by our "tribal" propensities; that is, those genetic patterns that evolved over the course of millions of years before *Modern Humans* arrived on the scene.

At the fundamental level humanity has the same goal as does all other life: perpetuate the species. But modern language provides another demand in order for *Modern Humans* to be successful: each individual person needs to become their best self so they can most usefully contribute to the "meme pool." The foregoing is judged to be true because every human being is unique and thereby has at least the theoretical potential to observe/discover something that could have survival value to the species. And they are most likely to live their life in such a way as to do this, and feed it into the meme pool, if they feel connected to the species and its survival. The foregoing is considered to be most likely to occur if they become their best self. And that is the message of *science of religion and ethics*.

But let's start at the beginning.

In the beginning was the word. As indicated it is my belief that *Modern Humans* began when the evolution of the language propensity reached a critical point. It is my working hypothesis that language and the brain co-evolved over the course of the last 2.5 million years so that some 30,000 to 60,000 years ago the basis was laid for a new paradigm for our species. From the time of the *Homo* separation from *Australopithecus* up until the cultural explosion, language was just one of five or so traits that accounted for our success as a species. (Others were unusual intelligence, bipedalism, opposable thumbs, use of tools, and social nature.)

And I follow the suggestion of others that the foregoing includes the evolutionary step of going from 24 chromosomes in apes to 23 chromosomes in Homo. For background see, "23, How Humanity Came to Be," James Hunt, 2015/16.

This transition culminated when the brain was able to freely use modern language. After the transition was complete everything else became just a resource for language to exploit. From that point on in order to understand humanity it has become necessary to understand symbolic language.

But language has been one of the great mysteries of philosophy and science. Many persons have done research on the various aspects of language, much has been written on the topic, and philosophers have considered its role in thought and our perception of the world. One widely quoted thinker is linguist Noam Chomsky who suggested several decades ago that language is too complex to be learned through reinforcement of correct responses at least in the way families teach it to their children. He proposed that there must be an innate language module that comes hard wired and each culture just plugs in its particular language. This idea has been widely accepted by those who study language even though it doesn't fit easily into an evolutionary model.

A book that laid the basis for a breakthrough in understanding language by exploring recent research, ideas, and thinking was Steven Pinker's book, *The Language Instinct* [8]. He examines the nature and development of language in a thorough and important way. However, when he discusses the brain's role in language he utilizes Chomsky's ideas as the explanation. And this is why he uses "The Language Instinct" as the title of his book.

A seminal work written even more recently that achieved the breakthrough in making language comprehensible was Terrence Deacon's, *The Symbolic Species* [9]. This book brings the most current knowledge of neurology, brain structures, evolution, anthropology, and all the other relevant fields of science together to present the best thinking possible at the time of my writing about what language is and how it evolved. His model depends completely on evolutionary processes and proposes how the incremental changes took place so as to develop the language ability. I would characterize it as one of the most comprehensive and well-grounded books on the physiology of language ever written.

Although there is still no universal agreement among scientists on the explanation for the cultural explosion that took place some 30 - 60,000 years ago Steven Mithen's *The Prehistory Of The Mind* [10] provides some interesting ideas. Mithen is an anthropologist and lays out in clear detail the best knowledge of human evolution since our branch separated from the other apes; that is, chimpanzees, gorillas, orangutans, and gibbons. He provides well-supported theories indicating that part of what separated the early *Homo* mind from its *Australopithecus* predecessors was a modular brain structure that divided the brain into several non-communicating intelligences: social intelligence connected with language, technical intelligence (for tool manufacture), and natural history intelligence (biology and geography for hunting and gathering).

His position (that I accept as a working hypothesis) is that it was the joining of these separate modules through the effects of language that produced the cultural explosion. I buy his explanation with the caveat that in my mind it was modern language made possible by this more effective brain that produced *Modern Humans*. And this laid the basis for all that has since happened throughout human history.

The above writers help us understand how the co-evolution of language and brains brought humanity to a new point in evolution. It produced modern language that provided the individual a potential that hadn't previously existed to live at a level of consciousness not available to any other species: to learn, create, discover, explore, accumulate, pass on knowledge, and be aware of our mortality. Deacon and Mithen postulate a time from 100,000 to 200,000 years ago for the completion of the evolution of the primary structures necessary for achieving languages at the symbolic level. This is the event that made possible the change of what "meaning of life" meant for human beings and started us on our current path some 10,000 - 20,000 years ago.

Before the changes in brain functioning turned *Homo sapiens* into *Homo sapiens sapiens* (that Mithen thinks happened when the natural history module was joined with the social module), and then into *Modern Humans* (when Mithen proposes that all cerebral modules were joined) our species was secure in an ecological niche that its predecessors had occupied for some 2-4 million years. This was the hunter-gatherer life style that provided a stable way of life congruent with the abilities and needs of proto-humans.

In those days our pre-human ancestors were hunter-gatherers by necessity -- this was the limit of their mental capabilities -- afterward hunter-gatherer societies remained because of custom and through lack of understanding about the need to change. Prior to the evolution of the modern language ability individual needs and social needs were narrowly proscribed (by their genes). Each individual fit into the hunter-gatherer society in a natural and normal way. And by so doing found their "meaning of life" like all the other plants and animals on earth that as indicated before is: "Eat. Reproduce. Die!" Meaning of life took on a whole new significance after the evolution of the language ability. And the hunter-gatherer life style can't provide it, though it laid the basis for what the Good Life is.

Of course the hunter-gatherer way of life continues in many places up to the present day, and many Americans think of it as an ideal state, or at least far better than that of modern society. However, in reality it represents an evolutionary stasis. It sustains the individual in an impoverished meme pool such that they are prevented from developing their "wisdom" potential. It maintains an environment in which the individual lacks the resources to significantly influence the memes their society has provided them. The combination of the need to move from place to place and the lack of a written language keep them from accumulating enough knowledge and experience to overcome the inertia of their society's customs, and permit them to break out of their historical patterns. In addition the group's folk religion to a large degree sustains them in their lack of awareness. Also, short life spans of 30 - 40 years help. To the degree that these things are successful in preventing persons from seeing their plight the individual's development is stifled and there is no motivation to change their society. As a result their worldview is restricted and they cannot achieve their full positive potential and consciously take part in maintaining and developing their species.

But it's not just the hunter-gatherer societies that fail to develop their members' potential. Up until the past several generations this practice characterized most societies. And even today the majority of members of every society are not able to raise their eyes high enough to recognize that they are controlled by the vestigial remnants of our "tribal" genetic propensities and to even yearn to achieve the "wisdom" potential which they may dimly see, but cannot properly interpret. However, individuals who are highly literate have the potential for dramatic and rapid change in the role they play in supporting the maintenance of the human species. (The miraculous recovery of German and Japanese societies after World War II because of their highly literate citizens, provides an inkling of this effect.)

Non-literate and static societies require special circumstances to change in such a way that they can provide the environment where their members are able to consciously promote cultural evolution toward an Enlightened Community. Until those changes take place both the individual hunter-gatherer and member of a static society are unable to understand the need for change, let alone being able to achieve it. They live a "pretty good life." They feel that their life is meaningful. But the truth is that they are very vulnerable to a neighbor whether from near or far who has discarded the hunter-gatherer/static society life style and therefore needs more land, more timber, more water, more minerals, more customers, and more converts -- and has the power and resources to appropriate these things, and lacks the moral development not to use that power to exploit.

After the brain and its language structures evolved to their current level, it is my contention that the individual's potential far exceeded the opportunities available. At that point the potential for incongruency between the individual and society arose. And we have been struggling with different permutations of this discord ever since. Subsequent to that time humanity has been in the process of creating an environment congruent with its new potential. At the same time we have been altering the memes that support the expression of our "tribal" genetic propensities and in the process of doing so continue to change the behaviors that are under our conscious control.

There is scarcely room for doubt that humanity as a species is working, though not consciously, toward a goal. Here goal is used metaphorically since technically goals are consciously developed prior to an action, while these changes are like all the other components of the evolutionary process, inevitable under the specific circumstance in which they occur, but not pre-planned.

Since the evolutionary changes that produced modern language, our species has been moving from the equilibrium of the hunter-gatherer life style toward a new equilibrium. The phrase that "history repeats itself" misses the key component in social change -- its direction. We can certainly learn from a study of history. Such study shows the dim outlines of the goal toward which *Modern Humans* have always labored. One thing is constant through peace and war, through reigns of terror and leadership of prophets, through civilizations and after their collapse. Humanity has been working toward the building of a community that includes all people and not only bonds all persons to each other, but nurtures individual freedom, opportunity for self expression, constructive use of each individual's abilities -- the "good life"; that is, achieving a *sustainable feeling that a person's life has meaning – a sustainable feeling of well-being.*

The above effort requires achieving a state of meme-based dynamic stability and it is an assumption of *science of religion and ethics* that humanity is indeed relentlessly moving toward this state to replace the gene-based dynamic stability of our pre-language days. If this assumption were true this would explain all the wars, cultural clashes, and exploitation of individuals and groups that have taken place over historical time. Many customs and patterns in every society or culture prevent this movement toward meme-based dynamic stability. Whenever this happens a counter-force is generated that will at some point destroy that culture/society, or at least the patterns that prevent progress. Sometimes these changes can be promoted as easily as developing a universal education system. Other times it is as destructive as the armies of Genghis Khan, or World War II.

Either way all that happens in individuals and societies is powered by the unstoppable force of the "wisdom" potential struggling to overcome the resistance promoted by our raw "tribal" genetic propensities.

Up until now humanity has lacked a "user's guide" describing the goal for which our species has been struggling, and as a result the goal of individual human lives. Nevertheless, it seems clear to me that *Modern Humans* have by trial and error moved relentlessly toward the goal for which a *science of religion and ethics* is working. Many historical events have delayed us in our attainment of this goal, but nothing has been able to change the trend. I feel safe in predicting that nothing will be able to, short of annihilation of the species. Any society that tries is doomed. If it cannot develop its members' full positive potential (that includes seeing all of humanity as "one") it will be destroyed or at least transformed. This was no less true of "Communist" Russia [11] than of Czarist Russia, "capitalist"

U.S.A., or imperial Rome, Muslim lands, or tribal Africa. For me a clear evidence supporting the foregoing predictions is the fact that the atrocities of the Holy Inquisition, and witch burnings were stopped not by outside forces, but by internal processes within the infected societies. And within our time this is true of the ending of the Cold War during which nuclear destruction of civilization if not Earth's current ecosystem seemed eminent to many thoughtful people.

Cultural evolution (change by evolution of memes) is the quality that best characterizes modern humanity. And the force that has been driving cultural evolution is the ability of memes to be changed by individual members of the society as they react to their changing environment and alter cultural memes as they project their unique perspective onto the words they use. As members of a community are able to achieve more and more of their potential they have a greater influence on the memes of their society. If *Modern Humans* (who evolved 30,000 to 60,000 years ago) are to endure, this is the force that needs to accomplish it. If all members of a society were to achieve their full positive potential this would maximize efforts to maintain and develop the human species.

Humanity has made wondrous strides, but has a major barrier to overcome before it reaches this new equilibrium. As indicated above it seems clear to me that we retain the essence of those instincts that guided primates when they lived in small roving bands. All of these drives or propensities (post-instincts) need to be mastered if we are to succeed in our efforts to reach a new equilibrium.

Our species, *Homo sapiens*, like all other species, started out with a certain nature resulting from its evolutionary history. Those individuals had drives and propensities related to instincts that existed millions of years earlier in the first primates. Since the evolution of the modern language ability these propensities have been affected dramatically and human nature has become more complex. We have been in the process of creating ourselves through cultural choices that expand the meaning of these propensities. Therefore, our new brains are pushing us toward a new synthesis, a new equilibrium. Our basic drives have been maintained: hunger, sex, thirst, sleep, comfort, and the like. But each of these drives is shaped by our social nature. However, these drives and all of our behavior are shaped by those other factors I'm calling propensities. Exactly what the specific propensities are I don't know, but I'll briefly list my best guesses about them and then discuss them in more detail. On the left below are the propensities. On the right is the potential toward which we have been struggling. All of the below listed raw "tribal" genetic propensities need to be brought under control of the "wisdom" potential in order to produce better societies. The foregoing will facilitate movement toward the goal of becoming an Enlightened Person (an individual who has achieved their full positive potential) who lives in an Enlightened Community (a society that promotes the belief and implements the idea that *human beings are the source of meaning and value* and that the individual person needs to be the focus for society's ultimate concern.)

	From: "TRIBAL" PROPENSITIES	TO: "WISDOM" POTENTIAL
1	Alpha male/alpha female (dominance/subservience)	Empathetic, cooperative, democratic interactions, and relationships.
2	Fundamentalist/Wisdom Quest Must possess Truth. Desire for the Absolute. Ends up with the relative.	Recognizes "Truth" is not attainable. Any position must be open to questioning
3	Sexuality -- diverse	Monogamy, or at least serial monogamy. (After an adolescent stage of sexual exploration and experimentation.)
4	Us/Them (Basis of prejudice, crime, and war).	All of humanity is us. "All for one and one for all."
5	Territoriality: trespass on my property at your peril.	We each have our private space, but the earth belongs to everyone.
6	Emphasis on "right brain."(Non-dominant hemisphere)	Emphasis on whole brain (both left & right hemispheres)
7	Adolescent males leave clan of birth and join a new one, or often set up their own.	Both male and female adolescents remain with family, but have multiple opportunities and options to explore the freedom this propensity encourages.

8	Work: everyone participates as appropriate and necessary. Everything by custom – group decision making or by alpha male.	Maximize creativity. Continuous self-growth. Necessary support is provided so each person becomes socially productive
9	Education: To fit into the group, and do the "right" things.	To become one's best self, maximize one's positive potential.
10	For Religion: Based on magic. Belief in miracles -- a persons' desire (wishing) controls what happens.	Inspired by a *science of religion and ethics*. A person's knowledge properly used and behavior properly directed influences what happens

People today are in a unique position in terms of the growth of knowledge. Enough knowledge has now been achieved so we can see the "light at the end of the tunnel" -- utopia resulting from achieving meme-based social dynamic stability. It seems clear to me that all human history since *Modern Humans* gained the symbolic language ability and up to this time has been prologue. Humanity has been in the process of creating itself. But only in the past several decades has it become possible to understand what has been happening. In the past humanity's achievements in inventing itself have been by happenstance rather than due to sensible planning. And always with an inner struggle to overcome limitations imposed by raw "tribal" genetic propensities. Nevertheless, this progress has been the result of a relentless inner urge (the "wisdom" potential) that under the proper circumstances guides behavior even though not understood by those countless persons who have collectively gotten us to the brink of success.

Of course as indicated before there has never been a carefully thought-out plan, based on theories, tested by empirical data, and therefore subject to change with more knowledge and experience. Only within the past hundred years have we gained enough knowledge and experience to even consider the possibility of assembling goals with an empirical, testable focus. Only now do we have the possibility of developing such. This book, *HOW TO LIVE THE GOOD LIFE: A User's Guide for Modern Humans*, is directed toward providing the first draft of a blueprint for such a plan. It would utilize stresses within individuals and within societies in general to show us where social changes are necessary in order to allow all individuals to become Enlightened Persons living in Enlightened Communities. A *science of religion and ethics* would be totally committed to clarifying what it would take to create a world in which all human beings achieve a rewarding life.

FUNDAMENTALIST/ WISDOM/SPIRITUAL QUEST

This propensity leads to the need for answers to the key questions. The desire that things make sense. Spirit causality (if a natural cause cannot be found, unseen, supernatural forces must be at work) has been the fall-back position since the earliest days of human existence. Because having "The Answer" is so important many individuals search, latch onto what they take as the best answer, and thereafter never question the truth of their answer, but do whatever it takes to defend their answer against any who would question it (including themselves).

A *science of religion and ethics* provides a way for anyone to have the feeling of finding the right answers but being able to change the "answer" without losing the feeling since the search doesn't leave them without a foundation. This is the process science has always promoted.

BELIEF IN MAGIC AND THE POWER OF WISHING

The most basic problem we need to learn how to deal with effectively is those patterns of thought that encourage us to believe in magic, and the power of wishing; that is, that a person's wishes control what happens by thought alone. These patterns of thinking make it more difficult to understand and utilize objective reality to achieve a person's full positive potential. I would associate magical thinking with the right hemisphere of the brain.

I think the power and attraction of the magic/wishing propensity makes it likely that it has been the sustaining propensity since the modern language ability evolved. I believe this propensity is based on those brain structures that produce a feeling of "hope" – for the rabbit, to run its fastest to escape the wolf; for the chimpanzee, hunting together to catch monkeys to eat. Once people became capable of formulating the question, "Is my life worth continuing now?" the genes have been hard pressed to ensure that the answer is, "Yes!" It appears to me that belief in magic and the power of wishing has provided a primary ingredient in coming up with that yes. Now we need to find a different solution. The Enlightened Person and the Enlightened Community provide the essence of that different solution.

SEXUALITY

Human beings, like all animals, have strong sexual drives that easily lead to sexual activity with different partners. For humanity this is best interpreted as a genetic propensity. However, it is my position that monogamy is superior to sexual promiscuity except in the early experimental years of non-reproducing adolescents, and in between long term relationships. Multiple simultaneous sexual relationships appear to be a distraction to creating true intimacy based on trust, full disclosure, and joint problem solving. In a society of equals where individuals are working to become Enlightened Persons monogamous relationships would seem to be the goal. (See "Shared Affection, Chapter Fifteen, Eighth Way of Wisdom.)

Terrence Deacon [12] builds a very strong case that the "marriage" ceremony provided the experience with symbols that became the foundation upon which language then developed. As a result the idea of proscribed conditions for sexual union may lie deep within our psyche. And monogamous relationships seem consistent with the ideas of an Enlightened Community made up of Enlightened Persons. But by the same token a momentary lapse, or sexual indiscretion doesn't represent a moral blemish, rather at most a need for greater social support to focus more clearly on the elements of wisdom. Anyone attempting to become and remain an Enlightened Person doesn't have time and energy to be promiscuous. In addition a life partner to help us deepen our understandings and expand our joy seems an extremely important ingredient to develop a person's full positive potential.

Different, but related to this issue, is the whole matter of reproduction. Our genetic propensity to reproduce is very strong. But our "wisdom" potential has brought us to the place where we also need to apply wisdom to controlling our reproduction. The out-of-control reproduction promoted by our genes and supported by some folk religions is merely another element of the problems that need to be mastered.

Since *Modern Human* individuals are defined more by their memes than their genes it is no longer necessary to feel that we live on in our children. We can now live on in the efforts we have made to perpetuate the memes of an Enlightened Community. And in such a community we are all responsible for the children and through that involvement can experience the unconditional love that is important for an individual's growth as a human being.

US VS. THEM

Another propensity that demands serious attention is the one that not only supports social classes, but also gives rise to prejudice, crime, and war. I believe this comes out of the "us" vs. "them" feeling. This propensity was no doubt of survival value in the 2-4 million years our ancestors were evolving as hunter-gatherers. It is totally out of sync with the current world joined together by rapid travel and instantaneous communication. (Not to mention A-Bombs, H-Bombs, germ warfare, international terrorism, and the like.) Modern technology makes our multi-racial, multi-ethnic, multi-lingual, multi-national contemporary world a source of infinite beneficial possibilities if properly used, or a potential wasteland if our "us vs. them" propensity is not wisely directed. New powerful images that can address these feelings at this basic level need to be developed and utilized. "Us" needs to be taken to include all human beings, but nothing else. (Cosmic consciousness, God, pets, all-living-things, planet earth, and the like needs to be seen as drawing their value from us; that is, human *beings are the ultimate reference system.*)

ALPHA MALE/FEMALE -- DOMINANCE/ SUBSERVIENCE

Another barrier to becoming an Enlightened Person is the remnants of the "alpha male/alpha female" instinct. Alpha males/females have a tendency to function on the moral principle: Do whatever you want that you think you can get away with. In small groups this propensity can be dealt with by the rules of behavior the group adopts and enforces. In humanity's proto-human stage roving clans were almost certainly led by alpha males within the context of social control. As the language ability evolved these males were able to control larger and larger groups. The larger their clan the safer each member was from other groups, and the uncertainties of their environment. However, at the same time within these larger groups the essential social control of alpha males/females became more difficult. Nevertheless, alpha males/females from the beginning were critically important. So they were highly valued if only in terms of the survival of the group. They had the pick of the food, work, and living space. Also, they were able to select a group of females to bond with and produce their children. The alpha female was head of this harem. Females to a certain degree achieved their standing in the clan through the male they paired with. However, at the same time it is very likely that females played a crucial role in the selection and continued rule of the alpha male. A given female as a result of her standing and drives either dominated other women or was submissive to them. The alpha female genetic propensity led these women to pair with alpha males. All women were in competition for the "best" men; that is, the best genes for their children.

The foregoing is a key factor even in today's societies, but the changes made possible by larger societies have made them more vulnerable to alpha male propensities even in the lowest ranking males when they feel they "deserve" a given woman, or job, and may kill or maim when they are denied this access.

The alpha male was the boss. He glowered and all the other members of the group jumped. The other males in the clan fit into a pecking order going down from the alpha male. As such they shared in the fertile females, work, food, and such, in accordance with their place in that pecking order. The male dominated. The female was submissive, except to other females where their own dominance hierarchy existed. We see alpha male/alpha female behavior demonstrated in almost every society by those males who seek power and control over others, and those women who pursue such men and pair up with them. Although such men and women may produce significant effects in their society, they can never become their best self and therefore an Enlightened Person unless they are able to regulate these drives. Nor can they be counted on to help build an Enlightened Community. They tend toward being absorbed in their own short-term wants and needs. (The need for power can never be satisfied. No matter how much power a person has there is still the possibility of losing it, the realization that somewhere there may be someone with more power, etc.)

It is this alpha male/female factor that led to development of social classes, military rank, and leadership in general. As the agricultural revolution was initiated it was laid on top of this dominance/submission propensity. Prior to the evolution of the language ability an alpha male was crowned through physical attributes. But in societies of *Modern Humans* social classes tend to be hereditary since language makes this possible. However, this hereditary pecking order is inherently unstable in *Modern Humans* for several reasons, of which two important ones are: Most males have at least some yearnings to be the alpha male, and a person never knows how and when such behavior will surface. Second, the language ability complicates the issue of who "can be" the alpha male. In addition social classes are hereditary, but the alpha male abilities do not necessarily pass from father to son, and especially not selectively to first-born sons. The hereditary approach becomes increasingly unsatisfactory as societies become larger, communication gets more difficult, the hereditary leader is more incompetent, and the lines of authority are unclear. The fact that the dominance/submission propensity is even more restrictive for women -- to utilize their full positive potential -- than for men has been an additional serious problem with this propensity. But most important, following this propensity carelessly cuts a person off from becoming their best self.

Most likely, physical strength and agility were important components of selection of the alpha male in proto-humans. But negotiating skills, ability to establish alliances, and talents to maintain order in the clan were equally important [13]. The development of folk religions with God as the "true" alpha male allowed the verbally gifted a natural place from which to achieve great power, even over the warriors. These things correlate with language ability and it is my guess that at some point language ability became more important than other characteristics in both alpha males and alpha females. Since the alpha male got the pick of females, which included the alpha female (and she played a key role in his selection), this process would have greatly speeded up the co-evolution of language and brain. When the relevant components of the modern language ability all came together *Homo sapiens* moved away from communication restricted to the social realm and moved toward *Modern Humans* communicating with words, sentences, paragraphs, and speeches within the total realm of our current awareness.

Even individuals in modern societies without any inkling of what they are doing, just naturally utilize the alpha male/female behaviors. Of course customs within a group can either support or diminish these patterns of behavior. Many tribal societies have essentially excluded authoritarian rule by the alpha male through group cooperation opposing such behavior [13]. On the other end of the scale are fundamentalists of every persuasion. They are controlled by dominance and submission. They almost always require women to follow a "traditional" role; that is, female submission. Such practices lead readily to spousal abuse and make it doubly difficult for their males to overcome this dominance/submission propensity.

Within small social groups the alpha male/female propensity is restrained by social bonds and group cohesion. In modern loose knit urban social structures there is often little effective restraint. In a modern industrial society, to avoid authoritarian behavior males who haven't learned how to restrain their alpha male genes frequently live in a constant state of tension and create instability around them. Possibly these are the so-called Type A males.

In a large society where everyone does not know everyone else and therefore "does not know their place" with each other, this issue has traditionally been dealt with through the custom of developing manners and instilling politeness. The practice of treating each other -- particularly strangers -- with courtesy prevents initiating a dominance/ submission confrontation. It exists for good reasons. Otherwise, every time two males meet for the first time it would be necessary to deal with dominance/ submission issues before other activities could transpire. Our language propensity allowed us to develop intricate social structures that require complex behavior that can be totally disrupted when the alpha male/alpha female patterns come strongly into play. Alpha patterns can lead to such inappropriate, disruptive behavior with employers; customers; passengers on trains; dealing with a person's dentist, physician, electrician, and such. They affect myriads of contacts with authority figures -- police, military rank, bosses, monitors, clerks, bureaucrats, priests, teachers, and such.

As a result a smoothly functioning society requires socially sensitive behavior. Manners and politeness have this function. They provide a clear social expectation of what each person should do in a given social situation. In this way a pattern is established that makes for smooth social relations. Those who violate the norms are seen by others as ill mannered and social pariahs. They tend to be shunned by others, and not invited to participate. They are excluded from the group. These patterns have evolved to help societies avoid socially destructive confrontations.

However, for activities that emerged recently (like driving cars) where appropriate behavior has not yet been fully integrated and completely accepted as social rules, people often display an "attitude" – they act rudely and thoughtlessly in situations that from the outside would appear to be similar to ones in which they are polite, say some version of "you go first." When two alpha males cross lanes on a crowded freeway and one person cuts the other off, they initiate a need for confrontation and dominance. They stop and confront. If one has a gun the bigger and stronger one may be left dead alongside the highway. In a world filled with strangers in which there are knives, guns, and paid goons, struggles for dominance can prove to be fatal.

Handling the alpha male drive differently has been one aspect of humanity's efforts toward creating itself out of its evolutionary roots. Democratic procedures have been a primary tool in this effort. Ideas of the Enlightened Community merely express more clearly and completely how this goal would be achieved. In an Enlightened Community the alpha male drive for power would be tempered by recognition that self-interest requires channeling this drive toward goals that are socially useful. More than that the goal of an Enlightened Community needs to be to empower every person to take an active, constructive role in the community that is neither destructively dominant, nor passively subservient. It is a basic assumption of a *science of religion and ethics* that dominance/submission propensities, like all drives, can be channeled so that they do not prevent the individual from being part of a utopia, working to become an Enlightened Person and build and maintain an Enlightened Community.

The foregoing process will be easier since not all alphas are the same (as is true for the individuals within any designated label). I use the term "Alpha C" (C for compassion) to apply to an alpha male/female who is in fact able to feel compassion. And of course there are many such individuals. And I use "Alpha E" (E for exploitation) to apply to alphas without the compassion component. (See Appendix E for more ideas on this.)

ADOLESCENT MALES: WHY SO STRANGE?

In proto-human clans the males were the hunters and the defenders of the group. The females the gatherers, cooks, and maintainers of the living space and caring for the children. Probably females were the inventors of agriculture, weaving, and medicine. But, more important, the females cared for the kids until they reached puberty. I believe that up until the evolution of the language ability males at puberty left the clan. And the adolescent females stayed in the tribe in which they were raised. Leaving the birth clan of course had a selective evolutionary advantage because it reduced incest and thereby worked to keep the gene pool diverse. Incest is also reduced by the human characteristic of being attracted to new (exotic) partners rather than members of the group the individual was raised with. (This promoted spreading of genes far and wide by those traveling adventurers who usually had great genes.) Young males came into the clan from other tribes and established their place in the pecking order as they matured. After the evolution of the language ability, groups increased in size and adolescent males started to remain with their birth family. I assume this was related to the tighter bonds that developed as a result of language plus the larger groups this also promoted. However, I would guess that adolescent males with an intense alpha male gene component would not have been able to adjust to living under their father, or other males. And, from time to time would break off from their birth group and move to new territory to set up their own group. I suspect this process had an important role in spreading humanity and genes over the face of the globe, especially those genes involved in language.

But was it the *Homo* male who left the group? In chimpanzees, baboons, and gorillas it is the female who leaves the birth group, and that may well have been the pattern for *Homo*. I base my assumption that it was the males who left the tribe on the fact that over the past several thousands of years at least within urban settings, adolescent males have been a mystery to their cultures. They go into some strange state that makes the elders scratch their heads and become convinced the culture is falling apart. I believe this state includes withdrawal from the family, rejection of its values, and other behaviors that in earlier times prepared them to leave their clan and go to another. Females (at least until recently in the U.S.) had no similar patterns. Rather, adolescent girls need the love and affection of their fathers and suffer various kinds of stress when it is lacking. They tend to display an early, almost compulsive -- but non-sexual, at least in terms of a male interpretation of sexuality -- interest in the opposite sex. Soon afterwards, they tend to lose their self-esteem, and become very pliable. They fit into a pattern to start rearing a family, and not make waves. They are ready to make the necessary adjustments to raise a family and submit to their mate.

I take as further evidence that it was the male who left the clan, the fact that it is a wide-spread practice in tribes and primitive cultures to go out and get their wives by abduction, war, or courting. Sometimes the bride is purchased or obtained through negotiation from neighboring tribes or groups. I see this as a sign that the adolescent female is not eager to leave her clan and to do so needs the pull from outside or the push from inside.

DEALING WITH PROPENSITIES

Are the above ideas about "tribal" genetic propensities accurate? None of them are based solely on firm research findings, since I'm not aware of such data. However, sociobiology has already said much on the bigger elements of this issue.[14] Surely, final answers will turn out to differ greatly on some points. However, there is absolutely no doubt in my mind that the broad outlines of these ideas are correct. On the specifics there needs to be questioning.

A *science of religion and ethics* needs to help individuals become more aware of their self-defeating inclinations that stand in the way of achieving what is in their long term best interests. This knowledge needs to be available so they can more effectively deal with these tendencies. Understanding that these propensities exist is not taken as justification for succumbing to them, just the opposite. Knowing about them helps us to become aware of the danger that we will succumb to such behavior and to do what it takes to interrupt or redirect these propensities. Because such patterns develop in puberty, or even before and are found in all adult human beings to varying degrees thereafter, they are something we all have to learn how to deal with, if we are to become Enlightened Person*s*. And, we need to learn to act in new ways never widely followed in any society or group before.

Propensities, including those discussed above, have contributed to the confusion of *Modern Humans*' efforts to find a new stability -- to replace the hunter-gatherer pattern (that is, gene-driven) with one that is compatible with our symbolic language ability. Nevertheless, in spite of the frequent failures of imagination and understanding throughout the course of human history, we have been gathering experience on all the things that don't work plus the things that produce improvements, such as democracy, education, progressive laws, and such. Also, we have been accumulating knowledge to allow us to take the steps that will lead to a breakthrough. The essence of this breakthrough as previously expressed is that a new state of equilibrium in social living is our goal. In this new stasis there needs to be congruency between the community and the individual as there was in the previous hunter-gatherer stage. This can best be described as the creation of an Enlightened Community made up of Enlightened Persons such that any conflict between the needs of the community and the needs of the individual can be resolved without triggering the "us/them" dichotomy.

We can even make out many of the specifics about what an Enlightened Person and an Enlightened Community would be like, and these ideas are presented in Chapter 2 [15] along with ideas about what needs to be done to achieve both. Since Western societies have built their primary institutions on the idea that there is an inherent conflict between an individual and their society, and non-Western societies tend to follow the practice of rule by the most powerful male, introducing the necessary changes will not be easy. However, the challenge of a *science of religion and ethics* is to uncover the knowledge necessary to build the structures that will allow these changes to be made so this congruency can be achieved.

WORK, EMPLOYMENT, JOBS

Understanding, at a fundamental level, the relationship between "meaning of human life" and symbolic communication has ramifications for every aspect of the problems we currently face and how to find the best solutions to those problems. Religion, gender, and ethnic groups have already been dealt with. Work, employment, and jobs remain as a very important area to examine. The tools we call the industrial/ technological/ information revolution are essential to the successful resolution of the "meaning of human life" issue. Many changes in customs, life styles, and memes were necessary before the industrial revolution was ignited. However, these changes relied heavily on our "tribal" genetic propensities rather than our "wisdom" potential. Because "tribal" genetic propensities limit a person's development, and yet still form the basis for modern employment this means that the whole industrial component of today's world needs to be restructured -- as does government, education, and religion -- if individuals are to be supported in developing their "wisdom" potential.

Before *Modern Humans* came on the scene with their advanced language ability, each proto-human's mental abilities were fully utilized living the hunter-gatherer life style. Tribal members worked cooperatively to hunt, gather, and create an environment in which all could share in the available sustenance; for example, I take it that eating together was a defining characteristic of *Modern Humans*. Without it we would have become a very different species. Although some members may have gotten larger portions and the best of the skins as discussed above -- re: alpha males -- sharing and cooperation comprised the milieu in which each person lived since human beings are social animals. With the evolution of *Modern Humans* and a vastly enhanced language skill, humanity was no longer limited to the hunter-gatherer life style. Other options became possible, in fact necessary.

It seems clear to me that work, jobs, and employment need to be altered so that they help all persons to become Enlightened Persons, and whatever changes are necessary need to be worked on until this is achieved. A critical challenge is to discover how to apply in today's societies an appropriate method of sharing that provides the success the model used by hunter-gatherer societies permitted.

To help each person achieve the foregoing would be a primary goal of a *science of religion and ethics*. The aim would be to develop Enlightened Communities so that all members would be able to participate in the work, the play, and the rewards of the Community. At the same time the goal would be to help individuals develop as fully functioning selves. A core part of this functioning would include every individual's involvement in the expansion of knowledge, and the production of wealth and services in their community. To do this successfully the tremendous potential of the industrial/ technological/ information revolution needs to be harnessed in such a way as to achieve congruency between individuals and society. (See Volume II, Chapter 34, "Work and a *Science of Religion and Ethics*," [16] for some specific ideas on this point.)

According to Robert Reich, Secretary of Labor under U.S. President Bill Clinton, work and working in the U.S. has been transformed in a basic way in the past several decades as a result of technology and globalization (*The Future Of Success* [17]). (See Volume II, Chapter 34-B [18] for key ideas from this book.) The impact of these changes is to make work the focus of individual lives in the name of "faster, better, cheaper."

Reich claims these changes are as fundamental and will be as sweeping as those that occurred when mass production was introduced in the mid-1800s. And these changes supplant the mass production paradigm. To the degree that Reich has properly characterized what is happening this is of seminal importance to a *science of religion and ethics*. It appears that the gains are currently overshadowed by the losses, therefore some limits need to be imposed on this pattern to prevent serious loss of quality of life by workers. It is after all quality of life that is the goal, not work.

However, something even more troubling in current U.S. industry involving the relationship of citizens and corporations is examined by

Barry C. Lynn in his book *CORNERED: The New Monopoly Capitalism and the Economics of Destruction* [19]. There he explores the history of industries' efforts to use monopoly to control markets and the dramatic changes in this that took place during the 1980s during the Presidential Administration of Ronald Reagan. Conservatives redefined free enterprise to mean the unfettered power of an individual to amass as much wealth as possible, while liberals sought to use planning and efficiency to lower costs, even if it resulted in the loss of some economic freedom.

Reagan's Administration was able to combine both of the foregoing by refocusing enforcement of antimonopoly laws so that growth of monopolies was encouraged and markets were narrowed in the name of producing cheaper goods. [19] Corporations grew dramatically in power. This growth of the power of corporations has changed significantly their role in the political realm where their power (money) influences every relevant law congress considers. And of course this just got much worse with the Supreme Court ruling (Citizens United vs. Federal Election Commission – No. 08-205) that corporations can spend whatever they desire to influence legislation.

As previously discussed a *science of religion and ethics* recognizes that work is essential in a community and some elements of the new paradigms appear to hold positive benefits. The elements that promote individual creativity and talent are among these. But the aspects of this change that focus on money that is destructive to family, community, recreation, and anything not directly increasing a person's work efficiency supporting money and power over individual well-being appears counterproductive. The challenge is to learn how to utilize modern knowledge and technology to enhance the quality of life rather than to numb the mind, and harden the heart to turn each person into a tool for producing goods and services at the cheapest cost possible even if that means starvation wages, destroying our ecology, exploitation of the vulnerable, and focusing the individual only on survival. This is a prime example of misusing economics by ignoring more fundamental values – that is, the teachings of a *science of religion and ethics.*

EVOLUTION OF MEMES AND SOCIAL CHANGE

With the brain's new ability to use, produce, and alter memes *Modern Humans* were able to master the new behaviors required by animal husbandry and agriculture, so these activities were invented. These life styles allowed permanent settlements and provided numerous challenges that gave individuals different ways to explore and to satisfy the possibilities of their newly wired brains. By developing and manipulating memes various communities were able to master care, breeding, and production of animals, as well as planting, growing, and harvesting to produce the food necessary to sustain life. Under normal circumstances these talents produced surpluses of food that freed some persons to explore their world in ways not possible to a hunter-gatherer society. This pattern of life also allowed them to increase their populations. In addition wholly new ways of living became possible. Although this period opened new doors for many individuals, it wasn't even close to providing the environment necessary for every member to develop their new capacities as *Modern Humans* in a fully satisfying way. As a result humanity continued into a period of diverse change and on-going instability. And, in the process more doors for individual achievement were opened.

Almost all of these changes were caused by or at least shaped by the new memes that became available as societies met and exchanged memes. This cross pollination of ideas, experiences, and discoveries came about because the various cultures took different paths as they attempted to fulfill their citizens' new needs for personal achievement and fulfillment. Generally speaking this pattern led to more rapid evolution of cultures. And, this period was characterized by a more rapid widening of the breach between the society and an increasing number of individuals. From time to time this evolution of memes led to ideas that conflicted with the religious ideas then binding the society together. If this conflict was not able to be successfully resolved, it normally promoted disintegration, or at least reforming of the society -- sometimes slowly, sometimes quickly. And this demonstrates the importance of studying and recording as much information on every clan, tribe, group, and society as possible. Every society like every person is a source of unique information and experiences. Each provides a resource of priceless value in learning what to do and what to avoid doing -- based on the effects of the beliefs and practices of that person or society.

However, historically one of the most priceless contributions made by any society was the invention of writing (using pictographs, hieroglyphs, ideograms, etc.) and then the alphabet. But as would be expected this process not only brought great rewards, it also -- since there are no unmixed blessings -- included detrimental elements that are only now being understood. For an interesting description of this process see, *The Alphabet Versus the Goddess* [20], by Leonard Shlain.

but regardless of what the range of effects were when an alphabet was adopted, explosive cultural change was one of them as writing vastly expanded the number of memes available in a society. This increase of available memes opened doors for individual achievement and fulfillment. It provided a way for persons to develop their individual personhood. Written language made it possible -- under the proper circumstances -- for individuals to extract themselves from groupthink and suppression of self, produced by the impact of the group's customs and rules.

Because of these things and thousands of others, individuals moved further in the direction of becoming their own person. In comparison to the pre-literacy period the relationship between the individual and their society became increasingly more flexible. Societies grew larger and social bonds became looser and frequently less satisfying for the individual and for society. As societies moved ever further in this direction, more and more they lost cultural unity. The congruency of life style and social needs achieved by our forbearers prior to the evolution of modern language became more and more eroded and lost. And, evolving societies continued into ever more uncharted territory.

There was a brief period of hope during the Enlightenment of the eighteenth century when the idea was developed that human well-being could be achieved through use of knowledge. And in the mid-1800s many persons shared the vision of utopia that included a life of culture and plenty on this earth.

But there was much to overcome. One effort that was promoted in the 1800s in England by writers such as John Stuart Mill (1806-73) led European societies to adopt the idea that there exists an inherent conflict between the individual and their society. This may have been done as a strategy to break out of the stifling social customs of the day when there certainly was a conflict between what individuals wanted and what the society permitted. In these circumstances such thinking did advance science, technology, and commerce. Also, it promoted individual freedom. It provided a barrier to protect individuals against some of the worst attacks by the repressive religions of the day. But this progress was achieved at a heavy expense. It enshrined the "tribal" genetic propensities in the context of a Judeo-Christian understanding of human nature. It increased alienation between individuals and society. It mis-focused serious thinkers so they failed to look empirically for the roots of conflict between individuals and society. As a result the advance of technology and industry was never able to be properly utilized for the good of all.

One issue that made progress difficult resulted because Western social institutions were based on the Judeo-Christian-Islamic idea that God provides guidance on how to live a person's life and that the human species lacks importance independent of God. As a result it was widely accepted that the individual and their life only had value based on their affiliation with a religion, nation, or family. (This is the path of the bee, the ant, the termite, and of course the path of our "tribal" genetic propensities.)

As a result by the late 1800s even those persons who believed in the ideas of the Enlightenment began to feel a deep pessimism about human capabilities that were widely accepted as being inherently limited. Therefore, many formerly liberated individuals began to return to the ideas of folk religions and to doubt that human beings have the potential to develop a livable world, let alone a utopia. Economic depression and World Wars -- especially WW II and the temporary loss of one of the most civilized nations in the world, that is, Germany, to despotic evil -- supported this sense of hopelessness.

During the Cold War that followed World War II, destruction of civilization by nuclear weapons seemed eminent. This did nothing to encourage humanity's faith in the potential of their mental powers and the value of knowledge and reason in spite of the almost miraculous growth of knowledge and economic well being during this period.

But beyond the explanations mentioned above it seems we need deeper reasons to account for such gross failure of vision and hope in spite of the tremendous potential of *Modern Humans* and their achievements in the evolutionary blink of an eye of some 30,000 - 60,000 years. I believe that part of the explanation is that all societies have lacked clarity about what it means to be a human being and what the universe is like. For persons taught that the goal of life is to please God and to spend eternity with Her [21], ideas proclaiming the value of our species in general and the individual in particular fell on deaf ears. Therefore, such persons spend their time in ways believed to be important to God, not in ways aimed toward the well being of the species. On the other hand persons who believe that the goal of life is to achieve personal happiness, find that every achievement only points out the deficiencies in their lives. This tends to be true because they are focusing on effects. Therefore, they tend to look for short term, self-serving activities, rather than investing their life in something inherently more satisfying.

An additional cause of this failure of vision relates to the "us/them" and "dominance/ submission" propensities. Historically, most leaders have pursued power as a goal in and of itself. This has happened not only in religion, politics, science, education, literature, and art, but especially in business. These leaders have seen the rest of society outside their group as something to exploit rather than as something to share the fruits of their efforts and abilities with. Also, they have tended to live in an environment of self-gratification, and with the vision of scarcity. Because they sought power -- that is always limited -- they have lived in a mental state of scarcity no matter how much power or wealth they achieved. Everything has been seen as being in short supply. In order for them to have "enough" others have to "not-have-enough." Exploiting others for a person's own gain seemed like a law of nature; that is, "survival of the fittest." The foregoing patterns have endured up to this time in all parts of the world. In Western societies it exists in every domain, but is especially blatant in the business community. The foregoing, I think, helps to explain why the wonderful potential of the industrial/technological/information revolution has been grossly misdirected up to this point, and in fact taken as the criteria for measuring progress, defining value, and even success. (See VOLUME II, Chapter 3, "The Enlightened Community." [22])

Another aspect of the preceding ideas encourages looking more closely at the relationship between a society and its alpha males. From the alpha male perspective a person could say that modern societies actually exploit these individuals' need for power and channel it into producing material wealth for the culture -- cars, oil, computers, software, and so on. Therefore, they work relentlessly to ensure that the things needed by an industrial/

technological/information society exist. But, however this is seen, there is an essential need for change to develop Enlightened Communities.

In an Enlightened Community there would be ways for everyone to contribute to the wealth and knowledge of the society and share in its prosperity and sphere of well-being. These ways need to be as satisfying for current humanity as the ways used by hunter-gatherer societies were for our early ancestors. A core element of this process would be to ensure that each citizen would be helped to become a true individual -- self empowered, well-educated, creative, an active participant, and so on. To achieve the foregoing persons need to be brought to their highest level of development. This can only happen when it is realized that a society exists for its citizens, not the other way around. Their well-being is the most important thing for a society. And, a by-product of this concern of the society for its citizens is the reciprocal concern of the individual for the continued existence and proper functioning of their community. More than that because they have been nurtured and expanded as persons they have the talents and ability to actualize their concern. In addition this development opens the door for others because there is always a social component to self development. It is this process that needs to lead to the expansion of life for everyone in every area of fulfillment.

If we can in fact produce Enlightened Persons and Enlightened Communities we will finally have reached a stable stage where each individual's life is congruent with the language ability; that is, the universality permitted by symbolic thinking rather than the "tribal" genetic thinking imposed by our genetic propensities. There will then be harmony between society and the individual. And this is humanity's goal that is now clearly in sight.

So once we understand the foregoing we now have the possibility for dramatic change. With the understanding made possible by our current knowledge we have the possibility of utilizing the fantastic power of the liberated human mind. When people who have had their talents developed, work together cooperatively and synergistically with other liberated human minds, current societies can be transformed (as envisioned in Chapter Two [15]). These ideas should give us the insights to utilize the powerful tools provided by industry and technology in ways to help transform societies into Enlightened Communities.

CHAPTER 2

SCIENCE OF RELIGION AND ETHICS OVERVIEW
Defining the Meaning of Human Life

"There is no field of experience which cannot, in principle, be brought under some form of scientific law, and no type of speculative knowledge about the world which it is, in principle, beyond the power of science to give." A. J. Ayer

An Enlightened Community is one that promotes the belief and implements the idea that human beings are the source of meaning and value and that the individual person needs to be seen as the focus for society's ultimate concern.

Science is the search for congruency.

The outline of my system is presented below, and then in more detail in the remainder of this book.

ASSUMPTIONS OF SCIENCE OF RELIGION AND ETHICS

I. Religious/ethical beliefs relate to everything concerned with maintaining and developing the human species; i.e., satisfying human nature. For individuals that means those beliefs that lead them to become Enlightened Persons.

II. Humanity itself is our ultimate reference system living immersed within a cosmos with Reality As the Objective Reference System.

 A. Human beings will never be able to discover Truth when it is envisioned as a Platonic ideal. However, it is a useful image to assume that we can fully understand every aspect of the cosmos by appropriately studying and modeling it -- as long as we keep in mind that we cannot! This process allows the achievement of Knowledge; that is, improved ability to predict the future. Thomas Kuhn [1] questions this assumption, but pragmatically his approach appears to be of questionable value.

  1. TRUTH is often thought to be achievable by experiencing Ultimate Reality, or Objective Reality. However, neither Objective Knowledge nor the will of God can be known because they require unmediated access to an Outside Reference System which by definition is not possible. That which is outside one's self can only be interpreted by human beings based on the relevant stimuli.
  2. KNOWLEDGE means information, data, understanding, and principles. It permits prediction, manipulation, and use of the forces, attributes, and patterns of the natural world -- utilizing what is known.
  3. WISDOM is that aspect of Knowledge which when applied to a person's life increases the probability that they will become an Enlightened Person.

III. A *feeling of well-being* is defined as existing when a person who is able to end their life does not do so for irrational reasons.

 A. The feeling that a person's life has meaning describes an emotion-state based on beliefs.
 B. The correctness of any given belief that supports a *feeling of well-being* depends on the degree to which it is sustainable in an Enlightened Community.
 C. Only empirical study can determine whether or not an individual's beliefs that support their *feeling of well-being* are sustainable.

D. Knowledge is not an end in itself, but has value to the degree that it helps individuals find Wisdom; that is, set goals and make life choices that increase the likelihood of achieving a *sustainable feeling that their life has meaning*, or the equivalent, *a sustainable feeling of well-being*.

    1. Those beliefs and actions will most greatly aid a person in achieving a *sustainable feeling of well-being* which moves them out of their raw "tribal" genetic propensities toward attaining their "wisdom" or "symbolic species" potential.

        a. Below are the currently proposed <u>Ways of Wisdom</u> judged necessary to achieve *a sustainable feeling of well-being*.

Eleven Ways of Wisdom4 – 4-15-18

1. **Recognize that human beings are – for us -- the Ultimate Reference System. (Chap. 8)**
2. **Endeavor to maintain and improve the human species. Support efforts to develop Enlightened Communities. (Chap. 9)**
3. **Seek to understand. Pursue Wisdom. (Chap. 10)**
4. **Recognize that all knowledge rests on assumptions and must always be open to questioning. (Chap. 11)**
5. **Strive to make the best choices possible. (Chap. 12)**
6. **Know and struggle to improve yourself; work to be physically and mentally healthy. (Chap. 13)**
7. **Develop and adopt a perceptual framework in which pain does not prevent the achievement of a sustainable belief that your life has meaning. (Chap. 14)**
8. **Help and be helped by other people. (Chap. 15)**
9. **Work to increase knowledge and all creative and artistic endeavors. Adopt an inspiring life goal. (Chap. 16)**
10. **Support efforts to ensure that every child is provided a loving, nurturing life and all the things necessary to become an Enlightened Person. (Chap. 17)**

11. Make of your life a *spiritual* quest[1]. Work to become an Enlightened Person. (Chap. 18)

Regarding the person I propose that the <u>individual</u> is responsible for all of their choices -- acts, thoughts, etc.

Second I propose that <u>one's society</u> is responsible for every choice -- act, thought, etc. -- of every citizen.

In my mind the above approach is the only way to build a utopia for all human beings while at the same time perpetuating our species. What do you think?

Science is the search for congruency (everything fits together in the natural world with no unexplainable gaps).

Religion is the search for meaning.

Both science and religion are necessary to provide a sustainable feeling of well-being to each and every person.

2. The Ways of Wisdom are attempts to specify the beliefs necessary to become an Enlightened Person and can only be fully actualized within an Enlightened Community.

   a. <u>An Enlightened Person</u> is someone who is achieving the closest approximation currently possible of a *sustainable feeling of well-being.*

   c. <u>An Enlightened Community</u> is one that promotes the belief and implements the idea that human beings are the source of meaning and value and that the individual person needs to be seen as the focus for society's ultimate concern.

3. The goal would be to have all the organizations of an Enlightened Community support in whatever ways are appropriate the ability of all persons involved to become their best self.

   a. The Wisdom Group is seen as the initial organization to bring individuals together to help them apply the ideas of a *science of religion and ethics.*

> b. When Wisdom Groups develop sufficient support they
> would establish a Center for the Practical Application
> of Wisdom to work on developing an Enlightened
> Community.

RELIGIOUS / ETHICAL

Religious/ethical beliefs within the domain of a *science of religion and ethics* are defined as those beliefs concerned with maintaining and developing the human species. For individuals this means achieving a *sustainable feeling of well-being.*

Traditionally, any efforts to involve science in the area of ethics have foundered on one problem after another. Initially this was because morality was either within the realm of folk religions – by custom the sole possessors of meaning – or Platonist rational systems. More recently it has been because this didn't seem possible due to the way the various philosophers discussed it, especially the English philosopher G.E. Moore who claimed it was a "naturalistic fallacy" [2] to think that science could be used to improve ethical choices.

Bart Kosko in his writings on fuzzy logic discusses other ideas that made it seem science and ethics could not be joined together. Kosko says, "In a sense that I will explain science has disposed of ethics. We have no final argument but force against the young men who run through Dostoevsky novels and shout 'Everything is permitted!'....Up close the social contract shades into gray and frays into whatever you want it to be." [3]

However, a *science of religion and ethics* says there is an argument other than threats and punishment for those who claim, "Everything is permitted." The answer is knowledge, information, facts, opportunities, Wisdom, human nature. This answer consists of first, developing a unifying principle of a compelling nature: *a sustainable feeling of well-being.* A *sustainable feeling of well-being* is based on those beliefs that lead a person toward developing their full positive potential. It is distinguished from a *feeling that a person's life has meaning* which boils down to having a good enough reason to live so that a person does not commit suicide or otherwise end a person's life for irrational or erroneous reasons. This also provides a compelling reason to avoid asocial and antisocial behavior.

There are some things that are essential for a person to achieve the state described by the concept *a sustainable feeling of well-being*. On the other hand there are some things that prevent, or at least make more difficult, the achievement of this state. Therefore, in terms of a person's most fundamental need, not all things are permitted. Discovering which things are permitted and which are not is the most important goal of a person's life and the lives of all people.

Kosko writes, "Science undercuts ethics because we have made science the measure of all things. Truth means truth of science. Truth means logical truth or factual truth. Truth means math proof or data test. The truth can be a matter of degree. But that does not help ethics."(p. 256) I think the concept *sustainable feeling of well-being* provides a way around Kosko's arguments. To more deeply explore this approach see VOLUME II, Chapter 18-B, "What Fuzzy Logic Can Teach Us About Ethics, Morality, and a *Science of Religion and Ethics*." [4] When the *sustainable feeling of well-being* concept is adopted religion/ethics/morals then becomes an area of relevant concern.

Kosko continues (p. 256), "The argument starts like this. Are ethical statements true? Are they false? Look at the ethical statement 'Murder is wrong.' Is it true?" Obviously, when Kosko considers whether or not murder is wrong, the issue boils down to what we take "wrong" to mean and our related assumptions. If we think there is some Absolute Reference System independent of humanity that we can use to determine right and wrong we are pursuing a dead end path. This approach ended with the death of God, or the recognition that God is a mystery, not a source of information or answers. But if we recognize that right and wrong relate to the fact that Humanity itself is our ultimate reference system-- who have evolved in this world and have the stamp of their evolutionary history imposed on them by that experience which thereby defines right and wrong, empirically, in this context -- we then have a way to evaluate such sentences. Ethical statements are expressions of opinion. They are opinions that can in principle be substantiated/disproven. Current science is developing and perfecting tools that could be helpful for the preceding effort. How does a person validate an opinion about an ethical statement?

By testing it against data just like scientists test any other opinion (which they call hypotheses, theories, laws). Is it true that aspirin cures headaches, small pox vaccinations prevent small pox, heavier than air craft can fly, that the universe is mostly made up of dark matter and dark energy? When we say a given choice is right if it leads toward achieving *a sustainable feeling of well-being* and wrong if it leads away from it, we have a criterion that can be used to evaluate choices and determine their truth value.

When we focus on *a sustainable feeling of well-being* then we have a criterion that permits direct empirical study. Such studies would refute Kosko's above conclusions about murder. We can test whether or not murdering (or for that matter lying, cheating, stealing, intimidating, abusing, mistreating, striving for power over others, etc.) leads a person toward or away from achieving *a sustainable feeling of well-being.*

I'm sure everyone has opinions on these things, but the point is this issue like any other can be studied to remove the more subjective aspects of opinions. Data can be accumulated, analyzed, and compelling conclusions drawn. Like any conclusion in science these are not final answers that cannot change, but they are answers to be used. When properly used these answers can help people make better choices in their lives.

The following quote puts ethical/moral matters into the proper perspective. "An ethics of daily practice...would need to employ almost a novelist's eye in order to uncover the implications of acts and choices so small that we rarely stop to observe them. It would take as its goal an examination of behavior that we automatically consider free from ethical content: what we read, what we wear, how we talk to our children, the furnishings we choose, even perhaps the daydream that passes unnoticed as we round a familiar corner." [5]

One consequence of the foregoing is the need to recognize that we need a lot of help in making choices. What seems essential to me is to focus more broadly and also very specifically on the area of choice. What are the rules for making the best choices possible? What is society's role in teaching these rules and then providing assistance to help individuals and groups actually make good choices and avoid bad choices?

Every choice is a "cause set in motion." It is essential that we monitor all choices even if sporadically to ensure that our choices are moving us in the direction we want to go. The foregoing is especially important if we have accepted the goal of helping to create an Enlightened Community and to become an Enlightened Person.

Making good choices is what the Ways of Wisdom are about, especially the Fifth Way: Strive to make the best choices. [6] The Ways of Wisdom provide a method to organize all knowledge. Persons will thereby be able to assess the value of any given data, fact, or assumption. The aim is to help individuals use the experiences and best thinking of all people to make every choice in their life. Each choice should help the person move toward achieving *a sustainable feeling of well-being.*

Kosko goes on (p. 262), "Reason ends in doubt. Science disposes of ethics. It strips moral claims of logic and fact and reduces them to feeling in words." Up to the current time Kosko is right. Reason does end in doubt. This is not just the doubt of realizing that Truth cannot be attained, but the doubt of not knowing what the proper way to live a life is. What is it about human life and human living that is important? How should we be living our life? What is the goal of life? How can we achieve that goal?

Western society has been guided by the current concepts and models of philosophy (the joy of free speculation), folk religions (transcendence through God), and science (the satisfaction of having Truth about the Cosmos) to their obvious limits/conclusions. We have found that these concepts and models lead into an abyss. We can stand at the edge of this abyss and wail and moan or we can start over.

I want to start over. For me starting over means utilizing the best thinking and experience from all of humanity to get clearly in mind the most fundamental issues. I think that "the meaning of human life" provides a way to usefully deal with these definitive questions. When we properly define and utilize "the meaning of human life" concept we see that the path leads not to doubt, but to clarity -- to clarity in choices, life goals, behavior, and how to achieve satisfaction, joy, excitement, creativity, enthusiasm, transcendence: the Enlightened Community made up of Enlightened Persons.

But to achieve the foregoing requires changes at the most fundamental level that clarify what the quality of human life means. We need to re-define science and understand religion and ethics in a new way. Science instead of being only the search for knowledge, truth, and understanding, needs to include the application of whatever knowledge and understanding we achieve to the improvement of the quality of human living. The best place to start is by defining science as the search for congruency. The goal of religion and ethics needs to be clarified in terms of the meaning of human life. It needs to be recognized as the area of science that deals with everything relevant to human living. It takes the goal of human life as being to achieve *a sustainable feeling of well-being*. And it studies beliefs to clarify which ones lead the person toward achieving *a sustainable feeling of well-being* and which ones do not. It would encourage the development of organizations to help persons to achieve *a sustainable feeling of well-being*. Empiricism provides the feedback to a science-based naturalistic religion and ethical system to guide each individual to become an Enlightened Person.

If contemporary society is to make a "breakthrough" and achieve something fundamentally new -- a paradigm for achieving the potential made possible when our species evolved the "language ability" (see Chapter 1 [7]) -- it needs to learn how to properly use knowledge. The foregoing can only be accomplished by establishing Enlightened Communities where necessary changes can be introduced as needed.

However, only individuals who have achieved *a sustainable feeling of well-being* can set up and maintain an Enlightened Community. Therefore, the need is great to produce Enlightened Persons. But, since no model currently exists, how do we learn what needs to be done in order to become an Enlightened Person? The answer to the foregoing question is not clear. Are the ideas included in the current Ways of Wisdom on the right track, or are they distractions, totally misfocused? It seems important for a Wisdom Group to move carefully and honor any resistance by the individuals involved.

Clearly, it is necessary that all persons decide for themselves whether they have found *a sustainable feeling of well-being*. Society may help the individual in every practical way to make their search as easy, direct, and fruitful as possible, but it cannot make fundamental decisions for them. The foregoing defines the essence of an Enlightened Community. Certainly, no one can find *a sustainable feeling of well-being* without help. But neither can it be found by accepting ideas that wear like robes that cover, but hide individuality. A *science of religion and ethics* is based on the core assumption that **the fundamental goals are the same for all**

people. But at the same time each person is unique. And a Wisdom Group needs to honor and promote these differences. It is also the uniqueness of the individual that is the strength of *Modern Humans*. It needs to be encouraged and developed if we are to endure in a chaotic universe.

However, since the state of having *a sustainable feeling of well-being* needs to also be determined by outside observers this is the evaluation used by Wisdom Groups, scientists, and all other persons. There is the potential for a difference of opinion on this evaluation so it is important that standards, procedures, behaviors, and such. be as clear as current knowledge permits.

The goal of a Wisdom Group needs to be to stimulate in each person a thirst for knowledge and an ability to distinguish between positive and negative answers and values. All teaching needs to be aimed at helping students ask better questions rather than expecting to obtain final answers. Care needs to be taken to ensure that the content of education is proven to the degree claimed. And it needs to always be made clear that all "facts" rest on unproven assumptions. (See VOLUME II, Chapter 10, "Science and the Search for Truth." [8])

It should be obvious that *a sustainable feeling of well-being* can only be achieved with knowledge. Just as certainly individuals will labor in a vacuum as long as knowledge is not used to help them attain *a sustainable feeling of well-being*. For all persons to achieve *a sustainable feeling of well-being*, it is necessary to recognize that the focus needs to be not on what humanity achieves, but on what each individual achieves.

A.J. Ayer [9] was right on the mark when he said, "There is no field of experience which cannot, in principle, be brought under some form of scientific law, and no type of speculative knowledge about the world which it is, in principle, beyond the power of science to give."

A *science of religion and ethics* presents a new paradigm, and a Center for the Practical Application of Wisdom would build on it. All of a society's assumptions need to be carefully examined to see how well they hold up. And, all parts of this process depend on the methods of science that have allowed humanity to make giant strides forward in understanding the world due to the ever increasing power of its tools and knowledge base.

Although science has increased our knowledge and mastery of the forces of nature, it has rejected that which is most important: the area of meaning of human life. By ignoring ethics which deals with meaning, or by accepting the validity of ethical systems based on untestable assumptions, scientists have been among those leaders who have missed the opportunity to help our species master our greatest hurdle. Humanity is in the process of creating itself and needs guidance on how to do that. To produce such a breakthrough is the goal of a *science of religion and ethics*.

This breakthrough would create a utopia leading to developing organizations to produce Enlightened Persons and Enlightened Communities. These structures would allow individuals to live the best lives possible totally bonded to their society yet totally developed as individuals. Nowhere has the necessary congruency between the individual and society yet been achieved. On the one hand the U.S. has been a pioneer in developing a model that is crucial in humanity's effort to create themselves in a way congruent with their "wisdom" potential. This is the model of the individual as being of the highest value and the importance of ensuring their right to make the choices about the things that affect their life -- what they read, their education, employment, religious affiliation, life style, and such. – everything where their choices do not harm others.

On the other hand because the U.S. has placed an unbalanced attention on the individual, it has greater incongruency between the individual and society (between independence and interdependence) than almost anywhere else on earth. In urban areas in the U.S. harmony between individuals and society is almost totally missing. It seems clear to me that the U.S. has reached a point where its citizens are in a position to see that a new approach is needed. We need to learn how to maintain the sacredness of the individual while at the same time allowing them to achieve total integration into society. In spite of our tremendous knowledge this synthesis is almost totally missing from modern life. Many modern persons would ask whether or not it's even possible for modern human beings to achieve the same level of congruency with the natural world and each other that existed prior to the evolution of the language ability, and yet maintain current levels of personal freedom and individual self fulfillment. Can we find a way to achieve congruency of life that maximizes growth and development of the individual, and of the community at the same time?

First we need to recognize that these two goals need not be in conflict. That is one of the most important messages of a *science of religion and ethics.* Unfortunately, this conflicts with some 200 years of thinking by many persons in Western society most respected in the reactionary areas of our culture — many religious, political, and business leaders who look to the past for answers rather than the future. So making this transition will not be a cakewalk. The key to this congruency needs to be to develop organizations based on a *science of religion and ethics* to provide well-grounded alternative visions.

But how can a *science of religion and ethics* be developed? To develop a *science of religion and ethics* a person merely needs to provide a unifying principle that ties all relevant behavior and experience together in such a way that the associated hypotheses can be tested empirically. Darwin's approach -- that changed biology from a descriptive to an empirical science -- might provide a useful model.

Unfortunately, my organizing principle for a *science of religion and ethics* -- meaning of human life -- is not supported with the overwhelming mass of carefully assembled evidence such as that Darwin presented in *Origin Of Species.* However, I do elaborate on the ideas presented here with the material assembled in VOLUME II [10]. Nevertheless, my efforts are probably more comparable to the evolution writings of Jean Baptiste Lamarck, or the work of Darwin's grandfather, Erasmus Darwin. As a result my model very possibly includes assumptions as erroneous as those that Lamarck based his theory of evolution on -- that changes in offspring were caused by parental behavior as they struggled to fulfill an inner urge -- an innate tendency toward perfection (a Platonist ideal) -- to fit their niche.

Regardless of how the foregoing turns out the establishment of a *science of religion and ethics* seems to me to be the most pressing need of humanity. I propose that every major problem in the world today is due to the lack of a *science of religion and ethics.* Current ethical systems based on non-empirically testable ideas do provide a storehouse of data to be analyzed and sifted for relevance. But developing an alternative system will be a mammoth undertaking. However, as indicated in my introduction, it is my fondest hope that after reading this book many members of local churches, synagogues, mosques, and such. might more clearly understand their mission and want to become part of a Wisdom network. Although folk religions in general are like folk medicine prior to the introduction of science there is tremendous variation within local groups. Some of them only need a convincing vision of a *science of religion and ethics* in order to move in that direction. However, speaking generally, folk religions can do some things very well based on folk remedies, and cultural wisdom. Other things are a disaster. One area of crisis/tragedy/calamity in the modern world is the inability of folk religions to apply the tools of science to their assumptions and conclusions. As a result this has led to their enmeshment in erroneous ideas about how the cosmos and human beings work. Individuals who are attempting to rise above the subjective, error-filled assumptions of their culture's folk religion often have no source of common wisdom to look to. There is no universally applicable foundation upon which to ground their life.

One reason for the foregoing situation is a lack of understanding by scientists and modern thinkers in general of the possibility and importance of a *science of religion and ethics*. Because the true function of religion/ethics in a society – to allow each person to find meaning in their life by working to maintain and develop our species – has been overlooked by social scientists and almost all other seminal thinkers up to this point, we have built social structures without foundations. Religious/ethics systems when they function properly are a bonding force in society, binding the individual to their society, and to all of humanity. They provide the symbols and concepts used for assessing and valuing everything else. They provide individuals a sense of well-being and focus for their life. It is the failure to develop a *science of religion and ethics* that has magnified all our other failures.

CHAPTER 3

HOW TO LIVE THE GOOD LIFE

From the perspective of a *science of religion and ethics* all current religious institutions are based on erroneous and outmoded ideas and models of human beings and the world. As a result they mislead, confuse, and induce all who are involved in them to fritter away their lives. For some people the effects appear minor. For others it is catastrophic. However, in reality it is disastrous for everyone because instead of functioning at the highest level of a person's potential almost all of us move along in low gear. Instead of achieving Enlightenment -- a *sustainable beliefs that a person's life has meaning* -- many persons experience hopelessness, depression, deprivation, and the lowest levels of achievement. Individuals exploit each other because they have been taught that they can benefit from doing so though they may be punished later if their behavior or thoughts are discovered. Instead of helping humanity move smoothly and honorably toward the Good Life they support or encourage activity that retards this movement. They add little, or more likely, show by example how not to live the good life.

Replacing folk religions is the greatest need for current societies. Alternative institutions need to be developed that help real people with their real problems. These new institutions need to dramatically improve the quality of each person's life. I see a Wisdom Group as the primary institution to initiate and support the vision of the Enlightened Person. The members of such a Group would then develop and work through a Center for the Practical Application of Wisdom to help each society become an Enlightened Community.

Lacking such groups and institutions neither the U.S. nor any other society will be able to coordinate and focus its intellectual and economic resources so as to produce the necessary changes. The goal of a *science of religion and ethics* is to encourage in every way it can the growth and development of such resources.

As indicated earlier a *science of religion and ethics* is based on the core ideas imbedded in the confusing concept, "the meaning of human life." I have proposed that the *science of religion and ethics* is the science concerned with definitive issues, particularly the concept of the Enlightened Person -- someone with *a sustainable feeling of well-being*, and how individuals can attain the beliefs necessary to achieve this state. A *science of religion and ethics* would provide a framework to allow all knowledge, wisdom, and understanding to be joined together into a congruent whole.

Because all human problems or concerns relate to the issue of meaning of human life it should lie at the core of religion/ethics. But can this key issue be tackled in a scientific way? For me the answer is: Yes! Meaning of human life can actually be used as an organizing principle or concept to create an empirical a *science of religion and ethics*. It would then provide the mechanism to tie together our observations, analysis, and synthesis. Although the complete description of "meaning of life" remains to be developed the first component as discussed earlier is the choosing of life over death when this is possible. In other words I define a person as having meaning of life when they decide to continue living. And I presume that this choice comes out of beliefs that may or may not be clear to the person involved.

However, this is just a first approximation to understanding since the reasons each person chooses as they do may be too many to fully enumerate. And obviously some reasons are vastly superior to others. In my mind the core of a *science of religion and ethics* would be clarifying superior over inferior reasons and helping persons move forward in doing so.

Although all the causes for choosing life over death may be unknown, the physiology behind these choices is another matter. It seems to me that the first and foremost element of meaning of human life involves a feeling of being part of a social group. Another might be in the area of transcendence -- looking beyond the moment to that which is of lasting value. These social needs are something all normal human beings in good mental health share. And these social needs are ones traditionally filled by religious organizations. But looking at these aspects of meaning of life helps us see that we need to not only focus on the individual, but also to focus outward onto the individual's society and then beyond that to all of humanity.

When we see people living hollow lives, we are not observing "human nature"; i.e., -- persons following their drive to maintain life with well-being. Rather, we are seeing reflected in the lives of individuals a society's deficient institutions, erroneous social theories, and mistaken ideas about how to live. When we see angry individuals, performing cruel and hurtful acts, we are seeing persons who lacked important nurturing and guidance in their early years, and who have not been shown ways to recover from those traumas and achieve love, tenderness, and closeness. In addition we are seeing persons who lack transforming visions that inspire and direct them.

"Human nature is not something existing separately in the individual, but [is]... a relatively simple and general condition of the social mind.... [Human beings] cannot acquire it except through fellowship, and it decays in isolation." [1] Therefore, no person can be studied independently of the society and family in which they were raised.

A *science of religion and ethics* should provide guidance to establish the agencies and resources to support individuals in their quest for meaning and a universal way to bind all people together. Specifically it needs to help to provide the paradigm to guide research in sociology, anthropology, philosophy, psychology, medicine, and the other sciences, as well as studies and research within a *science of religion and ethics* itself. A *science of religion and ethics* needs to then bring the results of all this research together and utilize it to improve the quality of human living.

At their best this is what religious institutions have always been for -- to provide ways to incorporate the wisdom and experiences of the past into the lives of current and future generations. In the process of doing this religions bind all the members of the group together and provide the feeling that the individual's life has meaning. Since modern thinking and understanding have shown the inadequacy of traditional religious symbols, the concerned person therefore needs to grapple to find new symbols and new formulations -- better ways to tie it all together. That is the real quest of this book!

A study of the way science works indicates that a person cannot determine by thought alone what behaviors, ingredients, social structures, and such will fulfill the requirements of the concepts Enlightened Person and *sustainable feeling of well-being*. As Einstein has said, "Through purely logical thinking we can attain no knowledge whatsoever of the empirical world." [2] Conjecture will not allow a person to decide which courses of action are absolutely necessary to become an Enlightened Person and achieve a *sustainable feeling of well-being*. And which ones, though enjoyable and useful, are not absolutely necessary. Or which ones may appear important, but turn out to be destructive or to misdirect the person.

Perhaps the factors that make up becoming an Enlightened Person are not the same for everyone. They may conflict and interact in complex ways. It may be that different personality styles require different behaviors in order to become an Enlightened Person. There could well be ingredients absolutely necessary to one person that would be harmful to others [3]. If the foregoing is correct, it will increase the difficulty of finding the components of an Enlightened Person. However, I am convinced that it can and needs to be done. But it can only be done by studying actual people's lives and actual societies. Anything said here needs to be tested by actual research and changed as the data requires. Every culture should be expected to provide useful insights to guide the restructuring of existing societies into Enlightened Communities.

If the components making up an Enlightened Person and the methods for achieving it can be isolated, and described, this information needs to be formulated in such a way that it would help anyone from any culture to move toward becoming an Enlightened Person. The Ways of Wisdom currently look suspiciously like idealizations of the present social and cultural goals of contemporary progressive Western societies. Undoubtedly, the views herein presented are overly dependent on one culture, and need more anthropological input.

A basic assumption of my approach is that at their core human beings need to feel worthwhile and that their life has value and purpose. This is what I call a state of *feeling that a person's life has meaning, or a feeling of well-being*. It is characterized by positive emotions such as joy, happiness, effectiveness, love, usefulness, and such This need for a *feeling of well-being* can overcome all our drives at least within limits. It can cause us to deny our sexual drive and become celibate. It can cause us to spurn food, and fast even unto death. It can cause us to undergo torture and deformity. Under certain circumstances it can move anyone to sacrifice their life and in other situations to commit suicide. It is the need that is with us all the time and causes the disillusioned, lost, betrayed, unfulfilled, and/ or discouraged person's feelings of hopelessness, despair, and uselessness.

For human beings the essence of the meaning of life is a feeling state -- a feeling state that depends upon the individual's beliefs. At its best this is a positive feeling that a person is important and that their life has value. We can only understand its complexity and parameters by studying individuals and societies. However it seems safe to say that meaning of life at its most fundamental level means love and physical affection showered on the individual by people they love and who care for them in return. These conditions tend to exist in all hunter-gatherer tribes of the world. In a small integrated group of individuals who share common beliefs this condition exists for most members almost all the time. As a result nearly all the members of the group experience a *feeling of well-being*. In fact they would not understand the question if they were asked whether or not their life had meaning. Existential separation can only come when a person is cut off and alienated from other people, when they see no reasonable hope for the future. The foregoing begins to occur with increasing frequency as a society becomes more and more complex and loses the cultural activities that make people feel connected. This condition was rampant during and after World War II because of the disillusionment the war caused about humanity's ability to attain the good life.

However, on the other side of the balance, a person would find that in a pre-literate tribe the area of the transcendent is not handled very well from the perspective of a *science of religion and ethics*. Information is not dealt with satisfactorily. There are no structures to gather, test, assimilate, correct, expand, and properly make use of information. Therefore, there is a severe limitation on how much of their positive potential each member of the group can achieve. They are totally preoccupied with the mundane -- finding and eating food, idle discourse, sexual activity, and taking care of other basic life necessities, or diversions. As indicated in Chapter 1 such individual's lives are focused on their raw "tribal" propensities. Knowledge is not pursued as a goal, so ignorance reigns. The individual's "wisdom" potential opened up by the development of the language ability is barely utilized. Members of the group have vast capacities and powers that are not realized. Whether they recognize it or not, some essential elements of their needs are not stimulated by their society and, as a result, are missing from their worldview. These missing components make them very vulnerable to losing their *feeling of well-being*. This can happen due to changes in the climate, invasions by other societies, disease, contact with new ideas, old age, and such. In the foregoing situations the *feeling that a person's life has meaning* is not *sustainable* even though it may last over a given individual's entire life. If it is based on erroneous or non-congruent beliefs, for a *science of religion and ethics* it is not considered sustainable since it is not a guide for others to achieve the Good Life. (On first exposure the preceding idea sounds like doublethink. However, it is a key idea that will be discussed more deeply in a future chapter.)

Current U.S. society values the pursuit of knowledge (at least in a general way), but almost always for the wrong reasons. Rarely, if ever, is it focused on the relevant aspects of the transcendent -- developing a person's "wisdom" potential. Modern people have lost the deep and nurturing connection with a group, clan, tribe, family, and such. And it is a core assumption of a *science of religion and ethics* that the absence of nurturing connections with other people is a major component of depression. Therefore, as indicated below, psychological depression surrounds us.

"We live in an age of depression. Compared with when our grandparents were young, depression is now ten times as widespread in the United States, and the rate is climbing. Nowadays, depression first strikes people ten years younger, on average, reaching into late childhood and early adolescence for its youngest victims. It has become the common cold of mental illness."[4]

"If we consider the <u>worst</u> mood these people [in the experiment] ever experienced, it appears that the dimension of <u>depression</u> is the most strongly represented. The words that make up this dimension are: depressed, gloomy, sad, empty, lonesome, helpless, discouraged, and hopeless. The experience of loss, separation, and mourning is apparently a more distressing experience than that of fear or worry." [5] I interpret the foregoing to support my analysis of the importance of having a *feeling that a person's life has meaning*. States of depression I equate with moving toward the lack of a *feeling that a person's life has meaning*. This state has been shown in the above study to be the most painful one to those persons studied, and I assume to essentially everyone else.

Susan A. Everson -- an epidemiologist at the Western Consortium for Public Health in Berkeley, California -- and her colleagues have recently published data about the relationship between depression and hopelessness. [6] Their studies suggest that the widespread notion that hopelessness represents an extreme form of depression is wrong. However, this research doesn't change the above conclusions about depression. Everson's work supports the idea that hopelessness -- bleak expectations about oneself and the future -- bode ill for physical health.

My position is that depression is more likely to occur as a person's *feeling of well-being* begins to diminish. This loss represents a failure in the society's and the individual's belief system. Although our culture tends to think of depression in terms of psychological illness and chemical imbalances in the brain, these overlook the obvious: all primates need nurturing touch and group acceptance in order to maintain a positive, energized life. All societies have tried to provide their members a viable feeling of worth and value, but from the perspective of a *science of religion and ethics* they have always failed to do so. A society that is not yet an Enlightened Community cannot provide this feeling to all members of the group. The foundation used by these societies to support a *feeling that a person's life has meaning* can disappear at any moment. Only an Enlightened Community would be able to provide sufficient support to its members so they can continue to correct the Community's errors and therefore maintain necessary procedures on a sustained basis.

Many individuals have thought that they could find an objective standard transcendent to humanity by which to attain meaning. But every step forward in knowledge and understanding has moved us in the opposite direction. The redness of a rose and the roundness of a sphere exist only in people's minds. Instead of showing the inadequacy of human beings as interpreters, the foregoing demonstrates that we must always work within the framework of human perceptions and interpretations.

Individuals can enjoy the beauty of an orchid and a musical composition not because of any inherent quality in those things, but because of the way human brains function, and therefore interpret/experience them. A thing, therefore, becomes meaningful only as it is meaningful to human beings. A meaningful life cannot rest on any standard independent of humanity. From this perspective human beings are the source of meaning and value and the individual person is taken to be the focus for society's ultimate concern.

As the foregoing ideas are studied it becomes obvious that *meaning of human life* depends upon a feeling state. These feelings are characterized by hope. In this way aspirations are nurtured that give a sense of direction and importance to each individual's life. There is no need to look for answers beyond the physical world. This book is concerned with developing a *science of religion and ethics* that would include every dimension of reality and promote the exploration of the full complexity of the Cosmos.

A science of religion and ethics need not be able to answer every question about which a person wonders. However, the questions that are not answered cannot be crucial to the issue of the *meaning of human life*. But they may require more knowledge and/or understanding than is currently available in order to be answered. In addition to the foregoing it is proposed that any cogent religious/ethics system is required to fulfill at least three other requirements:

1. **It needs to be of value to and able to be followed by all of humanity -- be universal.**
2. **Its premises need to be independently discoverable and its conclusions capable of being falsified -- be objective.**
3. **It needs to be comprehensive in scope, clearly stated, and internally consistent.**

REQUIREMENT FOR UNIVERSALITY EXPANDED

Any cogent religious/ethics system needs to be of value to and able to be followed by all of humanity.

Any religious/ethics system to be cogent needs to be universally applicable -- for all human beings. Persons are not justified in accepting a religious/ethics system as "The System" unless it is accepted and fully implemented by all people. Each person would need to be politically and physically free, satisfactorily educated, and accept the System not because of ignorance, but through understanding. Furthermore, until every person accepts and is able to follow its precepts, no system can legitimately be judged as complete by its supporters. Until the foregoing state exists it cannot rightfully be proclaimed "The System."

To accomplish the foregoing, a religious/ethics system needs to be able to help each person achieve a suitable, satisfactory level of education. These persons need to also have a firm contact with reality; that is, be in good mental health. A cogent system needs to be able to help any person become an Enlightened Person. No matter how prejudiced, sexist, racist, chauvinist, or otherwise self-destructive and asocial/antisocial the person, they need to be helped to achieve a *sustainable feeling of well-being*, or the religious/ethics system is imperfect. Since any irrationally harmful behavior to self or others results from ignorance (either in the individual or in society), such behavior needs to be able to be changed with sufficient knowledge.

REQUIREMENT FOR OBJECTIVITY EXPANDED

The premises of any cogent religious/ethics system needs to be based on falsifiable concepts that are independently discoverable and available to all persons.

Any religious/ethics system to be cogent needs to be based on objective (in terms of Human Beings as the Ultimate Reference System), not subjective events such as accident of birth. Its foundation assumptions must not be immune or shielded from questioning; rather they need to be open to being proven false. Like any scientific theory "The System" needs to be easily accessible to anyone. However, since it is concerned with all knowledge, it is not easily discovered any more than was uranium, the dwarf planet Pluto, calculus, or the theory of relativity. Every path followed consistently needs to lead to it. A person's position needs to not critically depend only upon desire, blind faith, or subjective, unrepeatable experience.

Unless basic concepts have testable implications and observable, experimental support it is difficult to separate them from erroneous beliefs. Without the foregoing, discrepancies are hard to recognize and correct. So if beliefs cannot be tested and validated, using them as the basis for life choices is problematical at best. For example, using an illustration from the natural sciences consider the situation where the question is raised whether the earth is flat or spherical. We need to ask how a person might choose between these ideas. Can either assertion be translated into a test that can be demonstrated or refuted? Or does it become obvious to a sensible, rational, knowledgeable person that either claim is irrational and/or invalid? In other words does a person's answer come out of their personal psychology, rather than from external observational data?

"The System" cannot be forced upon anyone. If it is correct it needs to be able to prove itself so in such a way that every person accepts it without resort to force, psychological trickery, subterfuge, group pressure, and such. In reality if a society possesses "The System," individuals from other societies -- if such existed -- would be able to enter it and become completely at home there without significant misgivings, longing to return to their former society, or feelings of disillusionment. The foregoing would be true because an Enlightened Community is able to fulfill all of a person's essential needs. To reiterate for the sake of clarity, fulfilling all of a person's essential needs does not consist of guaranteeing complacency by perpetuating the vegetable state (like dripping pleasure hormones into their brain). "The System" needs to fulfill people's aspirations and ensure that they are engaged in a spiritual quest. To accomplish the foregoing, "The System" needs to be able to replace the ideas of any parochial group, society, folk religion, or those spontaneously generated by a seeker.

"The System" needs to have a better foundation than common sense. Common sense cannot be looked upon as more than a collection of preconceptions defined by the limits of a person's experiences and knowledge. To say that a person can determine by common sense whether a given act, idea, or system is the best one is to deny the tremendous advances science has made ever since scientists gave up such methods.

The idea of determining whether a procedure, concept, or construct (such as a religious/ethics system) is "right" or "wrong" through logic is a smaller segment of the foregoing problem. As A.J. Ayer [7] makes clear, logic can tell us nothing necessarily true about the real world, the empirical world -- the world of "right" and "wrong" behavior. It is critical to understand that Aristotelian yes/no logic (law of the excluded middle) cannot be counted on to apply (be "necessarily true") in an analysis of real-world behavior.

Because the realm of logic is grossly misunderstood I will take a few words in an attempt to make some key points clear. Yes/no logic only truly, fully applies in the realm of mathematics. In the empirical realm thoughts are rarely completely true or entirely false, but are almost always somewhere in between. The empirical domain is the realm of fuzzy logic [8]. In the realm of science empirical assumptions must at some point be tested if they are to be used as a basis for valid conclusions. Until that satisfactorily happens any "then" statement coming out of an assumption must remain in question. The foregoing is especially true when "proof by contradiction" is used. Although proof by contradiction works well in the realm of mathematics, in the real world there can be serious problems. In a particular application proof by contradiction may lead to useful answers, but it can lead to errors and even absurdities (such as demonstrated in Socrates' arguments about virtue in Plato's "Menos Dialogue.") So we see that misapplication of logic outside the realm of mathematics has been common even before Aristotle formalized logic in the fourth century BCE.

REQUIREMENT FOR CONSISTENCY EXPANDED

Any cogent religious/ethics system needs to be comprehensive in scope, clearly stated, and internally consistent.

The System needs to be concerned with everything in some way and everything needs to in some way be pertinent to it. Unless a religious/ethics system is comprehensive and considers all things of which humans are aware, it does not provide an adequate framework for living in the world. Therefore, no component of history, emotion, science, art, or anything else could automatically be excluded from consideration because it was perceived as being too insignificant to matter. "The System" provides the unifying vision that fits all these things together into a congruent whole to answer the question, "what is the meaning of human life?"

In the *first requirement* the hypothesis is presented that a religious/ethics system needs to be able to be followed by all persons if it is in reality "The System." If a religious/ethics system is not clearly stated, no person can truthfully say whether or not they accept it or are following it. If it is so vague that any person can be said to be following it regardless of her or his beliefs or actions, then the religious/ethics system has limited validity and cannot be "The System."

It needs to avoid vague concepts that are undefinable and/or untestable such as God, eternal soul, Heaven, the Devil, Nirvana, Karma, and similar ideas. Since these concepts are actually being used in many current religions or ethical systems, I take that as evidence of the inadequacy of those systems. A religious/ethics system is not cogent if its key terms have different meanings for all who use them. If people interpret the basic concepts in different ways, no cogent system exists. This does not mean that everyone needs to believe exactly the same things and agree on every point. The foregoing is impossible since every assumption is open to questioning, and few ideas are proven beyond the shadow of a doubt. As a result just as early scientists were justified in thinking of light as either a wave or particle phenomenon since research and observation supported each view, a religious/ethics system needs to consider all the explanations consistent with the evidence.

However, if the core assumptions can be used as easily to prevent people from understanding the cosmos as from achieving understanding, then a cogent system does not exist. As indicated in the *second requirement* falsifiable concepts are essential to have a cogent system. Only if the statements and definitions of a religious/ethics system are clearly presented like those for the other areas of science is it possible to develop valid experiments or observations to test them.

A cogent religious/ethics system needs to be internally consistent. Only if the foregoing condition is met can a religious/ethics system be in harmony with itself. If one part of it supports cause and effect and another part denies it, internal consistency is lacking. If in one place it promotes the importance of the individual human personality, and in another supports isolation and repression of individuals, internal consistency is lacking. If it works to promote human well-being and ignores the well-being of the planet on which all human life depends, then internal consistency is lacking. If it claims to deal with all that is important in the cosmos and yet ignores the maintenance and development of the human species because it relies on historical mythologies, then its consistency with modern knowledge needs to be questioned.

CHAPTER 4

HUMANS AS THE ULTIMATE REFERENCE SYSTEM (MORE DETAIL IN APPENDIX B)

> *There is no quantum world. <u>There is only an abstract</u>*
> *<u>quantum mechanical description</u>. It is wrong to think*
> *that the task of physics is to find out how Nature is.*
> *Physics concerns what we can say about Nature.* [1]
> *Niels Bohr*

Humanity itself is our ultimate reference system(HBAURS) living immersed within a universe with Reality As the Objective Reference System (RAORS).

Throughout history people have believed that there is something absolute, or ultimate that exists independent of themselves that would make their life meaningful. The foregoing position implies or depends on an Ultimate Reference System that could be used as a criterion to measure and evaluate human life and human behavior. However, more thought and experience make it clear that human beings themselves are the source of meaning and value. They are as near as we can get to an "Ultimate Reference System." Therefore, I take the position that Humanity itself is our ultimate reference system defining meaning.

The foregoing means that it is the human species itself that provides the framework within which meaning of human life needs to be interpreted. And for each person this makes the answer to this question dependent upon empirical study and evidence. This means that life and living is an empirical process not a Platonist one.

Because the HBAURS concept stands in opposition to most of what we have been taught, it is easy to be confused by what it means. Some readers interpret it to mean that I am saying there is no way to use reality as a reference. To help reduce the likelihood that anyone interprets HBAURS in the foregoing way, I would like to present another concept which I hope will clarify matters. This is **Reality As the Objective Reference System** (RAORS). I take reality to be everything that exists -- chairs, cars, rivers, atoms, eclipses, stars, black matter and black energy, and of course all living things including humanity and all their physiological processes.

However, the foregoing is talking about existence, not meaning. The only meaning associated with the existence of a chair, star, or living thing is one applied by human beings. If we say a star or an elephant has its own meaning we are the ones deciding this, not the star or the elephant. If there are alien life forms capable of using symbolic language they would provide their own reference system which we might or might not be capable of comprehending. Therefore, discussing the meaning of anything that exists is talking about human nature, perception, and interpretations. As a result of the foregoing whatever meaning we assign is subject to change as we study and better understand our own nature and the rest of the universe in general.

I do not in any sense feel that there is "no way to use reality as a reference." Obviously, reality is the main resource for our efforts to understand and to correct our errors -- to ponder the ultimate.

However, from the perspective of a *science of religion and ethics* the ultimate of reality is not the ULTIMATE we have been led to believe in. My thesis is simple. The ideas we have been taught about ULTIMATE are as erroneous as most of the other basic ideas we have been taught. The "ultimate" we can reach is to develop ourselves as fully as possible (to achieve a *sustainable feeling that our life has meaning*) which includes using our accomplishments to help all other people attain a similar state now and into the future. And to do our best to ensure that humanity will prevail and maintain this vision. This is the desirable role of each individual human being when they are guided by their "wisdom" potential. This is the step that is now possible for human beings to take. And any who are able to help make it happen would become the greatest heroes humanity has ever produced. In Joseph Campbell's words, this is the "hero's journey."[2]

1. To see more on the above go to Appendix B-1.

Another issue that relates to reality and reference systems is the "laws of science." Julian Huxley reminds us that, "The laws of nature did not exist as such before individuals began scientific investigations: what existed was the welter of natural events, and the laws of nature are constructions of human thought which attempt to give comprehensible general formulations of how those events operate. Similarly gods did not exist as such before people built up theistic religious systems: what existed was the clash of natural forces, physical and spiritual, including those of the human mind, and the gods are attempts to give a comprehensible formulation of these forces of destiny." [3]

An additional area that involves reference systems is cause and effect. Traditionally, cause and effect have been fundamental concepts in Western thinking, but its meaning was significantly altered by mechanistic science. As Holmes Rolston [4] explains, "The medieval world had inherited its science and metaphysics from the Greeks and its religion from the Hebrews. Thomist philosophy coherently fused all three, employing Aristotle's four 'causes,' or explanatory factors in understanding a thing: (1) the *material cause*, matter, the stuff of which a thing is made; (2) the *efficient cause*, the affecting, mobile operating force that produces changes; (3) the *formal cause*, the plan or structure inlaid into a thing, and; (4) the *final cause*, a goal, the end state toward which a thing is drawn. The two earlier causes look backward to ask about generating antecedents. They look for a compositional substrate that has been pushed into its present conformation. Explanation is thus in terms of *physical origins*. The latter pair of 'causes' look forward to ask about plans, a will-be, a will-to-be, and a pull onward. The former pair features the objective side of reality, while the latter suggests a working at ends, rationality, intention, and, at length, subjectivity. In the medieval account, the first pair is secondary, necessary but insufficient for understanding. Explanation needs to subsequently be completed by setting forth the primary components that account for why things and events are what they are. Explanation is in terms of *significant endings*.

Rolston continues, "In terms of...[previous discussions], we can say that formal and final 'causes' tend to inquire into meanings and belong more to religion than to science, at least to physical science. In contemporary usage in science (though not in history), we would not refer to goals or plans as 'causes,' except somewhat awkwardly, because in strict science, at least since David Hume, we restrict the term 'cause' to material and efficient causes. The scientific revolution programmatically repudiates formal and final categories for understanding and did not base understanding and prediction on teleological factors, but on material and energetic propellants. Jacques Loeb, a physiologist, finds such explanation the key to all knowledge: 'What progress humanity has made, not only in physical welfare but also in the conquest of superstition and hatred, and in the formation of a correct view of life, it owes directly or indirectly to mechanistic science.'"

"This revolution in explanatory strategy can be diagrammed, perhaps over simply ... [as done below].

THE MEDIEVAL VIEW	THE NEWTONIAN VIEW
Secondary explanations	Secondary explanations
1 Material cause	3 Organic plan
2 Efficient cause	4 Intended goals
Primary explanations	Primary explanations
3 Formal cause	1 Matter
4 Final cause	2 Motion"

"Applied to the objective physical world, this move had spectacular results, seen in the successes of physics, chemistry, and astronomy. It was deployed with more uncertainty in the biological realm, for organic life did seem to be regulated by plans (formal causes), and organisms with a subjective life even seemed to select goals (final causes). Nevertheless, the apparent goal-directedness of 'organic machines' (as Descartes calls them) rested on physiochemical determinants. Life was a derived phenomenon overlaid on fundamentally mechanistic processes. The word *anima*, 'animating vitality,' is reducible to the word *vis*, 'force.' So it has seemed, and even in our own times half of bioscience (but only half) is based on this conviction. Thus, modern science began with a revolution in the sorts of explanation looked for, and while we may be glad for the resulting insights into the nature of things, we may also be wary of a blindness imposed by the governing blinkers. Physics achieves its successes, we remember, by clever decisions about what to leave out. Science involves more careful observations, but not simply so; it comes with decisions about what to look at, and what not to."

"In our century we are in another scientific revolution. The natural world, when looked at more closely, has defeated or shown to be inadequate many Newtonian presumptions. So even in physics we need to worry about what was getting left out in the earlier abstractions.... Beyond that still, we must eventually reckon with such phenomena as mind, society, and history, about which physics is silent." As Rolston points out below this is not strictly true. The Copenhagen interpretation of quantum mechanics puts mind into science because it acknowledges that physics is about what we can know about the universe not what the universe is. Although this principle has not been followed through to its logical consequences – *Humanity itself is our ultimate reference system*– it demonstrates the problem at the base of science, which has not yet been adequately addressed.

Continuing on Rolston says, "An allusion in the revolutionary sketch... [above] to primary and secondary qualities is not incidental. The Newtonian primary explanations were thought to correspond with what is really there in nature, *matter-in-motion*, while any secondary explanations are observer-dependent, the introduced products of subjectivity, appearing when mind interacts with matter. This switch in explanatory emphasis was to have far-reaching results. It yielded an enormous rise in technical power. But this know-how for manipulating the motions of matter came with a corresponding impoverishment of any sense of purposes, those upper-level explanations that were now said to be secondary, derived, subjective, and only apparent. The revolution that gained increasing competence over causes in the world came with a reciprocal loss, a decreasing confidence about meanings there. What was no longer looked for was no longer found."

And this returns us to the point that to assign a cause, or effect requires a Reference System, and mechanistic science as presented by Isaac Newton and other scientists of his day took objective reality to be the reference system. However, the newer physics in the Copenhagen interpretation of quantum mechanics completely turned this understanding around. Niels Bohr and Werner Heisenberg adopted a special version of the Humanity itself is our ultimate reference system concept. Based on the experiments performed by the physicists studying the quantum realm in the 1920s, the following conclusions were reached.

As Henry Stapp says in *Mind, Matter, and Quantum Mechanics* [5], "Bohr's Copenhagen interpretation, the nominal orthodox interpretation, rests on the idea that the aim of quantum theory is merely to describe certain connections between human experiences, rather than to describe a physical world conceived to exist and have definite properties independently of our method of observing it. According to this view, seemingly enforced by the difficulty of constructing a rational picture of the world compatible with empirical requirements, physics is actually about human consciousness."[5]

The very idea of reality became an open question:

As Roger Newton says in *The Truth Of Science* [6], "Bohr's reaction to such ontological questions was unequivocal. Always professing a lack of interest in *reality*, he placed his emphasis on *language*. 'What is it that we human beings ultimately depend on?' he asked,

We depend on words.... Our task is to communicate experiences and ideas to others. We need to strive continually to extend the scope of our description, but in such a way that our messages do not thereby lose their objective and unambiguous character.... We are suspended in language in such a way that we cannot say what is up and what is down. The word 'reality' is also a word, a word which we need to learn to use correctly."

"Accordingly, he came to the conclusion that there is no quantum world. There is only an abstract quantum mechanical description. It is wrong to think that the task of physics is to find out how Nature *is*. Physics concerns what we can *say* about Nature." [1]

Due to the foregoing the Copenhagen interpretation of quantum mechanics gave up cause and effect and took the statistical interpretation of quantum phenomena to be all a person needed to say on this issue.

My own position is that Bohr went too far when he expressed a lack of interest in reality – in his willingness to speak only of what humans could observe and measure and remain silent about the possible workings of the real world; that is, reality. In my mind this has led toward obscurantist positions. If we take cause and effect to be basic organizing principles to describe change in the universe, as I do, within the context of Human Beings As the Ultimate Reference System then I think we have a firmer foundation for clarifying these issues. But this does require redefining science (**as the search for congruency**) and recognizing its dependence on human nature rather than existing independent of human abilities and interests.

As I say above it is my own belief that Bohr also went too far in trying to avoid thinking about "how nature is." In his efforts to apply his own vision of how science works it seems to me that he ended up assigning nature some unnecessarily strange characteristics. Of course nature is whatever it is and when parts of it seem strange or paradoxical the problem need not reside in nature, but may be due to our limited abilities to understand anything totally foreign to our past experiences.

I take this to be the case with understanding the ultimately small components of the universe. At this point physicists accept that these components can be thought of as either particles or waves. I think it is safe to say that whatever the basic components of the universe are, they are neither waves nor particles, but something currently beyond human comprehension because this comprehension is too far outside any experience we've yet had.

2. *Should you have an interest in exploring a new paradigm for solving this problem, see Appendix B-2.*

TRUTH

Human beings will never be able to discover Truth (defined below), but they can move nearer and nearer to it by inquiring into the nature of things. This process allows the achievement of Knowledge and Wisdom.

TRUTH (total knowledge) is a concept based on the presupposition that individuals can directly experience, or understand reality, God, or some other absolute reference system outside themselves, rather than only interpret such things drawing from observations or feelings.

From a supernatural perspective Truth – God or something similar – provides the "foundation" upon which a given folk religion rests. One element of this is studied by Karen Armstrong in *A History Of God.* [7] There she traces how ideas about God have advanced as societies have accumulated a better understanding of themselves and the world around them. The most advanced religious thinkers recognize God as being totally unknowable. It seems to me that to rest the meaning of a person's life on something that is unknowable and thereby reject everything science and reason tell us about how to live a meaningful life is a frivolous choice.

Western science has provided us the key to unlock the puzzle of human knowledge. However, though science has provided the key, so far there has only been confusion about what the puzzle is that it unlocks.

In the world of classical physics Truth, that is, the Laws of Science, would explain and predict every future event. It would be a condition similar to the one described by Lincoln Kinnear Barnett as "...a final flawless concurrence of theory and natural process, so complete that every observed phenomenon is accounted for and nothing is left out of the picture." [8] Some scientists and philosophers thought this Truth answered all questions including those about human nature; that is, behavior, needs, and goals.

They thought these laws would permit every event or phenomenon to be explained completely. Everything would be explainable in relation to everything else. All the forces acting in the universe would be understood within the same system of laws whether supernovas or the feeling of rapture a person feels when gazing at a thing of beauty. They believed that there would be nothing that could not be predicted and explained exactly.

This system of laws would allow a person to predict where an atom, a person, or a galaxy would be at any given time in the future. However, today though many scientists still believe that science provides "Certain Knowledge," it is recognized that prediction has severe limitations. Chaos theory [9] demonstrates that this kind of prediction is not possible in the universe as we know it. If Truth in this sense actually existed, it would have to exist outside of humanity, individually and collectively.

As a result modern science takes truth to be "provisional and approximate." [10]

Nevertheless, there remains among many scientists a single-minded focus to know what the universe is like in spite of clear demonstrations by philosophers that Truth can never be achieved. How is it possible for science to maintain this effort in spite of David Hume's (1711-1776) and Immanuel Kant's (1724-1804) clear demonstrations going back over 200 years that Certain Knowledge cannot be obtained by humans through either science or religion?

Seminal ideas on this topic can be found in Thomas Kuhn's essay on the history of science [11] examining the way science actually has emerged over the past 400 years or so. His thoughts on how to interpret this information are very insightful.

Scientist's interpretation of science lies at the core of their approach. Because science was traditionally interpreted to have as its goal the search for Truth (Certain Knowledge) it instilled that perspective into scientists. This vision has energized and directed them individually and collectively ever since.

An underlying assumption of this approach is the widely quoted words of Henri Poincare:

"Scientists do not study nature because it is useful; they study it because they delight in it, and they delight in it because it is beautiful. If nature were not beautiful, it would not be worth knowing, and if nature were not worth knowing, life would not be worth living."[12]

Obviously Poincare has his priorities very confused just as he has his idea of what makes life worth living. The Third Way of Wisdom (Seek to understand; pursue Wisdom) and the Ninth Way of Wisdom (Work to increase knowledge and all creative and artistic endeavors; adopt an inspiring life goal) present an alternative view of the relationship between science and what makes life worth living. Certainly if a person can combine these ideas with their life work they are doubly blessed. But of even greater importance is the Second Way of Wisdom (Endeavor to maintain and develop the human species) because it provides the foundation for all the others.

Since leading scientists such as Poincare have presented a model of science that makes it appear to function outside the realm of community concern, this has distorted the history as well as the motives of science.

It has also provided the orientation for interpreting their history (primarily done in science text books, says Kuhn). Kuhn makes it clear how the foregoing has been accomplished. Scientists and those writing about science often confuse the relationship between truth and scientific achievements by ignoring their "failures" and writing them out of their history. They have succeeded in this approach because the scientific process really does provide data that leads to useful and satisfying knowledge; plus the individual scientist is not only intellectually challenged and fulfilled, they -- like the warriors who sacrifice their life in battle, confident that they will wake up in Valhalla -- never survive to raise questions about the broader aspects of what they have been taught. So the system has a vested interest in maintaining the conviction that there exists a linear progress toward Certain Knowledge, and a process to ensure that this training process is maintained.

Related to the matter of achieving Truth is the opposite side of the question. That is, whether or not there is any fact that is inherently unknowable or event that is unpredictable. This is something we can never know because there is always the possibility that any theory or position that says such is the case will be shown to be wrong by a completely new concept or advance of knowledge. It is therefore maintained here that a person needs to be careful when assuming that some individual fact is unknowable, event unpredictable, or feat unachievable. It is clear that what we can say about Nature to a large degree depends on our understanding at a given point in history. But regardless of this we need to make assumptions that go beyond our knowledge. And, although there may be absolute barriers, we need to forever remain in doubt as to just where those points lie.

> 3. For more discussion on knowing when something is unpredictable, see Appendix B-3.

Truth, for a *science of religion and ethics*, is considered to be forever beyond our grasp except in a tentative and general way. Also, it is not a primary goal in an Enlightened Community, and is not necessary for the creation of an Enlightened Community.

KNOWLEDGE

Knowledge means information, data, understanding, and ability to increase the odds of being right in our predictions. It permits the manipulation and use of the forces, attributes, and patterns of nature.

In spite of the fact that we can never be sure that a given event is inherently unpredictable, we can say that it is "currently unpredictable." An event is currently unpredictable, when: 1) Necessary predictive data cannot, or at least has not yet been gathered. 2) The ability to handle the necessary number of computations to predict the event exceeds the contemporary computation processes and equipment, or it takes longer to predict the outcome than for the real-time change to take place. 3) No way presently exists to reduce the problem to mathematical, predictive form.

With the advance of science humanity has become able to understand and predict more and more of the forces of the Universe. But even more importantly we can now recognize an ethical dimension to all problems that involve human life. An Enlightened Community takes the individual to be the highest value. As a result individuals are not seen as things to be thrown away when they are not functioning well, or worked on and fixed as though they were a watch. Rather it is critical that they be as deeply involved in the process of taking care of their problem as circumstances permit. Ideally they might become experts on their condition and guide the study and research to help learning proceed at the fastest rate possible. Or, if their talents lie elsewhere, for example, in fund raising, they might ensure that there would be researchers available to give this matter maximum attention. In this shared effort individuals contribute their problem not merely to help themselves, but as a means to help others and thereby fulfill their role as helping to perpetuate the species in such a way that all persons can achieve a *sustainable feeling of well-being.* The more severe their problem the more they have to contribute to human progress. AIDS provides a model for how a terrible problem has provided an entry into understanding human physiology at an almost unimaginable depth.

The foregoing might be called the "Christopher Reeve model," and his efforts to support work to find a cure for paralysis resulting from spinal cord injury serves as an example we all might follow to varying degrees.

WISDOM

Wisdom is that aspect of Knowledge which when applied to a person's life increases the probability that they will become an Enlightened Person with a *sustainable feeling of well-being*.

Knowledge and Wisdom draw their definition from human beings as the ultimate reference system. Knowledge and Wisdom mean what human beings understand. They are not about forever, but are very "here and now." They are the source of everything essential to develop a *science of religion and ethics* and to utilize its findings: provide guidance to individuals in making satisfying life choices, setting up and maintaining organizations, and such. It is the foregoing process that would help any individual to become an Enlightened Person.

IMPORTANCE OF MEANING OF HUMAN LIFE

The most basic need of every human being is to achieve and maintain their life with a feeling of well-being.

This is true because in a *science of religion and ethics* being alive (within the defined parameters) when a person is physically able to end their own life is defined as having a *feeling of well-being*. (Being dead is a little more complicated!) Only live people can do stuff, experience joy, have children, support a society and the species, and such. Although dead people may cast a long shadow this is true only because they once lived or their promoter lives/lived.

But what is actually being discussed when we talk about a *feeling of well-being*? A useful way to look at this is by examining some ideas explored by neurological researcher Antonio Damasio. One such source is his book, *Looking for Spinoza*. [13] Here Damasio relates the story of Spinoza and his concept of *conatus* – maintaining life with a feeling of well-being. This to me gets to the core of the definition of the meaning of human life. As Damasio's research shows [14], when the emotion-based component of our neural system fails, making choices based only on the reason-based components of our brains is almost impossible – at least in a timely fashion. In my interpretation the experiences and beliefs that program this part of our neural system produce a state of harmony – a feeling of well-being; that is, a feeling that a person's life has meaning.

Albert Ellis points out in Rational Emotive Behavior Therapy (REBT) that underlying a person's feelings and behaviors are their thoughts or beliefs. Beliefs guide our responses to stimuli, and cause them. The foregoing is the case when all physiological systems are functioning adequately [15]. And this is the component of the equation our "I" is most able to affect. Therefore, it is clear that the primary component – **belief** – of a *feeling that a person's life has meaning* is responsible for, but in some sense independent of the basic emotional component. This realization helps to clarify the role of happiness and satisfaction.

Another way to get to the same conclusion about feelings is to examine Victor Frankl's experience which David Morris relates, [16] "Frankl believes he survived at least in part because, at a critical moment, when he felt absolutely overwhelmed by exhaustion, pain, and despair, he found a meaning [belief] that allowed him to go on. He suddenly imagined himself behind a lectern speaking to a large audience on the psychology of the concentration camps. [17] Amid the wreckage of European civilization, this almost crazed vision of civilized, scientific inquiry recommencing its normal work in the aftermath of unprecedented disaster gave him a reason not to give in to his despair. It also provided an individual instance of the general principle he saw at work in the death camps and in the world beyond. For Frankl, the crucial key to survival – even in the face of an intolerable abyss of suffering – lies in our power to discover or to attribute a meaning to our existence."

To me the above is an example of the concept that beliefs precede feelings. Frankl had a vision that produced a belief. If he could survive the concentration camp experience and work to help ensure that such things could never happen again, his life would be worthwhile (the state of *feeling that a person's life has meaning*) and the suffering would not be totally pointless.

But normally a person is not aware of the beliefs that support their *feeling that life has meaning*. These beliefs are like automatic assumptions coming out of a person's experiences. My take is that Damasio provides the research that shows us how a person's beliefs support the *feeling that a person's life has meaning*. The following quote helps move us a little further toward some additional understanding of the "feeling that a person's life has meaning" concept.

"[Victor] Frankl found himself living in a political version of the irrational universe that postwar existential philosophy came to describe as absurd: stripped of his identity, reduced to a number, denied his basic human dignity and rights, confined in a senseless routine, brutalized and tyrannized. Kafka invented nothing more terrifying than what Frankl faced every day. Yet this personal encounter with pain was for Frankl not a confirmation of existential nothingness. It was a turning point. The challenge he faced was to find a personal meaning in an apparently meaningless and inhuman existence. 'Woe to them who saw no more sense in their life,' he writes of his comrades in the camps, 'no aim, no purpose, and therefore no point in carrying on. They were soon lost.'" [18] I think it is important to note that what Frankl calls "personal meaning" is in reality only the specific process by which he achieved a universal state (*feeling that a person's life has meaning*).

"Meaning of human life" describes a feeling state based on the interplay of a person's beliefs, their "tribal" genetic propensities, and their "wisdom" potential that results in their choosing to live rather than not. There are numerous relevant beliefs to consider. Some have positive value and some negative value. On the negative side are those that are anti-social such as: desire for revenge, to inflict pain and suffering on others, to perform a violent act where many may be killed in order to gain some recognition, and such. Other negative beliefs come out of unsustainable ideas because they conflict with current knowledge, are based only on authority and custom; or depend on accident of birth or other limiting circumstances.

A feeling that a person's life has meaning is necessary but not sufficient to ensure choices characterized as ethical by a *science of religion and ethics*. As discussed later the element of sustainability is required for the beliefs producing these choices.

However, even though an individual may not be able to make choices defined as ethical by a *science of religion and ethics*, they may still function at a very high level of productivity and effectiveness. They may be filled with enthusiasm, zest, ecstasy, or at least hope about the future. They may feel they are doing useful and important things and that their life counts. They may wake up feeling good about the opportunity to live another day. Persons fitting the foregoing description have a *feeling that their life has meaning*. A feeling that a person's life has meaning is in opposition to states of hopelessness, depression, despair, abuse of drugs, or a desire to commit suicide and end it all due to the foregoing states. Among the specific "...symptoms of depression [are]: lack of enthusiasm, poor appetite, feeling bored or uninterested, loss of interest in sex, trouble falling [down] or staying asleep, crying easily, feeling downhearted or blue, feeling low in energy or slowed down, feeling hopeless about the future, thinking of suicide, and feeling lonely." [19]

4. To see some ideas on levels of feeling that precede a sustainable feeling that one's life has meaning see Appendix B-4.

The measure of how correct one's worldview is, is the degree to which it would support and maintain an Enlightened Person and an Enlightened Community. All this requires following the path of wisdom – the path of science. Changing a person's mind, opinions, positions, and goals when new information and understanding calls for it is a key element of achieving the Good Life.

To change beliefs when they are found to disagree with a person's best interpretation of available knowledge and experience, a person needs to maintain the ability to recognize their ignorance and be able to change after receiving new data and better interpretations. This requires that the person's beliefs are not primarily dependent on authority and/or custom but depend on the best available knowledge about the Universe.

It is only possible to determine whether or not the beliefs that support an individual's *feeling of well-being* are <u>sustainable</u> by empirically studying the effects of those beliefs on one's self and on others.

Knowledge is not an end in itself, but has value only insofar as it helps individuals find Wisdom; that is, set goals and make life choices that increase the likelihood of becoming an Enlightened Person, and achieving a *sustainable feeling of well-being*.

One of the most important questions for a *science of religion and ethics* is, "What is knowledge and wisdom for?" Many thinkers of the past have believed, and some still believe that knowledge purely for its own sake is good and to focus on using it for some practical purpose demeans its value.

Also, scientists have tended to believe that knowledge is not <u>for</u> anything! Discovering and understanding is all the pay-off necessary.

A *science of religion and ethics* takes a different view – insofar as possible knowledge needs to be used to improve the quality of human life. However, as intimated earlier we need to recognize that research won't necessarily provide answers that have an immediate application. The most useful approach here is to go on the assumption that all knowledge has the potential to improve the quality of human life if we look carefully and long. Unused data, theory, or observation has not attained its potential worth. It may have brought satisfaction to the person who discovered it, and others who know about it. But it gains increasing value as it helps more and more individuals achieve a *sustainable feeling of well-being*.

CHAPTER 5

RELIGIOUS AND MORAL BEHAVIOR

For a religion of science and ethics religions' responsibility is to provide the social domain where meaning of life is provided.

In order to function as an Enlightened Person it is essential to use a person's "wisdom" potential to help achieve a *sustainable feeling of well-being*.

Since religious/moral behavior comes out of beliefs, it is beliefs that must be measured for their sustainability. Do a person's beliefs lead them toward becoming their best self? Are these beliefs and the behaviors they produce congruent with objective reality at its deepest level -- capable of satisfying; beneficial and lasting to other people, or at least not harmful to them in such a way as to prevent them from achieving a *sustainable feeling of well-being*; and do they have an intent consistent with the foregoing, or at least not cut a person off from achieving these things?

Being congruent with objective reality at its deepest level means acting so as to maintain and develop the human species. However, the foregoing is not easy to test empirically, but behavior can be measured in terms of its agreement with the underlying theories. And of course this testing needs to be done. An Enlightened Community would have the motivation, and the resources to do so.

The foregoing ideas provide the basis to understand why pursuit of our raw "tribal" genetic propensities are not likely to lead a person to achieve a *sustainable feeling of well-being* even though surrendering to a propensity may provide deep satisfaction at least for short periods since it resonates with something very deep in the human psyche (things that allowed our hunter-gatherer forebears to survive for 2-4 million years), However, the purpose of a *science of religion and ethics* is to make clear the ways to fulfill these propensities so as to support the maintenance and development of the species.

A path that has purposes that nurture self and others will come closer to helping a person achieve a *sustainable feeling of well-being* because every goal when reached lays the foundation for achieving long-term satisfaction rather than only immediate gratification followed by pain for self or others. Instead of doing things haphazardly that may be undoing the acts of others or cutting off future benefits, we are working in an integrated manner that is normally the most efficient, effective way to achieve goals.

There are many things in life that bring pleasure if they occur surrounded by the proper conditions. The former is true of shared time with friends, stimulating discussion, enlightening literature and plays, good music, delicious/nutritious food, nurturing sex with a loving person, and the like. Mere gratification, however, does not necessarily contribute to a *sustainable feeling of well-being*. Short-sighted goals may be accompanied by too many unpleasant results, such as a stomach ache from eating too much candy, lung cancer from smoking cigarettes, maintaining low self-esteem by engaging in sado-masochistic activities, losing friends because of childish behavior, and the like. Wealth, power, beauty, physical strength all have their value, but do not by themselves give a person a *sustainable feeling of well-being*. Each act or condition must take into account all its obvious implications so the act will give not only momentary pleasure, but lasting good feelings as well. This is an important part of a *sustainable feeling of well-being*. Also, a thing may be painful or unpleasant in some ways, but satisfying enough in other ways to offset this. An example of such an event is setting a track record in the mile race. Every step may bring almost unendurable physical pain, yet the satisfaction brought by breaking the record, or just being part of the race, may compensate a hundred times over.

EMOTIONS AND A SUSTAINABLE FEELING OF WELL-BEING

It seems to me that a *sustainable feeling of well-being* must include all the appropriate emotions. Since emotions as experienced depend on a person's beliefs, in order to have healthy emotions, a person must have healthy beliefs. Take worry as an example. Sometimes individuals spend hours in pain because they believe that worrying about a problem is helpful or necessary. Once they realize that worry is not only painful, but debilitating, they than can recognize that the goal is to do whatever they can to solve the problem and face whatever ensues with peace of mind and tranquility. So worry becomes a signal that a person needs to focus on their beliefs and work to get them in a better state. Intense guilt and shame are similar examples.

Ideally a person should take no action they realize would prevent others from achieving a *sustainable feeling that their life has meaning*. If individuals can determine that their actions will prevent others from achieving a *sustainable feeling of well being*, they must alter their actions to avoid doing so, or take parallel action that will prevent their act from doing so. We cannot kill, punish, or harm other individuals -- at least in the absence of unique, unpredictable circumstances.

When a society supports actions with irreversible negative effects on individuals, this prevents members of the society from achieving a *sustainable feeling that their life has meaning*. Until all people are secure, no person is secure. No one is immune from the acts of others and until each person is an Enlightened Person, they are at the mercy of those in too much pain to avoid violence, too confused to make wise decisions, too insensitive to be counted on.

There are many factors in a *sustainable feeling of well-being*. Some of these factors must be unique to each individual. However, in spite of the unique components of a *sustainable feeling of well-being*, I believe the primary elements are universal and apply to all human beings.

"One requirement for a happy life and satisfying society is the avoidance of acts that are known to be harmful and utilization of techniques found to bring desirable results." [1]

Although the foregoing appears obvious and is something most thoughtful people would agree with, close scrutiny will point out an interesting problem: We currently know very little about which "acts" (life patterns/behaviors) interfere with happiness and satisfaction, and which ones promote it. Part of the explanation for the foregoing is that the old ideas that taught that God provided all the answers have lost their power, but new answers have yet to be recognized and accepted. No one is focusing on this issue in a coordinated way. Even the fields of psychology are only peripherally involved in this issue. Yet, overcoming this lack of awareness seems to me to be one of the most pressing needs now facing humanity. An organized approach is essential because a single person's efforts, life experiences, and knowledge are too limited to spark the necessary social changes. In addition, the data is too confusing for any individual to put it all together perfectly by themself. The foregoing is a serious problem with my current formulation of a *science of religion and ethics*.

Restating the above issue of the requirement for a happy life in my own terms, I would say we need to clarify what the beliefs are that provide a *sustainable feeling of well-being*.

Victor Frankl tackled the issue of meaning of life by developing logotherapy. But he failed to realize that meaning of life has many components not just one, has an essential social dimension, and its primary components are universal requirements needed by everyone. He focused instead on the transforming effect some experiences can have. (For more about Frankl's approach see VOLUME II, Chapter 11, "Victor Frankl and the Meaning of Life," [2] or read him directly. [3]) Because of the foregoing he took the view that meaning of life somehow comes from outside the individual and that it is unique for each person. He thought in terms of specific events rather than universal categories. Therefore, he thought of meaning of human life as exclusive to the person who experiences it. However, it does not seem to me that Frankl's approach gets us very far. I think it is critical to realize that "meaning of human life": 1) has many components not just one, 2) depends on common human characteristics shared by all people and comes out of basic human nature, 3) has an essential social dimension that requires support from a person's community.

The foregoing description provides the basis for an empirical science. A feeling that a person's life has meaning undoubtedly has elements unique to a particular person. Also, it is irreparably tied into a person's raw "tribal" propensities. My study of humanity convinces me that there is a core of common attributes shared by all people; that is, their human nature. I believe that a person's society plays a key role in providing a *feeling that a person's life has meaning*. This depends on the beliefs taught by the society and the way the society is organized. My approach not only gives us a way to examine the things that provide a feeling that human life has meaning, it also gives us a way of judging societies based on how well their citizens achieve a *sustainable feeling that their life has meaning.*

It is my belief that a person's *feeling that their life has meaning* is sustainable to the degree that they are living congruent with the best of what it means to be a human being. However, this approach contains a two-pronged dilemma. First, what is the best of what it means to be a human being? Second, how do we achieve the foregoing condition?

As for being the best human being it is possible for us to be, I think this has a theoretical dimension that lies at the core of the problem. This is the idea that humanity is in the process of inventing itself and has been since the evolution of the language ability. As indicated elsewhere this means re-interpreting certain elements of our genetic heritage -- our raw "tribal" genetic propensities -- that can divert us from becoming our best self. It is now possible to understand how to realize our full positive potential; that is, our "wisdom" potential. I propose that humanity is now capable of developing Enlightened Persons and Enlightened Communities.

But at any given moment in time the necessary knowledge and resources will not be available to help all who desire it except in the way described in the Seventh Way of Wisdom [4]. This is as good as it gets. This is utopia!

Achieving this condition is the core problem for a *science of religion and ethics.* It is a process that must be determined empirically by gathering data. That method involves honest collection, correlation, and interpretation of facts obtained by actual study of individual people's lives. An extension of the methods of questioning and statistical analysis used by Dr. Alfred C. Kinsey and his group at the Institute for Sex Research at Indiana University should be valuable for the actual gathering of some of these facts. This technique might be combined with the knowledge gained from evolutionary psychology, psychotherapy, psychological research, and other data gathering methods to allow real progress in understanding human beings and determining the parameters of a *sustainable feeling of well-being.* Also, Dr. John Gottman's approach described in his book, *Why Marriages Fail Or Succeed,* [5] would seem to be especially valuable.

The focus for study of a *science of religion and ethics* would be: First, study individual lives to provide data that permits the researcher to determine the individual's beliefs, whether implicitly or explicitly held, that relate to their experiencing a *feeling of well-being*. Next use this research to determine how closely the person has lived according to her or his beliefs, how successful this has been in providing the *feeling that their life has meaning*, and finally determining whether the foregoing has universal significance. Since we are dealing with millions of variables, obviously we should not expect to come up with simple yes/no answers. Rather we would be working from fuzzy logic grids.

We rarely would have double blind experiments with one variable different in the control and test group in any meaningful way; therefore, conclusions would be less sure. Nevertheless, there are many other ways to test multi-causal phenomena. One example is use of propensity scores. [6]

At best we come up with probabilities, with clusters of behaviors, with ranges that interconnect with other behavior in complex ways. But all of these problems do not mean that we cannot draw useful conclusions from such studies. It merely means that conclusions are open to change and may be altered in important ways with more information just like the rest of science.

This information would need to be gathered from all age groups to determine how needs and values change with age. The data should be collected from all social groupings in order to determine the effects of social factors. These studies need to include all societies in determining the importance of variation in the factors. These projects would be used to search for the ideas or behaviors that cut people off from achieving their full positive potential, as well as those that encourage individuals to steadily mature and develop throughout their life.

Below are the Eleven Ways of Wisdom judged necessary to achieve a *sustainable feeling of well-being*. These are working assumptions -- open to revision, clarification, or replacement with updated information. Each of these Ways is discussed in detail later in the following chapters. The Ways of Wisdom as defined here have value to the degree that they are useful to individuals and as a starting point for experimentation, organization, discussion, and testing.

THE WAYS OF WISDOM

1. Recognize that human beings are – for us -- the *ultimate reference system.*
2. Endeavor to maintain and develop the human species. Support efforts to develop Enlightened Communities; that is, Communities promoting authentic happiness for all their citizens.
3. Seek to understand. Pursue Wisdom.
4. Recognize that all knowledge rests on faith/beliefs and must always be open to questioning.
5. Strive to make the best choices possible.
6. Know and struggle to improve yourself; work to be physically and psychologically healthy.
7. Develop and adopt a perceptual framework in which pain does not prevent the achievement of a *sustainable feeling of well- being.*
8. Help and be helped by other people. Recognize that all human beings are "us;" everything else is "them."
9. Work to increase knowledge and all creative and artistic endeavors. Adopt an inspiring life goal.
10. Support efforts to ensure that every child is provided a loving, nurturing environment and all the things necessary to become an Enlightened Person.
11. Make of your life a spiritual quest. Work to become an Enlightened Person. Use the fundamentalist propensity to produce Enlightened Communities.

The Ways of Wisdom express the things that, I believe, would collectively be able to help anyone achieve a *sustainable feeling of well-being.* However, anything that is listed must be supported by evidence or else it is merely conjecture. We can only discover what will bring a *sustainable feeling of well-being* by research and study. Armchair speculation may be useful in pointing out directions to search, but it is not proof in any way. There is no justification for accepting these conjectures if they sound wrong or are unacceptable for other reasons. All this writing is in one sense a blueprint and can be given no more credence then current evidence supports. As indicated below there will probably be changes in how the <u>Ways of Wisdom</u> interrelate as a person matures. Some things that at one time seem very important will at a later time appear less important and vice versa. But, having a *sustainable feeling of well-being* must remain as constant as our ability to develop, and this – like for all of science – requires a continuing series of paradigm shifts over a person's life and over the generations.

One person who has thought about the changes that accompany growing up is Dr. David Norton. He writes about "The Stages of Life: Childhood, Adolescence, Maturation, and Old Age." [7] He believes that, "It is no mere coincidence that the world's two great self-actualization doctrines, the Greek and the Hindu, share the thesis that personal growth proceeds by incommensurable stages ...." (p. 172) I don't believe in incommensurable stages (movement from one stage to the next with no intermediate positions). However, Norton's ideas provide some thought-provoking things to consider.

Also, Norton's characterization of Hinduism and Greek religions as incorporating self-actualization doctrines raises some interesting questions. Obviously, a *science of religion and ethics* is totally focused on self-actualization. Exploring where the Greeks and Hindus went wrong could be valuable to a *science of religion and ethics*. VOLUME II, Chapter 24, "What We Can Learn from The Study of Folk Religions and Other Worldviews," [8] is presented as a start in this process.

Norton defines Childhood "as essential dependence." (p. 172)

For adolescence, Norton says it "...begins in the discovery of autonomy -- 'I am alive; I am an authentic living being, not a derivation. From this moment forward it is I myself who must do my living; no longer is there any other who can do my living for me.' The implications of this recognition are revolutionary, transforming not merely the individual but the entire world. By this single recognition the world of childhood is exchanged for the world of adolescence." (p. 179) Helping this step to be successful is a core challenge of a *science of religion and ethics*. In my mind these characteristics related to the changes during adolescence appear as though they might help expand what I describe as the "tribal" genetic propensities and make it easier for adolescents to move toward their "wisdom" potential.

Norton discusses maturation "...whose definitive moral quality derives from its intrinsic obligation upon each individual to 'Become what you are.'" (p. 188) Although this initially sounds good, as indicated below in my mind it ends up being wrong.

According to Norton, old age "...is the stage that has no future.... it cannot 'look forward to life,' it cannot 'live by hope.'"(p. 204) In my mind an Enlightened Community would not lead to this state. Even at the moment of death, a person would recognize their connection with humanity and its unfolding potential.

Norton's ideas are not compatible with my own thinking about a *sustainable feeling of well-being*. But exploring his ideas in more depth may be of great value. For example, thinking of Maturation (mature adulthood) as relating to "becoming what you are" seems inherently wrong to me. In reality each person is a vast reservoir of potentials. Which of these potentials are developed and to what degree depends on the time and society in which they grow up. The goal of a *science of religion and ethics* is to help the person develop those potentials that move them toward becoming an Enlightened Person and avoiding those potentials that would stand in the way of becoming their best self -- not merely the vague "what you are."

Many times the correct choices are not self-evident to an individual, or to a community. But an Enlightened Community must organize its resources so as to do the best it can considering the time in which it exists. It must act so as to help each person make the best choices. And as indicated earlier when a person is able to correct errors as they are recognized, the path of error becomes the path of truth -- the path toward becoming and remaining an Enlightened Person.

CHAPTER 6

THE ENLIGHTENED PERSON

The <u>Ways of Wisdom</u> are attempts to specify the beliefs necessary to become and remain an Enlightened Person and can only be fully actualized within an Enlightened Community.

Because human beings are social animals they can only be fulfilled in their deepest needs within a nurturing, encouraging, growth promoting, supportive environment. This point has not been properly addressed up to this time. Since *Homo sapiens sapiens* evolved the language ability and became *Modern Humans,* they have had a potential that has never been fully actualized within any society. The hunter-gatherer way of life allowed total congruency between the individual and the group up to the time of the evolution of the language ability. After that it has at the fundamental level been a failure looking from the perspective of a *science of religion and ethics.* From within the group it often looks great!

Rather than helping humanity to reinvent itself, a hunter-gatherer group forces/allows its members to live in their pre-language style, and function at the pre-language ability level. It does not even develop the individual's ability to become literate and thereby directly tap into the knowledge and experiences of past generations and the rest of humanity's ideas except as captured in folk legends. Unlike in urban and industrial/technological/ information societies, individual members have no opportunity to rise to levels of their highest individual achievement and develop some of their greatest potentials except to the degree that these potentials fit into the hunter-gatherer mode of living. On the other hand urban and industrial societies have not provided an environment that allows full congruency between every member and the society. There is always an underclass that is locked out. Only now have we accumulated enough experience and knowledge to begin to understand how to go about building an environment that is congruent with our "wisdom" potential. Doing this will require bringing together all who share the vision as well as the appropriate available knowledge so we can focus successfully on this issue. The Ways of Wisdom are presented in the hope that they will help in this effort.

The first step in creating a community in which to actualize the Ways of Wisdom is to improve and distribute the ideas necessary to promote a *science of religion and ethics*. The next step is to develop small focused groups, that I call "Wisdom Groups." (See "Organizing for an Enlightened Community.") A Wisdom Group's primary goal would be to bring together persons interested in a *science of religion and ethics*. It is my hope that Wisdom Groups would develop to the point where they would be able to set up Centers for the Practical Application of Wisdom. These Centers would work to assemble a select team of persons committed to becoming their best selves while developing a *sustainable feeling of well-being*. In the process they would correct, expand, develop, and actualize the goals of this book. They would develop the variety of activities and experiences necessary to help a broader membership work toward achieving a *sustainable feeling of well-being*. Insofar as possible they would bring together the wise people of the community who accept the goal of developing a *science of religion and ethics*. A Wisdom Group would when appropriate initiate efforts to develop a Center for the Practical Application of Wisdom. All work to actualize these ideas will be difficult because without proven models many mistakes will be made. So getting started will require a great deal of caution as well as tremendous optimism and energy. However, these structures are needed to help thoughtful, gifted persons join their efforts to develop testable theories and do the tests; that is, gather and analyze data. And at the same time to apply this knowledge to developing Enlightened Persons and Enlightened Communities.

ENLIGHTENED PERSON: Such an individual is herein defined as a person who has adopted the goal of maintaining and developing the human species and has reached the Tenth Level of Human Development (see Chapter 19). This includes exhibiting the highest human attributes of warmth, physical affection, honesty, truthfulness, open-mindedness, and rational thought. Such a person would not be committed to any belief that would prevent them from achieving *sustainable beliefs that their life has meaning*.

What are the attributes of an Enlightened Person? They need to be individuals who can control their raw "tribal" genetic propensities and are working to fulfill their "wisdom" potential. This means they will possess a standard that will allow them to recognize the fallacies and untruths that are widely accepted and that will prevent them from accepting the same errors by another name. This standard will provide ways to help all persons achieve a *sustainable feeling of well-being*. Such persons will know themselves and be able to control their behavior and environment within the necessary limits. But this can only happen in a supportive environment!

Before the various aspects of the Enlightened Person are explored, it might be useful to approach directly a critical question: Can every person living today achieve a *sustainable feeling of well-being*? The short answer must be, No. We don't currently have sufficient knowledge to aid everyone in discarding the beliefs that prevent them from achieving a *sustainable feeling of well-being*. Neither do we have enough knowledge to make clear each step every person needs to take in order to become an Enlightened Person. However, a primary goal needs to be to learn how to enhance the lives of an ever-increasing number of individuals.

When thinking of a *sustainable feeling of well-being*, the skeptic might wonder whether or not "Enlightened Persons" are not actually boring, goodie-goodies; freaks; automatons; or peas from a single pod. What turns people into individuals and prevents their being slaves to their society, persons of no substance, stereotyped units? Is not part of what makes people interesting, vibrant, alive their irrationalities? If people always act rationally, logically, and without prejudice, would they not be rather dull persons?

Fortunately, the above need not be true. Although irrationalities make individuals unstable and apparently unpredictable, the behavior of irrational people is in reality often more stereotyped than the behavior of more rational individuals. Irrational individuals tend to be "driven" persons who fill their life with activity and drama. They have little insight into their motivations and real needs. Therefore, they fail to experience long-term satisfaction. They tend to have a limited repertoire of behavior. They lack the spontaneity, versatility, and passion that would characterize the Enlightened Person. A person need not, therefore, sacrifice oneself to be interesting to others. More important, people are not irrational because they desire to be, but because they don't know how to avoid it. Human beings become empowered and self-directed individuals as they learn insight into themselves, work through the traumatic experiences of their infancy and childhood, and receive medical assistance as necessary. Enlightened Persons' lives would be so full that the lives of current "interesting people" would seem shadow-like in comparison. To find peace of mind and yet remain creative, persons need to overcome their irrationalities. Such people will not only become more helpful to their fellow humans, but more interesting in every way.

A sustainable feeling of well-being depends on achieving congruence between a person's rational and emotional sides. To achieve a *sustainable feeling of well-being* a person's total being needs to be developed. Therefore, the development of both the intellectual and the emotional side of the individual (dominant and nondominant cerebral hemispheres) needs to be encouraged. Folk religions appeal to the emotions. They use processes that provide emotional sustenance (that is why they provide a *feeling of well-being*). Unfortunately, most of them provide this emotional support at the expense of both intellectual and emotional growth. They have not encouraged development of the individual's ability to think and reason. Therefore, emotional development has been kept at an immature level. As a result of the foregoing they have been able to get away with using symbols that cannot withstand critical examination (e.g., soul, immortality, heaven, hell, angels, Satan, free will, God, etc.)

Enlightened Persons cannot have their emotional and intellectual sides divided. In fact the development of both reason and emotion go hand in hand. Persons cannot be fully functioning, mature adults if either their emotional or intellectual development is stifled. Antonio Damasio makes that very clear in his several books and provides the research to support this. [1]

Individuals may become Enlightened Persons only as they master the ideas and procedures offered by a religious/ethical System that meets the requirements of a *science of religion and ethics*. Being able to accept a valid religious/ethical System requires adequate education and experiences. Also, it requires a satisfactory level of integration of a person's conscious and unconscious and freeing oneself of the effects of early psychic trauma. Achievement of the foregoing is part of the <u>Sixth Way of Wisdom</u>: Know and endeavor to improve yourself. [2] A Wisdom Group needs to help a person achieve the self-knowledge required by the Sixth Way.

Each person would thus be helped to become an Enlightened Person (motivated by wisdom and maturity) and therefore a responsible, trustworthy member of society. Otherwise there is the danger of getting something started that would be worse than the Holy Inquisition and *Nineteen Eighty-Four* [3] combined.

Traditionally, when philosophers, writers on religion, and intellectuals in general have discussed religious/ethical behavior or the ideal person -- here called an Enlightened Person -- terms such as selfishness vs. altruism, free will vs. determinism, good and bad persons, punishment, laws, the "soul," come out of particular assumptions in the religious/ethical domain. Therefore, it seems worthwhile to briefly discuss the foregoing concepts here.

A *science of religion and ethics* needs to either discard or define each of the foregoing concepts in a new way. Collectively they have been used to present an interpretation of an individual and of society that is grossly misfocused. These terms are flawed in various ways, one of which is to make it seem that cause and effect do not apply to the issues being considered. As a result concepts such as punishment, law, the "soul," good/bad persons, evil, free will, selfishness/altruism have not been open to empirical testing. Their effectiveness is not open to objective questioning in their normal usage. They need not make sense, or be supported by evidence. Any thought or idea relating to these terms can be voiced and has equal standing to anyone else's opinion. Loud-mouthed bigots tend to get the headlines and, therefore, the votes. Experiments, tests, accuracy, and clear definitions are irrelevant.

Looking first at selfishness and altruism we see that these terms generate a smoke screen that obscures thought. In a *science of religion and ethics* selfishness and altruism turn out to be the same thing. In an Enlightened Community when a person acts selfishly (to achieve their own best interest) at the same time they do what is best for everyone else (altruism). Best interest means long-term self-interest. What is good for oneself in the long term turns out to be the same thing as what is best for everyone else. That is a core assumption of a *science of religion and ethics*, and is open to testing.

When the clergy, politicians, and people in general talk about good persons and bad persons they normally are talking about a person who obeys society's rules and lives by the moral law of the particular society concerned. However, up until the development of a *science of religion and ethics* the criteria for judging good and bad had little basis beyond cultural relativity, and "tribal" genetic propensities. Somewhere in the package of rules are some that relate to the key issue: What it takes to have a smoothly functioning society -- don't murder, don't steal, don't lie, and such. But when it got to the application of these rules it turned out that offenders were not treated in the same way. Some were executed or suffered other severe penalties for minor infractions or no infractions at all; some had their wrists slapped. But in addition to the rules necessary to have a society pleasant to live in there were many other rules less obvious in their intent. These rules were designed to enforce the customs of the society. For these rules their justification was merely "because our customs and authorities say so."

In reality the way most of these rules played out they always favored those in power. The rules benefited the rich and exploited the poor. They put the force of law behind the beliefs of the folk religion dominant in the society. At one time in England it was a serious crime to publicly say God does not exist. And, even in 1998 a decree of death (*fatwa*) initiated by Ayatollah Ruhollah Khomeini, 14 February 1989, was still in force against Salman Rushdie for "insulting the Prophet Mohammed in his book *The Satanic Verses*." It was renewed in February 1998 with the words: "Any Muslim who hears an insult to the prophet must kill the person who commits the insult." And the world has accepted this morally bankrupt decree with little more than an embarrassed moan. [4]

Therefore, if the world is to progress in terms of individual fulfillment it seems essential to me that the United Nations needs to work out a way to declare the issuing of a *fatwa* involving bodily or property injury, as a crime against humanity and therefore a violation of international law.

Nevertheless, in spite of the *fatwa* against Rushdie, Muslims as a group are as moral as the members of any other folk religion. However, Islam like all folk religions is ruled by inconsistent and, therefore, conflicting beliefs not based on a scientific foundation. Because Islam is now controlled by persons of limited vision it may be a little more conflicted than other folk religions, but by and large all members of folk religions suffer from the same lack of congruency in their life and, therefore, conflicted citizens are produced. In all cases such persons perform practices that prevent not only themselves but others from achieving a *sustainable feeling of well-being*. Therefore, the term "good person," that attempts to make a positive statement, makes a negative statement. Persons who are held up as worthy of being honored and emulated are in fact moving in the wrong direction. Most Westerners would probably see this about Ayatollah Ruhollah Khomeini. However, there would be less recognition that this also applies to Mother Teresa. "Despite all the publicity she received and the massive sums she collected, the level of care provided by Mother Teresa for those in her charge was minimal. When asked by an Australian reporter why she did not spend more of her vast wealth on the relief of suffering, her reply was that her business was *'saving souls, not bodies.'*"[5] In addition she supported a worldview that opposes birth control, as well as the development of each person to achieve their full positive potential.

These "good persons" do bad things because they are ruled by irrational customs and authority. They lack the guidance of a *science of religion and ethics* and the support of an Enlightened Community. And their beliefs prevent them from working for either.

Bad acts, bad people, laws of society, guilt, and punishment as defined by political bodies exist outside of the realm of cause and effect. Therefore, punishment (even capital punishment) is considered to be the perfect response to sufficiently bad behavior. Those who judge people "bad" do not need to prove the value, the psychological or moral justification, or effectiveness of punishment; they don't need to consider society's responsibilities. They only are required to prove guilt. But in reality even that is not required since many innocents are in prison and many guilty individuals are found innocent and are treated as honored citizens and moved into positions of power. This has been especially true in the U.S. South, but it happens almost everywhere in the U.S.

Was an individual warped in their physical and psychological development during their vulnerable childhood? Physical and/or sexual abuse, being terrorized with lies and fearful stories at the earliest ages, absence of nurturing physical affection, all are taken as acceptable hazards of growing up. If the child fails to come out of this as a good citizen we blame the victim and make them the guilty party.

For a *science of religion and ethics*, "bad" is not a valid adjective describing a person except in the broadest terms (describing a habit of behavior) and then not to condemn the individual but the behavior, with the goal of helping the person recognize the mistakes in their actions. "Bad" needs to be replaced by more exact adjectives that describe behavior in ways that make more obvious the necessary and desirable changes to implement.

Once a society accepts the idea that there are "bad" people it is caught in the dilemma of explaining why. Are they "bad" because they chose to be, because they were innately bad/evil, or for some other reason? Therefore, the below ideas on "free will"/ determinism relate directly to "bad" people; that is, individuals who do cruel, illegal, or thoughtless things. It is a core assumption of a *science of religion and ethics* that it is counterproductive to say that anyone is inherently "evil" (or, "bad"), or beyond human help. Persons may be confused, misled, ignorant, and perhaps even physiologically malformed; but they cannot just be inherently bad. This would make badness an effect without a cause. A *science of religion and ethics* does not accept belief in effects without causes. An Enlightened Community cannot ignore cause and effect, scientific evidence, study, analysis. If an individual does cruel, illegal, immoral, or stupid things a core assumption of a *science of religion and ethics* is that ignorance is to blame, either in the individual, their society, or both. Therefore, in a *science of religion and ethics* laws and morality need to be defined so as to depend on cause and effect and as a result be open to scientific study.

Free will was specifically developed to exist outside the realm of cause and effect that equates with determinism. On the other hand due to the spin given to determinism -- in spite of its being the essence of cause and effect -- as it relates to human choices, has effectively resulted in moving it outside the realm of cause and effect, also. Because of its simplistic "Newtonian" interpretation determinism is often equated with predestination, fatalism: that we can ignore the specifics of how people make choices because choice is an illusion.

Free will states that a person's choices are not caused. They are "freely" made. Free choice (like quantum mechanics) exists outside the realm of cause and effect. As a result it can be said that if a person commits a bad act, they deserve and require punishment. It is believed that they could have done the "right" thing, but they freely chose to do the "wrong" thing. These ideas are discussed in more detail in the Fifth Way of Wisdom [6] wherein the traditional assumptions about determinism [7] are also discussed.

Those who argue that punishment (including capital punishment) is a necessary social tool to achieve good behavior realize that persons can many times be intimidated into refraining from certain acts or into performing certain acts, even when they have not internalized the values of their society. However, what is usually overlooked is that persons raised this way are a constant threat to themselves and society. They are taught that if no one is looking anything is permissible! They may at any time do things to harm others and perform self-destructive, antisocial acts. Therefore, this method is at best stopgap because a person can never be sure how long or the conditions under which it will be successful. Worse yet, this approach develops individuals unable to achieve their full positive potential. [8] However, all the foregoing is very easy for modern people to ignore because our society has already accepted as true that there is an inherent conflict between the individual and their society.

Societies that regard punishment as necessary because it reduces the number of bad acts and without it society would be destroyed, are ruled by a principle I call the "Doctrine of Fear." This doctrine comes out of our genetic heritage of dominance and submission -- punish those who do not obey the leader. It involves banishing, excommunicating, whipping, ridiculing, jailing, torturing, killing, and such, those members who do not do what the society says they should do. Obedience and submission to the rules and to those who command is the aim. Many proclaim that without punishment a society would experience chaos, and a society that is not yet an Enlightened Community might. However, the Doctrine of Fear needs to be discarded as a necessary, or even desirable way to organize an Enlightened Community. An Enlightened Person cannot be ruled by fear, but needs to be inspired by love, understanding, honesty, and commitment based on acceptance of the goals and institutions of the society.

It may seem much easier to "put the fear of God" into individuals rather than helping them become Enlightened Persons. But this takes us directly to the core issue. What is a society for? In my framework its transcendent justification for existing is to work in every way it can for the well-being of every one of its citizens in order to ensure the long- term survival of our species. Authority, fear, and control should never be seen as necessary methods for helping individuals become their best self unless they have already been alienated from their society and therefore need special assistance to overcome that alienation.

However, without a *science of religion and ethics* and the necessary organizations based on it no society can recognize its responsibility let alone achieve it. Until the institutions supporting a *science of religion and ethics* are established, the research done, and results experienced, many will continue to support rule through fear because that is the way they were taught to believe. Most leaders are functioning out of their alpha male propensity. Therefore, they are more interested in obedience than producing Enlightened Persons. But even if a person ignores the importance of an individual life, it should be obvious that fear and punishment fail far too often to be endorsed as practical methods for organizing society. A person has but to study the lives of those called "bad" to see where the Doctrine of Fear errs. [9] It rests on the assumption that punishment will change behavior in the desired way.

In truth, however, there is the possibility that for many persons, "Whether in its first or final stage, [crime] is essentially a self-destructive, probably masochistic need and is therefore more often satisfied than eliminated or even temporarily held in check by punishment. For that reason the use of punishment as a correctional device is self-defeating." [9] Equally important as Alice Miller [10] points out, physical punishment produces grave psychological scars that interfere with the healthy functioning of the individual. Such persons are convinced that they are somehow lacking as human beings and deserve every punishment and cruelty they can imagine. By their destructive behavior (either to self or others) these individuals show that they need help to overcome their deep-seated beliefs. A Center for the Practical Application of Wisdom would be one organization that should work to learn how to provide such help.

Everything about law would be refocused in an Enlightened Community. In theory a good law states a principle or method of action that a good person would follow if no law existed. Therefore, when a person breaks a law they are a priori considered to be a bad person. But in an Enlightened Community there are no bad persons. There is only bad behavior. Bad behavior is a consequence of ignorance, not some innate essence called "badness." Because law is based on faulty theory it has been almost totally misapplied. It often leads to persecution of the innocent and rewarding the guilty. Laws in a society that is not yet Enlightened are almost universally used as tools by which the rich and powerful exploit the weak and powerless. Also, laws act as excuses to perpetrate cruel and heartless behavior on whoever is vulnerable.

In a truly civilized society (an Enlightened Community) it is always to a person's long-term advantage to do right because that is what right is. It is impossible for "bad" persons to truly advance themselves and achieve what they need. They commonly believe -- because society reinforces their raw "tribal" genetic propensities for "us vs. them" and "dominance/submission" -- that wealth, power, fame, and such, will bring what they seek. However, even the most cursory thought will make clear that illegal or antisocial behavior will not fill a person's needs, except in a very short term, superficial way. Wealth, power, fame, and such are only means not ends. They may bring satisfaction because they can be used to do things that will give fulfillment; for example, build nurturing bonds with loving friends. But in themselves they are as worthless as addictive, pleasure giving drugs.

Laws used to justify punishment are considered to be essential in primitive civilized societies (societies such as the U.S., Europe and Japan, for example.). Because these societies lack a science-based model for human behavior they have followed archaic ideas about the effectiveness of punishment. Therefore, their primary socially approved method of dealing with aberrant behavior is to punish those who will not or cannot follow the rules. In a truly civilized society (an Enlightened Community) laws would be guides for social behavior. Violators and transgressors would not be punished. Rather, helping hands would be available to aid them in making appropriate changes, and this includes changing bad laws (such as current drug laws). This process would ensure that each person would to the degree possible be helped to develop their full positive potential. For an expanded discussion of these issues, see VOLUME II, Chapter 22, "A Close Look at the Criminal Justice System. [11]" Also, see discussion of the Santa Clara County Child Sexual Abuse Treatment Program and S.M.A.R.T. Recovery, VOLUME II, Chapter 23, "Human Centered Treatment Programs." [12])

Through processes like the foregoing ones justice would be ensured and tyranny prevented in an Enlightened Community. These processes would provide techniques that are more trustworthy and humane while at the same time less wasteful and destructive than prisons/ jails are, and punishment in general. These processes would make it possible to protect all the members of the community by a better method than punishment. The foregoing will be true because procedures will exist to help each person move toward becoming an Enlightened Person.

The concept of law as traditionally used in Western society focuses on three primary points: 1) that the person was capable of intent, 2) that they did in fact perform an illegal act, and, 3) prescribed punishment will be meted out. The foregoing demonstrates the primary deficiency of this approach. It is concerned with guilt, blame, and punishment. There is limited interest in understanding the causes and effects involved, particularly society's role in the process. Therefore, laws as now utilized give us very little hope for future improvement. They basically only "work" in those situations where the individual has already accepted the need to change their behavior. It is here proposed that being guilty and having intent are only part of the picture. Knowledge and ignorance are also of prime importance. They provide a way to consider society's share of the responsibility for the behavior under discussion. This would open channels to make whatever changes are necessary in society to prevent behavior that harms others whether asocial, antisocial, or otherwise, whether through innocence or intent. In most cases the need is not to guard society from individuals, but rather to guard both society and individuals from their own ignorance in order to help them avoid encouraging and/or performing hurtful acts.

Murdering, stealing, lying, hating, squandering, using addictive drugs, and such, are symptoms. These are things that exist because of erroneous beliefs. We need to work at all times in the most strenuous manner to expose these erroneous beliefs and limit their power to control behavior. Saying that murder is immoral or a crime is not very useful. Murder needs to be avoided for reasons far more fundamental than being illegal. It interferes with the perpetrator and victim becoming Enlightened Persons, and achieving a *sustainable feeling of well-being*; that is, living the person's life rather than just going through the motions.

Religion and ethics have been areas of confusion for anyone trying to understanding the good life. Religion/ethics have traditionally been interpreted as dealing with behavior that violates the rules of some Ultimate Reference System, normally God, but also systems based on rational "shoulds"; that is, Platonic ideals. A given act is wrong because God has said not to do it, or some act ought to be done because God says so. Or, in a rational-based system -- such as Kant's Categorical Imperative -- because it violates the logic of the system. Since the death of God and the exposure of the limitations of reason, modern thinkers have tended to take a relativistic approach to religion/ethics. They think of religion and ethics as being about a particular group's customs involving their behavior. Group A thinks eating some meat is wrong. Group B looks forward to its celebrations with baked ham. Most modern thinkers believe there is no objective standard by which to judge a person group's beliefs in comparison with another's. However, a *science of religion and ethics* is based on the idea that there are objective standards, not in terms of some external absolute, but objective relative to the human nature of our species, that can be empirically measured. And this book aims to show how that can be done.

WHAT IS THE "I" OR "SELF"?

All current folk religions propose that the essence of an individual is their "soul," a unitary, immortal spiritual essence. Of course such an idea has no standing in a *science of religion and ethics*. Therefore, a *science of religion and ethics* would ask, from a naturalistic perspective, what is an individual? Before determining how to achieve a *sustainable feeling of well-being* it is necessary to clarify what a person truly is. A person finds all kinds of ideas about the "I" presented in psychology, in philosophy, in folk religions, and in most writings that attempt to deal with anything that relates deeply about human beings.

One such discussion concerning the "I" can be found in an interview by Bill Moyer in his book, *"Healing and the Mind"*[13] There he is interviewing individuals who work beyond the limits of current medicine, but have sufficient credentials to avoid being called quacks or charlatans by most responsible persons. In this section he is interviewing Jon Kabat-Zinn, Ph.D. and founder and Director of the Stress Reduction Clinic at the University of Massachusetts Medical Center and Associate Professor of Medicine in the Division of Preventive and Behavioral Medicine at the University of Massachusetts Medical School.

They are discussing the "I" and over the course of two pages hash over the usual meaningless ideas about the "I": being independent of the mind, who is saying "I," that the "I" is not the body, but controls the body, and such.

Kabat-Zinn on a more useful note discusses "selfing" where the individual thinks of certain components of their "I" as their self: "I'm a failure; I'm no good, I'm inadequate, I'm unworthy." He points out that this identification has the potential of limiting a person's options and behavior.

The point of Moyers' discussion is to clarify ways to promote healing. But this discussion -- like the explorations of the "I" by psychology, philosophy, and folk religions -- leads nowhere in terms of understanding the "I." The above discussion involves persons who are both intelligent and thoughtful. Therefore, it does give some specific evidence of the confusion that still exists around the "I," "the essence of an individual." There should be little doubt that one of the biggest mysteries in the Cosmos is the riddle of a human being. What is an individual, really? Why do persons behave as they do?

Traditionally, societies have evoked gods or God to explain where human beings came from, why they're here, and what they are in the most fundamental sense. This supernatural heritage has always made it more difficult to understand the natural world because it misfocuses and confuses thinking. The mind-body "problem" has been an enduring problem bequeathed by those who thought in terms of the supernatural.

Speaking somewhat metaphorically we could say that specifically we have seventh century scientist and philosopher Rene Descartes to thank for this "problem." In an effort to liberate science from Christian control he made a "deal" that was accepted by the Church; which means the Roman Catholic Church which was the only Church recognized at that time). And for that he got the right to publish and be heard. Without that he would have been banned like Spinoza was and would have had limited influence on the very productive thinking going on at that time. Because of Descartes religion got the "soul" (meaning), and science got everything else (cause and effect). Probably at the time this was a good bargain because it allowed science to compile a tradition of success in understanding the natural world and gave humanity an area of study so far beyond the science of the day, that it still remains a collection of unanswered questions even in today's world. Nevertheless, it continues to be a popular topic of speculation among philosophers, scientists, and thoughtful people in general. Probably more hours of thought and conjecture have been consumed on this pseudo-problem than almost any other issue. Had things been different and Spinoza's "conatus" (maintaining life with well-being) been accepted we would live in a very different world. It seems to me that four hundred years of science makes clear that Spinoza was on the right track -- and still few modern thinkers even realize this!

In my framework (and Spinoza's) there is no mind-body problem. There is only the problem of understanding how the human body works including consciousness, choice, the feeling of well-being, and related problems. Traditional explanations involve forces and factors that transcend the natural world. The view taken by a *science of religion and ethics* is just the opposite. Human beings are in every way considered to be a part of the natural world. They are looked upon as being complex organic machines. [14] However, this complexity is not a trivial attribute. My assumption is that it is essential to the "I." Also, it needs to be taken into account in understanding the choice process.

Because of the complex nature of human beings, their choices can only be understood within the context of symbolic communication, chaos theory, and other theories that deal with the limitations of prediction. These matters are discussed more fully in the Fifth Way (strive to make the best choices possible). But for the sake of this part of the discussion I would like to focus on the role of prediction in understanding the "I."

It is currently known that any system that is turbulent or has feedback mechanisms -- though deterministic -- is inherently unpredictable except within some specific limits. The choices made by an individual are the epitome of unpredictability. Chaos theory makes clear the relationship between determinism and unpredictability. Chaotic phenomena are deterministic but unpredictable except within certain limits. Nevertheless, like any real phenomena human choice can be understood more and more fully as a result of greater study and experience. But to understand human choices a person needs to understand the "I." At the same time a person needs to understand that there is no part of the human being that is, in principle, beyond understanding, including their behavior.

An individual's behavior (including their choices) depends upon their physiological makeup, physical structure, biochemical composition, knowledge, experiences, and the environment itself. Every part and aspect of a human being is naturalistic and can be understood in terms of cause and effect. This behavior follows the laws of mechanics, electrochemistry, molecular biology, evolution, psychology, information theory, and related fields.

Another key component that affects behavior is the human ability to learn. Almost all organisms are capable of learning, but human beings exceed all others evolved on Earth primarily because of our language ability utilizing symbolic reference. Not only can people use this learning to modify and change their ideas, environment, beliefs, and choices, they can use this knowledge to change themselves in ways they judge worthwhile by actually modifying their physical structures. If we are to understand the nature of the "I," the function learning plays for an "I" needs to also be understood.

As discussed elsewhere a key element that relates to learning is the effect of symbolic communication. Also the language ability is a large part of a person's "I." In a very real sense humanity is in the process of creating itself. An essential part of this creation is to alter the "I" in many important ways.

This "I" has long bewildered humanity. The science writer, Lincoln Barnett, is concerned with it when he mentions the "ability to transcend ourself and perceive ourself in the act of perception [15]"; and when he quotes the physicist Niels Bohr, "we are both spectators and actors in the great drama of existence."[16] Also, as Barnett states, "Individuals' inescapable impasse is that they themselves are part of the world they seek to explore; their body and proud brain are mosaics of the same elemental particles that compose the dark, drifting dust clouds of interstellar space;

they are, in final analysis... an ephemeral conformation of the primordial space-time field."[17] Of course the preceding flirts with acknowledging that Human Beings Are the Ultimate Reference System, a concept that totally alters the way a person needs to understand the "I."

Confusion about the "I" or "self" has dramatically retarded people's ability to understand themselves and all their behaviors including how they make choices. This confusion has also made it more difficult to recognize the fundamental connection between science and the naturalistic core of religion. At this time adequate terms are still lacking to discuss this fundamental aspect of the human being. As a result people's thinking about the foregoing ranges from the sublime to the ridiculous with rare contributions that are helpful. However, this is rapidly changing and modern philosophy and science, especially evolutionary biology, are now closing in on this issue in helpful ways.

As indicated earlier there is still a widely held view within the human family that a person's "I" exists as a basic, unitary core within a person that is stable and perhaps eternal. This stable, unchanging "I" is often called a "soul." A soul is usually believed to survive the death of the body. Is the foregoing possible? Could an "I" be separated from the totality of the body? Many philosophers and nearly all religious leaders have thought so. Early philosophers such as Bishop Berkeley, Immanuel Kant, John Locke, and of course Rene Descartes included "soul" in their thinking. But modern philosophers generally recognize that past philosophers wallowed in meaningless semantics on this issue. Sigmund Freud was one of the first widely known thinkers to lift the veil and throw some light on what before had been in darkness. He focused on the human mind in ways that made it clear there is no soul. "Soul" cannot be meaningfully defined or discussed except when it is interpreted as meaning some attribute, or aspect of a person's physical being. It is clear that the "I" is tied directly to bodily structures. Change the body in any way and the "I" changes. To consider that such a fragile, ephemeral thing as the "I" could exist independent of the structures that produce and maintain it basically comes out of wishful thinking.

The nature of the "I" is still being clarified. However, even with current limited knowledge it has become obvious that the "I" cannot transcend death. In addition if the "soul" (the *Atman* in Hindu theology) is the part of a person's being that does not change and is the calm, dispassionate controller, then it does not exist. There is no such part of a person. The "soul" theory of the "I" turns out to be at most a satisfying myth -- a poetical, primitive, simplified, casual way to characterize a person.

However, like with most ideas (as Socrates so well demonstrated) it is easier to point out the errors in other folks' arguments/positions/ideas/religions than to avoid errors in a person's own. Some persons (like Socrates) attempt to avoid this problem by never taking a position. Others propose positions impossible to disprove. A *science of religion and ethics* is committed to the approach of science. The goal is to propose ideas that can be falsified. Only then can a person correct errors, develop better positions, and move toward congruency. Whatever tenets anyone proposes will be in error. But, do they lead persons to achieve a *sustainable feeling of well-being*? Do they enable a person to more accurately understand the cosmos? Do they facilitate living a better life, having more joy? Do they assist humanity in spreading throughout the cosmos? These are the important things. Being wrong is not the problem. Not being able to admit errors, learn from them, and correct them is the problem.

It is clear that the "I" is neither unitary nor permanent. But if the "I" is not unitary and permanent, what has led societies worldwide, throughout history to believe that it is? Why is it not recognized as composite and changing? Part of the answer is that an eternal, unchanging "I" is congruent with the supernatural foundations that support all current societies. There is a short-term, emotional benefit in thinking of the "I" as permanent and unitary. Another part of the answer lies in the fact that it feels like a person's "I" is permanent and unitary. All adults share the experience of growing from infancy into maturity, seeing all parts of themselves change, and yet feeling identification with each stage of their previous being. Since each new "I" incorporates in one way or another every earlier "I," that identity seems very natural. "I" was a child, but "I" grew up. "I" couldn't read, but now "I" can. "I" used to have two legs, but one of them got crushed in the accident, and so on.

If a person can experience that identification over such a range of change it seems a small step to suppose that some essential element of a person's being can even survive the death of the body. The error of this approach lies in failing to understand that the "I" a person feels is not a physical reality (nor a supernatural reality), but a mental construct (a collection of interlocking memes that form a Platonist ideal). Since it isn't physically real it is open to infinite interpretation and flexibility. The real "I" is a multifaceted, multidimensional complex consisting of "hardware" (the totality of the body) and "software" "files" (rules, strategies, patterns, knowledge, understanding, beliefs, values, etc). The "I" does not reside in any one place in the body, but is a person's totality at any given moment. However, some components are more critical than others.

To have a unitary "I" would require that the "I" be unaffected by the forces acting on the body. Some people accept the foregoing idea. People know that an arm may be removed and the "I" remains. But what has not been considered thoroughly enough is how the "before I" compares with the "after I." Is it the same "I"? A person need only observe such persons to know that it is not. Picture the sports car driver who lives to race. They lose an arm and commit suicide thereafter. The "old I" had not yet adapted to the "new I." On the other hand, take the person who proclaims, "I would rather die than be blind." They lose their eyesight and through training and support find they can live a full life without being able to see. Their "new I" replaces their "old I." A person can see that the "I" that is said to be independent of the body is hopelessly a result of an individual's physical being, their experiences, their knowledge, how well their various organs are functioning, and the other forces acting upon the physical body.

Here is another example: "I...[asked] if her injury had caused major changes in her life. Suddenly this composed, quiet woman, who had sat through her treatment almost in total silence, sobbed and sobbed. She told me that the high point of her life was playing the organ for her church choir. She lived for the twice-a-week practices and Sunday performances. Now, with pain immobilizing her elbow, she could no longer manage the keyboard. Her days held nothing that she looked forward to. The constant aching had robbed her of any hope. Life seemed empty of everything except pain." [18]

When a person's attributes change and their "new I" is in conflict with who they thought they were this becomes a problem for them; for example, during puberty, serious injury, and the like. This woman had achieved a *feeling of well-being* through her ability to play the organ and experience the joy of accomplishment and intimacy this allowed. Her "new I" could not play the organ so her *feeling of well-being* began to disappear. In an Enlightened Community or one attempting to move in that direction, support would be provided for persons like the former organ player to help them deal with such problems and move toward a *sustainable feeling of well-being.*

At another level a person might see the ex-organ player as representing a challenge and an area of responsibility for a Center for the Practical Application of Wisdom (CPAW). These persons require existential help. A CPAW would need to provide that help. As more effective services are developed, and become available to more and more persons, CPAWs will become of greater and greater value. As CPAWs grow in relevance, they will grow in size, support, and visibility. In my mind this is how a *science of religion and ethics* will become ever more important in the modern world. To the degree that CPAWs have structures to provide the searching person with better choices, they could attract and assist these persons. Ideally, these persons would then be helped to move in the direction of becoming their own best self.

Let us use the above case of the organ player as an example. She might be involved in a chronic pain eradication group and work with others to learn how to understand pain and how to abolish or at least reduce it. She might be pointed toward more serious and deeper aspects of her potential as a result of becoming a victim of chronic pain. Of course what this woman experienced might result from any occurrence that pushes an individual out of the humdrum rut of their unexamined life.

However, even though an "I" changes, there is still the reality of a person's feeling of continuity. The Spanish-speaking, twenty-five-year-old person feels identity with the little child who learned that language from her or his parents. The "I" normally changes so slowly that a person does not recognize that any change is taking place. Nevertheless, in reality every adult has been exposed at least once to the experience of actually feeling their "I" shift when they were mature enough to remember the experience. That universal experience is puberty. During puberty, the changes are so dramatic and so rapid that the individual often can actually experience a transition in their "I." Sometimes there is even the feeling of loss of identity. Since current societies do not have the symbols to properly discuss or interpret this experience, its actual significance is universally lost. Everyone agrees the person has changed from a child into an adult. But somehow all this has happened without changing a person's "I" -- since "it doesn't change!" A person remembers the anxiety, confusion, and other emotions, and totally misses the core of this experience -- the shift of a person's identity. However, the "I" has changed and this shift of identity demonstrates that not only can't the "I" transcend death, it can't even transcend puberty!

Therefore, what puberty and other traumatic experiences actually provide is a window through which a person can see how the "I" works. At these difficult times change takes place so rapidly that there is often a feeling of fragmentation such that the person does not know who they are. Organ transplant is another example of a traumatic event that may have a major impact on the "I." Just being confined in a hospital can change the "I" in important ways. Where a person has felt invincible and immortal this experience may put them in touch with their mortality and vulnerability. When an organ transplant is involved -- heart, kidney, and such -- there is the potential for even greater change in the "I." Where the culture teaches that the "I" is unchanging a person may not be prepared for the trauma these changes produce. Another example is "mental illness." Much of what is labeled as "mental illness" may actually be a period of rapid transformation of the "I," and the disorienting effects of this transition.

It is clear that the "I" is not independent from the things that go on around it because they are constantly altering it. Light, sound, touch; all these things change the "I." Things as minor as marks on paper can change the "I" in major ways. There are so many subtle forces that affect this "I" and produce tremendous change, that it is easy to see why studying the "I" is so difficult. Even the experience of Christian fundamentalists being "reborn" is an example of this change, and actually a useful model to develop. This kind of mental/emotional change is what many persons working to become Enlightened Persons would experience.

It seems reasonable to believe that a person's body, including every atom, could be exchanged for another identical one and the individual would neither lose identity nor form. (This is admittedly idle conjecture because the means do not exist to perform such a difficult task, and probably never will. But if it were able to be done a person could then be duplicated or transported over vast distances at the speed of light!) However, if the foregoing ideas are true then it is the unique arrangement and relationship of components and structures that must be what is responsible for a person's individuality. Change the unique relationship and you have changed the individual. And yet, "We are not today what we were a year ago, yesterday, or even an hour ago; we shall be different one hour from now, tomorrow, and next year from what we are this moment. Certain aspects persist as habitual attitudes, others are less stable; but either stability or volatility indicates only varying degrees of persistence and change. The basic factor of change permeates the entire individual." [19]

The "I" is affected, and forged by stimuli transmitted from the sense organs and the resulting interpretations, reasoning, and choices that are made. The "I" interprets these stimuli and makes choices, but only within the framework of its assumptions and physical structure. However, as has been said before, the "I" is too complex to be easily understood. The true dimensions of the "I" are just beginning to be recognized. Only with much research and analysis by seminal thinkers will it really be able to be understood.

Nevertheless, it is abundantly clear even at this point that the real "I" is a composite. But what are the actual components of the "I"? This has been discussed in a general way above. Another way to explore this term is to look at the ways it is used: "I am hungry." "I am going to kiss you." "I think murder is wrong." "I have black hair." "I am in love." "I can ride a bicycle." Probably all of these are examples of "selfing"; that is, thinking of one part of the "I" as the whole self. Here a person is actually looking at some of the different facets of the "I." However, each of these represents only a narrow aspect of the "I." None are the complete "I." The real "I" is the sum total of all these things and everything else that can be accurately said about an individual. At a given time there must be only one "I" for any individual.

One major component of the "I" is a person's consciousness. But what is awareness? [20] Frequently, this awareness is taken as actually being the "I." Also, it is often taken as being unique to humanity. However, why should a person think other organisms lack consciousness? It would be very premature to draw such a conclusion since our current knowledge is so limited. In reality, many organisms could have this awareness. [21] In fact it is my position that consciousness is necessary whenever a choice is made by any organism; that is, whenever a decision is not hard-wired and/or automatic. When more than one input and/or memory must be utilized to make the choice, I believe consciousness is evolution's way to make this possible.

However, there seems to be some evidence that at least for human beings we often only become aware of a choice after it has already been made. At any rate it currently seems likely to me that at some point as computers move beyond the "earthworm" stage and begin to utilize neural nets and other components so that genuine choices can be made, that they will begin to experience consciousness "naturally." This consciousness will expand as their ability to manipulate choices increases. And it is my prediction that their reference system (i.e., Computer as the Ultimate Reference System) will be quite different from that utilized by human beings!

"Common sense" tells us that a person's "I" is their awareness of their own being. However, as usual common sense is wrong. A person's "I" is more than awareness. A person accepts ownership not only of the conscious decision to walk around the block, but also of the involuntary reaction of withdrawing their hand from a hot stove.

Evidence that a person's "I" is more than their awareness is given by hypnosis. Subjects of post-hypnotic suggestion are either unable to give a reason for their behavior, or are entirely wrong in the reason they give. The foregoing occurs because their conscious mind is apparently not aware of the correct reason: the post-hypnotic suggestion. If the subconscious can cause a person's actions that are subsequently unexplainable to or mis-explained by the conscious part of the mind, the "I" must then be more than our awareness. Numerous brain studies add other dimensions to the foregoing. [22]

Looking at the phenomenon of the multiple personality helps to further clarify issues. Apparently the human brain under certain circumstances can generate more than one "consciousness," each of which may be totally disconnected from the other. There probably are some persons willing to propose that there are as many "persons" as there are consciousnesses that exist in one brain. However, I think the better answer is that there is only one "I" of which these different personality constructs are a part. Current psychological studies seem to suggest that childhood sexual abuse is a key factor involved in producing multiple personalities. That may be basically true, but I think the issues are bigger than this. My best thinking at this time is that the bulk of humanity has multiple personalities! In ways not yet well understood different memories, for instance, and such. are suppressed and isolated from normal awareness. These isolated areas may have their own awareness that "takes over" at different times for almost everyone and is not recognized as being a different personality. To the degree that a person compartmentalizes their thinking, to this degree these multiple personalities may exist even in "ordinary" people!

Psychoanalysts demonstrate other evidence that indicates many if not all human actions depend upon the part of our being that Freud labeled the subconscious. As the following indicates, Freud was actually trying to solve the problem of the "I" when he wrote about the various parts of the mind that we call "ego," "super-ego," and "id." In trying to determine the different aspects of brain function and how they influence an individual's actions and reactions, he clearly was working to develop a model that would describe the nature of a human being. And the foregoing is born out by Kabat-Zinn [23] who writes, "...when Freud was translated into English, he referred to what we call the 'ego' as 'das Ich,' meaning simply 'the I.' 'The I' got translated into this highfalutin idea of 'ego,' [that in Greek means self] that we then made into a separate thing."

It seems to me that study of Siamese twins might provide some additional help in understanding this matter. Because different sets of twins are joined differently, they are part of each other's "I" in many different ways. Perhaps a thorough study of such persons would help to clarify some elements of the "I."

Another major component of the "I" is a person's knowledge/ideas/beliefs/faith. All observation shows that a person's beliefs, for example, change and can change dramatically. But it is still possible (easy!) using current ideas of the "I" to think of it as constant while at the same time thinking of it as being a person's knowledge/ideas/ beliefs/faith. Such is the kind of confusion permitted by current thinking about the "I." Using the ideas presented here will avoid such confusion. However, to reach these deeper levels of understanding a person needs to recognize that not only are a person's knowledge/ideas/beliefs/faith (K/I/B/F) major components of a person's "I" that constantly change, but that each of these things are tied in a fundamental way to a person's society.

The degree to which a person is able to overcome their raw "tribal" genetic propensities and develop their "wisdom" potential depends to a great extent on the knowledge/ideas/ beliefs/faith of their community. It is in community that a person learns language and becomes literate, is provided with the experiences out of which they assemble a worldview, is furnished the educational tools that help them to increase their knowledge, and so forth. It is in community that a person learns, adopts, or rejects K/I/B/F. Community is the individual's fundamental source of information. The further a person's society is from being an Enlightened Community, the more difficult the individual's growth and development will be.

In addition, the further the society's K/I/B/F is from being congruent with the real world -- and fails to support humanity's efforts to redefine itself so as to achieve its "wisdom" potential -- the more incongruencies will be produced in the members of the community. Their worldview cannot be in harmony with reality and becoming their best self. This lack of congruency exists in every society today and has throughout history. When individuals recognize this lack of congruency they have two choices. They need to either choose to accept the incongruencies as the way things are, or work to find congruency. They may accept incongruency by thinking this is the way the cosmos is (Copenhagen interpretation of quantum mechanics). Or, they might just ignore it (people who accept the supernatural). Or, they might laugh it away; for example, "A foolish consistency is the hobgoblin of little minds." If people overcome all the barriers and decide to work to achieve congruency their great challenge is, how?

For me the path toward congruency is clear. A person needs to surround oneself with the best people a person is able to connect with. These are people who share a desire to understand and who are willing to develop the tools to achieve that goal. The next step is to find a foundation upon which to stand as a person searches for congruency. I have proposed that this foundation is the "meaning of human life." When properly formulated this concept provides an organizing principle for a *science of religion and ethics*. It also provides a spotlight to illuminate the path a person needs to follow in order to achieve congruency. I think this path needs to lead toward the Enlightened Community made up of Enlightened Persons, and the nature of both becomes clearer as a person pursues the <u>Ways of Wisdom</u>. [24].

Some people might wonder whether or not there are some potential dangers in the concept of the "I" as presented in this analysis. Part of the reason past societies have been attracted to the unitary, unchanging model of the "I" is that it appears to be easier to work with than a multicomponent "I" whose parts are constantly changing. A changing "I" is more slippery. How can a person be held accountable for their behavior if they are always changing? If the "I" is always changing why shouldn't a person go for immediate gratification and let a future "I" suffer the consequences? Why should a person sacrifice, or endure suffering today for bigger rewards in the future? ("I" suffer now. A future "I" reaps the rewards.) More to the point, if a person gives up the symbol of permanency (that at its most extreme says, "I" will transcend death), How can a society be established that develops goals and plans for working to achieve them? In my model of the "I," where does social responsibility come from? What about honest, hard work, keeping a promise, long range planning, concern for the well-being of a person's community and the species?

To me the answers are clear and positive. The "I" is altered from moment to moment. A person can change dramatically and almost infinitely. But at the practical level the change is normally so small that statistically a person really is the same "I." A person is 99.9% the same from month to month. And this is true throughout a person's life. But more important, if the best way to live a person's life is to achieve a *sustainable feeling of well-being*, each of a person's activities is not only what is best for the person right now (the person's "current I"), but what is best for the person tomorrow (for the person's "new I"). All of a person's changes help them become a better person. A person is not only better for oneself -- now and in the future -- but also better for all other people, better for society.

Recognizing clearly and explicitly that the "I" changes, helps to clarify society's role in this process. Society's role is not to punish or bully, but to educate and nurture. The goal of an Enlightened Community is to do everything possible to help each person become their best self, to achieve a *sustainable feeling of well-being*. An Enlightened Community does not easily ask its members to sacrifice their lives either by dying or by living as a zombie, brute, or grossly deprived person. War is not accepted as just another way to solve international problems. Peace and organizations to produce social harmony on a global basis need to be the goal. Work that is dangerous, boring, and/or difficult needs to have equivalent personal rewards that move a person toward a *sustainable feeling of well-being*. Part of this might be achieved by reducing such work to the minimum, possibly by distributing it among everyone. Persons doing such work need to be highly rewarded.

However, the foregoing may have become more difficult due to recent economic changes occurring in the world. If Robert Reich is correct in his model presented in *The Future Of Success* (see Vol. II, Chapter 34-A) [25], the move from mass production to small-scale production and businesses may hamper achievements in reducing work hours as incomes increase. Modern technology and globalization in the form of "better, faster, cheaper" may drive individuals to make their work the focus of their life thereby making it more difficult to achieve a *sustainable feeling of well-being*.

The culture of the society (its music, art, sophistication) should be maintained by everyone, not the enforced sacrifices of "the masses." Each person should have a chance to share in the pain and share in the resulting rewards. In an Enlightened Community all persons would work together to help each other. In addition it needs to be recognized that pain is part of life. As indicated by the Seventh Way of Wisdom [26], pain is not something to totally eliminate from life.

Also, risk-taking is part of the life process. Particularly for some persons, dangerous work may provide the essential zest to keep them functioning at the necessary level for their own well-being. Death, hurt, and neglect can always happen -- possibly even senseless, premeditated killing. However, in an Enlightened Community the foregoing experiences would exist as rare exceptions. When they do occur social energy would be directed toward reducing the negative consequences as well as understanding them and preventing recurrences. Prevention would be undertaken not by putting every wild person into a padded cell, but by finding ways to channel that boisterous enthusiasm so as to be valuable to a person's self and to society.

Understanding the "I" gives a *science of religion and ethics* ways to aid more and more individuals in developing their maximum positive potential. This understanding makes clearer what kinds of societies are needed, and how to build them. In addition this view of the "I" presents a very optimistic and hopeful model upon which to develop Enlightened Persons and Enlightened Communities. It implies that living a full and happy life is not difficult, it is simple. It points out that people have the potential for almost infinite change, growth, and development. It embraces the use of knowledge to help people change in positive and constructive ways, to become their best "I."

CHAPTER 7

THE ENLIGHTENED COMMUNITY

THE ENLIGHTENED COMMUNITY: One that promotes the belief and implements the idea that human beings are the source of meaning and value and that assisting each member to become an Enlightened Person must be the focus for society's ultimate concern. The Enlightened Community is in the tradition of what early philosophers called the "good society." See VOLUME II, Chapter 3-A [1] for more discussion about the Enlightened Community.

Plato in *The Republic* wrote about the good society and therein presents his vision of ethics. And in the 1800s communes -- thought of as utopian communities based on ethical behavior -- were widely discussed, and many established. However, with the arrival of the Twentieth Century this area has not been a major concern of writers. Probably this is because the good person and the good society seemed anachronistic as decade following decade were filled with the evil of wars, economic disasters, and the like. Plus, in more recent times discussing religious/ethical behavior seemed like a basically pointless activity since it was taken to be only culturally relevant. In addition, communes have been considered to be failures and the thought of developing broader societies based on such ideas seemed naive and unachievable. Certainly my definition of an Enlightened Community is outside of current mainstream thinking, as is also true of the concept of the Enlightened Person. Partially, the foregoing is true because most writers who address these issues utilize the God concept that focuses answers in an entirely different realm. Many persons who don't actually use the God concept have had their thinking affected by this idea such that they are pessimistic about human potential and indifferent about anything that proposes that all individuals might live an inspired life, or even that this is a meaningful goal. As a result they think ideas such as mine are grandiose, unrealistic, out of touch with human history, and the like. Therefore, such persons stand as roadblocks wherever they have the power to divert, or stop conversations.

Bucking the trend discussed above, two modern writers have addressed the area of the good society. Walter Lippmann wrote *The Good Society* (1943) [2], and John Kenneth Galbraith wrote *The Good Society* (1996) [3]. However, they both demonstrate the currently impoverished vision of this concept. They each focus almost entirely on the economic aspects of a good society. They take the approach that if citizens have economic well-being then everything else will take care of itself. In fact they both make strong statements against just what this book is attempting to do, use a *science of religion and ethics* as the foundation for a new civilization. (See VOLUME II, Chapter 3, "The Enlightened Community," for an in-depth discussion of Lippmann's [2] and Galbraith's [3] books.)

Although an Enlightened Community would rarely function as a commune, nevertheless, considering all of the foregoing, the most useful area of study for a Center for the Practical Application of Wisdom might be the work done in the area of utopian theory and communes. These thinkers have explored much of the relevant theory and concepts an Enlightened Community must consider. Better yet they provide empirical data some of that might be able to be utilized by a *science of religion and ethics*.

Of course it is most specifically the ideas on utopias that have been rejected by modern thinkers. In fact characterizing someone's writing as utopian is equivalent to calling it worthless. However, we must ask whether or not this rejection has been done for adequate reasons. The charge is made that human beings have been shown to be incapable of living a utopian life: **They are said to be too flawed, too imperfect, too short-sighted, and too "selfish."** But as I work to make clear in Chapter 1 human nature must be seen in an evolutionary context to be understood in this regard. The true culprit lies in current social, psychological, and religious theories that societies now utilize. Any close study of societies shows them to be based on serious errors. <u>In my mind these errors make it likely that our "human problems" lie in human societies, not in the individual human being</u>. It seems to me the blame lies in our institutions and the theories they are built on, not in "human nature." Likewise, any close study of human beings based on evolutionary psychology shows a deep potential waiting to be released. This is shown best in times of natural disaster, but is there under all circumstances.

In the spirit of the foregoing paragraph some material on communes is presented below, not with the idea that an Enlightened Community must be a commune, but rather for the theory and experience that seems to be relevant. It is drawn from a very valuable reference [4] by Rosabeth Moss Kanter. She describes her book as follows: "The focus throughout is on how groups are built and maintained.... I hope to demonstrate... that in the past a number of utopian communities have in fact been successes.... [But] there are important organizational considerations to be taken into account in building a viable community."[p. vii]

In applying the experiences of communes to thinking about the Enlightened Community it is essential to look closely at the theory that supported these communal efforts. Each of them conflicts in numerous ways with the assumptions of a *science of religion and ethics*. Therefore, the successes and failures must be analyzed in this light. And it is within this context that I measure success and failure. On the other hand actual data is the true criterion that must be used to assess the value of all the ideas in a *science of religion and ethics*.

Kanter says, "For the current communal movement to succeed, it needs thinkers as well as doers, intellectuals as well as activists, who will discover and report what is known, provide new ideas, warn of dangers, and suggest alternative directions. I hope the findings of this book can contribute toward that end."[p. vii] To the degree that Kanter's writings and information can clarify the value of the concept "Enlightened Community" and provide insights for achieving it, to that degree will her writings also perform an invaluable benefit to efforts to implement a *science of religion and ethics*.

Kanter writes in terms of utopia. I think in all cases where she uses this term it is compatible with my term "Enlightened Community," and the ideas she expresses are consistent with my thinking. She says, "Utopia [think: an Enlightened Community] is held together by commitment rather than coercion, for in utopia what people want to do is the same as what they have to do, the interests of the individual are congruent with the interests of the group.... Underlying the vision of utopia is the assumption that harmony, cooperation, and mutuality of interests are natural to human existence, rather than conflict, competition, and exploitation, that arise only in imperfect societies."[p. 1] And this is the underlying assumption of a *science of religion and ethics*. When an individual or society is controlled by raw "tribal" genetic propensities rather than their "wisdom" potential they are governed by "conflict, competition, and exploitation" (us vs. them) rather than "harmony, cooperation, and mutuality of interests" (they are us).

Kanter continues, "For the most part, the vision of utopia has been the vision of community."[p. 2] The whole idea of an Enlightened Community focuses on the importance of community. It is only within community that a human being can be fulfilled. It is only within an Enlightened Community that a person can receive the assistance necessary in order to become their best self. It is the mutual support coming out of the feedback loop between the individual and their community that makes possible the Enlightened Community and the Enlightened Person. The individual relies on their community for the wisdom and support necessary to move beyond debilitating ignorance. Society's influence on the infant is overwhelming. That is why I say we cannot help all who desire to become Enlightened Persons until we have Enlightened Communities.

The following words, in my mind, also capture the spirit of the goals of a *science of religion and ethics*. Putting them into practice would be a prime responsibility of an Enlightened Community. Kanter indicates that communes sought to provide "...a refuge from the evils of the factory system, characterized by dehumanizing competition and the excessive labor of the many for the benefit of the few."

"Horace Greeley, whose ideas influenced utopian experiments in the 1840s, captures many of the beliefs of these utopians: 'There should be no paupers and no surplus labor; unemployment indicates sheer lack of brains, and inefficiency in production and waste in consumption of the products of a national industry that has never worked to half its capacity and has resulted in social anarchy; isolation is the curse of laboring classes, and only in unity can a solution be found for the problems of labor; therefore, education is the great desideratum, and in association the future may be assured.'" [p. 5] Kanter's quote of Greeley captures perfectly some of the goals and issues that an Enlightened Community would be concerned about and motivated to deal with in better ways then currently exist.

Kanter remarks that, "Historically, three kinds of critiques of society have provided the initial impulse for the utopian search: religious, politico-economic, and psychosocial."[p. 3] Of course for a *science of religion and ethics* all of these things are part of the same issue and must be dealt with together.

"[The psychosocial] critique revolves around alienation and loneliness, both social isolation and inner fragmentation. It holds that modern society has put people out of touch with others and with their own fundamental nature."[p. 7] I would say that the foregoing is basically true and that this is the primary challenge of a *science of religion and ethics* and a Center for the Practical Application of Wisdom. However, as indicated in other places it's not that modern society has separated the person from the group. Rather, it's that society has not yet created an environment in that the goals and behavior of each human being are congruent with the goals and behavior of every other human being.

The following quote expresses the above ideas in more detail. It includes almost perfectly the goal of an Enlightened Community though "religious, spiritual values, and sinfulness" would be interpreted in the context of a *science of religion and ethics*. "[T]he initial impetus for the building of American communes [as indicated earlier] has tended to stem from one of three major themes: a desire to live according to religious and spiritual values, rejecting the sinfulness of the established order; a desire to reform society by curing its economic and political ills, rejecting the injustice and inhumanity of the establishment; or a desire to promote the psychosocial growth of the individual by putting them into closer touch with their fellows, rejecting the isolation and alienation of the surrounding society."

"[These three themes] stress the possibility of perfection through restructuring social institutions."[p. 8]

"The primary utopian idea is human perfectibility."[p. 33]

"The beliefs underlying the development of utopian communities stem from an idealization of social life, that holds that it is possible for people to live together in harmony, comradeship, and peace. Utopian thought idealizes social unity, maintaining that only in intimate collective life do people fully realize their human-ness.... [In the view of sociologist Charles Horton Cooley] primary groups are fundamental to the development of human nature -- to fostering sentiments such as sympathy, love, resentment, ambition, vanity, hero worship, and a sense of social right and wrong."[p. 32] There is more than adequate evidence from studies of communes and social groups to support the foregoing point of view.

However, it appears to me that up to this point communes have achieved their success by emulating the hunter-gatherer life style. They have not moved to the next level. At that next level each member of the group must be motivated and supported to achieve their full positive potential as made available by the language ability. This would be accomplished by helping to improve the Ways of Wisdom and as appropriate, utilizing them to guide behavior.

Kanter explains the importance of education in communes as follows, "Education has been central in utopian thought.... Many communities place great emphasis on their educational institutions, establishing schools that are often of such a high quality as to attract many non-utopian children from the outside, and providing continued opportunities for adult learning, including lectures and study groups."[p. 37] It is this feature that most strongly aligns the commune tradition with the goals of a *science of religion and ethics*. Whenever true education -- and such when not used as a code word for indoctrination -- is stressed in any society a force is liberated that must move toward a *science of religion and ethics*. The "wisdom" potential is stimulated, developed, and nourished by a liberal education, and every step encourages the next step toward wisdom even though the paths may be circuitous and even tortuous. Education is critical to a *science of religion and ethics*. It may well be that setting up schools will be an essential step in the development of an Enlightened Community. As indicated elsewhere these schools would include education to become an Enlightened Person. And it is through this process that the individual would develop all the potential inherent in their language ability. This would be done in such a way as to be fully congruent with their participation in an Enlightened Community.

"In a number of communities, perfectibility means constant attempts at self-improvement, constant striving for perfection in word and deed."[p. 37] And for a *science of religion and ethics* in general and a Center for the Practical Application of Wisdom in particular the perfectibility of the individual and of society is an essential assumption. However, until a person has a viable idea of better and worse -- "wisdom" potential vs.

"tribal" genetic propensities -- such effort is as likely to be destructive as constructive. Up to this time all such models have contained within their core assumptions detrimental ideas that have produced harmful effects on varying numbers of persons.

"Another utopian value is order. In contradistinction to the larger society, that is seen as chaotic, uncoordinated, and allowing accidental, random, or purposeless events to give rise to conflict, waste, or needless duplication, utopian communities are characterized by conscious planning and coordination whereby the welfare of every member is ensured."[p. 39] And this is equally true of an Enlightened Community. However, order would include a much broader range of behavior and social activities than permitted by any of the communes. The order would come out of the Enlightened Person's needs and the Enlightened Community's efforts to fulfill those needs in such a way that everybody benefited, or at least none would suffer.

"A third utopian value is friendship. Just as the social world can be brought into harmony with the natural laws of the universe, according to utopian thought so can people be brought into harmony with one another."[p. 43] And of course friendship at its deepest level and in its fullest meaning is an essential ingredient in an Enlightened Community. Almost everything done in an Enlightened Community would have friendship for the rest of humanity as a key element of its goal. To assure that every person is enabled to achieve this kind of friendship would be a fundamental value.

Kanter discusses unity of body and mind (harmony) as a utopian value. "Harmony [as a utopian value, means] the merging of values, ideas, and spiritual matters with physical events, the union of mind and body, spirit and flesh."[p. 49] To me the foregoing is the core of the concept a *sustainable feeling of well-being*. And, to achieve a *sustainable feeling of well-being* requires an honest congruency in knowledge, understanding, and ideas tested by their universal applicability.

"Utopians are characterized by a spirit of experimentation." [p. 51] And, as Kanter indicates, this is another utopian value. Not only are utopian communities major social experiments, in which unique forms of human relationships are explored, but within the communities themselves new ways of doing things are often explored that may better enable the utopia to implement its ideas. For example, "Job rotation ensures everyone gets a chance to do both the most attractive and the least attractive tasks, and the least attractive may sometimes get the highest reward in the form either of 'credit' against goods from the community store or of increased leisure time."[p. 43] In an Enlightened Community experimentation would be done in a much more rigorous way and firmly within the scientific meaning of this term. Such experimentation would be part of the empirical process that would justify the claim that a Center for the Practical Application of Wisdom builds solidly on a *science of religion and ethics.*

"Utopians value their own uniqueness and coherence as a group."[p. 52]

"In general it is important for utopians to believe that life is an expression of their ideas, that there is no separation between their values and their way of life. Utopian communities offer to members life's services -- food and shelter, a job, education for the children, care in old age -- in the context of an explicit set of shared beliefs about how people should live."[p. 54] And there can be no Enlightened Community that doesn't have these characteristics. But, at the same time, the Ways of Wisdom require additional elements including motivating each individual to become their best self and providing resources to make this possible.

"The ideas forming the communal lifestyle -- perfectibility, order, friendship, merging of mind and body, experimentation, and the community's uniqueness -- all represent its intentional quality, with harmony as their principal theme: harmony with nature, harmony among people, and harmony between the spirit and the flesh.... Some utopian ideas offer romanticized versions of social practices that may be described in quite different terms. 'Mutual criticism,' for example, can be viewed as 'brainwashing'; friendship can be used to justify the sacrifice of individual needs to collective demands; and emphasis on harmony can cloak an unwillingness to deal with conflict or with the fact that individuals have discrepant desires."[p. 54]

And the above paragraph provides hints as to why ideas about the Enlightened Community and the Enlightened Person must be seen as hypotheses to be tested and altered as the data exposes mutually contradictory values or behaviors. It is by comparing empirical observation with theory that ideas must be tested. We must always be alert to the danger of missing what is really going on because we have defined goals too narrowly, or sometimes too broadly.

"Utopian thought makes a number of assumptions that contradict other viewpoints.... It proposes, for example, that human relationships need not be contingent on competitive, win-or-lose assumptions, but rather that cooperation is natural and that any interpersonal tensions can be eliminated through social structural patterns or re-education.... that is, what people want to do is the same as what they have to do."[p. 55] "[T] hat conflict between values and practical realities need not exist; that a single, harmonious value-based way of life is practical."[p. 56]

The foregoing ideas are the assumptions upon which a *science of religion and ethics* is based. If these assumptions are wrong then all the ideas about an Enlightened Community and the Enlightened Person expressed herein are also likely to be wrong. If such turns out to be the case this book must either be revised to reflect the better data, or scrapped and chalked up to another example of castle building in the air.

However, after having said all that, we need to recall the message of Chapter 1: We all have raw "tribal" genetic propensities that can easily distract us from the effort of becoming our best self by using our "wisdom" potential to fulfill our "tribal" genetic propensities through interpreting them so they apply to the whole human species. The essence of an Enlightened Community is to help its citizens become Enlightened Persons utilizing their "wisdom" potential rather than to be victims of their raw "tribal" genetic propensities.

I think examining the Hutterites -- a group Kanter (for good reason) neglected to mention in her book -- demonstrates people's potential to be guided almost totally by their raw "tribal" genetic propensities. This 400-year-old fundamentalist religious communal group appears to be doing very nicely: growing, cleaving, and growing some more. I'm sure some people leave the group each year because they cannot handle the suffocation. However, I'm not aware of any psychological or sociological studies of these persons.

The Hutterites are discussed by Daniel Dennett in his outstanding book, *Darwin's Dangerous Idea* [5] where he refers to a useful article by David Sloan Wilson and Elliot Sober ("Re-introducing Group Selection to Human Behavior Sciences," in *Behavioral and Brain Sciences*, Vol. 17, pp 585-608). In this article it is mentioned that the Hutterites regard themselves as the human equivalent of a bee colony. Their success makes it obvious that this propensity does exist within the human gene pool. And, it is our "wisdom" potential that provides us the opportunity to avoid that pattern and reach a whole new level of evolutionary development. But up to this point our "wisdom" potential functions weakly and sporadically while our raw "tribal" genetic propensities continue to guide almost all of our daily choices.

"Whereas [Charles Horton] Cooley proposed that a person gains full humanity only through complete identification with a primary group, Freud indicated that mature human development requires separation of egos, independence of the self from the group. Because the group is an agent of repression for the ego, in Freudian thought there is an inherent and irreconcilable conflict between the individual and society. Only weak individuals exist solely through collective impulses. In short, Freud believed that strong emotional ties, similarity of life circumstances, and absence of private property -- all of which characterize the commune as well as the primal horde -- produce a uniformity of individual mental acts that he deplored: 'The dwindling of the conscious individual personality, the focusing of thoughts and feelings into a common direction, the predominance of the affective side of the mind and of unconscious psychical life, the tendency to the immediate carrying out of intentions as they emerge -- all this corresponds to a state of regression to a primitive mental activity.'" [p. 56]

Certainly, Freud raises some valid points in his concern about anyone existing "solely through collective impulses," "The dwindling of the conscious individual personality," or "predominance of the affective side of the mind." The Hutterites are living proof that these issues are not merely hypothetical. The light at the end of the tunnel means establishing an Enlightened Community and Enlightened Persons who would maximize their individuality and their intellectual development, not diminish them. However, these things can expand a person only with the support of their society. The society can only provide this support because the achievements of past generations have allowed them to reach the level of knowledge and understanding wherein each member will support all the others in developing their full positive potential. It seems to me that one of the serious deficiencies of Freudian theory is its focus on the individual and its failure to see the societal dimension of therapy and the good life. I think Freud was caught up in the alpha male propensity, and envisioned that state as the goal to achieve. Freud's student, Alfred Adler, however, was right on target. As indicated earlier Adler sidestepped Freud's misdirected focus and went to the core of the meaning of human life though he didn't use this term. But his message is clear when he says:

"It is not a question of any present-day community or society, or of political or religious forms. On the contrary, the goal that is best suited for perfection must be a goal that stands for an ideal society amongst all humankind, the ultimate fulfillment of evolution". [6]

Adler's social psychology seems to be very compatible with the idea of becoming an Enlightened Person functioning within an Enlightened Community.

I am in basic agreement with Cooley's remarks on Freud quoted above. I feel that many of today's problems come out of the core concepts of Western society developed by seminal thinkers such as Freud, John Locke, Adam Smith, John Stuart Mill, and the like. These concepts form a chasm between the individual and society that cannot exist if we are to have Enlightened Persons and Enlightened Communities.

Harmony between an Enlightened Person and an Enlightened Community is one of the primary assumptions of a *science of religion and ethics*. But this issue must be dealt with in a totally honest and scientific way. It must address all relevant issues in sufficient depth to ensure that hidden problems are not being created. It is critical that no area is being overlooked that might undermine the process of developing Enlightened Persons and an Enlightened Community. Looking at all the relevant areas is the point at which all previous efforts to build a better world have faltered and eventually, therefore, collapsed or become harmful. Hypocrisy is a key problem. When individuals are forced or encouraged to say or do publicly what they don't believe privately, a destructive pattern is being established.

"Discrepant desires" is a core ingredient of the foregoing. A *science of religion and ethics* holds that there is no conflict between an Enlightened Person and an Enlightened Community. However, the foregoing requires the goal of long-term satisfaction, not short-term gratification. And, moving from current conditions to this ideal state will not happen easily. Levels of Membership in a Wisdom Group (see introduction in Chapter 18, and more detail in VOLUME II, Chapter 1) [7] is one tool proposed for developing the knowledge and experience to build such a group. It would be aimed at helping more and more people reach a level where "discrepant desires" can be handled so as to keep Enlightenment developing.

"If utopian theories were fully tenable, then many more viable and longer-lasting utopian communities would be found than has been the case in the United States. Only a few dozen American communes have survived more than two or three years. The experiences of the few successful ones indicate the kind of social organizations that are important to implementing a utopian dream, as well as the limitations to utopian theory inherent in these very practices."[p. 56] "The dream of utopia must be compared with the realities of creating viable utopian communities."[p. 57]

"This period [the 1840s]... offered an essentially secular and optimistic culture. The feeling prevailed that the perfect society could be founded on earth and within the context of an established political order."[p. 62] And it is this vision that a *science of religion and ethics* seeks to restore. It has been essentially lost in the modern world because past utopian ideas relied on too many false assumptions. Now we have the knowledge and the experience to more properly focus the vision. Now we can implement the dream.

"Building viable utopian communities has proven to be difficult: translating the utopian dream into reality is fraught with issues that in time may even distort the original vision."[p. 63] To me part of the problem contributing to the foregoing arises because "Utopia" starts with the assumption that the proponent has a "true vision" that only needs to be implemented. Their idea of utopia is not presented as a hypothesis. There is no effort to test and correct it. In contrast to the foregoing, "Enlightened Community" and "Enlightened Person" must be seen as theoretical, testable, and able to utilize experience to make necessary revisions. The goal is to find out how to build societies made up of people who can develop and maintain a *sustainable feeling of well-being*. This is the kind of utopia a *science of religion and ethics* proposes. And it is not proposed that these communities would necessarily exist as separated groups. They would most likely be made up of people living in various degrees of connection in a larger community.

The foregoing will not happen in the absence of continuous effort. Because this effort involves working with several theoretical concepts with limited empirical data supporting them (Enlightened Community, Enlightened Person, a *sustainable feeling of well-being*, the <u>Ways of Wisdom</u>, etc.), attempts to clarify where the problem lies when things don't work will not be easy. However, to the degree that we can remember that we are involved in a scientific process with empirical, not absolute answers, or totally predictable outcomes, the more likely we are to maintain the necessary flexibility. Only such clarity and flexibility in our approach will make it possible to correct errors and omissions to help more and more individuals achieve a *sustainable feeling of well-being*. But it is also important to keep in mind that our efforts relate to the future of our species. Will it survive? Can we help ensure that future?

Kanter continues, "The Shakers, Amana, and Oneida, along with Harmony (1804-1904), Zoar (1817-1898), and Jerusalem (1788-1821), are among nine 'successful' nineteenth century utopian communities, lasting thirty-three years or more. They can be contrasted with twenty-one 'unsuccessful' groups lasting less than sixteen years, including Brook Farms, New Harmony, and other Owenite and Fourierite ventures. The differences between the success of these thirty groups lie in how strongly they built commitment."

"The primary issue with which a utopian community must cope in order to have the strength and solidarity to endure is its human organization.... The idealized version of communal life must be meshed with the reality of the work to be done in a community...." "The organizational problems with which utopian communities must grapple break down into several categories:"

"How to get the work done, but without coercion." "How to ensure that decisions are made, but to everyone's satisfaction." "How to build close, fulfilling relationships, but without exclusiveness." "How to choose and socialize new members." "How to include a degree of autonomy, individual uniqueness, and even deviance." "How to ensure agreement and shared perception around community functioning and values."[p. 64]

"These issues can be summarized as one of commitment; that is, they reflect how members become committed to the community's work, to its values, and to each other, and how much of their former independence they are willing to suspend in the interests of the group. Committed members work hard, participate actively, derive love and affection from the communal group, and believe strongly in what the group stands for."[p. 65]

Kanter's above ideas provide some important thoughts that are applicable to an Enlightened Community. However, one point mentioned by Kanter that is especially important to a Center for the Practical Application of Wisdom is, "How to include a degree of autonomy, individual uniqueness, and even deviance." The whole point of an Enlightened Community is to provide an environment in which each individual can become their best self. This is not a second-order goal. It is the primary goal.

Kanter's ideas make clear that communes are a useful area of study for actual empirical data that can be drawn upon prior to starting the process to establish an Enlightened Community. As indicated elsewhere a Center for the Practical Application of Wisdom would be the responsible body to analyze all available data and develop plans for establishing an Enlightened Community based on the best available interpretation of this data.

All the organizations of an Enlightened Community must ensure that their goals, procedures, and efforts support in whatever ways are appropriate -- considering their specific mission statement -- the ability of all persons involved to become their best self.

All current societies ask the members to live for somebody or something else. Usually, this is for family, church, nation, or often their work. A *science of religion and ethics* would work to change all this. But it's not clear precisely how this can happen. It is not self-evident how to build an Enlightened Community and exactly how it would function. Nor is it obvious how to develop Enlightened Persons when there are no such individuals to start groups or serve as models. One way to begin building an Enlightened Community and helping individuals move toward becoming Enlightened Persons is to start gathering the necessary data including practical experience. Part of this process might involve monitoring and collecting all the facts possible on social structures within the community. The goal would be to assemble information on everything that impacts development of each individual's best self. This data would be used to establish experimental, bootstraps procedures to utilize each individual's best impulses and strengths (their "wisdom" potential) to collectively help each other move in the right direction. The more groups that follow this path, the greater the number of individuals who will be helped to achieve a *sustainable feeling of well-being*. In order to follow this idea procedures would need to be developed to help groups utilize the theories and research coming out of a *science of religion and ethics*, psychology (including evolutionary psychology), sociology, anthropology, medicine, economics, philosophy, folk religions, and other fields of scientific study of human beings individually and in groups. All experiences possible would be incorporated into a feedback loop to provide raw data to help these sciences improve their theories and become more useful in helping to produce both Enlightened Persons and Enlightened Communities.

CHAPTER 8

FIRST WAY OF WISDOM: HUMANS ARE THE ULTIMATE REFERENCE SYSTEM

A more detailed description of each of the Ways and congruent methods of achieving them are presented herein and in following chapters. However, let me begin with a reminder that the current writing about the Ways contains much speculation. They are based on the best evidence I have been able to assemble, but they are a long way from being proven. And like all of science they have no more standing than the available evidence can support. These ideas are presented as falsifiable hypotheses. Everything about them is open to change as study, research, and more thought require. It is the quality and quantity of this research that determines the value of anything written. The goal of this book is to motivate study, experimentation, exploration, inquiry, and investigation relevant to each Way and all related or relevant ideas. This material must be assembled and organized so it can be used in the best way. Such information would help to determine the dimensions, exact components, value, and application in people's lives of each Way of Wisdom, or whatever ideas may replace them. Eventually, there should be vast files developed on each Way detailing the research findings to support, call into question, or replace it. These materials would bring together all the information available to clarify each Way of Wisdom, its value, and how to achieve it. VOLUME I is a beginning in this effort, and VOLUME II substantially expands on this material.

FIRST WAY OF WISDOM: Human Beings Are – for us – the Ultimate Reference System (HBAURS) living immersed within a universe with Reality As the Objective Reference System (RAORS).

Throughout history people have believed that there is something absolute, or ultimate that exists independent of themselves that would make their life meaningful. The foregoing position implies or depends on an Ultimate Reference System that could be used as a criterion to measure and evaluate human life, human behavior, and everything else. However, more thought and experience make it clear that human beings themselves are the source of meaning and values. They are as near as we can get to an Ultimate Reference System. Therefore, I take the position that Humanity itself is our ultimate reference system defining meaning -- and everything else.

The foregoing means that it is the human species itself that provides the framework within which meaning of human life must be interpreted. And for each person this makes the answer to this question dependent upon empirical study and evidence.

Because this concept stands in opposition to most of what we have been taught, it is easy to be confused by what it means. Some readers interpret it to mean that I am saying there is no way to use reality as a reference. To help reduce the likelihood that anyone interprets HBAURS in such a way I would like to present another concept that I hope will clarify matters. This is Reality As the Objective Reference System (RAORS). I take reality to be everything that exists -- chairs, cars, rivers, atoms, eclipses, stars, dark matter and dark energy, all living things including humanity, and of course everything else whether or not currently known.

However, the foregoing is talking about existence, not meaning. The only meaning associated with the existence of a chair, star, or living thing is one applied by human beings. If we say a star or an elephant has its own meaning we are the ones deciding this, not the star or the elephant. If there were alien life forms capable of using symbolic language they would provide their own reference system that we might or might not be capable of comprehending. Therefore, discussing the meaning of anything that exists is talking about human nature, perception, and interpretations, all of which come out of our evolutionary history. As a result, whatever meaning we assign is subject to change as we study and get to better understand our own nature and the rest of the universe in general.

I do not in any sense feel that there is "no way to use reality as a reference." Obviously, reality is the main resource for our efforts to understand and to correct our errors. But reality is not the Ultimate Reference System for many reasons. One, discussed later, is that we can't directly access reality, but only know it through experience and thought so it cannot be our Ultimate Reference System. Another is that our knowledge of reality changes as our understanding increases. But we must make all of our choices based on our current understanding. All of our motivation and knowledge are tied to what is known today. For these reasons Humanity itself is our ultimate reference system-- because we live our full life making choices and plans with the Reference System current knowledge makes available to us. It doesn't matter to us that five generations in the future society's understanding of reality may totally change the way people live and the goals they pursue. Our life has limits. It exists only now. The future is just an unknown, and our only tie to it is our own individual life and our relatedness to our humanity.

Because science allows us to better utilize our language ability we are getting better and better approximations to reality (at least insofar as it can be used to improve the quality of human living). But again, all of our interpretations are based on our current understanding of reality -- not on what reality truly is.

Some people have interpreted HBAURS such that they fear it would convince others to be satisfied with their current understanding of reality and overlook the need to compare all conclusions, ideas, assumptions, thoughts, and such to Reality As the Objective Reference System.

I take things to be just the opposite. Since HBAURS requires us to focus on quality of life, there then becomes a driving need to learn more and more about everything that exists. Every aspect of our life depends on understanding reality including the reality of ignorance, disease, hunger, and how our bodies and human societies work. This would require that insofar as possible every person's ability would be as fully developed as possible and utilized in this process. Not just to learn, but also to apply our knowledge because for a *science of religion and ethics* that's what knowledge is for.

CHAPTER 9

SECOND WAY OF WISDOM: ADVANCE HUMANITY

SECOND WAY OF WISDOM: Endeavor to maintain and develop the human species. Support efforts to develop Enlightened Communities; that is, communities promoting authentic happiness for all citizens.

A *science of religion and ethics* is based on the thesis that the best way to maintain and develop humanity is to establish an environment in which every person will have the opportunity to establish a life that will provide a *sustainable feeling of well-being*. However, the foregoing will not happen immediately. It will take great effort just to move toward developing a state where some members will achieve a *sustainable feeling of well-being*. But the goal is to develop societies where more and more citizens will advance the quality of their lives and the lives of all people. Certainly any given individual cannot be equally active or effective in all areas. The important point is that this Way of Wisdom supports the development of whatever ideas, structures, plans, and such. are necessary to help more persons direct their thoughts and energies toward maintaining and developing humanity. Fulfilling the Eighth Way of Wisdom (help and be helped by other people) will in itself be a large component of this Way. Currently, essentially everyone harms others, sometimes in ways that limit those persons' ability to achieve a *sustainable feeling of well-being*. Much of this harm results because individuals have not received sufficient guidance from their society to understand and guide their raw "tribal" genetic propensities.

As discussed in Chapter 1, these raw "tribal" genetic propensities include the "dominance/submission," "fundamentalist," "us vs. them," "world works by magic/wishing," "family separation at puberty – for males," "territoriality," "sexuality." Although there may be other propensities that have important effects, the foregoing ones are the prime ones I'm aware of that cause tremendous problems for humanity today. It is a basic assumption of this book that these raw propensities can be productively directed when a person's community presents clear ideas on how to incorporate these drives into becoming a person's best self. Part of this recognizes that humanity is in the process of inventing itself. Any given individual needs to buy into the value of this goal if they are to become an Enlightened Person and help create an Enlightened Community. Once they are committed to becoming an Enlightened Person, they could become an active participant in a Wisdom Group in order to discover how to stay on that path, and to help others do the same.

Sometimes persons harm others because they don't realize the effects of what they are doing. Here society needs to develop mechanisms for providing adequate feedback. Sometimes persons harm others because they are so mentally disturbed, or socially alienated they don't care, or don't know how to change what they are doing. Here society needs to establish resources to handle such situations. (See "Other Support Organizations.") At the beginning this will seem like an overwhelming task. Currently, most of society is in need of such help, and some of the help needed is not even available at this stage of human knowledge. But -- like for all things -- we need to do our best with the expectation that this will impact the problem positively and build a foundation that will support further growth.

Another area that will advance humanity involves gaining a greater control over disease, illness, disability, and death. Although it would be pointless to strive for immortality, all persons should attempt to be healthy, active, and effective. As such it might be useful to have a goal of extending life to 150 years. That would give persons the time to appreciate the fruits of their efforts. Obviously, merely to prolong the life of the old and enfeebled is no worthy goal. Provision for voluntary euthanasia is an essential component of the Enlightened Community. At the same time societies need to look into the basic mysteries of life and aging and learn how to retard aging to allow more years at a person's prime.

However, the foregoing is merely an example. A multipronged attack needs to be mounted against the ignorance that surrounds the species *Modern Humans.* There will always be unknowns, but it seems that ignorance about the workings of the human body should always be a top priority for study and research, theory building, and speculation. A greater share of our scientific energies needs to be focused on increasing our understanding of the human body. With such efforts society would learn ways to help more and more people achieve a *sustainable feeling of well-being*. Researchers need to strive to find out more about the basic mysteries of body functions. Society needs to learn how to increase intelligence, treat malfunctions, eliminate genetic defects, and such. Anything that prevents or retards the achievement of *a sustainable feeling of well-being* for anyone needs prime attention to overcome. And much of this work would be done with the involvement and assistance of those affected so that their lives would actually become part of this important effort.

Part of this process might include involvement in what I will term the "Christopher Reeve" [1] model for persons affected by conditions not currently treatable, or at least not treatable in such a way as to permit functioning within the normal parameters for a human being. The essence of this model is to take a person's condition as an opportunity to help humanity in general by providing the person's body in all its attributes to focus on this condition and support efforts to cure, overcome, live with the condition, and turn it from a liability into the channel a person uses to connect with and advance humanity. It thereby becomes a person's personal contribution to the process of developing humanity -- improving human life for all.

The elimination of poverty and the suffering it produces are vital to human advancement. Knowledge holds out the potential of providing unlimited wealth for every human being. [2] Humanity lives in a universe of potential abundance. An abundance of love, friendship, support, and nurturing will be forthcoming when we each learn how to experience and share these things. Also, material abundance – whatever is necessary to the Enlightened Person – is within our grasp. The only thing that keeps every person from sharing in that abundance is ignorance. (See VOLUME II, Chapter 14-A, "Bionomics – Economics and the Enlightened Community," that builds on the ideas of Michael Rothschild.) [3]

Developing knowledge and using it more effectively is the essence of a *science of religion and ethics* and the Enlightened Community. Many aspects of the foregoing issue are considered in the Eighth Way of Wisdom (Help and be helped by other people.) However, much of the poverty and suffering of humanity is due to a lack of understanding of things outside of human beings. The possibility of each person achieving a *sustainable feeling of well-being* did not exist until our knowledge base reached a critical level. That has only happened at this time because Western science has provided the knowledge necessary to develop the requisite tools, and capitalism made it possible to build and use them in the production of industrial, science, and consumer goods. These have allowed goods and services to be so efficiently and abundantly produced that people need devote little of their time to this end. As a result people have more time to develop their minds and engage in satisfying activities. However, people need to realize that technology must be used to improve the quality of human life. Unfortunately, the negative impact of capitalism and new technology has frequently not been taken into account. [4] (Also, see below and VOLUME II, Chapter 28, "Managing Change In an Enlightened Community.") [5]

The Organization to Enhance the Quality of Human Life [6] would function to help all persons fulfill the needs involved in this <u>Way</u>. An Organization to Enhance the Quality of Human Life would provide the structures to allow persons individually and in groups to gather the data and, to supply the knowledge to help more and more persons achieve a *sustainable feeling of well-being.*

The Knowledge Bank -- that brings together everything that is known or speculated about -- would be one of the resources of an Organization to Enhance the Quality of Human Life. (See VOLUME II, Chapter 19, "The Knowledge Bank and an Enlightened Community.") [7] Also, an Organization to Enhance the Quality of Human Life would provide every person a way to channel their insights, unique experiences, and such into society's knowledge base in order that it would not be lost -- so that it would achieve maximum utilization to ensure the survival and development of humanity.

The Organization to Enhance the Quality of Human Life would have the flexibility necessary so that regardless of the individual's specific circumstance they could be shown a way to be part of the Knowledge "Revolution." Some persons might assemble teams and coordinate the myriads of details needed to accomplish a particular task. This could even involve hiring scientists to find a cure for a particular disease, achieve a project goal such as establishing a colony on the Moon, develop a way to guide the evolution of all species in order to keep Earth a desirable place for human living despite the changes it experiences, and such. (Keep in mind the issues raised in VOLUME II, Chapter 28, "Managing Change in an Enlightened Community" which starts with the following:

A science of religion and ethics "must find a new way to manage change so it occurs in a more satisfactory way. Exponential "progress" can prevent quality living just as surely as the stagnation during the Dark Ages did. The current pattern cannot be tolerated in an Enlightened Community. In current society any given change is resisted by some element of society. Parts of society even attempt to prevent discussion of some kinds of change. Other elements of society blindly cause changes as rapidly as they can with little consideration for the possible consequences of this change. Neither approach is appropriate for an era experiencing an information explosion. The destructive impact on the ozone layer due to modern technology is only a small glimpse of the possibilities of the future." [5]

One exciting method to promote this <u>Way</u> might be to combine recreational games and "research." Currently there is so much talent wasted (not directed toward helping individuals achieve a *sustainable feeling of well-being*) it is criminal. It is proposed that a Center for the Practical Application of Wisdom would significantly impact this problem. However, there will probably always be room for improvement in this area. One way that comes to my mind is to establish "Discovery Games" that not only provide enjoyable times with friends, but actually produce knowledge that becomes part of the database available to humanity.

Suppose a couple of friends, or a group have a tradition of meeting socially on a weekly basis for several hours or so. Instead of only playing cards, bowling, or watching athletic events on TV, for example, they might also select a "Discovery Game" packet from a list of available offerings from their local Organization to Enhance the Quality of Human Life. These game packets might be put together by sponsors overwhelmed by too much data to adequately process in a timely fashion. Suppose the group selects as their game, analyzing data from space probe X. They might study records made by this space probe, but not yet analyzed by scientists because of lack of time. The group could search for gems in the mountain of data and bring these to the attention of "Game" monitors or sponsors. Their findings would increase the efficiency of project scientists studying this data while providing increasing numbers of persons a way to experience the joy of discovery. This process could also ensure that individuals do not feel alienated, but recognize that they are useful members of society. When properly established and functioning this project might provide a way to process the current and soon to increase vast storehouses of unexamined data. Currently it takes years, possibly decades for this material to be made available to humanity. Many areas of social concern -- for example the relationship between specific beliefs and the individual's behavior -- have never been properly analyzed due not only to lack of desire and/or vision, but even with such motivation, there still would be a lack of available talent to perform the analysis. Also, see VOLUME II, Chapter 32, "Science for Everyone."[8]

Another method of advancing humanity would be by using the principles of federal union to develop a world government for all the people of the world starting with those nations most experienced in democratic government. This goal was first propounded by Clarence K. Streit in his book *Union Now* [9]. The importance of this goal will depend upon the ease with which individuals can become Enlightened Persons. The more difficult the task the greater the importance of international federal union. It is an important goal any way a person looks at it, though. The world needs to be governed by a political body organized on a more basic foundation than alliances such as NATO or the United Nations. The advance of science and religion requires a better functioning political foundation. The perpetuation and expansion of the good life for all persons demands international federal union -- maximum freedom, no wars, one currency, no borders, improved communication, protection of the individual. Hopefully, better communication and data-gathering would mitigate the effects of pressure groups, "good old boys" clubs, and such.

However, one caveat on the idea of universal federal union: It is critical that local governing areas have the broadest range of independence compatible with the safety of the individual. This opportunity to be different is essential if we are to have a broad range of human experimentation, variety, customs, and such to draw from to cope with the unknown and the unexpected. This suggestion comes out of ideas discussed in VOLUME II, Chapter 14-A, "Bionomics: Economics and the Enlightened Community." [3] Michael Rothschild [10] considers economics and evolution as equivalent systems whose primary difference is their time scale. To me this brought to mind the point that an extensive gene pool is very difficult to change even when superior mutations arise. The foregoing is true because of the mass, or the inertia of the size of the pool to be affected. A similar problem can arise with businesses or any human organizations. The bigger they are the more difficult they are to change. Presumably in an Enlightened Community made up of Enlightened Persons this would not be the case. However, becoming too big to change needs to be guarded against to reduce the potential of catastrophic collapse. Preventing monopolies would help achieve the foregoing.

Humanity might also be advanced by adopting a world language not of any country. This would allow all the people of the world to converse with each other, experience greater camaraderie, and read all the literature of the world by knowing just two languages. By understanding the people of other cultures a person becomes able to share in their knowledge, experiences, and insights. The more people who thus understand each other the more secure is human well-being. With the free exchange of persons allowed by political union a common tongue that could be used all over the world becomes even more important. Also, every person might be motivated to learn two languages, but expecting them to learn more seems unrealistic to me (as a single language American!).

Perhaps study of human brains and how they process language might permit the development of a new language very different from any now in existence. This language might vastly increase the ability of people to think, communicate, and act. For more discussion of the preceding topic, see VOLUME II, Chapter 25-A, "A Universal Language and a *science of religion and ethics*." [11] However, with the advent of computer real-time translation, even language may soon cease to be an impenetrable barrier to communication to persons lacking a common language.

Also, humanity would be helped by universal adoption of the best measuring systems. An example is the universal adoption of the Celsius temperature scale and the metric measuring system. Metric units are so easy to use and are so necessary to international commerce that a person cannot justify the continued use of any other units, at least not by saying, "Change would be difficult." Of course this primarily applies to the U.S. since the rest of the world has already adopted the metric system. And the difficulty the U.S. has had in changing to the metric system is an example of the difficulty of changing vast governmental realms and bodies where democracy is practiced, and short-term self-interest of individuals rule political decisions that have long-term consequences.

Striving to reach the stars is another necessary avenue of human advancement. Only if humanity is spread over a large portion of the Universe, will it be secure from local cosmic disasters such as the passage of erratic suns, collision of Earth with a large meteor, solar energy fluctuations, and such. Also, only by moving into space can the chance of being destroyed by alien life forms be reduced. (It is admitted that the latter possibility is quite remote. Any intelligent life form that has mastered the ability to move among the stars would surely nurture the miracle of life wherever it is found, not destroy it. And unintelligent life forms would be unlikely to be dangerous to earth life.)

Moving into space might eventually aid in preventing the overpopulation of Earth, particularly as human beings live longer and longer life times. This will probably never be a very important motive, but it could conceivably become a helpful one (perhaps by exiling those persons who are unable to see Earth as a closed system with limits -- just kidding!). Obviously, the only reasonable way overpopulation can ultimately be prevented is by limiting births.

But more importantly people will eventually be halted in their efforts to understand the Universe if they do not advance beyond the limiting conditions encountered on Earth. To understand the Universe, humanity needs to at least to some extent advance into it. And to understand the Earth and everyday problems, human beings need to understand the Universe. Striving to reach the stars will also furnish another constructive outlet for human energy. A society advances or it degenerates. It cannot stand still.

This Way would draw from all human wisdom to increase the likelihood that significant energy will not be wasted on trivial pursuits while at the same time ensuring that every issue of potential importance has its task force working to deal with it in a timely as well as productive manner. Every person who shares the vision would be engaged in the active pursuit of this goal, and will in the process be helped toward becoming their best self.

Because current folk religions focus their primary attention on what happens after a person dies, there is little concern for helping each person to become their best self in a way that takes responsibility for maintaining and developing the species. As a result few people use their life in such a way as to combine their joy with promoting the future of humanity. The goal of a *science of religion and ethics* would be to change all that. It would support every individual to develop their "wisdom" potential and achieve a *sustainable feeling of well-being*.

CHAPTER 10

THIRD WAY OF WISDOM: SEEK TO UNDERSTAND. PURSUE WISDOM

All we are and all we become depends on our knowledge and understanding, and our ability to apply Wisdom to this knowledge and understanding. Primarily we depend on our society to help us take the path of Wisdom. When we are lucky our society provides us knowledge, data, and experience in such a way as to permit us the best understanding currently possible. That is Wisdom. This Wisdom helps us to see that for all practical purposes we live in a boundless universe, with infinities in every direction we look. However, because our knowledge is always finite, therefore our understanding is always time-specific and open to change.

But when our knowledge is combined with Wisdom then it can serve us in achieving a *sustainable feeling of well-being.* All data becomes knowledge as it is compared to or measured in terms of a reference system. Therefore, it is critical to find the best reference system available to use in the interpretation and application of data. It is our wisdom that allows us to find the best reference system. In the absence of an adequate reference system all data, experience, and knowledge may be misapplied, or misunderstood and lead someone in the wrong direction. It is the search for an Ultimate Reference System that has been at the core of the Wisdom quest throughout human history.

However, until modern time almost all searches started at the wrong point (God), and have, therefore, led to wrong conclusions. Unfortunately, up to this time those who have rejected God as the Ultimate Reference System have done little better than those who accepted God in clarifying what beliefs provide a *sustainable feeling of well-being.* Their thinking tends to be so misfocused by the God concept that they have been diverted from understanding the goal of their search.

Once a person has found the best reference system their wisdom permits, then they need to interpret their available data in terms of this reference system. A *science of religion and ethics* utilizes Human Beings As the Ultimate Reference System. For anyone accepting this approach it will be clear that the next step is to learn everything they can, particularly those things necessary to use that knowledge to help achieve a *sustainable feeling of well-being.*

Mastery of the general ideas of a *science of religion and ethics* might be the most productive step possible in achieving this <u>Way</u>. However, there are many ways to achieve knowledge. To the degree that a person's society has organized its data in useful ways that are open to revision with additional understanding, to that degree will the individual benefit from mastering such knowledge. Insofar as the society has misfocused its data, to that degree will the person be misled by their society unless they can find a way to escape such deception or learn how to recover from it. Nevertheless, normally the individual will benefit by pursuing formal education. This is particularly true if such teaching includes a good portion of science, history, comparative religion, critical thinking, logic, reasoning, questioning, analysis, and study of real things, primarily left brain activities. The broader their studies and the more sources they draw from, the more likely they will be able to correct the errors that are included as part of any teaching.

But until a person achieves the wisdom to determine what their knowledge is for they will primarily be assembling data and will be misguided on how to use it to help them become their own best self. It is with knowledge that we tap into the abundance of the universe. With knowledge we learn how to use the unlimited power of the sun. We learn how to produce bountiful food that is healthy, nutritious, and tasty. And with knowledge we learn how to create and maintain a joyful life not only for ourselves, but also for all people on this earth.

By mastering the knowledge slowly accumulated by our species over its history we prepare ourselves to achieve each of the <u>Ways of Wisdom</u> in general and in particular the <u>Ninth Way</u>: *Work to increase knowledge and all creative and artistic endeavors. Adopt an inspiring life goal.* To fill our brain and mind with good, clear knowledge is a long step toward Wisdom. This is the point where efforts to achieve wisdom using so-called "wisdom traditions" get a person off track and end up leading not to wisdom, but to positions that are fundamentally based on intuition and tradition; that is, are not theory-based, and therefore not falsifiable. They are not based on wisdom in the context of a science of religion and ethics. Rather they are narrowly focused insights about how to use the mechanisms of the brain to achieve simple goals. Under certain conditions these practices utilizing mysticism can produce an illusion of great understanding.

These traditions are sometimes represented as relying on "objective" knowledge because if the student follows the training faithfully they often achieve the predicted results. But these results tell us how the human brain behaves or can behave under certain circumstances. They don't tell us how to increase the food supply, cure disease -- except in a very limited way -- produce nuclear energy, or maintain our species in this chaotic universe. However, they normally have a story designed to convince their students that the foregoing things are unimportant or possibly should not even be thought about. This issue is discussed in greater depth elsewhere.

With Wisdom based on knowledge -- rather than the illusion of wisdom provided by severing the brain from outside contact as mystical experiences depend on -- we can make ourselves immune to all the systems that depend on ignorance, confusion, and error. As we gain sufficient knowledge based on empirical data we increase our ability to achieve true Wisdom. With true Wisdom we can evaluate and rate all ideas and thereby move toward total congruency so that all of our knowledge and all of our activities support each other and help us become Enlightened Persons.

CHAPTER 11

FOURTH WAY OF WISDOM: FAITH / BELIEF

"If error is corrected whenever it is recognized as such, the path of error is the path of truth." **Hans Reichenbach** [16]

<u>FOURTH WAY OF WISDOM</u>: Recognize that all knowledge rests on faith/beliefs, and must always be open to questioning.

THOMAS HENRY HUXLEY ON FAITH

Below is some material that expresses the issue of justified and unjustified faith very well. This material presents T.H. Huxley's views and was provided by Bill Schultz [1], founder of the Agnostic Church, in an e-mail message in which he draws from a site on Thomas Henry Huxley [2] who coined the term "agnostic."

"Preachers, orthodox and heterodox, din into our ears that the world cannot get on without faith of some sort. There is a sense in which that is as eminently as obviously true; there is another, in which, in my judgment, it is as eminently as obviously false, and it seems to me that the hortatory, or pulpit, mind is apt to oscillate between the false and the true meanings, without being aware of the fact.

"It is quite true that the ground of every one of our actions, and the validity of all our reasonings, rest upon the great act of faith, that leads us to take the experience of the past as a safe guide in our dealings with the present and the future. From the nature of ratiocination, it is obvious that the axioms, on which it is based, cannot be demonstrated by ratiocination. It is also a trite observation that, in the business of life, we constantly take the most serious action upon evidence of an utterly insufficient character. But it is surely plain that faith is not necessarily entitled to dispense with ratiocination [just] because ratiocination cannot dispense with faith as a starting-point; and that because we are often obliged, by the pressure of events, to act on very bad evidence, it does not follow that it is proper to act on such evidence when the pressure is absent."

Although Huxley pretty much says it all above, I will examine this concept in more detail because of its importance.

As Huxley implied above there are different varieties, or levels of faith and belief. On one end of the spectrum are blind faith and unquestioned belief. These are the forms of faith/belief that need to be avoided by any who seek to achieve a *sustainable feeling of well-being.* On the other end of the scale are faith and belief such that a person's basic ideas can change when data and experience require. This is the kind of faith/belief that of necessity underlies a person's working assumptions. This faith provides the framework in which the individual will interpret their experience -- that is used to improve knowledge, ideas, models, and choices as learning occurs. This includes the faith underlying all science that there is a reality that our senses allow us to perceive and that reason can be used to understand that reality, and so forth. New experiences and new information bring new knowledge. But unless the tentativeness of a person's understanding of all things is recognized, it may be almost impossible to see the need to change ideas as knowledge grows. It is the working assumption of a *science of religion and ethics* that a *sustainable feeling of well-being* cannot be achieved unless a person's ideas and beliefs can change. *Sustainable* can only be achieved when a person's fundamental assumptions are congruent with reality and with each other -- that means they incorporate the rule to change with new information. They need to be satisfying while also being flexible. A person's ideas need to be free to change with new information and insights because we can never have more than part of the picture. Positions cannot be rigid but must be able to evolve when data and better paradigms become available.

FUNDAMENTALISM

However, there is another dimension of faith and I take *fundamentalism* to provide the best example of this. Because of insufficient study this parameter is poorly understood. But a close look at fundamentalists may provide some useful clues. Most fundamentalists would agree that their position rests on faith. However, at the same time they believe that their position rests on objective knowledge as the quote below from *Fundamentalism Observed* [3] indicates:

> "One of the distinguishing characteristics of fundamentalism is the tendency to make the cognitive dimension of religion foundational and determinative.... [F]undamentalism is not distinguished by the specific content of its orthodoxy... or necessarily by its epistemological presuppositions per se... but by the priority of 'correct belief' itself. The fundamentalist orientation therefore is not an emotional one but a strongly rationalistic one where religion is based on a standardized, objective knowledge.... Fundamentalism seeks to be a 'true science,'.... For the fundamentalist, 'holding right views' and uniformity of belief is normative for all other elements of religious self-understanding. It follows, therefore, that doctrine is not the historical product of... [the religion's] experience but what *determines*... [the religion's] experience, that religious truth is a fixed body of eternally valid propositions, that religions are contraposed ideological entities, and that the theological task is apologetic rather than exploratory or critical." [4]

As indicated above once a fundamentalist's brain is locked onto a particular orthodoxy -- usually the one they were born into, but more rarely one they find on their own but accept as being true -- they are almost totally incapable of discarding it. Still, science demonstrates that change is possible at least to some degree. Science is able to appeal to the same inner yearning as fundamentalist religions do and thereby turn this characteristic from a negative for humanity to a positive.

A *science of religion and ethics* is presented as a way to formulate this aspect of science to describe, understand, and satisfy this drive in a way that would be consistent with a person's "wisdom" potential. It would satisfy the underlying need of a fundamentalist by providing a rock-solid foundation -- that is, the process of correcting errors by empirical testing of beliefs -- for making life choices plus a support group to assist and encourage evaluations and desirable changes.

But what is the relation between faith/belief and the scientific method? As is described in another quote from *Fundamentalism Observed* [4], scientists have traditionally said that the goal of science is the search for truth, to find objective knowledge.

"For scientists of the early modern period, such as Francis Bacon (d. 1626), the task of science was the discovery of the Laws of Nature. They understood the world to be organized by rational principles established by an all-knowing God and 'truth' as objective and available to the 'commonsense' reason of the sincere seeker. In this view, human senses apprehend facts, and reason discerns the underlying order in them. The task of science, then, is to catalog, organize and derive theories about the true facts of the Cosmos. By the late nineteenth century, the Baconian system was still the dominant scientific orthodoxy of the day, at least among ordinary, educated folk.

"However, marshaled against this system by the late nineteenth century were various intellectual forces, one of the most influential of which was the legacy of the eighteenth-century German philosopher Immanuel Kant.

The intricacies of Kant's critiques of pure and practical reason were lost on popular scientific culture in America, but they created a thought world accessible enough to challenge the Enlightenment's wholesale confidence in human reason and commonsense induction. By placing the subject at the center of the process of perceiving and knowing the world, Kant had called the whole scientific enterprise into question. Objective truth is filtered through subjective experience and perception, he argued, and thus scientific knowledge is always shaped by the cultural and historical content in which it emerges. We cannot know 'absolute realities.' The 'theory-in-itself' can never be apprehended but comes to us only through the welter of our sensory experiences. The order we perceive, the forms and categories through which we understand, are not demonstrably present in the natural world itself but are instead inherent in the ability of the human mind to reason.

"And just as science depends on human reason, so also does moral philosophy [and religion]."[4]

Scottish philosopher David Hume has similarly written closely reasoned words demonstrating that no amount of observation proves a scientific generalization. (See VOLUME II, Chapter 10, "Science and the Search for Truth. [5]")

POST-MODERNISM

These ideas laid the basis for post-modernism, which has pretty well brought sociology and anthropology to a standstill. However, they have had much less impact on the natural sciences except in physics where they influenced the theories explaining quantum phenomena. The foregoing dichotomy developed because the natural sciences tied "objective knowledge" to "reality" and therefore were forced to alter ideas as knowledge accumulated. The life sciences and folk religions have never been grounded on firm theories, so measurements of "reality" have been tied to more subjective aspects of the world driven by feelings and our raw "tribal" genetic propensities. As a result change is both easier and more difficult depending on circumstances. However, in the realm of folk religions this has resulted in less pressure to alter their fundamental ideas like God, soul, Heaven, Nirvana, and such. But because of the foregoing patterns thoughtful people have found it easier to ignore the fact that the foundation of science is based on faith and therefore its knowledge is vulnerable in the same way that religion is.

Thomas Kuhn, in his book, *The Structure of Scientific Revolutions*, provides a carefully constructed argument showing the primary way science has maintained its vision of a straight-line movement toward Truth. [6]

As indicated earlier a better definition of science would be: **Science is the search for congruency.** [7] When the foregoing is recognized we see that a hidden element becomes central. That hidden element is that Human Beings Are the Ultimate Reference System. It is this insight that provides a foundation for a *science of religion and ethics*. It also allows us to put the post-modernist view into proper perspective.

Because scientists have traditionally said they are searching for truth -- that is, objective/ certain knowledge -- they frequently think they have found it. The laws of physics are such examples. Of course, as indicated elsewhere, the Copenhagen interpretation of quantum mechanics, the current paradigm of physics, went to the other extreme and focused only on measurements, and attempts to leave "reality" out of the picture. In the process it still blurs the point that behind every measurement is a trail of assumptions, and assumptions depend on faith/belief. Equally important, people generally are not even aware of most of their assumptions. The foregoing has routinely diverted scientists and others from better understanding and utilization of the world around them. In our time post-modernists have attempted to utilize the insights of Kant and Hume to advance current understanding.

But, in spite of the validity of Kant's and Hume's observations, post-modernists' efforts to build on them have been grossly irrelevant. The truth of post-modernism is a truth that misses the point by much more than the error it replaces. Post-modernists got fixated on the erroneous assumptions of science and religion and missed the opportunity to understand the actual relationship of objective reality and human life. It's true that the theories, laws, and hypotheses of science reflect the society in which they developed. But these theories also need to account for the real behavior of the objective world. It is this element that allows science to grow beyond the prejudices and the blindness of any culture and move closer to congruency with objective reality. This is an element that is seriously hindered in folk religions, particularly because they are almost totally ruled by "tribal" genetic propensities: primarily "dominance/submission" and "us vs. them."

Classical scientists assumed a materially based, mechanical Cosmos. They labored long, and looked more deeply into the nature of the Cosmos than had ever been done before. But because at the fundamental level they searched for TRUTH rather than "Congruency," they were laboring without a valid foundation. When a person works for Congruency it becomes more obvious that the observer needs to be included in the equations in ways the Copenhagen interpretation doesn't make clear. The goal of congruency makes the observer not just the recorder, but leads to the recognition that the justification for all scientific effort -- just like any other human effort -- is the maintenance and development of the human species.

A perceiver is needed not just to measure what the instruments record, but also to test for congruency and assess its presence or absence within the full range of human knowledge. Once a person accepts that Humanity itself is our ultimate reference system it becomes clear that the goal is Knowledge and Wisdom, not TRUTH. Knowledge and Wisdom are tied to the knower. This requires seeing measurement as a means to improve the quality of human life, not as an abstract behavior with no explanation beyond the personal satisfaction this behavior provides. Most people who think the goal of science is to achieve TRUTH think of this as meaning to understand how the Cosmos is. They see Truth as existing independent of the observer. However, Knowledge and Wisdom do not exist independently. Knowledge and Wisdom depend on human nature, and in that capacity they serve humanity well. They help individuals achieve a *sustainable feeling of well-being*. Knowledge allows whatever is known to be used to improve the quality of human life. When this step is made science takes on its true responsibility and becomes part of a *science of religion and ethics*. Its goal is dramatically altered, and the "soft" sciences (anthropology, sociology, and some parts of psychology) would thereby be turned into "hard" sciences. The practices for the current hard sciences would remain almost totally unchanged. However, all fields of science would be joined together in a way that is currently lacking.

Science, like religion, has often included a broad streak of arrogance. Scientists have usually thought they were closer to understanding reality than they were/are/can be. However, as Thomas Kuhn says, "We may... have to relinquish the notion, explicit or implicit, that changes of paradigm carry scientists and those who learn from them closer and closer to the truth." [8] But regardless of the foregoing to shrug off the efforts and findings of science as cultural relativism is even more arrogant. To believe that any interpretation has as much validity as any other makes "validity" a meaningless term. Ideas and concepts have value to the degree that they help us understand, utilize, and predict. Many interpretations are worthless or even harmful. An interpretation has validity to the degree that it is congruent with all our other ideas, or measurements -- and leads to deeper understandings and insights (helps people achieve a *sustainable feeling of well-being*). Interpretations such as "scientific creationism" (the belief that God created all living things just as they are now only a few thousand years ago) that divert people's thinking or makes understanding impossible is not just a matter of bad ideas. They are bad from a standpoint of human well-being. These ideas prevent people from achieving a *sustainable feeling of well-being*.

Most modern thinkers realize that in order to accept a folk religion's supernatural system, unquestioned faith and belief are required -- the leap of faith. Many of these thoughtful people seem to want to protect science from a similar fate by banning "faith" from in any way relating to science. However, it seems to me that the problem is just the reverse of the one that bothers these people. Because scientists have not recognized that their ideas about the Cosmos are beliefs, they have sometimes shown as much reluctance to change their ideas as have those who accept the ideas of supernatural religion. They thought their conclusions were based on objective knowledge and weren't able to see the underlying assumptions accepted on faith. As a result they often had difficulty realizing when change became necessary. They did not see their ideas as tools, but rather as "truths of the Cosmos." And, worse in my mind, because they were focused on finding Truth they weren't aware that their own life suffered because it was not well focused, and particularly for this reason failed in their responsibility to do whatever they could to ensure that their knowledge was used to improve the quality of human living. These lines of thinking are among those that have led me to the conclusion that it is essential that we recognize our fundamental ideas have a belief component. Only then can we develop rules and procedures to ensure that ideas based on blind faith, and beliefs based only on authority and custom are not judged as having the same merit as ideas based on faith and held tentatively, even when supported by evidence that seems unshakable.

In science, faith and beliefs are supported by multiple lines of evidence, experimentation, and reasoned thinking with each step tied securely to the steps that precede it. When the system works these beliefs change as the information upon which they are based changes.

On another front of this issue, is the situation that people who favor blind faith and unquestioned belief have not been challenged to justify their type of faith/belief. No responsible body has promoted and encouraged individuals to move to higher order beliefs. It has not been widely discussed that using blind faith and unquestioned beliefs – for example, when using a "Holy Book" – to guide a person's life is foolish and deplorable. Rather it is commonly accepted that unquestioned belief – turning a person's life over to God, following the words of a "Holy Book" unquestionably, and such – is a virtue. Rarely is it recognized that to believe something with more conviction than the evidence warrants is immoral.

Why is it so common to base a person's life on blind faith? Part of it is regression to childhood (where questioning authority is inconceivable) when confronted by a problem apparently beyond a person's ability to solve. Part of it is the wisdom to survive in a cruel and overwhelmingly powerful society. The latter situation relates to the militancy and willingness of true believers to commit violent acts. Folk religions often attract a large following of people drawn to authoritarian behavior and violence, and thereby these groups become the accepted spokespersons for their society because they suppress everyone else. Those with alternative positions are intimidated or even executed. Healthy, responsible people don't see any effective way to confront the militant's zeal and power.

However, as explained earlier the above practices have sometimes been allowed by those in power because there was no satisfactory alternative. Many people have a very real need to devote themselves to understanding the Cosmos and make this the core of their lives. But science has been virtually the only alternative to folk religions to fulfill such a need. And it attracts primarily an intellectual elite who tend to be closer to anarchists than troops willing to march in lock step into the face of death. As a result there has been no practical alternative to allowing fundamentalists of each culture to promote blind faith and belief based on authority. That is the only way someone can wholeheartedly accept any given folk religion. From the standpoint of the rulers these groups are not all bad because they can normally be channeled so that they support the power structure rather than threaten it.

But from the perspective of a *science of religion and ethics* folk religions have almost always grossly misused the fundamentalist propensity. The people making up such groups are a reservoir of energy and commitment to what is of ultimate value – maintaining and developing the human species. However, so far they have been seduced into supporting what is relative (a given culture's folk religion), rather than what is truly of ultimate concern (the perpetuation of the species in such a way as to allow each person to achieve a *sustainable feeling of well-being*).

Folk religions have always used these individuals to erect barriers to divert and delay human progress. This is done because those in power tend to see certain changes as threats to their control. Therefore, many liberating changes necessary to move toward the light at the end of the tunnel are violently opposed. Through this process fundamentalists' energy is used to suppress the "wisdom" potential. Their energy and commitment thereby results in suppressing human creativity, effort to understand the Cosmos, work to advance education, and in many cases to even ban representational art!

If it were possible to develop organizations based on a *science of religion and ethics* that would appeal to the fundamentalist propensity, and help them become Enlightened People this would remove the final barrier that retards human development in reaching the light at the end of the tunnel. Because of the firmly grounded knowledge base providing the foundation for a *science of religion and ethics* its approach and resources should help any person who desires to be a force for good in the world to know how to do so.

On a different front stand the post-modernists. Because traditional science has not accepted a role in defining the meaning of human life, and thereby recognizing its role in understanding truth, we see many thoughtful people lured into post-modernist notions. Science's failure to recognize the place of faith in human understanding has also encouraged this approach. Faith and belief have been interpreted by skeptics to mean an unquestioned acceptance of ideas based on authority, custom, or something similar. As a result of such convictions modern thinkers have been slow to recognize what happens when they ignore the element of faith inherent in all searches for ultimate answers. Such people end up taking their positions too seriously that can result in suppressing individual thought rather than encouraging it.

Here is an example of the foregoing, "A nineteenth-century woman who complained of pains incompatible with current medical knowledge about the nervous system... ran the serious risk of finding her illness dismissed as imaginary." [9] The previous quote provides an opportunity for a useful insight utilizing the history of medicine. Although science has mainly ignored folk religions, it adopted the religious model of seeking truth and seeing itself as the definer of what constitutes knowledge. [10] Religion asserts that it is the reservoir of ultimate Knowledge and Wisdom. Anything it can't explain isn't important. Science takes the same approach since many scientists are also motivated by the fundamentalist propensity to find true beliefs. At any given time its basic interpretations are considered to be full and complete although there may be some "minor" problems still waiting to be understood. Anything that doesn't agree with these basic interpretations is banished as superstition, error, falsehood, unimportant, or something similar.

When it is understood that all knowledge is based on approximation, conflicting data can be looked at with a totally different mind-set. It can be recognized, as most young scientists do, that observations that don't fit current theories offer a way to refine, correct, or replace those theories. In addition it can be realized that these changes can make our understandings more useful.

The following quote provides an enlightening characterization of science and helps to show how overlooking the role of belief in human thinking has produced a significant flaw in established science. "Normal science has been described, in an influential book by Thomas Kuhn [6], as mostly a mopping-up exercise. Kuhn means that during most periods and in most fields there is an accepted theoretical framework of scientific thought -- a paradigm, as he calls it -- that commands general acceptance, and scientists normally work on small, still unexplained problems (known as 'puzzles') that explore and fill out and confirm the prevailing paradigm." [11]

Kuhn's ideas as discussed elsewhere provide a helpful guide in understanding the scientific effort and uncovering some clues for how to incorporate a *science of religion and ethics* into the broader science. As he makes clear we are inherently blinded and cannot see totally different ways of explaining the problem if we think we have the theoretical framework established and merely need to tidy up a few loose ends. Over and over we see the foregoing happening in science. Some idea gains acceptance. This hypothesis/theorem/law/principle is like a clearing in a jungle of ignorance. All the other explanations, unexplainable data, and deficiencies are left as patches of weeds throughout the clearing, or are embodied in the growth that surrounds the settlement. Eventually it is realized that the weeds remain and the boundary isn't growing. So a better hypothesis/ theorem/ law/principle is searched out to replace the existing one. The new one dispatches some of the patches, extends the boundary of understanding at least at some points, and starts the cycle over again.

Physicist Richard Morris sets out [12] to clarify how science actually works in contrast with the way science philosophers such as Francis Bacon and Karl Popper proposed that it should work. He draws on the history of science to demonstrate the "primacy of theory -- the creations of the human mind." He points out that, "All-embracing theoretical visions can be accepted long before there is any evidence to confirm them, while we remain skeptical of the findings of experiments that seem to have no solid theoretical foundation. Anyone who delves deeply in the nature of science cannot help but come to the conclusion that we find the products of the human imagination more convincing than the things we observe. In the end, only experiment can determine whether a theory is true or false. But that is the end of the creativity process in science, not the beginning." [12] It seems to me that Morris' conclusions put Kuhn's ideas in a context that would suggest that the process Kuhn uncovered may be an essential process in the way science has to work. This process allows scientists to avoid being immobilized by the present ignorance or made permanent victims to the current beliefs. But it may also show the effects of a fundamentalist genetic propensity in scientists and how this propensity can be tapped for the good of humanity rather than serving as a barrier as it has up to now for religious fundamentalism.

The quote on myth that follows may demonstrate another aspect of this problem to ponder. "One important social function of myth... is to blind us to what it cannot explain." [13] This is an interesting idea. There is some level at which science could also be said to "blind us to what it cannot explain." But it seems to me the goal of a *science of religion and ethics* is to be as aware as possible of what is known and what is not known. A *science of religion and ethics* needs to encourage science to realize its goals should be seen as the search for congruency, not truth; for a better understanding of everything in order to improve the quality of human life, and only incidental to that a final understanding of how the Cosmos works. Therefore, science might be able to treat the inexplicable with more seriousness than is usually mustered. If a person's explanations divert attention from important issues that are being overlooked, then they are a mixed blessing at best.

However, as implied above it is worth keeping in mind that the steady accumulation of knowledge that science has provided especially over the past 400 years, may depend on, as Thomas Kuhn proposes, accepting the best paradigm available and collectively as well as single mindedly working on it as if it is true. This paradigm allows us to look more deeply into some aspect of how nature works than any other approach is likely to be able to.

I think the challenge for a *science of religion and ethics* is to point out the blind spots in currently accepted paradigms in order to help society explore the best way to address them. I would think that a footnote for all myths (and perhaps all scientific theories) should be provided to point out how these ideas divert a person's thinking and prevent a person from seeing important issues. This would be particularly appropriate for the Copenhagen interpretation of quantum mechanics.

With the better understanding of the Cosmos and humanity's place in it that a *science of religion and ethics* provides, science/religion achieves a more central and better-grounded role in society. When we understand that: <u>Science is the search for congruency</u>, everything then fits together. We can make better use of the insights of philosophers David Hume and Immanuel Kant that science can't provide Truth, and/or Objective/Certain Knowledge.

Physicist Roger Newton clarifies the issue of truth in his book, *The Truth of Science* [14]: "When we speak of the truth of something, the first point to note is that this something has to be a statement of an *assertion*; contrary to frequent usage, it makes no sense to speak of the truth of a fact or of a property. 'The "facts" themselves... are not *true*. They simply *are*, William James reminds us. To insist on this is not pedantry or hair-splitting. Formulating an assertion is attempting to communicate and therefore requires transmissible concepts and language: truth thus cannot be separated from human concepts and our linguistic apparatus. The history of philosophy is permeated with controversies that are of purely linguistic origin.... Awareness of the pitfalls of language should make us cautious when dealing with 'truth.'" [14]

Although we can't achieve truth some people would still maintain that science can provide "objective knowledge." They believe that if a measurement is made over and over and the same result is achieved to many decimal places each time, this is evidence that "objective knowledge" exists and has been found. However, measurements don't in fact provide "objective knowledge" since "objective knowledge" would mean knowledge that we can obtain directly from the Cosmos with no interpretation, evaluation, or imposition of our own human reference system on objective reality. Is this in fact what we do when we make a measurement? Obviously not. Depending on the measurement there is a wide variation in the interpretation involved, but it's never knowledge obtained directly from the Cosmos. It is filtered by our sense organs like everything else we perceive. The fact that the measurement always – or nearly always – comes out the same is no more relevant than the fact that every time we look at a tree we perceive it to be the same.

As previously indicated the post-modernists have made the foregoing their battle cry. But for them this only leads them to cultural relativity.

The idea that "everything" is relative is a common belief among not only post-modernists, but also the many students taught by them. Such people do not recognize that human beings share an innate human nature possessed by all healthy human beings that makes their values empirically understandable, not relative. Human Beings Are the Ultimate Reference System, and they have clear ethical needs. A *science of religion and ethics* depends on understanding human nature with congruency as the unifying principle. This is true because the concept of congruency forces us to seriously think about the meaning of faith/belief as it relates to knowledge, interpretation, analysis, and Wisdom. As a result it makes clear that we need to recognize that Human Beings Are the Ultimate Reference System, and values are not, therefore, relative. Rather, congruency mandates that knowledge be used to provide every person a *sustainable feeling of well-being*. When Truth is being discussed, we are looking outward for the reference system. When faith/belief is being discussed, we are looking inward.

This clearer understanding of the basic issues can provide a new foundation for science/ religion and society in general, as well as the individual person's life. The foregoing is necessary if Enlightened Communities made up of Enlightened People are to be developed. Our progress in the foregoing direction is greatly assisted by ideas presented by Hans Reichenbach in his book, *The Rise of Scientific Philosophy*. [15] He makes clear the reasons for the delay in applying the empirical approach more widely. His book is analyzed in VOLUME II, Chapter 10, "Science and the Search for Truth." [5] And some of those ideas are shared below.

The critical issue in faith/belief is that no idea, position, concept, theory, law, and such be held more firmly than the evidence warrants. The foregoing is essential for achieving a *sustainable feeling of well-being*. As Reichenbach says, "If error is corrected whenever it is recognized as such, the path of error is the path of truth." [16] I take "truth" in the foregoing quote to actually mean knowledge. And this needs to be the goal of anyone working to support the establishment of a *science of religion and ethics* and applying its findings.

"It is impossible to have a knowledge of the world that has the certainty of mathematical truth, it is impossible to establish moral directives that have the impelling objectivity of mathematical, or even of empirical, truth.

This is one of the truths that scientific philosophy has uncovered." [17] I agree with Reichenbach's foregoing statements, but not the inferred ideas. One of his key contributions is to show very clearly that there is no "mathematical truth" in the world of matter and energy, only in the world of language. Mathematics has no direct tie to the real world that would make "mathematical truth" a meaningful concept for discussing the empirical world we live in. Furthermore, as I have tried to make clear, an empirical *science of religion and ethics* is possible that would "establish moral directives" of a compelling nature, more compelling than any mathematical formula. But these "moral directives" are not iron clad; they are theory-based and empirically supported like the rest of science. That is why the <u>Fourth Way of Wisdom</u> is important. Faith/ belief cannot be avoided. Reichenbach makes obvious that everything that is known is to some degree tentative. Whatever a person accepts can never be completely proven. Human beings cannot achieve Truth; even the idea that there is such a thing is based on human nature.

The thoughts someone holds today may be largely false or misstated. Current goals may be misguided. Present methods may be ill conceived. It may even be that all people cannot achieve a *sustainable feeling of well-being*. However, people cannot wait until all the evidence is in before acting because all the evidence will never be in. People need to act then on the basis of current knowledge, and this requires faith. Human beings cannot escape faith. Every act, every deed ultimately depends on faith and belief for there is no other source in the final analysis.

Percy Bysshe Shelley thought there were three levels of belief (determined by the source of belief): He believed that the most correct beliefs are based on direct perception; next are those based on reason applied to our perceptions. The weakest beliefs are those based on the testimony or authority of others.

It seems to me that Shelley puts an interesting slant on the idea of beliefs. However, I would disagree with the order Shelley arrived at. Exchanging the order of his first and second sources appears to me to be better. It seems to me that direct perception is vulnerable to misinterpretation and that unless a given perception fits with a person's past experiences there should be a tendency to doubt what has been perceived, especially if it happens fast and only once. The most obvious example comes from a magic show.

We see things appear and disappear, move through solid surfaces, stand unsupported, and such. It is the rare person at a magic show who trusts the evidence of their senses and believes that the woman really was sawed in two.

These perceptions violate a person's other experiences. So the person's reason leads to doubting them. The same is true for other events that violate a person's reason, or understanding of how things work. So actually we are justified in having more confidence in a belief when perception is supported by reason than in a perception as an isolated source. When a skeptical person experiences or hears about mystical events that violate the laws of science they look for other explanations. The true believer accepts them uncritically as evidence of the supernatural.

Edmund Carpenter [18] even proposes that, "It's not easy to experience the unfamiliar, the unnamed. We say, 'If I hadn't seen it with my own eyes, I wouldn't have believed it.' But the phrase really should be, 'If I hadn't believed it with all my heart, I wouldn't have seen it.'"

Certainly, Carpenter's point has a kind of validity. But once we get past the shock it's clear that the facts are not as stated. The truth lies somewhere in between. Our beliefs influence what we see in varying ways. But blind faith and unlimited belief are not necessary for most of what we see. Nevertheless, the truly unfamiliar and unnamed may be "unseeable." And it is only as our reason constructs a way to tie it into the other things we "know" that interpretations may provide a way to "see" it. It seems to me that this is the case for quantum phenomena. We all have experienced particles – rocks, balls, bullets – and waves in liquids. We bring those images with us to the quantum world. But it seems clear to me that whatever quantum phenomena are, they are not waves or particles. Rather, whatever they are is beyond our current ability to envision -- to "see."

As for Shelley's third point that testimony or authority of others should lead to our weakest beliefs, I tend to agree with that. However, most of what we believe *is* based on the authority of others. Think of anything you believe. I doubt if you will move back to why you believe it more than three or four levels before you get to a belief you have accepted based on the authority of others, or unquestioned experience. The reason we accept it is because we trust the motivations and abilities of those "experts," parents, teachers, leaders, friends, and such. But eventually we learn that even the wisest person still knows very little considering all the things there are to know. Also, anyone can make mistakes. In addition in current societies even the best of us may sometimes lie. For these reasons and many more it needs to be recognized that there is a need to question all authority, especially our own, even though we still need to make choices and act based on our current understandings and beliefs, almost all of which are based on testimony or authority.

Therefore, each of these degrees of belief still need to be judged on the basis of their congruency with everything else we believe. How well does a given belief fit with everything else we believe? Are they congruent, or are they in conflict?

The important point is on what a person bases their faith. A person's faith needs to be worthy of the individual as a rational, intelligent animal with a "wisdom" potential. It cannot be a faith that denies a person's intelligence, ability to reason, and to think. It cannot be a faith that leads to torture, exploitation, suppression of thought, and all the other destructive things "people of faith" have practiced over human history. It cannot be a faith that overlooks someone's emotional side that their power and energizer, source of their strength and sustaining energy. It cannot be a faith based on ignorance, childhood conditioning, or driven by their raw "tribal" genetic propensities.

And a person's faith should be no stronger than the evidence that supports it. On some things we can be pretty sure: that in normal circumstances the ground will support our next step, that evolution explains the existence of current living organisms, that George Washington lived. Other things are very doubtful: that the Cosmos is a product of intelligence that is aware of and cares about human life, that extra-sensory perception actually exists, that Jesus of Nazareth existed as a living human being.

A primary reason that the Fourth Way of Wisdom is focused on faith and belief is to develop a way to handle these concepts. This cannot be done by ignoring them, discarding them, or improperly defining them. Rules or guidelines need to be developed to help guide us in discriminating between growth-promoting and growth-inhibiting ways to utilize faith and belief. These rules would clarify how to use the words faith and belief, as well as how to ensure that empirical evidence is used to clarify when faith/belief is based only on authority/tradition and when it involves working assumptions to be changed if evidence makes this necessary.

When the Fourth Way discusses the necessity of faith and belief it is not promoting blind faith, unquestioned belief, or unreflective acceptance of unacknowledged assumptions. Rather, it is just the opposite. It is discussing the faith and belief involved in the assumptions that underlie people's best interpretations. Faith and belief need to be based on knowledge and understanding. A person's faith should not prevent them from questioning anything. Knowing all positions rest on faith and belief should make it easier to see inconsistencies, incongruencies, and errors in thinking. When error and incongruencies are recognized or alternative explanations are presented, change to better positions should be promoted if we are to accept the Fourth Way. Our faith and beliefs need to be congruent with all human knowledge and experience and not diverted by some culture's glittering trinkets. This faith needs to incorporate the goal of human progress that would allow each person to achieve a *sustainable feeling of well-being*. And the foregoing would only be possible as a person feels a connection with all of humanity.

People's faith needs to be able to be examined in the light of day. We need to look at all the facts and be able to acknowledge each one of them. We need to have a faith supported by the best knowledge available. And it needs to always be compatible with humanity's highest attributes: reason, a *sustainable feeling of well-being*, intelligence, universality, and our struggle for congruency. The goal, then, is to ensure that knowledge and choices are consistent with the evidence supporting them, and that they can change as evidence grows. Those beliefs that cannot stand up to this standard have no standing within a *science of religion and ethics*.

CHAPTER 12

FIFTH WAY OF WISDOM: MAKE BEST CHOICES

"There are no unmixed blessings." "There are no unmitigated miseries."

FIFTH WAY OF WISDOM: Strive to make the best choices possible.

Can a person actually make a choice? What does it mean to make a choice? Why does it matter if someone makes the best choices, rather than the worst choices?

As previously discussed in the examination of the "I," it is my position that people make genuine choices, based on their beliefs, knowledge, understanding, convictions, assumptions, and so forth; their physical makeup; and the conditions of the moment. People's choices determine whether or not they achieve a *sustainable feeling of well-being*; therefore, choices are of the greatest importance. However, since knowledge and understanding are usually key components of choices it is essential to bring as much knowledge as necessary to the degree possible to every choice.

Part of the issue of choice is addressed by the Third Way of Wisdom (Seek to understand). Another part is addressed in "Organizing for an Enlightened Community" where a specific structure, Choices Are Us, is proposed so it would be available to help in this process. It is the first priority for a Wisdom Group and/or a Center for the Practical Application of Wisdom to provide all the help possible for each member to achieve congruency and be able to make the optimal choices. Congruency does not require that all of a person's ideas about the universe are correct. It does require that people strive to make the best choices based on the information available to them. This includes replacing current ideas/beliefs with better ones when they are discovered (better in terms of their congruency with other well supported ideas). Also, making choices that are congruent with each other is part of what is necessary to help each person become an Enlightened Person and able to make the best choices. However, our current ideas about the "I" need to be improved. New ways of looking at the "I" are needed. Some ideas for better understanding the "I" have been presented earlier. However, the ideas that relate more specifically with choice-making are discussed here in more detail.

In order to make the optimal choices it is essential to discard the concept of free will and correct the errors involved in the way determinism has been applied to the individual choice issue. One way to better understand the need for these changes is to examine the "I" as it relates to the free will/determinism issue. Both of the foregoing concepts have been pernicious and destructive to individuals and to society because they prevent people from making the best choices. The foregoing occurs because of the assumptions about the "I" imbedded in the free will/determinism concepts. As we move toward better definitions of the "I" we can sidestep these negative aspects of the free will/determinism concepts. When determinism has been applied to human choice it has traditionally resulted in a belief in predestination and fatalism [1]. Predestination and fatalism say we cannot actually make choices, or in any way affect what happens because everything has already been determined. This belief is truly immobilizing. Belief in predestination and fatalism can lead people to make unwise choices.

Early science tended to support the foregoing interpretation because it was widely believed that everything could be known and predicted. Science replaced the all-knowing, all-powerful God with the inextricable, unavoidable Laws of the Universe. Until the Copenhagen interpretation of quantum mechanics was adopted scientists assumed that human beings live in a deterministic universe, that is, everything is caused. Therefore, it seemed reasonable to assume that every behavior of every human being was as predictable and necessary as predestination/fatalism required. What got overlooked was, what does determinism actually mean as it relates to human behavior? The question could not be properly framed in earlier times because of the underlying assumptions about determinism, the universe, and human beings. Early scientists were not in a position to recognize that *human beings are the ultimate reference system*. Also, they hadn't yet discovered <u>chaos theory</u> (that the behavior of complex systems is not predictable except within narrow limits of space and time), and fuzzy logic (that shows that when the universe is analyzed in terms of dichotomies -- Aristotelian, "yes/no," logic -- error is introduced that can lead to untrue and ambiguous answers).

The primary negative aspect of free will as it relates to human choice is that it promotes confusion about choice and individual and societal responsibility. Free will is supposed to help individual persons recognize that they freely make their own choices and can therefore act as they choose. This idea is certainly an improvement over the idea of being a puppet totally controlled by outside forces, the traditional interpretation as to how determinism applies to human beings. However, because it denies the reality of cause and effect it almost immediately moves into the domain of the irrational. This happens because it functions within a domain not open to study or experimentation since cause and effect are denied.

When free will has been applied to human choice it has often resulted in belief that an evil act = evil person = need for punishment. Because punishment is used, even capital punishment, guilt or innocence is of critical importance in a traditional society. This is demonstrated by the following quote: "... [Torture] was an authorized means of gaining a confession [during the Middle Ages] at a time when confessions suddenly became crucial. The Fourth Lateran Council in 1215 had outlawed the older judicial practices of establishing guilt, such as duels, oaths, and ordeal, so that henceforth a legal conviction required either the testimony of two eyewitnesses or a confession." [2]

The idea of confession and establishing guilt are key issues that anyone seeking to develop an Enlightened Community or become an Enlightened Person needs to address. I have written on these in Chapter 6 and Chapter 7, but feel it is necessary to address it again here. Once we are able to put aside the misleading focus of the free will/ determinism debate and look at the critical issue of choice, we have a totally different perspective on guilt and confession. It can be recognized that knowledge and understanding are key issues in interpreting these ideas. To me guilt is only important in terms of what changes need to be made to ensure that people make better future choices; that is, that they do not repeat, or better yet, do not commence antisocial/asocial, abusive, wounding, harmful behavior. The foregoing considerations include what changes need to be made in the person and what changes need to be made in society.

It seems to me that confession also has a role in a *science of religion and ethics*. A person's confession needs to be an essential part of the change process for making better choices in the future. However, it would not be a confession in a legal sense: "If you confess that you stole the money (whether you did or not is not important to us), we'll give you a reduced prison sentence." Or, in a religious sense, "You did a bad thing; therefore, you are a bad person." It is a confession in a therapeutic/social sense. It explores all the steps -- beliefs, mental/physical conditions, inadequate social support, and such -- that led to making that choice. But most important it requires the clear recognition as to why that choice was a mistake and how it formed a barrier preventing the person from moving toward achieving personal power and a *sustainable feeling of well-being*. The person involved needs to understand the ways in which their behavior was self-destructive. And, they need to have available whatever tools are necessary insofar as social and personal resources allow -- whether educational/therapeutic/ medical/ social/and so forth, to change whatever led to the choice. This needs to lead them to be "reborn" by discarding and replacing their self-destructive beliefs so they can subsequently avoid such mistakes.

The person's guilt would only be important in terms of their achieving the necessary understanding of society's and their own responsibilities for their choices and what would be necessary to sidestep similar choices in the future. Death, or any punishment for that matter, could never be the sentence for a "guilty" person. Any pain inflicted on them could only be the incidental pain that growth and change entail.

In current society choice and guilt are tied together. Guilt is considered to be important in order to ensure that a person deserves the punishment assigned to them. Confession is considered to be important to guarantee that they are guilty. Western tradition has demanded punishment when people are disobedient. This comes directly out of our dominant/submission "tribal" propensity. As a result, numerous problems have been introduced into the process of dealing with persons -- in a democracy; i.e., in a society of equals -- who break the law, or rules in general. The importance of knowledge/ignorance in affecting choices has been misunderstood, and more specifically society's responsibility for the knowledge/ignorance of its citizens has not been understood. As a result, antisocial/asocial choices have been dealt with in ways that are frequently counterproductive to society and to those involved. The foregoing issues combined with current adversarial theory -- in which the people and society are seen as inherently in conflict -- work together to help produce today's serious problems.

The combination of utilizing the social practice of punishment and the model of adversarial relationships has produced a situation that will not be easy to improve. The person placed under arrest usually feels obligated to do anything they can – hide the truth, lie, bribe, flee, intimidate witnesses, behave violently, and so forth – to avoid being found guilty. Everyone has been exposed to the idea that they can personally benefit from doing things that harm others. It is widely believed that there is nothing wrong with making such choices if a person can be sure they won't get caught. The more alienated a person is from society and/or functioning out of their alpha male/alpha female power drive, or us/them propensity the more they are likely to succumb to such behavior. In all these cases when a person is not able to self-correct to avoid making bad choices that harm others, then the society needs to work to bring about the necessary changes.

The free-will concept makes choice and responsibility somewhat mysterious. Choices just seem to happen (freely!). At the same time responsibility has no intellectually meaningful definition. However, as previously indicated the definition of responsibility that comes out of Western moral theory about the nature of human beings tends to equate choices that harm others with being bad/evil. In addition, it equates behavior that is considered bad/evil with the need to be punished. The foregoing theoretical considerations provide the foundation on which all of our basic societal institutions rest. The theory is nonsense. However, it has practical effects that are detrimental to both people and society. This theory leads to the assumption that people are responsible for their choices some of the time, but not all of the time (not when they were ignorant of the effects of their behavior, or insane, under unusual stress, under the influence of drugs -- when they were not capable of premeditated intent). It considers society to be responsible for the person's choices none of the time. When a person intentionally harms others or is considered to be responsible for choices that lead to harming others, they are thought to deserve punishment: fines, prison, death, and the like. It is this moral theory that provides the mechanism used to hide society's immoral goals and/or its side of the responsibility for a person's choices.

It is also the moral theory based on free will that spawned the fatally flawed adversarial system. It incorporates the idea that a person and society are inherently in conflict. It encourages belief in the idea of the person against society, and society against the person. The foregoing belief is made easier because our alpha male/female drive that promotes dominance/submission interactions and our "us/them" feelings play out as adversarial relationships. For the alpha male the short answer would seem to be that such drives needs to be surrounded by feedback mechanisms to ensure that the person does not act against their own long-term self interest by destroying their support group. And of course this requires that the members of the support group are feeling their own personal power and not just enthralled by the achievements resulting from their leader's power. This issue requires maximum study and thought. This drive often produces pressures that pit what a person considers is best for them against what is most desirable for the group. This phenomenon will be a key problem to overcome in some people to help them become Enlightened Persons and in producing Enlightened Communities where everyone works together in a cooperative manner. To properly focus the us/them propensity it is essential to help people – the younger the better – to realize that their true allegiance is to their species – to all human beings, including themselves – and more specifically to help perpetuate the species in such a way that everyone achieves a *sustainable feeling of well-being.* Any other loyalty needs to be subservient to that.

The foregoing is just one example of the idea discussed elsewhere that our species is in the process of remaking itself by altering behaviors that once had value, but now get in the way of achieving a *sustainable feeling of well-being.* This is especially true of the genetic propensities that support adversarial relationships. Instead of being adversaries, I see the needs of the Enlightened Community and the Enlightened Person as being totally congruent. Human beings are social animals. To be their best self they need love and the acceptance of other people. People will sacrifice up to and including their lives for the good of their community. The goal of a *science of religion and ethics* is to make such sacrifices few in number and justified when they occur by building societies in which what is good for the person is good for the community, and what is good for the community is good for the person. That is the definition of an Enlightened Person and an Enlightened Community.

When there is a problem such that a choice does not achieve the foregoing effect, my claim is that the cause is ignorance. The solution requires knowledge. Finding the proper knowledge is the joint responsibility of the person and the community. Evil act = ignorance = need for knowledge (for society and for the person). Current religious theory allows society to avoid any accountability. Because society's responsibility is not recognized there are limited mechanisms for correcting societal errors and improving social and personal choices. In my model there is a totally different moral theory. For me all choices are based on knowledge/ignorance. Harmful choices, erroneous choices, and the like come out of ignorance. I believe that a physically and mentally healthy, socially connected person will, normally, learn from their mistakes and improve their behavior.

My model of choice assumes that everyone is always, all the time, under every circumstance responsible for every choice they make or don't make. This means that when a person harms others their choices had reasons/causes and until these reasons/causes can be learned and ways found to impact them positively the person is a threat to themselves and others. At the same time the community is always, under every circumstance responsible for every choice of every member of the community. The community provides the environment in which the individual grows from helpless embryo to self-empowered mature adult. This environment plays a critical role in who the person becomes. The community provides the memes, the support structure, and the wisdom that forms the person's initial worldview and way of interacting with their surroundings. The community establishes priorities for research and expanding knowledge. When the society assumes no responsibility for its choices and how these choices relate to the choices of its members, it has no means to evaluate what it is doing and determine when and what changes are needed. Such a society demonstrates its inadequacy and need for change. Since ignorance is the problem, knowledge needs to be the solution. And the society is 100% responsible for working to correct these shortcomings.

Unless the "I" is more fully understood, it is not possible to develop a meaningful/useful definition of choice and responsibility – as was discussed earlier. Such an understanding of the "I" opens the way for finding solutions to each specific problem. This use of the "I" concept is probably one of its greatest potential values.

Traditionally when the statement "I make choices" has been examined the focus was on the "choices" rather than on the "I." Mostly this was because everyone thought they knew what they were talking about when they said, "I." The error of this assumption is demonstrated by the fact that most members of every society still think that people have an immortal soul that is the "I," and that the "I" is unitary and eternal. If they had even a glimmer of understanding of what the "I" is they could not possibly accept this error.

If the "I" concept discussed here were to be adopted by society, it seems clear that the free-will concept would be discarded and the interpretation of determinism applied to human choice would be corrected. Then the harm produced by past definitions of free will/determinism could be avoided in the future. It would be recognized that human behavior is caused, and at the same time it would be understood that individuals make choices. These two ideas are not in conflict. Furthermore, it can be seen that it is absurd to consider that any given behavior is predestined. Neither science's Laws of the Universe nor the God hypothesis provide the Ultimate Reference System necessary to make fatalism and predestination meaningful concepts. Human beings turn out to be the Ultimate Reference System, and predictability does not exist as predestination/fatalism would require. Human behavior is not predictable for several reasons, one of which is that every choice is made by a different "I." As a result, each choice is a unique event and science can't predict unique events. Also, it seems obvious to me that the person needs to be recognized as being responsible for any choice they make. Lack of responsibility would mean severing choices from the laws of cause and effect. There would then be no way to utilize knowledge in order to improve the situation. I hope the ideas presented here make it clear that people are responsible for their decisions in a way that those promoting either free will or determinism never realized.

However, being responsible for a person's choices does not mean being punished for those choices. Rather it requires the person to change so as not to be a threat to self and to others. An important point to understand is that the "I" can both change and be changed. And a better "I" makes better choices. There is hope for anyone. Also, it seems clear that society bears responsibilities that have not been acknowledged. Whenever there are mechanisms in society for judging people and their behavior, and then rewarding or punishing them, more care needs to be taken to ensure that the judgments and societal actions are congruent with the real world. Societal decisions need to be constantly monitored to ensure that changes are made when incongruencies between goals and results are discovered. It becomes obvious that there is a societal responsibility to help people change their "I" so they can achieve a *sustainable feeling of well-being.* The foregoing will benefit all of society because the more Enlightened Persons there are, the more everyone will be helped to become more loving, more productive, more fulfilled.

If the issue is analyzed from the foregoing perspective it seems to me that a better way is provided to deal with the major concerns of society. A clearer understanding of what is involved in making choices will provide new answers in the areas of law, courts, jails/prisons, punishment, and the concomitant human behavior as well as religion, child rearing, schools, government, economics, employment, corporations, entertainment, news media, war, culture, philosophy, literature, sociology, anthropology, psychology; that is, in all areas of human endeavor.

Now, returning to what it means to say, "I make choices." As described a choice is made based on the relevant components of the "I" and the universe at the moment of decision. Some of these components relate to the actual nature of the physical body making up the "I," some to knowledge (or ignorance) – of which memory is an important component – some to understanding (processing), some to immediate outside influences, some to how well the organism is functioning (has it been traumatized in some way that interferes with processing information, therefore increasing bad choices).

From the foregoing analysis it seems clear that a person can only make the choices they make. But what does this mean? At one level the statement is a truism. One point that is essential in understanding this issue is the realization that an "I" is a mental construct made up of myriads of parts as previously described. All these separate parts interact in complex ways, with feedback loops, for instance, to keep the system functioning and to make choices. This complexity provides the "I" with a potential that goes beyond the visions of even the most imaginative mystic. Current science, philosophy, and religion are a long way from understanding how decisions actually are made. Information theory and computer science provide some tantalizing hints. Current brain study points out some amazing suggestions. Philosophy provides some useful speculations. Nevertheless, understanding of this issue is just beginning, particularly in a practical way that can help people make better choices. However, now it can be seen that this is an area that can be fruitfully studied and that demands greater attention by all segments of society.

Therefore, even though the key mechanisms involved in choice are not known, the key facts are understood. First, in order to improve choices everyone should be taught in a way that enables them to recognize and experience their personal power. If our best knowledge were used, people would not be taught that they are helpless entities controlled by forces beyond their influence. At the same time those who are obsessed to seek power over others by their alpha male/female propensity would be helped to find ways to free themselves from the destructive elements of this drive. This ability to learn and change is the key factor for a *science of religion and ethics.* An Enlightened Community does not use shame, blame, guilt, punishment, and the like. Its prime concern is helping as many people as possible achieve a *sustainable feeling of well-being.* Another critical factor is knowledge. First, there is knowledge of the choice process and the essential steps to follow. Obviously, people can make better choices by learning how to examine issues in more depth, living congruent with reality, focusing on the most important matters, avoiding being unduly influenced by irrelevant issues, allowing time to integrate major factors before making final decisions, getting help from others who are successful problem solvers, and so forth. Second, there is practical knowledge about how the universe works and that points the way to achieving a person's desired outcome. As part of the latter process it is important to have social structures because most of us can't hold all the relevant factors in our heads at the same time even if we know them on a good day. (See "Other Support Organizations -- Choices Are Us.") The help of these groups is most needed when particularly important choices are being made that may exceed the abilities of the person involved.

In making choices, as in all human behavior, it is essential to understand that there can be no perfect choices -- ever! "There are no unmixed blessings." "There are no unmitigated miseries." All choices produce both positive and negative results, and it may not be obvious which is which for decades, if ever. Our goal is to maximize the benefits and minimize the disadvantages. The foregoing indicates that George Wilhelm Friedrich Hegel's philosophy of "dialectics" is a simplification of what really happens. Even though this is the way our brains tend to process memes, in reality there is not just thesis, antithesis, followed by synthesis. Rather, any cause produces multiple effects. And every effect has multiple causes. From a particular perspective some of these effects are beneficial (positive) and some are harmful (negative). From a different perspective it might be the opposite. The more knowledge we have about the circumstances involved and the more control we have over those circumstances, the more favorable can be the outcome. However, there is no way that any cause can produce only positive (or only negative) effects because in a multicausal universe some aspects of a choice are to a given person's advantage at a specific time, and for other persons and/or other times some aspects are in opposition to it. But even more important, we never know with absolute certainty the long-term effects of any choice at the time it is made. So, if we try only to make choices that have positive effects, we'll end up only making forced choices, spending most of our life in limbo, and with choices that will be worse, not better. Therefore, it is essential that we make our best effort and then pay attention so we can make corrections as we progress in order to circumvent negative spots as they become recognizable. Unless we realize that these hazards will appear, we will not be aware of them as early as possible – when we are most likely to succeed with corrective action.

CHAPTER 13

SIXTH WAY OF WISDOM: IMPROVE YOURSELF

<u>SIXTH WAY OF WISDOM</u>: **Know and endeavor to improve yourself; work to be physically and psychologically healthy.**

The first, most important level of self-knowledge is knowledge of how one's mind works.

"Imagine this. You are paddling a little rowboat against the current in a small lake. Your friend, sitting across from you, is busily conversing, and you are using all the energy you can muster to keep the boat moving. The two of you are heading across the lake for lunch. It's a bit late and you are very hungry. Out of nowhere, crunch! Another boat has collided with yours, apparently moving into your path. You are furious and spin around to attack the boat's pilot. But no one is in the boat, that is drifting by itself across the lake. What happens to your attack? Unless you are a very tense person, your attack will dissipate. You realize that no one is at fault, so there is no one to blame. While you may still be a bit frustrated, it is likely that your blood pressure will normalize quickly and you will continue across the lake. No explosion will disrupt your continuing actions." [1]

However, if the person rowing the boat *is* a tense person they may turn on their partner, "Why did you let me run into this drifting boat?" Or, if the rower doesn't want to attack the partner, there is always God. "Why, God, did you let this boat drift into my path?" If they are an atheist then there are one's genes, or one's mother, "Mother, why didn't you teach me better so I would be more careful and never make mistakes?"

<u>But if an individual is ready to step out of the callow behavior of blame and deal with what is actually happening, and over which they have some control, then they are ready to recognize that emotions are not caused by</u>

what happens "out there," but come out of beliefs as we interpret the things life throws our way.

And this takes us to Rational Emotive Behavior Therapy (REBT) developed by Dr. Albert Ellis [2], and put into a very useful and usable form by Dr. Michael Edelstein [3]. A *science of religion and ethics* takes as its foundation the ideas proposed by Ellis. Therefore, an individual's beliefs are seen as a primary element to be studied to understand their behavior and emotions. And these beliefs are evaluated based on their effects. When the effects are not consistent with the individual's goals, and the maintenance and development of the human species, then it needs to be recognized that the relevant beliefs need to be examined and changed. That change needs to be guided by the best empirical evidence about the beliefs that support a moral behavior. Recognizing that an individual's beliefs are the key to everything else is the fundamental approach of a *science of religion and ethics*. And, as long as memes are a factor in controlling choices this approach is equally necessary in situations where the individual has been so impacted by trauma or deficiency that their behavior is not within the normal range. A critical part of the foregoing includes making choices to seek effective treatment, following the necessary procedures, and using all the available knowledge and resources available in the society and the world.

Next and of vital importance is to learn to integrate all parts of one's being. People need to learn how to tune into the part of their mind that lies below the threshold of the conscious but is involved in much of their behavior. The best ways to control all parts of one's being by becoming more unified need to be found. In addition people need to understand themselves in relation to others. The value of a given trait, ability, characteristic, or interest for the person and for society depends in important ways on how it relates to the given place and time of their life. "In the world of the blind the one-eyed person leads" (in spite of Voltaire's inspired writing about a contrary example -- *Candide*).

In the following discussion the term body will be used. Within that term is also included what has traditionally been called mind or spirit. "Mind," "spirit," and "soul" are psychological constructs and exist as vaguely defined structures and functions within the body. In a *science of religion and ethics* it is assumed that the mind, spirit, and soul are formed of the same stuff and function within the same laws as the rest of the body that very likely exist at a deeper level than current understanding has reached. Antonio Damasio has much to teach us in this realm and is well worth study. [4]

We need to know or be able to learn as necessary all the pertinent details about our physical, psychological, biological, chemical, and functional characteristics. We need to know what our body is -- its enzymes, hormones, antitoxins, cells, organs, systems, and everything else because this provides the foundation for how we need to understand our personhood.

How to maintain good health is currently a complex question that is answered differently by different groups and those with different worldviews. I take the approach that the methods of science provide the best way to address this issue as these methods do for any other issue. But like all areas of science the domain of our understanding needs to be expanded.

Each practitioner brings their own worldview and experiences to how they define and interpret physical health. The worldview provided by a *science of religion and ethics* should allow health to be approached and dealt with the best way possible. Certainly the field of medicine currently incorporates much ignorance, blind faith, misinterpretation, charlatanism, exploitation, misuse of power, and such. Partially, the foregoing is true because most people in Western society (the clients if not the caregivers) accept folk religions that continue to provide a supernatural, noncausal worldview. A good example of this is presented below.

A news article [5] reporting a study dealing with the relationship of longevity and beliefs provides an example of the kinds of issues that should be dealt with by a *science of religion and ethics*. This study was done by William Franklin Simpson, a scientist on the faculty of Emporia State University of Emporia, Kansas. He compared the life span of Christian Scientists (graduates of Principia College in Elsah, Illinois, a Christian Science school) with liberal arts graduates of the same year from the University of Kansas. Although Christian Science practitioners abstain from alcohol and tobacco, according to Simpson's research they die at a younger age than do people who use current medical technology. Mary Baker Eddy, founder of Christian Science, taught that illness was just a product of the mind. She taught her followers to avoid medical therapies and to treat illness with prayer.

Simpson's research should be seriously considered by any who would avoid modern medical treatment in favor of some "holistic" approach, or other nonscientific method. Of course it needs to be replicated and involve more subjects to clarify the conclusion. And, a *science of religion and ethics* needs to utilize such studies to provide the best foundation and focus possible for dealing with all health issues. (See VOLUME II, Chapter 20, "Health, Medicine, and a Science of Religion and Ethics.") [6] The Enlightened Person needs to utilize this information as they strive to be in as good health as contemporary medicine allows. And part of doing that is to adopt and follow the best available worldview.

Another component of good health is regular medical examinations. If people are to be healthy there needs to be some way of discovering those types of difficulties that develop so slowly or unnoticeably that people do not realize their presence. Of course significant improvements in blood tests, and similar procedures are essential. In addition when medicine is placed on a more personal basis, as genetic tests are making more and more possible, rather than depending primarily on norms and averages, more subtle difficulties will come into view to aid each person in achieving a constant state of good health. This will help more people maintain a healthy, active body until death. Probably all people would need to have their own expert health diagnostic system (CTRES -- Computer Tutor, Recorder, and Expert Systems) that would include full information on their genome. This would allow immediate treatment and professionals would only be needed when their instruments indicate the need. (Also see VOLUME II, Chapter 19, "The Knowledge Bank and an Enlightened Community.") [7]

Being in good physical condition is a goal to be sought. Those seeking to achieve a *sustainable feeling of well-being* should do their best to achieve and maintain it in order to get the most from life. However, the foregoing is considered more deeply as part of the Seventh Way of Wisdom (Develop and adopt a perceptual framework in which pain does not prevent the achievement of a *sustainable feeling of well-being*) and the Second Way (Seek to maintain and develop humanity). Under the latter Way it might be possible that a person's poor health can turn into a bonding gift to humanity where the pain is balanced with joy.

People need to know their capabilities: their physical strength, how fast they can run, how far they can jump, how much pain they can withstand, and such. Sports are one of the best ways for people to learn their capabilities. However, these sports should be selected for all-around good health. They should be those that allow the body to be tested and kept in good working order while enhancing joy, love, appreciation, and respect of other people.

The usefulness of sports should not be judged merely to show the better coordination and physical perfection of one person over another. Surely those so gifted and motivated should have the chance to demonstrate their abilities and accomplishments just as artists have their chance to utilize and develop their skills and interests. However, sports on a different plane -- a more important one -- needs to be organized for a different purpose. This purpose is not to glorify the best people, but to allow all people to test and gain confidence in themselves. The goal is not to demonstrate perfection, but to maintain the body at a good working level.

Participation in physical activities provides a way for a person to learn that a *sustainable feeling of well-being* does not mean complete satisfaction during each moment of life. Here people should learn self-reliance as differentiated from group support. Enlightened Persons know that there is always someone to help them when they need it. But here people learn how to judge when they need help. People need to learn that though they are completely exhausted -- when every step is made only with the utmost effort, the lungs seem to be aflame, the muscles ache from the effect of strain -- they can go on by their own effort. And that simple tenacity is often the primary tool of achievement. In this situation no one else can pick up the responsibility. Others may encourage, but only the person can achieve. If they persevere they have developed and thereby gained in personal power and self-esteem. If they quit they have delayed an opportunity to advance their development and experience the joy that comes from pursuing a difficult task to its successful conclusion. Of course, this physical trial by ordeal needs to not surpass the capabilities of the person concerned in such a way that it stunts rather than helps them. And we must not fall into the trap of sacrificing the many so that the few can "succeed," or to sacrifice the few so the many can "succeed."

Exercise is definitely necessary for a healthy body. In addition to the more strenuous sports mentioned above to help people discover their capabilities, all exercise should be encouraged that aids in maintaining a good physical and mental state. If someone does manual labor they, perhaps, get enough exercise. However, as work becomes more sedentary, workers need to look elsewhere for their exercise. One source is games (that is, making exercise fun) such as tennis, volleyball, golf, swimming, horseback riding, hiking, bike riding, and such. Other people might involve themselves in compact exercises such as calisthenics, aerobics, and such. Another source that might complement the foregoing at least for some people is combining exercise and music: ballet, tapdancing, square dancing, and all other forms of dance. In addition to promoting good physical health, dancing might -- at least in some cases -- aid in the integration of physical development to help people who missed stages in their bodily integration -- especially in infancy -- (e.g., the crawling stage, sufficient holding and nurturing touch) learn how to overcome these deficiencies. Surely different approaches will benefit different people.

Perhaps, in many cases several hours of strenuous work each week could be performed. This might lighten the load of others, and prevent some people from working like beasts of burden the bulk of their lives. All people may have to shoulder part of the hard work of the world to ensure that no one becomes overly burdened with psychologically unimportant work.

However, "psychologically unimportant" is a technical concept. It includes the idea that a person goes through many stages of maturity and is therefore capable of learning and gaining from many diverse occupations and activities. What would appear to be completely boring, unrewarding, exhausting, and such cannot be judged psychologically unimportant at face value, but only in relation to the person who is performing it, and the results of the activity for them.

WHAT ABOUT NUDITY AND THE BODY?

When thinking of health, one can hardly avoid thinking of nudity. A big stimulus to having a healthy body is having a healthy body judged to be important by some respected person or persons. When we are naked, one's body naturally becomes more important because instead of wearing false shoulders or bustles we need to present exactly that body that we possesses. We, therefore, have another benefit for keeping a healthy and beautiful body and to make the body attractive by developing it.

But, at the same time one needs to realize that every healthy human body is beautiful. However, this is not to say that some are not more beautiful than others. All people will vary from the ideal. Each of us has our special beauty and all of us are average or below average in most of our attributes. Scars, birthmarks, amputations, and all deformities are part of us, and have their own unique beauty when seen through loving eyes. The biceps may not quite match those of Hercules. The breasts may not rival those of Aphrodite. The torso, legs, head, and such may lack the shape and proportion that are considered ideal. However, the most ordinary body is still a thing of beauty when filled with a loving spirit. One need only open one's eyes and cast off the limiting misconceptions of a narrow-minded culture to see that this is true. In this regard plastic surgery in all its aspects needs a philosophical underpinning. We need to find guidelines to clarify how far it is wise to alter one's appearance to fit some imaginary ideal. Like all aspects of the Ways of Wisdom the final answer is an empirical one. What are all the effects and consequences of such surgery? What things move one toward a *sustainable feeling of well-being*, what things have no effect, or move one away from it?

The same thing is true for nudity. However, it would seem clear that an Enlightened Person needs to discard the idea that the nude body is indecent, whether in the flesh, in pictures, or in sculpturing. There is overwhelming evidence that the nude human body is not obscene per se. Is it per se sexually stimulating? It is often looked upon as such by non-nudists. However, there is no reason for it to cause more sexual stimulation than does the clothed human body, and viewed under the same circumstances probably cannot. It has been demonstrated by many groups and millions of people that the puritanical idea that sexual stimulation and nudity are in some way inherently related is completely false. The suggestively clothed body is far more sexually exciting than the nude body!

The nude body must not bring shame into one's mind. Being able to accept one's body is a sign of good mental health and is necessary to continued development. If individuals need to make any mental reservations at all about their bodies, they are not free. Also, nudity represents another form of ethical maturity. Accepting it allows one greater freedom of thought and action.

FOOD, SUBSTANCE ABUSE, SLEEP, DREAMS

FOOD/SUBSTANCE ABUSE

The food one eats and substance abuse both can have significant effects on an individual's health. Most people agree on the obvious: Misuse of drugs and food can be unhealthy. Don't smoke or abuse drugs or alcohol. Eat a healthy diet. And so forth. However, when one goes beyond the foregoing platitudes we encounter tremendous disagreement and ignorance on the do's and don'ts of nutrition and drugs.

Opinions about what is a healthy diet vary tremendously. Most of the reasons depend on anecdotal reports, intuition, mysticism, beliefs. Some make an effort at using science. But the test groups are usually quite small, or have no double-blind element, so the conclusions can at best be guidelines to use until better information is available. Yet no rational person can doubt that the food and substances we take into our body are capable of profound effects. The fact that we have no coordinated program to better pin down these relationships should cause shame and concern in the mind of any politician, scientist, or health or governmental official having responsibilities in this area.

To examine ideas about healthy diets let's take as an example "vegans." These are people who do not eat dairy products, honey, white sugar, or any kind of flesh food -- beef, pork, chicken, fish, or any other. Nor do they use leather products or materials tested for safety on animals. For me this is an inherently wrong approach. I think the goal of good health requires that one be as broad in their diet as circumstances and trustworthy data support. I think it is very likely that vegans are on the right track in terms of good health, a sustainable economy, and ecology. Nevertheless, by their rigidity I think they may have made the leap from wisdom to dogma.

When one steps across the threshold from reduced consumption to abstinence, an unassailable argument, or position is required. I have not -- up to this point -- heard an argument that moves one from moderation to abstinence other than a religious argument; for example, it is morally wrong to eat these foods and therefore should not be done. I find this argument less than compelling.

Rather, I think one's goal should aim toward being able to eat every food -- barring health or other compelling reasons, either due to the nature of the food or the particular constitution of the consumer. Of course we normally tend to think of those foods provided to us when we were children as being best tasting and most desirable. Those foods encountered later tend to be considered weird, unappetizing, not-to-be-eaten at least upon initial encounters. However, we can learn to eat (if not be moved to rhapsodize about) any food commonly consumed if we approach it with an open mind and moderation. Taking only a tiny bite that is increased slowly over time, is in my mind the secret to success. It seems to me this approach would be a natural behavior for an Enlightened Person.

Extensive research needs to be conducted to determine the long-range effects of all foods and substances on different human bodies. This data needs to be individualized to achieve its greatest value. The foregoing should be tied into one's CTRES (Computer, Tutor, Recorder, and Expert Systems) to achieve an individually tailored guide that is current and continuously updated.

SLEEP

Proper rest is also an important factor in health. The mystery of sleep, considering how much of each day an individual devotes to it, is probably percentage wise one of the most under-studied biological phenomena involving animals. For people sleep seems to be pretty much of an individual thing. Yet, there must be underlying truths about it that are applicable to everyone. How many hours of sleep does an individual need per day? How do people determine if they are getting enough sleep?

Or better yet, can it be determined whether or not someone is getting more sleep than they need? Surely there is some optimum amount of sleep a person needs to satisfy very vital biological needs. What are these needs? Does more sleep than the optimum help in any way? Does it hinder? Is an individual healthier who spends more time sleeping? Only research will give the answers to the mysteries of rest and sleep. Research into the broader and deeper aspects of this problem is very necessary. And the foregoing information will vary greatly from person to person. Therefore it should also be personalized by one's Computer, Tutor, Recorder, and Expert Systems so as to apply as perfectly as possible to them.

Fortunately, in recent years sleep research has established a foundation of understanding. Dr. William Dement who set up the Stanford Sleep Clinic has been one of the founding members of this effort. His book *The Promise of Sleep* [8] (discussed in detail in Chapter 36, "The Promise of Sleep," of VOLUME II) [9] presents many important facts and ideas for any person desiring to live a healthy, happy life.

One of Dr. Dement's central points is the need for more sleep research. The small cost of this research will provide enormous benefits in terms of better health and safety for individuals and society in general.

HERE ARE SOME OF DEMENT'S FINDINGS:

It is impossible to get too much sleep. (p. 434) [8]

An individual has body cycles such that "clock-dependent alerting" will tend to keep the person awake at some times and help them sleep at others.

Medical doctors are by and large ignorant of much of the recent sleep research findings. As a direct result of this lack of understanding, sleep disorders cause numerous deaths each year both directly and indirectly that could be avoided with proper treatment. However, lack of sleep in healthy people is an even bigger cause of accidents. It is responsible not only for countless auto accidents, and airline accidents, but also was the primary contributor to the Exxon Valdez, space shuttle Challenger, and Three Mile Island nuclear reactor accidents.

Almost everyone needs around eight hours of sleep per day. There are simple tests to determine if one is getting adequate sleep. When one gets insufficient sleep, a sleep debt is accumulated that needs to be paid off on an hour-for-hour basis by sleeping more in the future if one is to function at their best. One can either catch up voluntarily, or during recovery from illness provoked by the condition.

"When we don't have enough sleep, we have a sour view of circumstances: We are more easily frustrated, less happy, short tempered, less vital...grumpier." (p. 272-273) [8]

Although we still don't know why humans (and other animals) sleep, studies demonstrate that lack of sleep has significant effects. As Dement says (p. 260) [8], "There is plenty of compelling evidence supporting the argument that sleep is the most important predictor of how long you will live, perhaps more important than whether you smoke, exercise, or have high blood pressure or cholesterol levels."

DREAMS

What about dreams? There are many cultures and numerous people who believe that we need to pay constant attention to our dreams if we are to live well. In some cultures an individual may kill another person if they dream that the other has wronged them, or plans to. Freud attempted to bring dreams into the realm of science in his book, *The Interpretation of Dreams*. [10] Dr. William Dement (mentioned above) participated in the initial research on rapid eye movement (REM) sleep and its relationship to dreaming. Current studies lead some people to believe that dreams are not stories about events in the world. These people interpret recent studies to support the idea that the dream state is part of a process to file and store experiences into long-term memory.

Based on the available information it is my belief that we do not yet understand what dreams are for and/or why we have them. Greater understanding of this universal phenomenon seems important. It seems to me that we currently have the tools to understand the purpose of dreams if they have any purpose. Gathering enough of the right data from sufficient individuals and properly analyzing it should make clear whether or not dreams relate to secondary effects of other brain functioning such as memory, or other elements of the individual's life.

Whether or not dreams do in fact have meaning hidden in them, my own experience leads me to counsel caution in attempting to interpret one's own dreams. Taking them as messages to use in making personal decisions can be dangerous. I believe that people can put themselves into self-destructive, even life-threatening situations by doing so. With proper support dream analysis may have value. However, in the absence of solidly based outside help, dream interpretation may be more harmful than astrology, Tarot card readings, and other similar processes that appeal to our magic/wishing propensity. In the foregoing an individual projects their inner processes onto an external screen that may seriously mislead them. This is particularly true for the person who is already mentally unbalanced.

SELF-CONTROL/HYPNOSIS

The preceding discussions deal with one phase of self-knowledge. Another phase is what has traditionally been called self-control. As discussed in VOLUME II, Chapter 27, "'Will Power' and Free Choice," [11] it is clear that self-control is a flawed concept. However, we do make choices and choice management is part of the procedure to make the best choices possible. (See the Fifth Way.) [12] Part of this process involves developing conscious control over many parts of one's being not normally so controlled. This requires as much self-knowledge as possible and permits one to live a more integrated life. Using one's Computer, Tutor, Recorder, and Expert Systems as a feedback source would seem to be very helpful here. Most people utilize only a small percentage of their abilities, and bring insufficient facts to bear on their important decisions. The foregoing is of great importance for anyone working to achieve a *sustainable feeling of well-being*. Each person has tremendous potential. Everyone has the potential to develop into a fantastic, excited and exciting human being to the degree that they tap into their "wisdom" potential. A prime goal needs to be to help people move to this level of self-development. Self-hypnosis is one technique for allowing one to more fully control one's being. Biofeedback is another. Meditation and yoga also provide time-tested guidelines so long as they are not overused to thereby create a distortion of reality.

DEEP THERAPY

If an individual is to know themself and become psychologically healthy they need to also become aware insofar as is possible of the knowledge and trauma stored in their subconscious, and body structures. One's nonconscious mind determines many of one's acts in the absence of awareness. To become more aware of when the foregoing is happening in ways that are not in one's best interests would seem to require some form of deep psychotherapy. Although Freud's psychoanalysis was the first such technique, his processes have not worked as he envisioned. Nevertheless, his naturalistic model of mind helped scientists recognize that mind can be studied and understood. Before his time scientists as well as philosophers tended to accept 17th Century French philosopher Rene Descartes' division of the world into two parts: the natural world and the "soul," with the former being the realm of science (i.e., cause and effect) and the latter the realm of folk religion (i.e., the realm of meaning). Freud was one of the first scientists with access to a large audience to seriously question Descartes' model. Although the psychoanalytic approach Freud invented -- like all scientific efforts -- has not turned out to be the final answer, it achieved some spectacular successes that led us in the right direction.

There are probably many reasons why psychoanalysis has not always been successful. Alice Miller points out in her recent books, such as *Thou Shalt Not Be Aware,* [13] deficiencies in psychoanalytic theories around child abuse. Another equally important issue deals with assumptions about the goals of therapy. Psychotherapy is a process of revealing. It allows people -- at least in some instances -- to discard irrational ideas that have halted their progress and narrowed their outlook. It accomplishes this by showing the client the forces that have shaped them, thus sometimes making it possible for them to overcome those factors. However, while to reveal past trauma and ignorance is important, the thing that is vitally needed is to replace ignorance with mature and sustainable beliefs. All science-based therapies need to be combined with a valid *science of religion and ethics* to enable it to help people rise above old ideas and transcend debilitating beliefs.

But psychotherapy has additional difficulties. Even within an Enlightened Community contemporary psychotherapy would still often fail. Its theories and techniques are in need of further development. As new drugs and methods are discovered and knowledge is increased, people will find better ways to achieve self-knowledge, and reject self-destructive behavior. Victor Frankl's development of logotherapy was focused on some of these issues. However, he too left out the social dimension.

Alfred Adler focused on social psychology, but I only recently learned that he had come to basic conclusions perfectly in tune with the conclusions of a *science of religion and ethics*. My early study of Alfred Adler and Adlerian psychology convinced me that Adler's social psychology was interpreted in terms of family therapy wherein the person was helped to better function as part of the group, but said nothing about the need to improve the group. In reality he was focused much more broadly and actually laid out many of the key issues that lie at the base of a *science of religion and ethics*. The depth of his understanding is made clear in an article by Guy J. Manaster, Zeynep Cemalcilar, and Mary Knill [14]. They quote Adler as follows: "Social interest means... a struggle for a communal form." Then they go on to say, "From this one might infer that social interest is only a here-and-now concept that advocates conformity and belonging to a limited social group. Adler attempted to eliminate this common misunderstanding by saying:

> *It is not a question of any present-day community or society, or of political or religious forms. On the contrary, the goal that is best suited for perfection must be a goal that stands for an ideal society amongst all humankind, the ultimate fulfillment of evolution."*

In my mind Adler says it all above when he says, "ideal society," "all humankind," "the ultimate fulfillment of evolution." These are the concepts upon which a *science of religion and ethics* is built. Though I never had the good fortune to read about this part of Adler's thinking before reaching similar conclusions, I am heartened by finding such a core of similarity in our thinking.

The position of this book is that people need to be helped as a whole and in every phase of their life. They need to have assistance beyond mere recognition of their ills. They need help to realize their potentialities and also help to overcome their limitations. As scientists – especially neuroscientists like Antonio Damasio with a philosophical bent – uncover how the brain and the body in general really work as opposed to how past philosophers thought it works, we increasingly are learning the biology of mental health. When components of the brain are damaged or destroyed or just malfunction it becomes clear that there are limits to any person's ability to function in the way discussed by a *science of religion and ethics*. This is where our social abilities become crucial. We need to do the research to learn how to correct such conditions, and provide the necessary social support until that happens.

This requires changing societies not just the individual person since no society currently exists that satisfactorily empowers its citizens. These changes will not be easy, but they need to be made regardless of the difficulties. Each society needs to become an Enlightened Community that would provide resources to help all people deal with all mental health issues including ones such as Freud discusses below. [15]

"In the ordinary way it is apparent that by flight into neurosis the ego gains a certain internal 'advantage through illness,' as we call it: Under certain conditions a tangible external advantage, more or less valuable in reality, may be combined with this. To take the commonest case of this kind: A woman who is brutally treated and mercilessly exploited by her husband fairly regularly takes refuge in a neurosis, if her disposition admits of it.... Her illness becomes her weapon in the struggle against him, one that she can use for her protection, or misuse for purposes of revenge. She can complain of her illness, though she probably dare not complain of her marriage.... Whenever this external or 'accidental' advantage through illness is at all pronounced, and no substitute for it can be found in reality, you need not look forward very hopefully to influencing the neurosis by your therapy." [15]

However, convincing people to undertake therapy can sometimes be very difficult. An example of this is mentioned by Ludwig Eidelberg [16] in a "case history" he discusses about a person who came to him for psychoanalytic treatment. The patient was disturbed by a few minor difficulties that he wanted to overcome. However, he feared to try psychoanalysis for fear it would end his desire for homosexual behavior, a condition he considered to be necessary to maintain his creativity thus giving purpose to his life. And this certainly might have been a problem since traditional psychotherapy interpreted homosexuality as a condition needing to be "cured." It is hoped that personal development encouraged by membership in a Wisdom Group (VOLUME II, Chapter 1, "Levels of Membership in a Wisdom Group") [17] will not be diverted by similar errors. Rather it is hoped that a nurturing community will be provided that recognizes each person's full humanity while supporting them to become their best self.

In spite of the many barriers that stand in the way of helping a given person do all that is necessary to become an Enlightened Person, the task is critical. The glimmer of hope that needs to inspire the process is the realization that anyone who has not achieved a *sustainable feeling of well-being* will over and over confront the pain and despair resulting from the deficiencies of their religious position and their self-destructive life patterns. If a Center for the Practical Application of Wisdom is available at those times of intense depression, and similar states to provide tangible help, then many people can be encouraged to start the process.

Deep therapy at one time was the only technique available to help people understand themselves well enough to discard the irrational and incongruent ideas that have an obvious role in producing their pain, and causing them to be immobilized. However, recent advances in rapid-change technologies -- such as neuro-linguistic programming and outgrowths of those techniques -- demonstrate new potentials and new possibilities. It now seems more likely than ever before that any person who desires will be able to break their bondage to their past and achieve a *sustainable feeling of well-being*. Nevertheless, it will be a mammoth undertaking to build a world where every person has good mental health [18].

Freud realized that psychoanalytic processes were too time-consuming and too limited in availability to heal all the people with obvious mental illness [19], let alone every person. But with rapid-change technologies, and improved psychoactive medications it might be possible to reach everyone. When a person's average life span was only 30 or 40 years it would have been impossible for all people to achieve adequate self-knowledge and good mental health sufficient to develop their "wisdom" potential, especially if they were raised in a non-Enlightened Community. But humanity's longer life span and increasing level of education and prosperity now provide time and resources for more people to achieve a *sustainable feeling of well-being*.

Today, people spend thousands of hours attending all kinds of educational classes and activities to increase their competence and understanding, but they are often unable to use their education. In some cases they actually fill their life with socially destructive, and therefore self-destructive behavior. However, even normal people spend the bulk of their life at such a low level of fulfillment and productivity any help they provide for developing the species is only by accident. When people achieve a *sustainable feeling of well-being* they will add their energy to the rest of humanity's. Their ongoing feeling of joy that comes out of their fulfillment and their productivity in every area of their life should more than compensate for the time taken to help them achieve a *sustainable feeling of well-being*. The entire life of a person who has become an Enlightened Person would be rewarding to themselves and humanity in ways we currently can't even imagine.

However, much of the time taken now to carry out successful therapy is used just to overcome the social problems mentioned earlier, and related problems such as another one mentioned by Freud: "Analysts who know anything of the dissensions commonly splitting up family life will not be astonished to find that those nearest to patients frequently show less interest in their recovery than in keeping them as they are." [20]

With organizations to overcome the foregoing difficulties therapy will not take as long. Furthermore, as indicated before, rapid-change technologies, improved medical treatments, and other advancements will dramatically change the picture. And since this is one of the most pressing goals of a *science of religion and ethics* the combined efforts of all who have been liberated should provide an irresistible force to expand the percentage of people who achieve good mental health.

MEMORY, INTELLIGENCE, ART

Another area of self-knowledge involves memory. Memory, it seems, can be greatly developed with appropriate techniques. [21] Also, people need to learn their own intelligence, aptitudes, interests, and such. However, these things only become meaningful as they are related to and compared with other people. It is only as people come to know themselves in relation to others that they come to know themselves at all. The foregoing is how people become able to achieve the greatest good for self and society. People need to know their abilities as compared to others' abilities to discover the best way to develop their life. If people understand their strengths and weaknesses as well as their deepest interests they will be more likely to achieve a *sustainable feeling of well-being*.

In addition, it is important to be able to obtain pleasure from doing everyday things. Such activities comprise the major portion of almost everyone's life. These can be accomplished partially by learning to achieve the most from each act that needs to be performed. Also, people can learn to see most routine acts as having something pleasurable, interesting, or life-enhancing in them – especially if those acts are helpful to others.

A definite part of knowing oneself consists of being aware of those things that bring pleasure to oneself. Sensual experiences are part of this pleasure: an appreciation of beautiful music, nature; paintings, photographs, sculpture; the exquisite smell of a rose or the exhilarating "taste" of cold water on a hot day; the stimulation from a caress by a loved one; and countless other pleasurable sensations.

People who are demoralized and bewildered can often be completely revitalized and refreshed by beautiful music. Music has the power to soothe. If a person learns to really enjoy good music they are assured of many hours of satisfaction. Music is a truly wonderful part of our humanity. To be able to appreciate it seems to me to be important.

However, we need to remember the other side of the music coin that American composer, Aaron Copland, [22] mentions: "The sound appeal of music is a potent and primitive force, but you must not allow it to usurp a disproportionate share of your interest. The sensuous plane is an important one in music, a very important one, but it does not constitute the whole story." By understanding music, a person can get much more from it.

Music is also a key to understanding in more depth how the mind works. Robert Jourdain [23] provides details in clear ways to support this position in his seminal resource about music. The table of contents provided here (chapters 1 - 10) gives a hint of the range of material covered in this book. "From sound [chapter 1]... to tone [2]... to melody [3]... to harmony [4]... to rhythm [5]... to composition [6]... to performance [7]... to listening [8]... to understanding [9]... to ecstasy [chapter 10]." However, the simplicity of the table of contents may mislead the unwary about the breathtaking scope and importance of the material provided by this fact-filled, in-depth examination of music and the human mind.

The natural world is another source of beauty. Waterfalls, mountains, forests, canyons, a star-filled sky, ocean waves crashing on a shore -- all these and a million more can be a continuous source of exhilaration. These things probably mean something different to each person, but the important thing is that they can mean something vibrant and wonderful. Each experience can provide many hours of submersion and awe.

Also, art forms have the power to help us experience a plethora of emotions, and they, too, can be enjoyed to a greater degree if we learn how to properly evaluate them. However, figuring out how to "properly evaluate" art is a topic all of its own. *ART & PHYSICS: Parallel Visions in Space, Time, and Light* by Leonard Shlain [24] provides some interesting, stimulating, outrageous, and possibly insightful data and ideas about how to evaluate art. (See VOLUME II, Chapter 31, "Art and a Science of Religion and Ethics.") [25]

But, of course, utilizing the experiences discussed in the foregoing paragraphs will not be completely possible so long as a large percentage of the world's population lives only for the next scrap of food and has little ability to plan for the future. As a *science of religion and ethics* develops, and replaces those folk religions that repress creativity and personal development, humanity will more and more realize its full potential. An ever increasing number of people will achieve all parts of this Way of Wisdom as is true of all the other Ways.

INTIMACY, PHYSICAL AFFECTION, NURTURING TOUCH

A core necessity of psychological health is the ability to experience intimacy and affiliative love. (See VOLUME II, Chapter 5-A [26], "Intimacy and a Science of Religion and Ethics" and Chapter 7, "Romantic Love and a Science of Religion and Ethics." [27]) The foregoing concerns reside at the core of the Eighth Way: Help and be helped by other people. However, it is an example of the fact that each of the Ways moves into the others as they are expanded to their full dimensions so that collectively they are joined at irregular boundaries.

As *In Search of Intimacy* [28] points out, America is the land of lonely people. "Surveys show that in any given month at least one in four Americans is lonely." But "Loneliness is a healthy hunger for *intimacy and community* -- a natural sign that we are lacking companionship, closeness, and a meaningful place in the world." [28] When the hunger for intimacy in infants and children is not satisfied, or is not handled in a healthy way I believe this lies at the core of many troubled lives. However, it is my guess that many Americans -- especially males -- never recognize that the painful feeling they often experience is loneliness. Our cultural models make it easy to interpret these feelings as something else: a need for sex, dissatisfaction with one's achievements, a need to exercise, see a movie, ride a roller-coaster, and such. In addition this deficit leads to a high percentage of all crime committed by vulnerable males. Most asocial and antisocial behavior has a similar social origin. An Enlightened Community would ensure that any person at any time could accurately interpret and respond to their inner signal of loneliness in a wholesome way and do what is life enhancing for them and society.

But intimacy has another dimension. Perhaps one of the deepest truths about human beings is the truth of their mammalian nature that requires nurturing touch in order to experience and develop into their best self. Physical affection, touching, fondling, cuddling are essential elements in this development. Until a given person recognizes and fulfills the requirements of this truth we cannot expect them to move very far toward becoming their best self. Unfortunately, when infants are not provided nurturing touch, but instead are slapped, whipped, battered, sexually abused, and/or ignored they can often experience touch as a negative rather than positive experience. Or, they may pursue a thousand different paths in a vain attempt to fulfill this essential mammalian need. (See VOLUME II, Chapter 4, "Nurturing Touch and a Sustainable Feeling That One's Life Has Meaning.") [29]

Psychological health requires a clear understanding of the role played by material goods in becoming an Enlightened Person. Some people cannot distinguish between necessary wealth and wealth used for little more than ostentatious display. They think that the only thing that prevents their happiness is fear of hunger, lack of new clothing, need of a nicer house, and such. They see a person living in a big house on a high hill with a couple of luxury cars in the garage and they assume that the owner is living a life of uninterrupted bliss. Many people, especially in the American culture, have the false idea that wealth and happiness are directly correlated. The foregoing brings to mind the poem "Richard Cory" by Edwin Arlington Robinson:

> Whenever Richard Cory went down town,
> We people on the pavement looked at him;
> He was a gentleman from sole to crown,
> Clean favored, and imperially slim,
> And he was always quietly arrayed,
> And he was always human when he talked;
> But still he fluttered pulses when he said,
> "Good-morning," and he glittered when he walked,
> And he was rich -- yes, richer than a king --
> And admirably schooled in every grace:
> In fine, we thought that he was everything
> To make us wish that we were in his place.
> So on we worked, and waited for the light,
> And went without the meat, and cursed the bread;
> And Richard Cory, one calm summer night,
> Went home and put a bullet through his head.

It is essential to realize that wealth does not provide a *sustainable feeling of well-being.* Those who amass wealth through their own efforts are in almost every case pursuing their alpha male/female propensity. No rich person has ever achieved the goal for which all of humanity seeks. Therefore, they are as much in need of the assistance a *science of religion and ethics* can provide as anyone else.

Although wealth is a necessary ingredient in becoming an Enlightened Person, it is a wealth not directly related to amassing piles of gold and collections of merchandise. Rather, it is the material resources to obtain an adequate education, the tools to pursue a life goal, to be able to travel to the degree necessary, and devices to lighten life's burdens to permit time and energy to engage life and the joyful living of it. In an Enlightened Community every person needs to be ensured a satisfactory livelihood. Stated simply, production is wealth. As previously indicated wealth is many things. It is much more than two cars in every garage and a chicken in every pot. Nevertheless, every person needs to have the opportunity to produce so that the whole community will benefit and all people will be able to maintain their life at an adequate level. (See "Organizing for an Enlightened Community" [30] for more on this. Also, note VOLUME II, Chapter 34, "Work and a Science of Religion and Ethics.") [31]

MAXIMUM SOCIAL INTEGRATION WHILE BECOMING ONE'S BEST SELF

To be psychologically healthy one needs to be part of a nurturing society. And, total fellowship is the goal of this Way. But what does such fellowship mean? In every case up to now solidarity has been based on getting a person to submerge themself within the group. This has taken advantage of their "tribal" genetic propensities. There has been little room for nurturing the person's full talents and abilities. Only those talents that satisfy group values and immediate needs were encouraged. At some level every culture realizes that to educate a citizen beyond some level is to lose them as a blind follower of custom and authoritarian decrees. These approaches by such cultures can be studied, but primarily to learn how to avoid their mistakes. Because of the vast differences in the ideas among cultures much can be learned by such studies. As in all other areas better answers can only be determined by empirical study. But this is where clarity about the way the biology of one person differs from another becomes critical.

It is likely that what is needed for one type of person will be inadequate or wrong in some ways for other persons. They may need something very different. How to fit all this together will certainly not be easy. Also, integration of all these different needs -- so that the person as well as everyone else benefits -- will be a challenge. But in many ways it is the range of these differences that make an Enlightened Community possible. Nevertheless, total integration of every person into an Enlightened

Community will be difficult to achieve but, I think, not impossible. When people have clarity about their "wisdom" potential they will be better able to see how to achieve solidarity with their species and fulfill their own greatest needs at the same time.

A pre-literate society provides the direct contact and interaction that normally gives each member a *feeling of well-being*. As a society grows and becomes more complex the opportunities are expanded for people to achieve higher levels of development because of the existence of more sophisticated memes. They are thereby able to better utilize the brain capacity made available by the evolution of the language ability. At the same time it becomes easier for individuals to lose the *feeling of well-being* because of the loss of social support. The process of losing the *feeling of well-being* can easily be recognized because it is accompanied by a state of severe depression and/or self-abusive behavior; for example crime, general hostility, irrational use of power over others, self-destructive use of drugs and alcohol, and such. Every society has deficiencies and is, therefore, unsatisfactory to various kinds of people. As a result only the lowest level of the *feeling of well-being* is available to some members of the group.

All current and past societies are characterized by having both positive and negative elements. Some of these aspects are hurtful to some members of the society and have diverted them away from becoming their best self. At the same time the discoveries and efforts of each community have collectively helped move humankind toward the ability to assemble an Enlightened Community. Each culture has made discoveries and developed ideas that have helped other cultures advance further than they could have without them.

The deficiencies of Christianity are legion and many of them have already been explored. On the other side of the scale Christianity has played an essential role in moving humanity to the position where society can now adopt a more universal view based on a more accurate understanding of the human condition and the Cosmos in general.

Every worldview up to this point has been deficient. I claim that all history since the evolution of the modern language ability has been a struggle to find a solution to the question, what is the meaning of human life? Because hunter-gatherers function like pre-language *Modern Humans* and die young they have been pretty successful in ignoring this question, and living within the range of their raw "tribal" genetic propensities either suppressing or narrowly focusing their "wisdom" potential.

However, once a group has been forced out of the hunter-gatherer mode they have had to struggle with different aspects of this question. For 10,000 years the struggle has been intense. But thanks to the efforts of all those who have gone before we are now poised on the brink of success.

A *science of religion and ethics* needs to provide the tools to achieve that success. The fundamental ingredients of this approach are theory, empirical study, and experimentation -- the essential tools of science. We need to study every person, every culture, every worldview in as much detail as time, money, and circumstances permit. Over time, this study would produce a vast library. The goal is to have a complete collection of the total history of humanity and every individual person in as much detail as possible. Its volumes of interconnected ideas, experiences, times, places, consequences, and such would provide the source from which information would be assembled to guide each person on their journey to become an Enlightened Person. By organizing and distilling this data, best guesses, hypotheses, and such we should be able to help each person avoid getting stuck in a local low/high energy point and prevented from moving toward achieving a *sustainable feeling of well-being*. Some brief study of current and past worldviews is presented below as an introduction to this process. Additional material can be found in VOLUME II, Chapter 24-A, "What We Can Learn from the Study of Folk Religions, and Other World-Views." [32]

A LOOK AT SOME WORLDVIEWS

To know and to improve oneself it is essential to have at least some understanding of the various religious positions and worldviews and how they relate to achieving a *sustainable feeling of well-being*.

A simplified version of such a study is presented here as a way to initiate the foregoing process. A more in-depth study is presented in VOLUME II, Chapter 24-A, "What We Can Learn from the Study of Folk Religions, and Other World-Views." [32]

STOICISM: I'll begin by exploring some comments on Stoicism: "... [F]or our purposes we can consider Stoicism a fairly unified body of thought that promised its adherents, when they attained the rare state of wisdom, a complete freedom from anxiety, dread, and evil.... Epictetus.... taught that by a supreme act of will we need to in effect expel from our mind every possible distraction from what he repeatedly calls, 'the sphere of the moral purpose.'" [33]

"Marcus Aurelius implicitly assumes... that the mind or soul attains true freedom only when retired to its own inwardness untouched by things of the world."

"The ultimate victory of soul over body thus finds its characteristic expression for Stoic philosophy in the triumph over pain." [34] "The disdain with which this pagan philosopher [Marcus Aurelius] speaks of the body sounds like the severer excesses of theology.... 'A poor soul burdened with a corpse.'" [35] Epictetus' goal seems to be part of a common thread throughout human history. The belief is that achieving a mental state from which all "distractions" are expelled is a worthy goal. In these worldviews living is a distraction. There seems to be something very seductive about this idea since it lies at the core of most mystical religions including Hinduism and Buddhism. But as indicated below, I think, it is a misfocused goal. It builds on the "tribal" genetic propensity to believe in magic and the power of wishing, but distorts it in ways symbolic language permits. To use the mind to retire into oneself and become "untouched by things of the world" is the exact opposite of how a *science of religion and ethics* interprets the goal of the "wisdom" potential. The intent of a *science of religion and ethics* is to provide a better goal, a better answer, a path toward completely utilizing our "wisdom" potential to develop all parts of our mind and body and our social nature to maintain and develop our species.

HINDUISM AND BUDDHISM: In a similar way Hinduism and Buddhism divert people into mysticism and prevent them from achieving a *sustainable feeling of well-being*. See VOLUME II, Chapter 24-A. [32] In some forms of Buddhism the mysticism is less obvious. But they all develop a state of mind that is impervious to the growth necessary to become an Enlightened Person. (And since the goal of Buddhism is claimed to be "Enlightenment," the same as for a *science of religion and ethics*, this provides an opportunity to compare the path of mysticism with the path of science;

that is, understanding physical reality so its activity can be predicted and its forces utilized to maintain and develop the human species.)

As indicated in the foregoing it is my assumption that mystical traditions build on and expand the brain mechanisms responsible for the belief in magic and the power of wishing to the degree that any other aspects of the body not related to this are ignored. As a result the person is cut off from their "wisdom" potential and becomes the outward manifestation of a minor brain structure that exists as one of our "tribal" genetic propensities. Nevertheless, both Hinduism and Buddhism have centuries' worth of experience with meditation and other techniques for body control and integration. When properly used these skills should be an important part of the process to achieve a *sustainable feeling of well-being.* However, possibly as a result of these beliefs mathematicians of India had the mental stimulation to envision zero and pass it on to Western society. Without zero, mathematics would have been stymied and existed as only a shadow of what we have today. As indicated previously, Buddhism and Hinduism are examined more fully in VOLUME II, Chapter 24-A, "What We Can Learn from the Study of Folk Religions, and Other Worldviews." [32]

ANCIENT GREEK: The ancient Greek cultures lacked the potential to provide their members a *sustainable feeling of well-being* because, "...in spite of the keenness of observation, the extraordinary power of logical reasoning and the great freedom of speculation attained by the Athenian... industrial craftspersons were only just above the slave in social rank, their type of knowledge and the method upon which it depended lacked prestige and authority." [36] The Greeks, therefore, made the knowledge and interests of the craftsperson inferior, unworthy, unimportant. Yet, it is these skills and interests that led to the recognition of the importance of study of empirical processes, the core of modern science and the ability to construct the tools with which to conduct such study. Since ancient Greek thinkers scorned the empirical process their efforts to understand the cosmos were based almost entirely on rational speculation guided by debate. Nevertheless, at a fundamental level their worldview was proscribed by custom and authority. They perpetuated slavery, suppression of females, and rule by the elite. As a result, injustice was a necessary part of their philosophy. The "sustainable *feeling of well-being*" concept was beyond their comprehension. Therefore, their destruction or change was inevitable. However, the Greeks discovered many of the key ideas necessary to develop the concept of a *sustainable feeling of well-being*. According to Alan Cromer [37] the seminal concepts of objectivity and deductive reasoning were contributed by the Greeks. Without the Greeks Cromer postulates that these concepts, essential to the development of modern science, might never have been discovered.

My own opinion is that humanity's "wisdom" potential would eventually have found a way to reach these or similar tools even in the absence of the Greeks. But, regardless of whether this is true or not, all of humanity has much to be grateful for because of that fruitful era.

MEDIEVAL EUROPE: Its members were not able to have a *sustainable feeling of well-being*. These societies did not possess the technical knowledge, social structures, or spiritual level necessary to provide it. They made it impossible to attain such things because they had accepted resistance to change as a necessary part of their worldview. "... [T]hat that had rested upon custom was to be restored, resting no longer upon the habits of the past, but upon the very metaphysics of Being and the Universe. Metaphysics is a substitute for custom as the source and guarantor of higher moral and social values...." [38] They were merely finding a different way to provide a *feeling that one's life has meaning*. A *sustainable feeling* based on a system of beliefs that is *sustainable* was not possible until these early ideas were overthrown, hence change was necessary. Nevertheless, medieval Europe's contributions were critical parts of the mosaic that allowed us to reach our current level of understanding.

AMERICAN INDIANS: These societies lacked the technological (including medical), psychological, philosophical, and religious knowledge necessary to protect themselves from invasion and control. Because their societies could not withstand this external impact and protect them from its effects their societies were shaken down around them. They lacked the knowledge necessary to cope with new situations as they arose. And their societies could show them no way of obtaining this knowledge. Also, their societies could not free members from bondage to a limiting worldview. Their lives were proscribed by "tribal" genetic propensities. They could not prolong life, develop each person's full positive potential, or move all members of their society to become Enlightened Persons. Although, many were content with their lot (just as are many of the members of any society) they had not attained nor could their society help them attain a *sustainable feeling of well-being*. But American Indians contributed in numerous ways to those things that have made it possible to develop a *science of religion and* ethics. The model provided by the Five Nations may have been used to craft the U.S. development of government by federal union, a critical idea in the development of the modern world.

CHINESE CULTURE: The Chinese culture achieved an awesome stability lasting thousands of years. It brought a unique degree of culture, peace, and well-being to a gigantic geographical realm. It made discoveries and had a level of understanding rare at that time. However, that stability was purchased at a fantastic price. It excluded empirical science as well as democratic institutions that would allow the social and personal development necessary to produce Enlightened Persons, or build an Enlightened Community. They contributed key elements to the effort of developing a *science of religion and ethics*, but they, like every other society, by itself, could never have produced it until they departed their historical path.

Although the above societies and all the others not mentioned brought important contributions to the modern world to increase the likelihood that Enlightened Persons and Enlightened Communities would be produced, their demise was assured. The only question was how they would go and when. The foregoing discussion could be extended till it included every religion, philosophy, and society up to this time. They all have lacked in numerous essential ways the necessary tools required to provide a *sustainable feeling of well-being* to their citizens. However, they all aided in giving us knowledge. So, it is only by pooling all of our experiences, knowledge, and understanding and thereby dramatically altering each society that any society has the chance to become an Enlightened Community.

By considering **NAZI GERMANY** or **STALIN'S "COMMUNIST" SOVIET UNION** the picture can be clarified. Hitler and Stalin developed systems based on brute force and psychological knowledge. They utilized peoples' alpha male and "us vs. them" propensities in the least desirable ways possible. Murder, torture, intimidation, terror, isolation -- the Doctrine of Fear at its worst -- were used to perpetuate a society of oppression. There are some who fear that these methods really might be successful in stopping human progress, as postulated by George Orwell (*Nineteen*

Eighty-Four). [39] I believe the opposite. These techniques cannot stabilize a society that shows itself to be deficient by using them. This type of society is even more subject to change than a free, democratic one. Within a broader context democracy is the "wisdom" potential's discovery for countering the raw "tribal" genetic propensity of dominance/submission. It provides a way to involve everyone in the process of governance and make revolution unnecessary. A democratic society has inherent stability like a gyroscope because it provides a way to cope with changing times and incorporate "revolutionary" leaders to focus their energy in positive directions to improve their society without destroying it.

THE THEOCRACIES OF ISLAM: Of course we are not out of the woods yet, and there are many current threats to humanity's moving toward the light at the end of the tunnel. One of the most obvious is the religious terrorists of Islam. It is on a par with the threat of alpha males/females engaging in unrestrained capitalism that is now also strangling human progress.

However, as I've said before it seems clear to me that humanity is moving toward a goal. (See Chapter One, "Humanity's Goal Can Now Be Seen.") [40] Since the evolution of the language ability upset the hunter-gatherer stability provided by their genes, the species has been moving toward a new equilibrium. For *Modern Humans* history does not repeat itself except in those areas controlled by our "tribal" genetic propensities. A close study of history -- at least in my mind -- shows, dimly, the outline of the goal toward which *Modern Humans* have always moved. Through times of war and times of peace, whether led by ignorant tyrants or enlightened rulers, whether under the domain of "God" or controlled by evil forces, during times of widespread empires or the chaos following their demise, our species has been moving toward a universal civilization made up of all members of the species, in which all people are recognized as having equal value, all are able to develop to their maximum capacity, and each person achieves a *sustainable feeling of well-being*.

As this Way of Wisdom is developed it will undoubtedly be divided into hundreds if not thousands of specific behaviors arranged with interconnecting branches and hierarchies so that true guidance will be provided to help any person who desires to achieve a *sustainable feeling of well-being*.

CHAPTER 14

SEVENTH WAY OF WISDOM: MASTER PAIN

<u>SEVENTH WAY OF WISDOM</u>: **Develop and adopt a perceptual framework such that pain does not prevent the achievement of a** *sustainable feeling of well-being.*

Modern thinkers tend to talk about happiness and satisfaction when they discuss what life is all about. Pain is seldom mentioned except as something to avoid. They think pain interferes with happiness so it can be ignored in their goals. I believe that a *science of religion and ethics* cannot become a total worldview unless it is able to deal effectively with the issue of pain.

One thing that needs to come out of an analysis of pain is a better understanding of the term, *sustainable feeling of well-being.* The study of pain makes clear why the "feeling that a person's life has meaning" concept is more basic than happiness or even satisfaction.

The key to understanding why the "feeling that one's life has meaning" is more basic than happiness lies in psychological research popularized by Albert Ellis' Rational Emotive Behavior Therapy (REBT) [1]. Barring gross upset of our brain's functioning due to biochemical malfunctioning [2], or destruction of brain structures Ellis teaches us that our feelings come out of our beliefs [thoughts] rather than the stimuli we encounter. Since happiness and satisfaction are feelings, they are tied into some belief. The belief is more fundamental than the feeling. Therefore, with a *sustainable feeling of well-being,* the belief components are the key elements and they are what lead to satisfaction, happiness, joy, exhilaration, exuberance, depression, anger, suicide, and so forth.

Below is an article [3] that discusses serious spinal injuries. It is presented in order to focus on some important considerations in the issue of living with pain:

<hr />

"STUDIES SHOW REBOUND BY VICTIMS OF SERIOUS SPINAL INJURIES," 20 JUNE 1995

"I'd rather be dead."

That was the reaction of many, including medical professionals, when a riding accident three weeks ago transformed "Superman" actor Christopher Reeve into a quadriplegic who may be on a ventilator for the rest of his days.

"Some of my colleagues say, 'If it ever happens to me, don't even put me in the ambulance,' said Dr. John Haughton, a physical medicine specialist who works with spinal cord injury patients at Whittier Hospital in Haverhill, Mass.

Other experts have repeatedly described Reeve's broken neck as just about the worst thing that can happen to someone.

But recent studies, as well as interviews with several Ventilator-dependent quadriplegics, paint a surprisingly positive picture of what most people instinctively regard as an unthinkable existence.

"The main theme, I think, is that persons with high quadriplegia (high-up spinal injuries) are active, involved people who are satisfied with their existence and happy to be alive," said Gale Whiteneck, director of research for Craig Hospital in Colorado.

Whiteneck and his colleagues surveyed 124 victims of spinal cord injuries, including 26 who were -- as Reeve may be -- permanently dependent on mechanical ventilators to breathe. Only 17 percent said their quality of life was poor, while 84 percent said it was average or above average. Overall, 93 percent said they were glad to be alive.

"I never wanted to die, not for a minute," said Gene Doran, the victim of a well-publicized accident in which a three-inch nail fired by a carpenter's stud gun pierced his neck while he was getting a haircut in Andover.

Since the 1986 accident, that led to a $15.35 million settlement, Doran has lived in a specially built house in Andover with nurses and aides around him 24 hours a day. (See VOLUME II, Chapter 29, "How Much Is a Human Life Worth?"[4]). They feed him, suction out secretions that would otherwise clog his lungs and perform the two or three hours of tasks needed to get him from bed to wheelchair every morning.

"I was very independent since I was a teen-ager, and it doesn't need to be said how difficult it is to become dependent on just about everybody you can think of," said Doran, who served with the First Air Cavalry in Vietnam and was a top salesperson for John Hancock Insurance Co. "But I like life. I have children who need my help, great family support, and I am at no loss for friends."

Spinal cord injury patients "are very unhappy in the beginning, and some of them have told me they don't want to be resuscitated if their heart stops beating," said Dr. Mehdi Sarkarati, chief of the spinal cord injury service at the Veterans Administration Hospital in Boston.

Sarkarati said he tries to ease patients out of that hopeless attitude, and in time their life becomes better and they look back and they say, "You were right."

The VA center follows more than 900 patients paralyzed from spinal cord injuries, and officials said they could not remember losing a patient to suicide in recent years.

In the few scientific studies, a majority of these patients describe their lives in positive terms. Last year, researchers at the New Jersey Medical School reported on "life satisfaction" among 42 ventilator-dependent patients and 45 who had similar paralysis but could breathe on their own. A surprising 70 percent of those on breathing machines said they were generally satisfied -- a higher proportion, surprisingly, than among the quadriplegics able to breathe normally.

"There are several possible reasons for that finding," said Dr. John R. Bach, a physical medicine specialist who headed the study.

"For one thing, people dramatically scale down their expectations and shift priorities in life."

"It may be that the ventilator serves as a daily reminder of the tenuousness of human existence," wrote Bach and co-author Dr. Margaret C. Tilton. In addition, they speculated, the psychological mechanism called cognitive dissonance may play a role: "They overcame the greatest of obstacles and challenges simply to be alive: Therefore life must be meaningful and satisfying."

The study also surveyed paraplegics' caretakers, and Bach said the patients in the study expressed greater optimism than their caretakers thought they would. Bach, who trained in a New York hospital on a unit that had about 50 ventilator-dependent patients, said he was not surprised.

"Every day I would go there and the nurses were always bitching and complaining and seemed so unhappy, but the patients were incredible -- they were happier than the people taking care of them," he said in an interview.

Reeve, 42, shattered the two vertebrae just below his skull when he fell on his head during a riding competition in Culpeper, Virginia, on May 27. Damage that high in the spinal cord is apt to destroy the connections between the brain and most nerves below that point, leaving the victim with no sensation or motor control in most of the body -- including the nerve pathways needed to regulate breathing.

It is still too soon to tell how bad Reeve's paralysis will be in the end. Doctors at the University of Virginia Medical Center, where Reeve is recovering, said he is now able to move both trapezium muscles, the large muscles on the right and left sides of the upper back that control the shoulders.

"That's a positive sign," said Dr. John A. Jane. "It means that impulses are getting through the area of injury and he is consciously moving this part of his body."

Reeve's accident made him one of the 7,500 to 10,000 people who suffer spinal cord injuries in the United States each year.

Christopher Reeve died 10 October 2004.

The above report lays out well many of the issues that need to be considered when people experience debilitating injuries. Clarifying the primary factors causing each person's feeling that life even in this condition is worthwhile would be essential for our purposes. The article mentions several reasons that might explain these paraplegic's positive outlook. It seems to me that the most likely one involves the person's beliefs about their children. The injured parent has a strong belief that their child/children have a need for them. In my mind this is one of the strongest motivations a person can experience, and it is the one that has been generalized to parents, mates, clan, church, and nation. Reports from other sources regarding Reeve's circumstances may help put these findings in perspective. He is elsewhere reported to have originally expressed a desire to die. However, because of his wife's loving message that his life was important for her and similar expressions from his children, he changed his mind. In the previous article Gene Doran is quoted as expressing a similar idea: "I have children who need my help..." I would expect to find something comparable in the other cases studied.

Another important factor involves nurturing. A quote from a valuable reference source by Nancy Segal [5] is provided below that gives an interesting perspective on being disabled as well as on the relationship between nurturing and quality of life.

"I am proud to be disabled, really -- it is a natural part of the human experience." [6]

The above words were spoken by athlete Scot Hollenbeck who includes among his accomplishments setting records in the 1992 Paralympic Games in Barcelona. He earned the world records in the 800-meter and 1,500-meter wheelchair races. His time in the 800-meter race was the first time a wheelchair racer performed better than a regular racer in this event. His paternal twin brother has provided deep and ongoing support for his efforts.

However, I take this in the context of Segal's remark, "The successes of many of the injured twins may have been largely due to the love and encouragement of their twin brothers and sisters." [7]

In the spirit of the above point it appears that the people mentioned in the previous article discussing Reeve are receiving a higher level of care and concern than the average person. Perhaps as long as this continues they would feel their value and thereby maintain a *feeling of well-being.* Remove that support and the situation might dramatically change. It seems likely to me that many of these people are receiving more care and support than they ever did prior to their injury.

A different dimension of this issue is presented below [6] in a startling discussion of conjoined twins (twins who are physically joined together and therefore always at each other's side).

"According to Dr. Alice D. Dreger of Michigan State University, many people believe conjoined twins experience 'living hell,' but she finds this view to be narrowly conceived. The Schappell twins, Lori and Reba, tell a different story from the dismal world that is often envisioned.

"Thirty-six-year-old Lori and Reba (Dori) Schappell of Reading, Pennsylvania force hard looks at life quality and life satisfaction under conjoined twins' extraordinary circumstances. These twins are the only living adult conjoined pair in the United States joined at the head. They have individual brains, but their shared blood supply and brain tissue makes separating them impossible. Reba is much shorter in height, requiring her to sit in a special stool, steered by her sister. Reba is also paralyzed from the waist down and was born with some internal organs outside her body.

"The words of the Schappell twins and other conjoined pairs have echoed in the popular press, confirming difficult challenges, but revealing astonishing achievements. I spoke with Lori and Reba by telephone on June 18, 1998. Their achievements are extraordinary irrespective of their physical situation, and some of their stories will sound familiar, as well as amusing, to twins everywhere.

"They were born in Reading Hospital, in Reading, Pennsylvania, on September 18, 1961. Their mother, who had delivered three previous children, found this pregnancy uneventful. Lori and Reba cannot pinpoint their first awareness of their unusual twinship, but they always knew they were 'different.' Their presence brought unkind comments and stares, but they were taught to ignore them."

"Lori was responsible for arranging the telephone interview with me. She is the 'open, extraverted twin' who fields questions about conjoined twinning. Reba is the 'shy, private twin' who will only discuss her budding musical career, but who will assert herself when the situation demands it. According to Lori, 'She [Reba] always encouraged me to pursue my career [as a ward clerk or nurse receptionist], and now I want to focus on hers.' Today Lori accepts occasional part-time positions, freeing her to concentrate on her sister's singing engagements. Reba received a 1997 L.A. Music Award for best new country artist, and is now producing a CD, *Momma Taught Me*.

"The twins' behavioral differences are extensive -- Lori likes to watch television, Reba does not; Lori loves to shop, Reba does not; Lori craves sweets, Reba does not. Perhaps their physical proximity fuels their psychological separation, over and beyond what ordinary twins experience; their behavioral differences recalled those revealed in many conjoined twins' biographies. The Schappells' physician, Dr. John M. Templeton, Jr., a former pediatric surgeon at Children's Hospital, also found the twins' differences striking. He mentioned Lori's earlier computer interests and Reba's former medical ambitions. Reba, once an aspiring physician, designed support equipment for physically disabled individuals.

"When I asked the twins to list some similarities, Lori replied, 'We have the same last name and we love each other.' They call their relationship a 'compromise,' a plan any couple must learn, 'only we learned it from the beginning.' What is the most important message the twins would like the world to hear? It is that they are *handicapable*, a term coined by Reba. Handicapable means that they are successful, but slower, at doing what other people do. We may wrongly think of these twins as impossibly doomed, rather than as people simply trying to live their lives.

"My conversation with Lori and Reba ended humorously. They recalled Reba's attempt to pay for a gift, an alcoholic beverage they wished to bring to a friend. The cashier requested proof of age, but when he saw Lori's face he decided that she looked old enough -- and allowed her to pay instead! I suspect that identical twins differing in dress or demeanor have similar stories to tell [6]."

The material on Reba and Lori forces me to totally reexamine my assumptions about the good life. I think their lives make clear that the human mind is capable of finding meaning in a person's own life in ways far beyond our normal expectations. Obviously this is an area in need of far more thought and study.

To help provide a better basis for understanding what pain has to teach us, additional material from a seminal book about pain is examined [8]. "This book tells a...story. It describes how the experience of pain is decisively shaped or modified by individual human minds and by specific human cultures." Also see VOLUME II, Chapter 12, "The Meaning of Pain," [9] for a more detailed analysis of pain utilizing this book. *The Culture of Pain* by David Morris [8] deals with pain in ways that must be considered if people are to find out how to come to grips with issues relating to pain.

"It is the neglected encounter between pain and meaning that lies at the center of this book...." [p. 3] And this is the core issue I am attempting to deal with here.

"*Philoctetes* [a Greek tragedy by Sophocles c. 409 BCE] makes us feel the power of pain to reduce a life to utter emptiness and misery." [p. 254] And this is the challenge. What does pain have to say about a *sustainable feeling of well-being*? For me the evidence is overwhelming that a person can experience a *feeling that their life has meaning* while experiencing great pain. But can a person in extreme pain achieve a *sustainable feeling* -- based on a system of *sustainable beliefs* -- *of well-being*? This issue and its ramifications seem to me to be one of the prime reasons for studying pain and attempting to understand it better. Of course when we examine pain as it relates to meaning of human life we see Buddha smiling at us since the primary message of his teachings was to provide guidance in transcending pain. "The Buddha reduced his world view to four points: (1) life is suffering (dukha), (2) suffering arises from desire (tanha), (3) eliminate desire and you eliminate the suffering, and (4) live a decent life and meditate to help eliminate desire." [10] For more on this point see VOLUME II, Chapter 24-A, "What We Can Learn From the Study of Folk Religions, and Other World Views." [11]

Christians often preach that suffering is the lot of humanity and it is to be accepted with gratitude. They say that the greater our suffering on Earth the greater our reward in Heaven. Buddha taught the opposite. Suffering is to be avoided by giving up desire. But a *science of religion and ethics* teaches that suffering is neither to be gratefully accepted nor singlemindedly avoided. Suffering/pain it seems to me is an essential issue to understand if a person is to achieve a *sustainable feeling of well-being* just as are joy and pleasure.

We cannot live a full well-rounded life by making our primary life goal the avoidance of suffering, or by accepting it as a first order good [12]. As we pursue the true goal of life, to achieve a *sustainable feeling of well-being*, pain and pleasure become signposts along the way. A Buddhist can no more achieve a *sustainable feeling of well-being* than can a Christian. Each has a grossly inadequate model of the Cosmos in general, and human beings in particular. Therefore, they pursue goals and follow paths that guide a person away from consciously working to maintain and develop the human species rather than toward it.

Desire is how we know we are alive. Healthy desires, like healthy diets enrich our lives and help us move toward a *sustainable feeling of well-being*. Unhealthy desires come out of our personal ignorance and society's ignorance, and they need to be avoided or replaced.

Many people experience a *feeling of well-being* in spite of (because of?) almost unendurable pain that they tie into supernatural concepts. It seems to me that whatever can be achieved through ignorance (the supernatural), must be able to be achieved through knowledge, else what kind of knowledge has been achieved? David Morris provides the key to how knowledge can be used to focus pain so that a *sustainable feeling of well-being* is achieved/maintained: "Emmanual Levinas in his essay, *Useless Suffering* (1982), [8] proposes a way of understanding that begins from the premise that pain is utterly negative, absurd, and evil.... Suffering, he proposes, opens up an ethical dimension.... My own useless suffering... takes on a changed meaning if it becomes the occasion for your empathic, even suffering response. This is what Levinas calls a suffering for the suffering of someone else." [p. 287] In thinking about the foregoing it seems erroneous to say, "Pain is utterly negative, absurd, and evil." Pain normally performs an essential role in life. Any effects of useless pain -- chronic pain that performs no currently understood biological function -- presumably comes out of a malfunction of an essential, healthy defense mechanism.

But putting the above aside I am excited by Levinas' idea of focusing on the pain that promotes community. Coming together with others because of our compassion for their suffering seems real and important. The foregoing approach of sharing our pain with others should be extended. If this approach can be properly developed, I think, humanity will be aided in making a critical step forward. It seems to me that this is one of the issues that is most important to explore as part of this Way.

And this solution applies not only in situations involving great pain, but also in any situation where the person is cut off from a normal way of life due to accident, genetic condition, disease, deformity, or even criminal behavior and drug abuse in general. If this circumstance can be taken by some segment of society as an opportunity to learn from this person's condition how to make the life of others better, then this condition takes on a positive dimension. *I may suffer. But my suffering will ease the suffering of others. And others are here with me now to demonstrate their appreciation, while supporting me in whatever ways they can.*

"People continue to make self-destructive choices in pursuing goals that give their lives meaning."[p. 266] For me the purpose of a *science of religion and ethics* is to help people avoid making self-destructive choices as they attempt to achieve a *sustainable feeling of well-being*. This is the primary goal of the Fifth Way of Wisdom (Make the best choices possible).

"Tragic choices and tragic events are by definition unhealthy. Yet tragedy would tell us that we might be much healthier as a culture if we did not turn away from suffering, if we stopped trying to cancel pain and to prolong life at all costs, and if we gave up trying to ban or to remove from sight everything that frightens us with the premonition of our own death."[p. 266]

The concept "tragedy" moves us out of reality into the realm of mythology. It seems clear to me that a more realistic way to look upon pain is needed. And as indicated above I believe using an approach along the lines suggested by Levinas has great merit. This provides a way of conceptualizing pain that has nothing to do with tragedy. This useful approach would permit a person to achieve a ***sustainable feeling that their life has meaning*** even if they are experiencing intense pain. This approach would allow a person to utilize pain without welcoming it.

An Enlightened Community would want to do everything possible to prevent useless pain and to eliminate it or at least limit when it exists. However, such a Community must also teach ways to accept pain with equanimity when it occurs. But perhaps more important the person must learn how to avoid letting the threat of pain deter them from the greater good. One model for doing this might be dancers and athletes [p. 194]. And, a person could add mountain climbers, fire fighters, explorers, or anyone on a frontier where the body is actively used as a tool for work or exploration.

It seems to me that the beliefs that support achieving a *sustainable feeling of well-being* must produce a willingness, when circumstances require, that a person give their life if it will accomplish something of sufficient importance to the development of humanity.

Life is not only a matter of being comfortable, though all people need comfort in their lives. Life is about using the opportunity of our own existence to add to and utilize the store of human knowledge and experience to perpetuate the species so more people can do the same. There will always be times when people have to choose between sacrificing their life in order to actualize their beliefs (memes), or not. We must be alive in order to become Enlightened Persons. However, we must recognize that our death is part of our life. The **sustainable** in a *sustainable feeling of well-being* means congruency with the most worthy attributes of the human species -- and the universe of which death is a fundamental part -- helping humanity and ourselves move toward the light at the end of the tunnel; that is, the state in which human beings have reached dynamic stability based on memes.

Needless suffering, unnecessary death, pointless joy and happiness based on ignorance, should not be promoted. The goal of a *science of religion and ethics* would be to help people distinguish between the foregoing things and choices that lead to a *sustainable feeling of well-being*.

Certainly a *science of religion and ethics* must incorporate those people who are in pain, or those who are disfigured, diseased, disabled, immobile, grossly unhealthy, and such. These people must be included as active participants in society and as candidates for a *sustainable feeling of well-being*. But before a society can successfully achieve this, it must learn how to become a community where all people are joined together by their concern for each other. Ways must be developed to provide support to help each citizen be all that they can be.

"Civilization... not only insulates the upper classes from discomfort but is built upon the pain of the masses." [p. 271] To the degree the foregoing is true, I think civilization needs a new perspective. To me an Enlightened Community must be structured so that all people share fairly in the rewards of society as well as the pain of maintaining the society. The idea that the many must suffer so that the few can maintain culture, sophistication, and civilization strikes me as being wrong. The foregoing model of the upper classes comes out of humanity's "tribal" genetic propensities. It is not congruent with the effort to rise to a higher level of existence -- a community of equals -- to achieve our "wisdom" potential.

"We need to acknowledge that pain can serve multiple purposes and hold multiple meanings beyond its basic function as a signal of tissue damage." [p. 279] Shared pain can be an intense bonding experience as long as all members take part in it. However, only people kept in ignorance can feel bonded to others who would benefit from their suffering, but refuse to share in it.

"Nietzsche... in 1874.... managed his ailments in a manner both idiosyncratic and typically shrewd. 'I have given a name to my pain,' he wrote, 'and call it *dog*'.... the useful point to grasp... is that Nietzsche has in effect taken charge of his pain. He has assigned it a personal place and meaning. His crucial move, in fact, is to assign his pain a position of inferiority... Nietzsche decides, typically, that he will be the master rather than the slave." "Too many patients implicitly accept a definition of their illness that enslaves them and makes pain the master." [p. 284]

The foregoing seems like another seminal ingredient for developing a framework in which to experience and deal with pain. Nietzsche shows us a way to put pain in a perspective that does not leave us as the victim. This is easy to talk about, but how easy is it to do? How well did it work for Nietzsche?

On a different point: "... [H]ow we experience pain has almost everything to do with how we understand it." [p. 289] For me the foregoing is a critical message that must be heard and appreciated. It becomes clear that a framework is necessary in which the person can interpret pain. This framework needs to give pain a positive effect rather than a negative one. This interpretation should also inspire people to broaden the scope of their vision to give it more breadth and depth. Life is not just about joy, sunshine, flowers, and "living happily ever after." It is also about pain, suffering, and death. But the foregoing is not oppressive if our pain, suffering, and death allow us to be drawn into community, shared fellowship, and our efforts utilized in the maintenance and development of humanity.

CHAPTER 15

EIGHTH WAY OF WISDOM: HELP AND BE HELPED BY OTHERS

<u>EIGHTH WAY OF WISDOM</u>: **Help and be helped by other people. Recognize that all human beings are "us;" everything else is "them."**

Human beings are social animals. They have not evolved to live alone. Unless a person bonds with other people, they cannot achieve a *sustainable feeling of well-being*. Humanity may go on to eternity; however, the existence of an individual personality is very, very finite. The only true satisfaction comes from being actively involved in developing our "wisdom" potential as we help others do the same.

It is essential to realize that the very growth of a baby into a fully actualized human being is only possible within a community. Psychological research indicates, and a person's reasoning accepts, that infants raised in the absence of people would not become human beings (except in the most "animal" meaning of that term). They would function at the most primitive level of their "tribal" genetic propensities, close in many ways to chimpanzees. They could not speak, or use the parts of the brain that develop when language is mastered. All the cultural evolution that has taken place over the past 10,000 - 40,000 years would be swept away. They would not even have the potential to develop their "wisdom" potential barring a dramatic change of their circumstances.

Without language, without human contact, important parts of the brain do not develop. Raised without human contact -- but with sufficient nurturing contact to survive -- people would be grossly deprived and culturally malformed. The amount of a person's potential that is developed is almost totally dependent on the society in which they are raised. As said before many times we can only become an Enlightened Person if we are part of an Enlightened Community. Who we become depends on the specifics of our nurturing -- (See VOLUME II, Chapter 4, "Nurturing Touch and a Sustainable Feeling That a Person's Life Has Meaning," [1]) that discusses the importance of physical affection – holding, touching, cuddling. Intimacy and affiliative love are key ideas related to the concept of bonding. Achieving intimacy and maintaining it are discussed in greater detail later. For references see [2] and [3].

In addition to having a loving partner an essential component for becoming an Enlightened Person is to help other people and thus foster commitment between others and ourselves. This sense of commitment lies at the core of a *sustainable feeling of well-being*. Any person lacking this commitment will have their life significantly diminished from what it might have been. Nurturing connections with other people are essential in order to achieve good mental health. To achieve necessary social bonding, appropriate living conditions would be very helpful. (See VOLUME II, Chapter 21, "Living Space for the Enlightened Person." [4].)

Although people need to be part of a community they must not lose their individuality and identity in order to be part of that society. This is the challenge that has always confronted *Modern Humans*, but now we have a true opportunity to solve this problem. This is the dilemma that has troubled our species for at least the past 10,000 years. This is the problem we have been trying to solve since the evolution of the language ability. To achieve the unique potential we have as a species we need to build societies such that no person can be allowed to become simply a cog in the machine. Individual ants, bees, and termites exist as exchangeable units in a social machine. They have no value or existence independent of their place in their society. The language ability gives humanity the opportunity to follow a very different path. The goal towards which humanity struggles is to produce a society in which each person has the potential of being a key element in maintaining the species' existence. For humanity all people need to achieve their personhood and goals as differentiated from group goals. They need to function in ways that utilize their unique talents, creativity, abilities. They need to provide what only they have to offer their community that no other person can. As indicated elsewhere this is a new challenge that no other earthly species faces. It is only possible to achieve such personhood in an Enlightened Community.

People will achieve a *sustainable feeling of well-being* most easily who have been raised in a nurturing environment wherein they can develop their self-esteem, personal power, ability to love. This involves physical affection, opportunity to develop their minds, and to use their talents and abilities in effective ways from the first moments of their birth. The closer their community approximates an Enlightened Community, the more direct will be their journey toward a *sustainable feeling of well-being*. A fundamental assumption of an Enlightened Community says that it is the individual human being who is most important, not societies, not the species, not the genes. For it is only by making this assumption that all the evils are avoided if we start with any other assumption that I am aware of.

People are most likely to love humanity if other people have treated them with love. The more harsh and abusive their environment, especially their early environment, the more likely they are to be criminals, cruel, deceitful people, and/or in other ways less than model citizens. However, such people are not "bad." There is no such thing as a "bad" person, although anyone can do bad things. They, like any person at any time, have the potential to change their life and become an Enlightened Person. All that is needed is the right experiences. But these experiences may include social intervention to change the deepest elements of their physiology. Many people have not gained insight into themselves or found worthwhile goals to pursue, hence, are making an unsuccessful attempt to live in the right way. They, like all people, need to have reasons for that faith if they are to have faith in humanity. They need to draw material and moral support from their society. People cannot continually be beaten down and still be expected to continue loving. Children cannot be physically and sexually abused and be expected to grow into nurturing and loving adults without special assistance. People cannot be placed in the dim, dusty recesses of a cave-in-prone coal mine for their entire lives and expected to be able to practice the habit of nourishing love unless they are provided sufficient support. Even though some people may be able to overcome the foregoing experiences through their own efforts -- and the luck of being raised in a good family (including the right genes) and having supportive friends -- most cannot. However, the Sixth Way of Wisdom (Become psychologically healthy) aims to provide guidance to interested people so they will be able to get whatever help is necessary to function at their maximum level.

The Eighth Way of Wisdom provides the plan for achieving all the social support needed. Organizations (especially the Wisdom Group and Center for the Practical Application of Wisdom) need to be formed to help achieve this Way. Also see "Organizing for an Enlightened Community" [Chapter 19]. Centers for the Practical Application of Wisdom [Chapter 20] would be formed to ensure each person the opportunity to develop in the best and most rewarding way insofar as current knowledge permits. These groups would ensure that each person is offered the opportunity and support to achieve a *sustainable feeling of well-being*. They would ensure that no person is left to struggle, seek, and die alone. By introducing people to the Ways of Wisdom and helping them to achieve these goals, society would thereby provide the security, opportunity, and feeling of usefulness people so vitally need.

A Center for the Practical Application of Wisdom (CPAW) would provide all the resources possible for in-depth study of each person to help them understand themselves fully, and learn the best paths to pursue. This group would guard people against spending an entire life as a beast of burden; a contented cow; an ant/bee/termite; or leading an undirected or misdirected life. A CPAW would ensure that all interested people have the opportunity to attain worthwhile goals. Every attempt would then be made to help them achieve their full positive potential. At the same time it needs to be kept in mind that trial and adversity if not too great have often been important ingredients shaping the lives of admirable people.

To achieve the foregoing people would benefit from having their own "electronic helper" (Computer Tutor, Recorder, and Expert Systems -- CTRES) to accumulate detailed records. This data would be integrated, assimilated, and made available in every way to help the person. These records would include their entire life story: their medical records, their educational records, their most intimate, traumatic, important experiences as revealed by intense therapy, cross-references to their family's records, and so forth. All people might be assigned a universal code to ensure that their records would always be available.

In an Enlightened Community there would be no secrets. The prime purpose of personal records would be to help each person and humanity.

Records would benefit the person in an almost infinite number of ways. No matter where the person went a physician seeing them would be able to study their complete medical history and therefore know the best way to treat them. Such records would aid the person in all parts of their lives. This data would permit their Computer, Tutor, Recorder, and Expert Systems to make not only health suggestions including diet, exercise, and mental health, but help in the area of friendships, romance, finances, jobs, and such. Also, records would be an aid to humanity because these records would provide a resource for study and analysis of the different effects of similar factors in many different circumstances. These would be one source of data for researching the components of a *sustainable feeling of well-being*, for Discovery Games, and for factors too diverse to categorize.

Many thoughtful people fear any organization at all. They are worried that it will degenerate to exploitation and tyranny. People reared in the shadow of John Stuart Mill, Adam Smith, the Holy Inquisition, Nazi Germany, Communist Russia, fundamentalist religions, and such have learned to fear organization. Any person aware of humanity's alpha male/female propensity to focus their energy on dominating others when inadequately socialized, will recognize a fundamental justification for this fear. However, we have an overwhelming amount of evidence that such societies need not exist. (See VOLUME II, Chapter 18-A, "What Other Animals Can Teach Us About Morality.") [5] Certainly an Enlightened Community would not permit insufficiently socialized males or females to attain positions of power (at least not unmonitored power over others) in the community.

A *science of religion and ethics* needs to recognize that human organizations are essential. Organization is a central assumption of this book: The goals and conduct of an Enlightened Person and an Enlightened Community are not in conflict. **If this assumption is in error then everything else I have written needs to be viewed with deep suspicion**. And of course since neither Enlightened Persons nor Enlightened Communities currently exist – or at least none that I'm aware of -- suspicion is essential. However, be that as it may organizations are necessary to bring together and pass on the best thinking of the best people who have lived up to a given time. Without such organizations there is absolutely no chance at all for people to achieve a *sustainable feeling of* *well-being*. Properly structured organizations help us organize knowledge and experience so that each person can benefit from what those who have gone before have learned so they are able to build on these experiences. This building is what most noticeably separates science from folk religions.

Individual people become human in society. In "bad" societies, they tend to become "bad" people (Nazi Germany and the Ku Klux Klan provide food for thought on this point). Our species' "dominance/submission" and "us/them" propensities combined with the alienation that characterizes urban communities, provides the soft underbelly that makes exploitation, brutality, terrorism, and many of the other ills that flesh is heir to easy, or at least easier. It is only knowledge, experience, and social support that make us immune to the folly of our predecessors. Although people may rightfully fear organizations such as those proposed here, they need to also recognize the risks in failing to develop adequate organizations. It is clear to me that Wisdom Groups and Centers for the Practical Application of Wisdom (CPAWs) would only work for the good of humanity if their leaders have achieved a *sustainable feeling of well-being*.

Alpha males/females seeking power are susceptible to every temptation. (See VOLUME II, Chapter 18, "Ethics, Morality, and Science.") [6] Only Enlightened Persons will be able to avoid becoming oppressive -- a condition that has dominated all organizations, past and present, designed to help human beings. However, unless we can build social institutions that allow each person to be fully bonded to society without becoming "ants" the species has missed the opportunity provided by symbolic language. This failure by our species is not acceptable for me. We can do better. We can be better. We can develop structures to build on personal strengths and develop ways to prevent personal deficiencies from hurting, misdirecting, and killing others. We can fulfill the potential produced by the evolution of our language genes. CPAWs need to work to develop the resources and commitment to achieve the foregoing.

Also, see Fifth Way of Wisdom: Strive to make the best choices possible. Since people cannot know their capabilities when they are born groups like the CPAW are needed to make sure that the opportunities exist for each person to learn and experience what is necessary to become an Enlightened Person.

CPAWs would ensure that people have the opportunity to do the things they most desire to do and that they are best suited to do. At the same time they would be helped to maintain individuality and universal social bonding. Nevertheless, people need to remain on the alert in case a particular CPAW is taken over by "alpha males/females." The alpha male weakness for dominating others shows up in almost every paragraph of human history, even the history of science. Can democracy and good mental health overcome the "dominance/submission" propensity powered by our genetic propensities? Obviously, this is an open question that can only be answered empirically. Can society achieve a *science of religion and ethic's* goal to produce Enlightened Persons? To do so it needs to nurture the flame of the "wisdom" potential that exists within each person and work in every way possible to keep this potential from being overwhelmed by the flood of pressures constantly emanating from human beings' raw "tribal" genetic propensities.

To produce Enlightened Persons, certain rules would need to be followed. People would need to voluntarily associate themselves with a CPAW. Voluntary association might come about in a manner similar to that in a psychoanalytical case history mentioned by Robert Lindner [7]. A person came to him to be treated for impotence and depersonalization, but during the course of treatment was also cured of Communism [8]. Or, under certain circumstances it might need to be more coercive. Such an example is the formerly existing Children's Sexual Abuse Treatment Program of Santa Clara County where parents convicted of incest had the option to participate in the program or go to a state penitentiary. [9] Unfortunately, this program ended due to lack of participation when incest became a hot-button political issue in an era focused on punishment, not rehabilitation. And even worse than that in a contentious divorce, incest charges became a sure-fire way for an angry spouse to solve a child custody issue.

But regardless of the specifics of the treatment process, the mechanism is the same -- dealing with the relationship that exists between a person's irrational beliefs, genetic propensities, and the symptoms that plague them. To be cured of one, people need to be cured of the other. Everyone who has not yet become an Enlightened Person has difficulties they recognize as such and that they will, under the proper circumstances, accept assistance in handling. In the course of solving problems of which a person is consciously aware it is possible and necessary to help them deal with their irrational beliefs, or pursuit of irrational goals, most of which are powered by their raw "tribal" genetic propensities.

However, the values and ideas that support a person's worldview are vital to their self concept. Their harmful beliefs can only be changed if other beliefs that are equally satisfying to them replace their current ideas. People cannot give up their irrational beliefs unless they find a more satisfactory position to replace those ideas. And even more important, positions, beliefs, and ideas that are emotionally loaded cannot be shaken by reason and logic. Deep therapy in an environment of social support may be necessary in many cases to allow a person to discard the irrational ideas of their childhood and overcome the effects of the traumatic experiences of their lives.

CAPITALISM AND THE ENLIGHTENED COMMUNITY

What is the best way for an Enlightened Community to structure its economy? How can it most effectively help all members earn a living? Although most people who have worked to improve human societies have thought some form of socialism needs to control the economy, it seems to me that a mixed system with socialism for basic services – roads, schools, fire, police, and such – and some form of capitalism for the rest of society's needs would be better. When the proper regulatory guidance is given by a society the corporate structure and profit motive provides the flexibility and options necessary for each person to be a productive member of society. Benefit Corporations would be an ideal model for reforming corporation to make them more socially responsible. See Appendix D. Also co-ops and …. **add another**.

But when regulations are missing or even unwisely favor corporations in a Pre-Enlightened society, especially its economy, a dangerous situation is established. These are the conditions that have destroyed societies throughout history that Jared Diamond laid out so well in his book, *COLLAPSE: How Societies Choose to Fail or Succeed*, [10] and in my mind, are now moving the present world dangerously in that direction. It is my belief that the foregoing has been promoted in the world starting with the election of Ronald Reagan as U.S. President in 1981. According to a book by Barry C. Lynn, *CORNERED: The New Monopoly Capitalism and the Economics of Destruction*, [11] Reagan directed the Justice Department to base anti-trust decisions on a goal of efficiency as measured solely by lowered costs. This favored monopolies since the standard practice of a monopoly is to gain control by lowering prices in order to drive out the competition and, after that set prices to what the traffic will bear.

Reagan's changes were a revolutionary overthrow of U.S. antimonopoly laws, which I believe laid the basis for the Great Recession of 2008 and the concomitant power corporations now wield not only in the economic world, but in the political realm. Lynn opens a door into a domain that seems worth exploring in further detail by those interested in building a fair economy where all can benefit from their efforts. Dealing with this would be critical to development of the society proposed by a *science of religion and ethics*.

However, the foregoing doesn't alter the fact that corporations do have the capability to utilize many different skills and abilities. They have the potential to be structured so as to work with and help develop Enlightened Persons. They do need a broad range of talents thereby providing opportunities for many different kinds of people during many different stages of development to do the work that fits for them and that they can do best. Or, if this is not possible then to earn sufficient salary so they can put in the least amount of time necessary, allowing a maximum of free time to use as desired. And more will be said about this in later pages in the discussion of adopting policies of no growth – in population and the economy. Of course all of this requires that appropriate regulations be developed and properly used.

As indicated elsewhere (Volume II, Chapter 34, "Work and a Science of Religion and Ethics"), [12] the foregoing approach conflicts with the paradigm Robert Reich describes in *Future Of Success* [13] underway in the U.S. since the '70s and predicts will be adopted by the rest of the world over time. This is due to technology and globalization leading to products and services powered by what he characterizes as "better, faster, cheaper." The foregoing places a person into a life that is driven by work, and all other issues – family, friendship, recreation, education, and such – become valued only insofar as they support that goal.

It is crucial to recognize that Reich [13] is describing a society in which the citizens are living a life guided by economic materialism with no other basis except possibly in a future heaven after death. Success in life means material success. More and more the U.S. has been moving to permit this as the only option. There is no room for mental illness, universal education, and anything else that gets in the way of bottom-line profits. The prison system has been expanded and focused so as to make it easy to take those who do not cooperate, permanently out of society into an expanded prison system. There they are subjected to either meaningless warehousing, or transfer to prisons run by profit-making corporations using poorly maintained workers to produce low cost items for our consumer-driven economy. This turn of events definitely is a challenge to the ideas and goals of a *science of religion and ethics*. It will certainly pose a hurdle in moving toward the light at the end of the tunnel.

But of course the essential foundation for this whole distortion of human society lies in unregulated alpha males/females. Current societies permit such people to achieve total control rather than being controlled by the more comprehensive long-term needs of humanity.

As Reich struggles to point out, concerned people may want to limit some of the effects of this new paradigm. However, be that as it may, it seems worthwhile to examine economics as it has commonly been discussed in introductory university courses. Economists have long talked about supply and demand, inflation, theory of marginal productivity, free trade, export-import balances, gross national product, using a person's selfishness and greed to satisfy the needs of others, and such. These economists, however, have treated economics as something it is not -- a system of sufficient validity to replace a *science of religion and ethics* as the science that lays the basis for understanding and recommendations about the way people treat and judge each other.

A quotation by George Soule exposes the fallacy of unwarranted faith in economics. He writes, "It is one thing to be able to say, given certain premises, that certain conclusions must follow; quite another to be sure that the chosen premises are typical of the objective world, or that what is excluded from any particular logical process may not be more influential in determining the future than what is included." [14]

The science of economics contains much of value, and has even greater potential for the future when guided by a *science of religion and ethics*. However, while economists may teach that increasing the unemployment rate will reduce inflation, it is beyond the capacity of economics to decide if this is the best way to reduce inflation. Or, whether reducing inflation is the most important goal. How a society should apply knowledge from economics to achieve societal goals lies outside of economic theory. Economics is only a tool (like the rest of the sciences) for reaching the goals of a *science of religion and ethics* that comes first and economics afterward. Society first needs to decide what its goals are and then it can use knowledge of economics to help achieve those goals. The machinery of economics does not operate in a vacuum. People's ideas, emotions, and beliefs influence the way an economy functions and needs to therefore be influenced by ideas that go beyond the "laws" of economics. See VOLUME II, Chapter 14, "Bionomics -- Economics and the Enlightened Community," [15] where an analysis of Michael Rothschild's *BIONOMICS: The Inevitability of Capitalism* is presented. It provides a new paradigm vis-à-vis capitalism and its role in a modern society.

An extremely exciting development in the area of economics is being explored by the Evolution Institute [16]. Co-founder David Sloan Wilson gets to the core of the matter when he says, "Economic theory was originally inspired by physics and led to a huge body of formal theory based on assumptions that are required for mathematical tractability but make little sense from a psychological or evolutionary perspective.... For decades these assumptions were justified by the apparent success of the policies based upon them. Recent failures in economic policy have provided a sobering wake-up call: *Effective public policy needs to be based on a more realistic conception of human nature than economic theory has provided in the past.*" [17] [Emphasis in original.]

Sloan continues, "There is widespread agreement that economic theory must become based on a more accurate conception of human nature to successfully guide public policy. That is the objective of behavioral economics, which has become prominent within the larger field of economics. However, behavioral economics needs to become more broadly based in the human behavioral sciences, which in turn must be grounded in evolutionary theory. The purpose of this working group [of the Evolution Institute] is to properly ground the field of behavioral economics in evolutionary theory. This objective, in turn, will require an integration of subfields within the human behavioral sciences, including evolutionary psychology, cognitive psychology, applied behavioral analysis, sociology, cultural anthropology, and neurobiology. These subfields need to be brought together before they can be related to an applied science such as behavioral economics." [17]

Associated with all this is the question, must there always be poverty? A person in poverty is apparently not productive enough to share adequately in the wealth of their society. Is the foregoing realistic? Poverty does not seem to be necessary in the modern world. Science and knowledge hold out the potential of unlimited wealth for everyone. It seems to me that all people could be productive enough to live comfortably if their efforts were properly utilized, and if they had the benefit of a *science of religion and ethics* and the structures required to achieve its goals.

In an Enlightened Community all people need to have the opportunity to be productive, the chance to contribute to the economic well-being of their society. At the same time they need to be able to maintain themselves at a satisfactory level of income depending on their goals, motivations, productive capacity, level of preparation and training, type of work, amount of time devoted to work, and similar things. To put ideas about income and productivity in an Enlightened Community into the proper perspective, see VOLUME II, Chapter 34, "Work and a Science of Religion and Ethics," [12] and "Other Support Organizations -- Organization for Universal Employment" in Chapter 20.

All people in an Enlightened Community need to be able to develop as people. They need to be helped to become aware of their capacity and capabilities. This is important so that they may achieve the most by finding a creative outlet and doing the necessary work that best expands them as a person. Also, they should be doing work that they enjoy, or if the foregoing is not possible, work that takes as little of their time as possible, but is productive enough to allow them a satisfactory living. For many people once they obtain a certain minimum amount of material goods their rate of needs would decrease. After fulfilling basic needs, some people might want to spend only a few hours a week at work they find uninteresting in order to earn the necessities of life. The rest of their time they might spend at the things that would make their life a wonderful and enjoyable experience. This will not come about automatically, but only with the utmost planning, cooperation, commitment, and effort.

To the degree that Robert Reich and Barry Lynn have correctly assessed what is happening in the U.S. economy and therefore the world economy it is critical that fundamental changes be made. And these suggested changes actually fit exactly with the goals of a *science of religion and ethics*. The core of this is steady-state economics and population.

"No growth" – in population and the economy – needs to be the aim of a *science of religion and ethics*. Both of these have been non-discussable in the political realm for the past several decades. But we need to now change that. Fortunately, "Mother Jones" in the May/June 2010 issue [18] has opened the conversation on both of these. On the economic front Clive Thompson gives us some good foundational material. He mentions Peter Victor's book of 2008 [18] and Tim Jackson's in 2009 [20] as well as related ideas worth study on this. They also mention Herman Daly [21] who has written widely on steady-state economics. These authors provide a good foundation for thinking about growth in the economic realm and how to adopt a whole new paradigm -- no growth!!

In the cited issue "Mother Jones" provides some in-depth thinking on the population problem by reporter Julia Whitty. Although her article provides less than promised in the title, at least it takes a serious look at population matters by sharing what she saw in her visit to India and verification of the decades' old observation that the best way to reduce population is to educate a female. [22] But part of promoting that strategy is to have micro-loans available so these women can apply their new knowledge and ideas to start a business and increase their wealth as well as the wealth of those around them. Reporter Whitty does a good job of sharing her visits to people and places relevant to this issue. All of this needs to be more deeply dealt with by a *science of religion and ethics*.

Getting back to the overview, it now seems clear to me that in an Enlightened Community there needs to be governmental planning. This would involve the investment of a portion of the national wealth for the achievement of certain long-range goals that keep the economy and society progressing -- toward allowing more and more people to achieve a *sustainable feeling of well-being*. Examples might be: better health, cost-effective ways to use solar energy, purification of sea water at a cost to make its use practical, harnessing thermonuclear fusion, space travel, producing adequate healthy/nutritious food available to everyone, gathering basic knowledge about all life to maintain robust ecosystems, and such. Investments in government-planned projects might -- particularly in times of recession -- make up a significant part of the national budget.

Effort needs to be focused not just on things that require only a few people working on a limited budget. It should also be focused on projects that may require huge expenditures of wealth (spread over a correspondingly reasonable length of time). But the point is that this knowledge, structure, or capacity is essential in order to achieve and maintain an Enlightened Community. It needs to have a productive payoff that contributes useful social resources and/or knowledge and leads to more efficient results. It must not be a black hole (such as a war of aggression) with immoral goals that waste lives, creative energy, and resources. Examples from U.S. history of positive governmental planning include the construction and development as well as the building of many dams in the 1930s and the road improvement program of the 1950s. This governmental planning of the future might require comparable expenditures of resources before profitable results could be achieved.

These projects would be like a bank in which worker hours and creativity could be stored, and tools for future prosperity could be developed. These would be part of the effort to ensure employment to all workers and make them productive when they might otherwise not be so. Plus this would help harness creative energy and direct it toward improving the quality of life for everyone. In important ways the foregoing describes how science and technology work when functioning at their best.

SHARED AFFECTION

Human beings are social animals. We need other people to function at our best. We need to have friends to rely on, soul mates to provide nurturing love, companions to talk to, and allies to help us in time of need.

Many troubles can befall us when we are isolated from others, but when we have a community and good friends to stand beside us we can overcome the perplexities, complications, hardships and pitfalls of these situations. We should all have pals and closest of all a mate.

But as Polly Young-Eisendrath warns in _YOU'RE NOT WHAT I EXPECTED: Love After The Romance Has Ended_, "But consider the possibility that... [marital] intimacy has never before been tried. Only in the last few decades have married people sought intimacy. Previously they viewed marriage as a contract and the relationship mostly as a form of business. If it was enjoyable, that was lucky, but generally it was not expected to be."[23]

There are few things more psychologically rewarding than the joining together of two people in shared love. But this union of minds and bodies is not the same as the love in fairy tales and "true" romance novels where the characters do not defecate, belch, sweat -- in short, live. Fairy tale romance images come out of our "tribal" genetic propensities. However, like all the rest of human living an affiliative relationship between two adults changes dramatically when it is based on the person's "wisdom" potential rather than their "tribal" genetic propensities. Up to this point society is still presenting models of relationships coming out of our "tribal" genetic propensities. Therefore, it should be no surprise that most marriages in the U.S. end in divorce and those that continue are rarely very satisfactory to the people concerned. But there is much to learn and be learned about in this whole process.

One interesting area of research involving affiliative love is that initiated by John Alan Lee, a sociologist at the University of Toronto, Canada. The core of his approach involves dividing romantic love into different ways of loving. His research has led him to postulate various love styles used by people in different affiliative love relationships. VOLUME II, Chapter 7, "Romantic Love and a Science of Religion and Ethics" [24] tackles the area of affiliative love using Lee's ideas and research as a starting point in moving this toward congruency with our "wisdom" potential.

Dr. Young-Eisendrath's book quoted above is another resource that needs careful study. She is a Jungian analyst who does couples therapy in association with her husband to help their clients reach "mature dependence." This is a bond between equals utilizing their close relationship as the ground of the self. "It is a willingness to give as well as take, and to value a friend as much as oneself." It develops when a couple has "survived the breakdown" of their romance and "the disillusionment of seeing each other as disappointments." [25] Through therapeutic understanding of the dynamics that establish false expectations for marriage, and the projections onto the partner of a person's own images, the "romantic aura" is replaced by a new pattern never before available in human history, mature dependence. It is very unlikely that any couple can achieve this state without a shared desire to reach it, and possibly then only with therapeutic assistance.

There are multiple challenges in the area of romantic love. This may be an area where the Knowledge Bank, an improved model of affiliative love, and complete personal records can be beneficial. When the factors are understood that make two people attractive to each other in a sustainable way (congruent with our "wisdom" potential), a computer program might be developed to permit such people to obtain information about each other. Thus, a person will not need to search haphazardly throughout life to find a mate, or to marry for the wrong reasons, or not at all. (Also see "Other Support Organizations -- The Computer Connection," in Chapter 20; and VOLUME II, Chapter 8, "Finding A Partner to Love.") [26]

Another important area is explored in VOLUME II, Chapter 5.A, "Intimacy and a Science of Religion and Ethics," [2] that draws heavily from *In Search of Intimacy* by Philip Shaver and Carin Rubenstein. Other elements of intimacy, love, and romance are discussed in VOLUME II, Chapters 6, 7, 8, and 9. [3]

One part of the effort to help people find love would be to guide them toward understanding what a successful love relationship consists of and how they can achieve what is necessary. The second is to put them in contact with people with whom they have the potential to develop a nurturing, satisfying, growing relationship.

As indicated in VOLUME II, Chapter 7 and 8, [3] finding, developing, and sustaining a loving, nurturing relationship and marriage would be enhanced by learning what such a relationship requires. A difficulty exists in doing this because all the ways we learn about love are flawed and depend on our raw "tribal" genetic propensities. These processes prevent developing the "wisdom" potential as it relates to love. If we are looking for a particular thing and what is needed is the opposite, our success is unlikely. My guess is that most people in modern society have all kinds of erroneous ideas about what they actually need in order to have a fulfilling affiliative love relationship and marriage. Fairy tales, romance novels, television, movies, and current wisdom in general are less than helpful in this regard.

As indicated earlier Dr. Young-Eisendrath presents an interesting model that points out where some of the serious problems come from that get in the way of marital love relationships. And since her goal is exactly the same as mine -- that is, determining how two adults can establish and maintain a marriage relationship based on complete equality between the partners -- her book is examined in depth in VOLUME II, Chapter 9-A, "Analysis of *You're Not What I Expected*." [27]

Once we understand our own needs, shortcomings, possibilities, and such then it would be useful to have a way to tap into the massive resources of our community and find the ideal mate (our soul mate). For this only a computer with an adequate support network will do the job. The power and potential of computers could, if properly utilized, guide anyone to an enduring and wonderful love. This data can be analyzed by computers to help people meet others who share the attributes, interests, life-style, and such necessary to build a loving, supportive relationship. This whole process needs to continuously be studied, expanded, and changed as experience accumulates and errors and deficiencies in existing ideas are found. Centers for the Practical Application of Wisdom would have a primary responsibility for the foregoing with their "Knowledge Bank" as its central tool.

Since the sexual drive is such a basic motivating force -- healthy, important, a potent factor in joyful living -- a few comments about it are in order. It would seem difficult to find any idea held by decent people more foolish than the one that states that marriage and sexual intimacy can only decently exist together. However, one belief that might qualify -- at least among religious fundamentalists -- is that masturbation is wrong. This idea has probably been one of the most erroneous and destructive ideas that has been promoted in any society. The stress accumulated from sexual tension has often provided the final push that has led the vulnerable person to tragic behavior. As for marriage, it should rest on a firmer foundation that coitus. And sexual intercourse like food is necessary to healthy development. Abstinence as a sexual practice is comparable to abstinence from learning to read with equally self-destructive and socially destructive results.

Many reasons are given why sexual intercourse without marriage should be avoided. These almost always go back to a culture's concepts of morality. In some cultures this is supported by the threat of death for transgressors. In other cultures it boils down to more pragmatic arguments often with a moral basis (soiled merchandise, virginity is a virtue, there is only one true love, and such). But usually the argument includes issues of practical concern (pregnancy, sexually transmitted disease, exploitation, and such) the cause of which could be overcome with proper effort. The current moral arguments can probably only be discarded as the Judeo-Christian-Islamic traditions that foster them are replaced. The practical issues require a more focused effort by society to solve.

Certainly, a more realistic attitude concerning the sexual aspect of a human being's life is necessary. Sexual intercourse should not be seen as an ominous, all-consuming, degrading act that some folk religions make it out to be. Nor should it be seen as Freud interpreted it, as the most basic and intense social drive for the individual. As pointed out elsewhere the drive for social bonding and physical intimacy is humanity's most basic social drive. Rather, sexual activities should be recognized as a vital, healthy, important part of a caring, romantic relationship in marriage or -- as indicated below -- without marriage. "... [T]he following advantages have been claimed for.... [pre-marital coitus]" [28]

1. It may satisfy a physiologic need for sexual outlet
2. It may become a source of immediate physical and psychological satisfaction
3. If there is no guilt, it may increase a person's ability to function more effectively in other, non-sexual fields
4. It is more valuable than solitary sexual activity for developing a person's capacity to make emotional adjustments with other people
5. It may develop a person's capacity to make the particular sorts of emotional adjustments that are needed in marital relationships
6. It may provide training in the sorts of physical techniques that may be involved in marital coitus

7. It may test the capacities of two people to make satisfactory sexual adjustments after marriage
8. It is easier to learn to make emotional and physical adjustments at an earlier age; they are learned with greater difficulty after marriage
9. Failure in a pre-marital relationship is socially less disastrous than failure after marriage
10. Pre-marital coitus may lead to marriage
11. In at least some social groups, an individual may acquire status by fitting into the group pattern of behavior"

Regardless of the validity of any or all of the above benefits, a relationship between people either married or unmarried needs to be a sharing process if the couple desires to achieve a *sustainable feeling of well-being*. And it needs to be mutually beneficial, fulfilling, and satisfactory for the same reason. It needs to not be a bullying, threatening, scheming, dishonest kind of relationship if it is to be mutually satisfactory, at least for Enlightened Persons. These behaviors all make it unsatisfactory for both parties in different ways, and unworthy of a person. To achieve the goals of this Way of Wisdom any relationship whether viewed as a lifetime union or not, needs to contain the key factor of a lifelong relationship; that is, the model that it is a relationship between equals and all feelings and behaviors come out of this recognition -- trust, confidence, mutual satisfaction, and so on.

In addition we might seriously consider the ideas of Terrence Deacon [29] that marriage is a deeply symbolic act that involves not only the person, but also their community and may even have been the practice that started our species on its journey toward symbolic language. If this is the case its roots are very deep and may influence us in ways not always obvious.

RECEIVING VS. GIVING

One of the prime ideas that gets in the way of helping others is the idea of exploitation. I define exploitation as taking advantage of another; unfair exchange; taking without giving comparable value. Western culture teaches that human beings have a natural bias to exploit other people. The claim is made that this desire to exploit others is always lurking in any interaction. We can fight it sometimes. But we need to always guard ourselves against it and we need to always expect it in others.

At a certain level the foregoing is true. Because of the raw "tribal" genetic propensities, particularly the "us vs. them" and "dominance/submission" drives, some people have a strong propensity to dominate and treat others without empathy, compassion, and such feeling of fellowship. When a person has not been sufficiently socialized this may lead to behavior where they take advantage of, that is, exploit others. U.S. cultural values have supported these propensities particularly as part of the "business ethic." As a result this component of learned behavior encourages exploiting others. These propensities need to be refocused for anyone who desires to become an Enlightened Person and help create an Enlightened Community.

In U.S. society people are taught by parents and other family members to be dominant or submissive. Based on their own personal drives they respond to these teachings either positively or negatively, or in varying degrees. However, this "dominance/submission" behavior is not congruent with becoming an Enlightened Person and building an Enlightened Community. An Enlightened Person needs to be aware of and fully develop their own personal power. They need to develop the capabilities made available with the evolution of symbolic communication if they are to achieve a *sustainable feeling of well-being*. Since in an Enlightened Community the individual person is considered to be the only worthy focus of ultimate concern, developing Enlightened Persons is crucial.

Current research makes clear that this dominance drive can be encouraged or discouraged depending on how a society treats it; that is, depending on the culture's memes. "In egalitarian societies, men intent on commanding others are systematically thwarted in their attempts. The weapons used by their supposed inferiors are ridicule, manipulation of public opinion, and disobedience... the would-be chief who tries to order others around is openly told how amusing his pretensions are. The power of leaders is thus delineated by an alliance from below." [30] Hopefully, in an Enlightened Community effort to redirect dominance drives would be carried out in a more integrative manner that would help such people channel their drives so as to be productive for themselves and for the Community.

It is my contention that no one can ever better themself by exploiting another person. No goal or benefit directed toward gaining a *sustainable feeling of well-being* can be achieved by taking advantage of someone else. I believe just the opposite.

Any act knowingly done to exploit another must erect a barrier in the path leading toward a *sustainable feeling of well-being*. Any act unknowingly done will normally have the same effect. It indicates a lack of knowledge, sensitivity, and support. These deficiencies will prevent the person from advancing in the right direction until changes are made.

People will not have achieved a *sustainable feeling of well-being* before they discover the greatest satisfaction of all, loving other people with complete devotion and doing all things to help everyone become an Enlightened Person. (Also see VOLUME II, Chapter 6, "Love and a Science of Religion and Ethics.") [31] "There comes a time in the development of ourselves when receiving from others, that is the essence of selfishness, gives way to the irresistible urge to give to others -- to grow beyond the limits of a person's own skin, whether in the creation of a family or the building of a good society." [32]

This love of other human beings must not be what psychiatrists call "reaction formation" [33] but an honest, healthy love. Otherwise, it will be deficient. For example, it may be superficial and stereotyped. Or, it may be devious -- "The reason I must burn you at the stake and watch your pain as the flames slowly roast you alive is because I love you and this is the only way you can be cleansed of your sins" (one of the rationalizations of the Holy Inquisition.)

Helping other people because of love needs to always be more than heaping acts of kindness on them regardless of their level of development. The person who has not yet achieved a *sustainable feeling of well-being* may not be able to appreciate or benefit from some acts of kindness. People need to be helped to develop their higher self, their "wisdom" potential, and not be diverted into their raw "tribal" genetic propensities. Human life can be filled with happiness and joy when people live within the context of a *science of religion and ethics*. A way needs to be found to clarify how all people can experience love of others. If suffering is only lessened, additional change is needed. People need to be helped with their material and emotional needs. Also, they need help to satisfy their intellectual requirements and yearning to be creative. The foregoing, plus whatever else is necessary, needs to be done to help each person achieve a *sustainable feeling of well-being.*

We cannot obtain lasting satisfaction except by doing those things for others that can help them move toward a *sustainable feeling of well-being.* This does not mean that a person should not be concerned with themselves, just the opposite. Love of others is in fact the highest form of self-love. That which is truly best for others is also what is best for us. Of course until we live in an Enlightened Community we cannot always provide others what they truly need. In these cases we just have to do the best that circumstances allow. And to act so that we continue on our path toward a *sustainable feeling of well-being.*

When people achieve a *sustainable feeling of well-being,* they are as rich as a person can be. They have all their core needs fulfilled and are focusing their life energy in ways that are vitally important. This will continue to be true not only throughout their life, but throughout the life of our species. People need to give and do for the sheer pleasure involved. When people are found who want only to take, an Enlightened Community needs to try to help them achieve a higher sphere of existence. "... [P]eople who want always to receive and never to give are cases of arrested development. They are to be pitied and helped to develop..." [34] Helped not by speeches and chastisement, but by effective, appropriate aid. They need to be helped to attain the physical necessities of life and more important helped to attain the values of the mind. Anyone will be deterred from movement toward a *sustainable feeling of well-being* until they understand the truth in the statement: the most enduring satisfaction comes from loving and helping others.

CHAPTER 16

NINTH WAY OF WISDOM: INCREASE KNOWLEDGE

NINTH WAY OF WISDOM: Work to increase knowledge and all creative and artistic endeavors. Adopt an inspiring life goal.

An inspiring life goal is taken to be a critical part of achieving a *sustainable feeling of well-being*. Such a purpose might help to provide the center around which all the other Ways could be organized to fit into a person's life. This kind of goal would seldom be far from a person's mind. It would energize their life and sustain them in their darkest hours. It would move them into ever new realms as they pursued the twists and turns required in their on-going effort to move ever closer toward their goal. However, ideally this goal would be of such a nature that it could never be reached, but should have multiple preliminary goals to be mastered and achieved on the path toward it.

People are always wondering what is on the other side of the mountain, and just going and learning brings pleasure. The search itself brings personal rewards to the seeker. The new fruits discovered over the mountain bring something to everyone and this can be infinitely more rewarding.

Someone takes a brush and various paints, or a hammer, chisel, and stone, or a myriad of other things and with them, perseverance and creativity produce an exciting and pleasing result that brings a great feeling of accomplishment. What has been created can inspire, excite, and in general produce positive benefits for the rest of humanity.

For this Way, however, it is the feeling within the individual that is being focused on. To the degree that it gives humanity something, it also fulfills the Second Way of Wisdom (Seek to maintain and develop humanity). The spice of a *sustainable feeling of well-being* is the discovery and creation of new things. This is the Way that makes all the other Ways possible. The prospect of the continued discovery and creation of new things makes life challenging and interesting. Everyone who in any way can enjoy these pursuits should have the opportunity. Those who lack an obvious focus for their interests should be helped so they will be able to find the joy of discovering and creating.

Whether this <u>Way</u> is achieved by the creation of paintings, poetry, music, literary prose; the discovery of a new biological species, subatomic particle, comet; or better way to clean a sewer is to a certain extent unimportant. The important thing is that it is enjoyable and pleases the person involved, and is not knowingly hurtful to anyone else. When this situation exists, humanity cannot help but benefit. If every person adds but one pebble to a pile, how rapidly would a mountain rise.

But it is essential that the person revel in their activity. They need to feel good as a result of what they have produced. Some of our greatest geniuses never achieved more than a fleeting moment of joy from the inspired, seminal creations they produced, or that they worked on. Sometimes this was due to an overdeveloped sense of self-criticism. Other prodigies could not revel in their creations because these works were seen only as tools to achieve power over others. Whenever faulty thinking prevents the person from enjoying and sharing their creations they need to work harder on the Sixth Way of Wisdom (Work to be psychologically healthy).

The "Knowledge Bank," the universal computer information reservoir, mentioned under the Eighth Way of Wisdom (Help and be helped by other people) would be useful in achieving this <u>Way</u>. It would aid people in gathering new information in order to pursue their interests and achieve a positive result. The individual would be helped in the preceding way to find everything known including aesthetic material in its most useful form in order to increase the person's opportunities and fulfillment. See VOLUME II, Chapter 31, "Art and A Science of Religion and Ethics." [1] And the "Organization to Enhance the Quality of Human Life" discussed in "Organizing for An Enlightened Community -- Other Support Organizations," and the Second Way of Wisdom (Seek to advance humanity) would also be useful here. The Second Way and Ninth Way are actually opposite sides of the same coin. An Organization to Enhance the Quality of Human Life would help in the achievement of this <u>Way</u>

by providing a structure that any interested person could utilize to fulfill this Way.

Creative endeavors should lead to expanding human learning.

A key question that comes up when we consider increasing knowledge and understanding of the Universe is whether or not humanity should avoid exploring areas thought to be harmful -- "Forbidden Knowledge." The answer would seem to be an emphatic, no! Human beings can never be sure what knowledge or research is going to pay off the most. Therefore, humanity should never brand certain paths as off-limits in the absence of overwhelming evidence. If such an area is found the conclusion that it embodies overwhelming danger needs to be always open for reconsideration. However, we need to of course travel dangerous paths with care. At the same time it appears to be obvious that the highest priority should be to take routes that appear likely to be most rewarding. But it seems necessary to assume that humanity will be able to use all knowledge in some way. It is up to society to find the usefulness of each discovery/ insight/creation. Discoveries are just as useful, that allow humanity to advance to further knowledge as data that itself is used to help us predict, or improve human well-being. Also, discoveries that clarify a threat to humanity are of vital importance.

Up to this point human activity has not been guided by the realization that Human Beings Are the Ultimate Reference System, that the goal of a person's life is to maintain and develop the species, and that this can best be done when each person achieves a *sustainable feeling of well-being*. Therefore, the process of searching for knowledge and dealing with new discoveries and applications of that knowledge has tended to neglect personal and social long-term satisfaction. At the same time legitimate concerns such as environmental and ecological problems have been pursued irrationally and in a mis-focused way occasionally.

Examples of the foregoing in my mind include the heated arguments about the use of fission reactors to produce electricity carried out since the late '40s. Many people have been deeply concerned about any use of radioactive materials. Yet, radioactivity is a powerful tool that has benefited almost all areas of research and knowledge. As a result society should be supporting tremendous study into all aspects of radioactivity. A prime area of research should include the total understanding of all things involved in causing harm to the human body and the discovery of prevention and treatment procedures. Advance in one area has always demanded advance in many other fields. And this goes back at least to the time when tools allowed over-hunting that may have been a primary factor in making agriculture necessary.

It is very likely that an important step forward for humanity involving generation of power through fission reactors has been stopped by people acting under the banner of ecological concerns. They focus on the harmful effects of nuclear reactors, but fail to put it in the context that every mode of producing electricity (coal, hydro, natural gas) has an ecological price -- just like every other behavior (performed, or not performed). They claim to be working for a world fit for humans to live in. But whether through ignorance or stealth they have an agenda that does not in fact have human well-being as its concern. The environmental movement grew out of recognition by many thoughtful people over the past 200 years that unregulated technology can cause wide-spread destruction to this wondrous planet that is our only home and has the potential to make it uninhabitable. However, as this movement has grown in power and prestige it has attracted people whose goals are actually to return the earth to a period of "primitive beauty" when fewer than 10,000,000 humans occupied it and lived much like gorillas and chimpanzees do today.

A superb example of the foregoing point is provided by the Pirahã People, an indigenous hunter-gatherer tribe in the Amazon, who many people would hold up as a model of the Good Life. I hope my discussion in the Sixth Way makes it clear I do not share that opinion.

More recently the human intervention altering plant and animal genomes in order to increase their value to humanity has been attacked. This area of research has the potential to end hunger and create abundance, not only of food, but also for medicine, building material, manufacturing, solving the problem of carbon dioxide in the atmosphere, and an unlimited number of other things. Legitimate questions need to be raised about many of these procedures. But blanket opposition is reminiscent of a Luddite mentality.

It seems to me that human beings need to begin to take cautious, but responsible steps to guide earth's evolution so this planet will continue to be our home and to maintain a wide diversity of species because that is important to human well-being.

Neo-environmentalists are opposed to any such effort. They act as though they are intent on keeping the Earth "the way God made it." They are ready not only to oppose pollution, but to also oppose any effort by scientists that they interpret as "manipulating nature."

The following article discusses an example of this phenomenon where an experiment in which a minor quantity of tiny particles of iron were released into a small area of the Pacific Ocean to test their effects on increasing the growth of plants in an otherwise barren area; it was opposed as "manipulating nature." [2]

"MANIPULATING ENVIRONMENT FOR SCIENCE GOES TOO FAR, SOME SAY"

By Chris Woolston, 18 July 1995

For better or worse, the recent iron experiment in the Pacific could represent the future of ocean science.

"In the past, ocean scientists went out to pick up the clues Mother Nature gave us," said participant Eden Rue, an analytical chemistry graduate student from the University of California, Santa Cruz. "Now we're actually manipulating environments and making predictions."

But this vision of the future concerns environmentalists and even a few scientists.

"Where do you draw the line between a major experiment and an insult on the environment?" asked Sallie Chisholm, a professor of marine sciences at the Massachusetts Institute of Technology. Chisholm said she supports the iron experiments -- she had students on the cruise -- but she sees a clear need for caution.

For others, the iron experiments clearly cross the line. "You can't have scientists running around manipulating nature," said Kelly

Quirke, a spokesperson for Greenpeace. "That lack of humility is only going to get us into deep trouble."

Researchers maintain that the iron experiments are harmless to the ocean environment. The effects on nature are short-lived, but the improvement in scientific knowledge could be permanent, they say.

Kenneth Coale, the chief scientist on the research cruise, stressed that the experiment was far from a large-scale disturbance. "Globally, it was inconsequential," he said. "It was nothing compared to what's produced at the Santa Cruz waste treatment plant every day."

Kenneth Bruland, a chemical oceanographer at the University of California, Santa Cruz, agrees.

"It's really still a small scale experiment," he said. "This experiment bridges the gap between the scale and complexity of a bottle experiment and the scale and complexity of the whole ocean."

"Such bridges," he maintains, "may be the only access scientists have to the inner workings of life in the ocean."

Environmentalists like Kelly Quirke of Greenpeace talk about the need for others to demonstrate more humility. However, he expresses the neo-environmentalist's own total lack of humility. They have the "Truth" and they are willing to go to any lengths to impose it on others. They should rightfully be concerned about all the things people have done/are doing that degrade our environment. But when they express the view that we must leave the earth alone and it will take care of us, they are spouting erroneous dogma. Any serious study of Earth's history makes it clear that random events favor species randomly depending on the specifics of the event and the characteristics of the species. If we think nature will favor our species selectively we are expressing dogma, not evolutionary history. Human beings have a special ecological niche because we have the power to control evolution within the limits of our constantly expanding knowledge.

I believe that an ever increasing amount of human planning and behavior needs to reflect an acknowledgment that evolution, like national economies, needs to be guided by human intelligence if we are to develop and maintain conditions such that increasing numbers of people will achieve a *sustainable feeling of well-being*. All such decisions need to incorporate a prudent humility based on the recognition that no matter how much we know, it is always less than what we don't know. Therefore, the potential for disaster is very real if we act too fast and in too many directions simultaneously. We should not fail in our responsibility to study so we can better avoid disaster. We need to keep the channels of communication open so every voice can be heard and all wisdom utilized. And we need to work to maintain balance in the world. This balance needs to sustain the conditions for human life -- and not just to live, but also to live well. (For more on this topic see VOLUME II, Chapter 28, "Managing Change in an Enlightened Community.") [3]

However, if the goal of helping all other people become Enlightened Persons is kept clearly in mind then every step taken in increasing knowledge will always consider how this knowledge can be used to help people, not to harm them. And, we need to constantly consider that failure to act has moral implications in terms of maintenance of our species in such a way that each person can achieve a *sustainable feeling of well-being.*

CHAPTER 17

TENTH WAY OF WISDOM: PROVIDE EVERY CHILD A NURTURING HOME

TENTH WAY OF WISDOM: Support efforts to ensure that every child is provided a loving, nurturing environment, and all the things necessary to become an Enlightened Person.

Perhaps the best place to begin the search for a foundation for this Way is to start where I started. That was by studying Alice Miller. Some of her core thinking is provided below [1].

The things that Alice Miller discusses in her book, **"The Newly Recognized, Shattering Effects of Child Abuse,"** are probably the core requirement for an Enlightened Community and an Enlightened Person. Unless a society takes these issues into account it will spend most of its energy, resources, and creativity trying to overcome the effects of poor child rearing.

She tells us, "For some years now there has been proof that the devastating effects of the traumatization of children take their inevitable toll on society. This knowledge concerns every single one of us, and -- if disseminated widely enough -- should lead to fundamental changes in society, above all to a halt in the blind escalation of violence."

She points out further that "Childhood abuse in all its forms including neglect, indoctrination, and perpetuating ignorance is the greatest barrier for anyone preventing them from achieving a *sustainable feeling of well-being*. In order to build a better world we must fill it with better people. 'Better people,' includes having a more nurturing childhood. But this doesn't mean a childhood filled with idleness (endless TV) and mindless pursuits (all games and no study). Rather it means a chance to nurture curiosity, experience personal power, and obtain clarity about what life is for. It also means being able to do things in the world that are valued by others."

However, there is one critical area of child rearing that Dr. Miller has thus far totally overlooked. That is the area of nurturing touch. She speaks eloquently and focuses on every dimension of abuse. But probably because of her own up-bringing she misses an equally important point.

We must do more than avoid abusing children physically, psychologically, socially, and sexually. As indicated in the Eighth Way, "Intimacy, Physical Affection, Nurturing Touch," and VOLUME II, Chapter 4, "Nurturing Touch and a Sustainable Feeling That Your Life Has Meaning") [2] they also must have physical affection; that is, nurturing touch and loving support if they are to be fully prepared to embark on the road toward becoming an Enlightened Person.

CHAPTER 18

ELEVENTH WAY OF WISDOM: MAKE YOUR LIFE A SPIRITUAL QUEST

ELEVENTH WAY OF WISDOM: Make of your life a spiritual quest. Work to become an Enlightened Person. Use the fundamentalist propensity to produce Enlightened Communities.

Related to the belief in magic and the power of wishing propensity, but different is the human fascination with the unknowable. Human beings have a need to identify with the spiritual, and the transcendent -- with the eternal, with the ultimate, with the infinite, with truth/Truth. This is commonly called a spiritual quest. Up to the present this need has almost always been filtered through the individual's magic/wishing propensity and this has been one of the primary ways that societies have been diverted from developing a naturalistic religion and ethical system to replace supernatural religions. This has prevented the development of clear societal goals that are compatible with our "wisdom" potential provided by the language ability.

But equally important to all of this has been the fundamentalist propensity. Up to this point the spiritual quest has been mainly diverted into what is currently being called fundamentalist religions. There are two conflicts for a *science of religion and ethics* here: 1) People following this path are deeply committed, fully focused, energized, and almost single-mindedly directed. This represents a tremendous human resource. As discussed in Chapter 11, "Fundamentalism Observed," the fundamentalist propensity has been almost completely diverted to stopping human progress toward the light at the end of the tunnel. Science was largely presented in a way they couldn't get fully involved in and committed to. 2) Because of their search for what is fundamental up to today most of these people end up getting trapped in the relative; that is, cultural relativism based on their religion. This may have happened because nothing objectively better was available to them. Hopefully a *science of religion and ethics* will change that.

A *science of religion and ethics* must provide guidance in satisfying this longing for transcendence, this spiritual quest. And it must be done in a way that prevents the person from becoming lost in an overwhelming jumble of fantasy and make-believe with no beacon to guide their journey. This is the kind of challenge that the Ways of Wisdom need to address. A *science of religion and ethics* proposes that this feeling of transcendence needs to be achieved through the process of seeing oneself first and foremost as a member of a biological species. All else flows from that. [1] Our active, loving participation in human society -- in the creation and maintenance of an Enlightened Community -- needs to provide the Enlightened Person a deep sense of transcendence as real and vibrant as that often achieved through illusion; for example, a connection with God or other aspects of the supernatural.

A *science of religion and ethics* proposes that because of the importance of this matter and the fact that up till now it has almost always been satisfied through a supernatural approach, perhaps this area needs special focus. My own take is that mysticism utilizes the "tribal" genetic propensity to believe in magic and the power of wishing. Whatever circuits in the brain support the belief in magic propensity can with training and practice be expanded to create a very powerful result, the "mystical mind." A well-developed model for how "the mystical mind" works has been developed by two scientists, Eugene d'Aquili and Andrew B. Newberg in their book, *THE MYSTICAL MIND: Probing the Biology of Religious Experience.* [2] These authors propose very specific brain mechanisms for all the various feelings usually perceived as mystical that come out of meditation, religious ritual, near-death experience, and such. However, after laying a firm foundation for the naturalistic understanding of these experiences they veer off in a post-modernist direction and take the position that the universe demonstrated by these experiences (especially deep meditation) cannot be explained away as "just the workings of the brain." They justify their conclusion based on the observation that this experience is sometimes perceived as being more real than the experiences of "baseline reality" (d'Aquili and Newberg's term for what we experience through our regular senses). They propose that a phenomenological interpretation is all we can rely on to decide which is the "real" universe. And, since these mystical experiences are perceived as being more real than baseline reality, the conclusion mystics draw from them of the reality of God, Nirvana, and other supernatural concepts must be taken as seriously as the world the rest of us experience. They propose that these things have just as much justification for being considered real as the universe science has studied since Descartes divided the world between "the soul" (the world of religion, the world of meaning), and everything else (the world of cause and effect, the world of science).

Of course this is all very relevant to a *science of religion and ethics*, which takes the position that the ambiguity that has existed between the area of folk religions and science has continued partially because of a lack of clarity about Ultimate Reference Systems. And, when we recognize that Human Beings Are the Ultimate Reference System, but all data, experiment, and theories must be tested against objective reality insofar as current knowledge, understanding, and instruments permit, then the existing ambiguity will be removed. (For an in-depth study of this topic drawing heavily from *The Mystical Mind*, see VOLUME II, Chapter 37, "Mysticism and a Science of Religion and Ethics.") [3]

A *science of religion and ethics* starts with the assumption that those who develop their talents to have mystical experiences and who test and verify mystical hypotheses in their own experience through methods such as meditation, are people exploring the functioning of their own brains. It would seem best to see the assortment of sights and sprites experienced by shamans in their trances as examples of how the human brain functions under certain conditions, and this is the approach that d'Aquili and Newberg do take. A *science of religion and ethics* takes this to be very important since this issue lies at the base of all folk religions, and much of the thinking within psychology and philosophy. As far as psychology goes this area of study might end up providing an empirical basis for some of Carl Jung's ideas that d'Aquili and Newberg do incorporate into their hypotheses. A *science of religion and ethics* proposes that all these experiences have nothing to do with how the outer world works, a position also agreed with by d'Aquili and Newberg. It is only the manner in which they interpret "what is real?" that moves their interpretations of mysticism outside of the realm of a *science of religion and ethics.*

Newberg and d'Aquili term the state achieved during deep meditation as "absolute unitary being." They propose that this is one of the states all mystics achieve although it is differently interpreted based on the traditions of the practitioner. After a two-page description of the initial neurophysiological effects produced in the brain during deep meditation based on their research and study they then describe their interpretation of what happens next. They say, "At the same instant that the right orientation association area is totally deafferented [disconnected from outside influences], the left orientation association area is likewise totally deafferented…. We propose that the total deafferentation of the left orientation association area results in the obliteration of the self-other dichotomy at precisely the same moment that the deafferentation of the right orientation association area is associated with a sense of absolute transcendent wholeness. All the events from the moment of spillover in the hypothalamus with resultant maximal firing of both the arousal and the quiescent system to the total deafferentation of both the right and the left orientation association area may occur so rapidly as to be experienced by the subject as instantaneous. We believe that this results in the subject's attainment of a state of rapturous transcendence and absolute wholeness that conveys such overwhelming power and strength that the subject has the sense of experiencing absolute reality. This is the state of absolute unitary being. Indeed, so ineffable is this state that for those who experience it, even the memory of it carries a sense of greater reality than the reality of our everyday world." [4]

Like all who immerse themselves in folk religions such people end up living their life at the level of their "tribal" genetic propensities and have no chance to fulfill their *Modern Human,* "wisdom," potential. I take this process to involve getting caught in a closed loop within their brain. This process prevents them from moving to a higher level of brain functioning that is involved in finding and utilizing knowledge to expand their full positive potential – to develop as a fully functioning human being rather than an outward projection of a small brain structure (the magic/wishing structure).

Of course for mystics who utilize this "tribal" genetic propensity, my naturalistic view of the world will not be deemed an adequate basis for understanding their mystical experiences. A naturalistic interpretation of this experience conflicts in a fundamental way with their interpretations of what they have been taught about spiritual experience and phenomena. My explanations of spiritual experiences and events are based on material existence and phenomena (e.g., the brain). Mystics drawing on the supernatural (as projected by their raw "tribal" genetic propensities) provide a nonmaterial explanation for these phenomena. And of course this supernatural vs. materialistic interpretation of the universe is the essence of the left brain/right brain conflict.

But in the final analysis the foregoing boils down to an argument over how the human brain works. This is an argument that only science can resolve. However, it is worth noting that post-modernist forces have been for some time working to redefine science in such a way that folk religions exist in a separate, but equal magisterium (to use Stephen Jay Gould's term [5]). This is the explicit goal of d'Aquili and Newberg in *The* Mystical Mind. As they say [6] :

"We have seen that neurotheology [i.e., theology based on how the brain functions during "religious" experiences] is itself a metatheology that contains both the constraints upon and the rules for mythmaking, the generation of specific theologies, the formation and purpose of religious ritual, and the experiencing of the spectrum of religious experiences and altered phases of consciousness. Neurotheology has shown that the products of the mystical mind are real, at least as neuropsychological states. But the phenomenological analysis, that we have been forced to employ as a complement to our basic neuroevolutionary and neurophysiological approach, has powerfully demonstrated that hyperlucid states of consciousness and other products of the mystical mind must be understood as either more real or as real as baseline reality when recalled from baseline reality.

"Thus, it seems that in spite of the fondest hopes of eighteenth century *philosophes* and nineteenth-century materialist scientists, religion and theology will not go away. The reason is that, if we take external reality as primary for our ontology, then God appears to be 'hard-wired' into the brain. On the other hand, if we take subjective awareness as having ontological primacy, then a phenomenological analysis of altered phases of consciousness reveals that certain individuals experience God, as the absolute unitary being (AUB), as a primary epistemic/ontological state. While the state of AUB occurs in very few individuals, other hyperlucid states occur in many. These non-AUB hyperlucid states are not understood to be the direct experience of God... but they are, nevertheless, extremely powerful unitary/epistemic/ontological states. Since neuropsychology not only can document the possibility of these hyperlucid states existing in terms of what is currently known about neurophysiology, but also is now beginning to demonstrate their reality (as neuropsychological states) in current brain-imaging studies, contemporary philosophy and science are forced to take them seriously. One can no longer dismiss the description of such states in the world's religious and mystical literature as the 'silly imaginings of religious nuts.' They must be accounted for and their claims and practical implications carefully examined."

In my mind these authors have described two separate issues. I take Freud's hypothesis that human infants being born helpless and cared for by powerful giants for so long develop a propensity to believe in an all-powerful giant out there in the universe. In addition to that there is a "tribal" genetic propensity to believe in magic and the power of wishing.

Although d'Aquili and Newberg ground their argument on phenomenological interpretations, a *science of religion and ethics* takes an empirical, pragmatic approach and takes the experiences of the mystics as data. A *science of religion and ethics* does not accept that "God is hard-wired" into the brain. Rather, it proposes that belief in magic/wishing exists in the brain as a propensity that makes a person vulnerable to the God concept as well as other mystical images. There is no scientific basis for d'Aquili and Newberg's conclusion because they provide no theories with testable consequences.

Science must account for everything within a context of replicable experiments to the degree possible. There are numerous aspects of brain functioning that are relevant to this issue. Other data is provided by the study of poorly functioning brains. In some forms of psychosis a person's brain malfunctions due to various chemical imbalances. Similar imbalances are caused by LSD, mushrooms, and many other chemical substances. However, the point here is that psychotics do not need to meditate or ingest psychedelic drugs in order to have supernatural, mystical experiences. They can experience the feeling of direct contact with Truth on a regular basis. Newberg and d'Aquili take the position that the foregoing states are not perceived as being "real" as are the mystical states they describe. At this time I do not accept this as relevant to the argument. I take all these things as being descriptions of how some brains work under certain circumstances and this has no relevance beyond that, except in the area of psychology of belief: Why do people believe what they believe?

However, the primary issue is that all <u>abnormal brain states</u> are only exaggerated or diminished normal states. I believe that all people's brains provide them with a propensity to believe in magic and the power of wishing. Our very humanity makes us all vulnerable to believing in magic and that our wishes control the outside world. It is easy for people to accept the idea that we or others can have a direct connection with God or some other source of Truth. The foregoing explanation is proposed because the appeal of the mystical is very broad, powerful, and lasting throughout the human family. And all of these speculations and suggestions regarding a propensity to believe in magic and the power of wishing are open to testing and experiment if anyone is motivated to do so.

Belief in magic and the power of wishing attracts some people from the very core of their being. The interest in transcendence and the spiritual quest has usually been combined with the human propensity to believe in magic and the power of wishing. However, the mystical approach is not essential to the feeling of going beyond our place and time. Transcendence and the spiritual quest need not be in conflict with a natural world and human limitations. Any thoughtful person must at least at times focus on the mystery that surrounds us individually and collectively. At such times we may be stunned by the experience of amazement inherent in being part of a universe infinite in time and space (infinite in relationship to the scale of human power, life, and scope).

We may be awed by a rainbow, a musical event, the roar of a storm-driven surf, the vastness of the universe. But from a naturalistic perspective, interpretation of any experience needs to be applied tentatively with no more conviction than the evidence warrants. We should strive to remain open to all the interpretations that relate to the mysteries of this universe in which we find ourselves. There are questions in every direction we look.

However, we need to accept the limits of our ability to understand, and give those interpretations the most credence that have the best knowledge and evidence supporting them.

When mystics try to interpret their feelings and experiences as direct contact with Ultimate Reality and Truth, it is my assumption that they have succumbed to a sophisticated interpretation of their innate human propensity to believe in magic and the power of wishing. An inquisitive person wants to know what is beyond the next hill, and the one beyond that, and so on and so on. The promise of directly experiencing Truth may cause the vulnerable person to forgo rational, empirical approaches because they experience the frustration of knowing that a finite mind can never experience Truth without resort to magic. They realize that no matter how many questions they find answers to, that will only open the way to new questions. Yet, the mystic who experiences Truth has not only answered the last question, but the ones beyond that!

This is a powerful attraction. Just contemplating it might produce ecstasy! Imagine: No doubts. No blundering. Promises like that cannot be made for empirical processes. Certainly empirical scientists would never make such statements. Rather, they would say, "If you study hard, work diligently, and focus your entire life, you may wrestle some small answers from the universe's infinite storehouse of secrets." The only reason science attracts any interest at all is because the curious person who is also a skeptic finds that the Truth provided by supernatural mysticism (belief in magic and wishing) is in reality an overpowering feeling that leads to a collection of non-answers. They are too ambiguous, too limited to be of more than psychological value. Any answer that goes beyond the physical manifestations of the experience moves immediately into the realm of the objectively unverifiable. Frequently, these answers conflict with the truths of a person's own life experience. They are subjective and have no self-correcting mechanisms. They are often self-serving in the sense of perpetuating a person's current beliefs or deep desires. They cannot be differentiated from lies, deceit, malfunctioning brains, or misunderstandings about how the brain naturally works.

On the other hand, the small, seemingly insignificant answers of science make a real difference in human understanding, in human living. They connect things together in a new, more satisfying way. They provide insights into the workings of the universe beyond the dreams of even the most inspired supernatural mystics. They are objectively verifiable by anyone willing to take the time and effort. A self-correcting mechanism exists to find and rectify errors.

Scientific understanding helps broaden the range imposed by our current genetic boundaries and move humanity further toward developing our "wisdom" potential. This understanding advances technology and lightens the burdens of day-to-day living. It allows us to combat poverty, hunger, disease, and all the forces that diminish the value of human life. It makes us more secure as people and as a species. It fills our life with new possibilities and excitement. It permits ever-greater numbers of people to advance their understanding. Take for example learning how to master the body. What mystics take decades to accomplish can be achieved in a matter of weeks through biofeedback and other processes utilizing science and technology. And these processes expand a person's mind rather than narrowing its focus. Science like democracy allows more people to participate in the "thinking" of the world.

The answers of science build on each other to join seemingly unrelated areas. Collectively, these answers produce a unity that mysticism promises, but only science delivers. The findings of science provide knowledge. And it is this knowledge that allows true wisdom and the formulation of a *science of religion and ethics* -- to provide a user's guide for *Modern Humans*. And this is a spiritual quest that moves us beyond our raw "tribal" genetic propensities and toward the achievement of our "wisdom" potential.

And it is the quest to become a spiritual being that lies at the core of the Enlightened Person. Working with others to actualize the Ways of Wisdom and thereby achieving our full positive potential is to realize our complete humanity. Also see "The Enlightened Person" in Chapter 19 on "Organizing for an Enlightened Community Made Up of Enlightened Persons." The foregoing requires that we use our lives to maintain and develop the species. To do this we need to fulfill all the potential of our genetic heritage current knowledge allows. To the degree that each day of our life is committed to and focused on maintaining balance and maintaining our vision we are doing all that is possible to live the life of an Enlightened Person.

CHAPTER 19

ORGANIZING FOR AN ENLIGHTENED COMMUNITY MADE UP OF ENLIGHTENED PERSONS

These organizations need to have a triple focus. First, they need to do whatever is possible to ensure that a *science of religion and ethics* is properly grounded -- improve the ideas presented in this book and correct errors, provide missing components, and expand ideas so they can actually be used. Second, they need to do as much as they can to move themselves and as many people as possible toward becoming Enlightened Persons. Third, they need to help their society move toward becoming an Enlightened Community.

ORGANIZING FOR AN ENLIGHTENED COMMUNITY: IT ALL STARTS WITH A SINGLE PERSON!

1. THE WISDOM GROUP AND CENTER FOR THE PRACTICAL APPLICATION OF WISDOM

What will it take to put into practice the ideas of this book? What are the actual components of an Enlightened Community and the Enlightened Person? How can an empirical element be introduced into this discussion so we can rise above subjective evaluations about specific behavior and use of resources? I believe this aspect needs to come from actual study of people and societies. The accuracy of conclusions about which beliefs are most likely to produce an Enlightened Person and an Enlightened Community depends on data. Any conclusion is no better than the evidence that supports it. Clearly, this is a complex enough issue that it will be easy to go astray particularly considering that in our upbringing we have all been immersed in ideas so far off the mark.

Another question is, What needs to be done to actually develop an Enlightened Community made up of Enlightened Persons? Obviously, even with perfect theories and data we could not change an existing society into an Enlightened Community overnight. A skeptic might say it can't be done over any period of time. But if it can be done it can only be done by establishing organizations to promote such change.

How can someone start the process? At this time the idea that we could have a *science of religion and ethics* conflicts with the ideas most people currently accept. My efforts are a feeble first step. They are ideas with no existing organizations to provide the necessary framework for Wisdom Groups capable of growing into Centers for the Practical Application of Wisdom that can aid in defining concepts and focusing the gathering and analyzing of data. Our situation is not even comparable to the time of the metamorphosis of chemistry out of alchemy and astronomy out of astrology. Though alchemists and astrologers had mystical goals they at least had developed empirical experiences and studies that merely had to pass through a transformation from a supernatural to naturalistic focus. There might be experiences here that could provide some guidance, but not much since we are in a quite different situation. However, whatever help the foregoing provides, a great deal of caution as well as tremendous optimism will be needed in starting this effort. So, with cautious optimism we need to slowly construct both the mechanisms for producing Enlightened Persons and Enlightened Communities while at the same time working to clarify all relevant ideas to develop a *science of religion and ethics* and to assemble Wisdom Groups capable of producing Centers for the Practical Application of Wisdom.

Somehow we need to establish groups to develop Enlightened Persons, and at the same time encourage efforts to improve theories and goals. However, it is not obvious how to do this. We are trying to develop Enlightened Persons, but we're not sure what that means. There are no such people to start the group or serve as models, yet there are thousands if not millions of people who think they are Enlightened. In addition it is not totally clear how to build an Enlightened Community and exactly how it would function. We need to rely on experimental, bootstrap procedures in which we utilize our best impulses and strengths to collectively help each other move in the right direction. See later in this chapter Ten Levels of Human Development and VOLUME II, Chapter 1, "Levels of Membership in a Wisdom Group") [1] for some suggestions on the foregoing.

I believe the first step in establishing an Enlightened Community made up of Enlightened Persons is to set up small, experimental groups to explore the possibilities. I call such organizations Wisdom Groups. It seems to me that Wisdom Groups would most likely be set up by people who had studied this book and were in general agreement with its goals. They might meet in all the ways that people who share common interests meet and when two or more connect in the right way would decide to establish such a Group. However, another way that Wisdom Groups might be established would be through existing organizations. Every organization resists change and is almost impossible to refocus. This is why it is usually easier to establish new organizations to do a job than try to restructure an existing one. However, there may be times when an existing church/synagogue/mosque, fraternal group, educational organization, or similar group would have a leadership core that sees merit in the goals of this book. They might with the cooperation of membership decide to restructure the organization as a Wisdom Group, or at least spin off a Wisdom Group. This might lead to the establishment of a Wisdom network consisting of such groups.

It is possible that the best way to start a Wisdom Group would be to gather a group of at least three to six people to study and master Rational Emotive Behavior Therapy. (See *A Guide To Rational Living*, or perhaps even better, Michael Edelstein's *Three Minute Therapy*) [2]. The ideas that Dr. Ellis presents in the foregoing book, and that Edelstein simplifies are an essential first step for any who would accept a *science of religion and ethics*. Until they master this understanding there is little chance they can move further in their growth toward a *science of religion and ethics*.

A Wisdom Group would bring interested people together to share their ideas, their dreams, their hopes, their joy and enthusiasm. It would function in whatever way the participants agreed on. The core of its efforts and activities would be to explore and actualize the vision of a *science of religion and ethics*. I expect that they would explore the ideas presented in this book and at some point examine how to actualize these ideas or the improved ones that came out of the group process. They would work to help each participant achieve good mental health.

Wisdom Groups would provide the energy to organize a larger, more outer focused group, herein called a Center for the Practical Application of Wisdom. These Centers would be the custodian of the vision of a *science of religion and ethics.* The effort to establish a Center for the Practical Application of Wisdom would begin once the Wisdom Group reached a sufficient size and level of wisdom. One goal of a Center for the Practical Application of Wisdom might be to expand the range of activities and experiences available to help members work toward achieving a *sustainable feeling of well-being.* Insofar as possible a Wisdom Group would bring together the wise people of the community who accept as a working hypothesis the idea that Human Beings Are the Ultimate Reference System, that is, those who have a high level of good mental health and contact with reality.

It seems to me the best structure for a Wisdom Group would be to have levels of membership. People would then be able to utilize a self-correcting structure that incorporates the knowledge and wisdom of humanity to achieve total congruency, and become their best self. Levels of membership would help each person master whatever knowledge, skills, and experiences are necessary in order to move toward their life goals. Each level reached would represent a real achievement. The person's goals would truly be for their own benefit. However, the better the person they become the better it is for everyone else, also. In order to ensure that the foregoing is the case it needs to be recognized that in the area of value and meaning each person needs to be the final interpreter of "Truth." [3] No organization, community, group, and such can say what "Truth" is. However, it can say what is required of members of this particular Group. A good organization can help a person in the search, and encourage study, discovery, and synthesis. It can help a person develop their humanity and live a full life. However, a group attempting to develop an Enlightened Community cannot adopt conclusions and require that the person agree with all these answers as a condition of being accepted into the group.

It is too easy for group conclusions and requirements to become rigid, simplistic, and selectively reject those people with the greatest potential. Also, organizations that think they can provide "Truth" (except as a moving target, provisional and approximate) in fact promote hypocrisy, a big step toward causing a person to lose their bearing and become vulnerable to all other forms of dishonesty. Any community that exploits its members, begins by encouraging them to be hypocrites. After that lying, stealing, and abusing in all kinds of situations becomes possible. Levels of membership might help develop a flexible way to deal with the foregoing issues.

THE ENLIGHTENED PERSON

How to become an Enlightened Person cannot be taught in one course, or measured simply. It needs to be measured in progressive increments the way growth takes place. As indicated elsewhere humanity is in the process of creating itself out of its genetic heritage using its "wisdom" potential based on symbolic language. As a result of this reinvention process of what we are, our vision of the nature of *Modern Humans* needs to remain open to change and reinterpretation. This requires that a person be educated and socialized so that they are flexible enough to deal with these new insights. In addition to this a person under any circumstances is always in a state of becoming. They are constantly changing -- growing, maturing, and sometimes backsliding. People would normally come to a Wisdom Group in the early stages of their development. Their habits of thought may be poorly developed. They may be and probably are loaded with erroneous information, ideas, and patterns of thinking. They very likely still utilize immature behaviors and possess irrational values. They may be only starting to integrate new ideas into their life. They may not yet understand the implications of their new ideas and how these ideas relate to the concepts they were raised with. They may not have mastered both the scientific and philosophical ways of understanding "Truth." For science this is to see "Truths" as provisional and approximate -- to be questioned with an open mind so they can be changed when necessary -- and for philosophy to see "Truths" as concepts defined pragmatically.

Some candidates for membership might not have integrated their new values into their life in terms of how they use their time or in their interpersonal relationships. Others may be developed philosophically, and understand the goals and need for a Wisdom Group based on a *science of religion and ethics*, but have no experience with or understanding of organizations and how to be effective in them. Some may not have developed their left brain sufficiently to refocus their raw "tribal" genetic propensities.

The foregoing problems take time and effort to overcome. One class meeting, or one therapy session will not produce the necessary changes. People need other people to serve as models in order to get a clear vision of what it takes to become and live as an Enlightened Person. They need honest feedback given with love. They need guidance and encouragement. They need education, therapeutic assistance, and experience. But equally important they need to be able to put their insights and criticisms where they will be heard and produce any changes necessary in the ideas and functioning of the Wisdom Group.

Very likely there need to be different paths for different kinds of people. If the Myers-Briggs Type Indicator [4] has any reality behind it at all, and I believe it does, then people may differ in important ways. As a result the behaviors, knowledge, experience, and so forth. I suggest below as criteria of evaluation for levels of membership may also differ significantly among people.

Therefore, for the concept of levels of growth/maturity/commitment to hold up under careful scrutiny it may need to be broadened, or alternative paths developed to accommodate different types of people (*Type Talk* [4], or, analysis in VOLUME II, Chapter 26, "*Type Talk* – Personality Types and the Enlightened Person.") [5] Also, left brain people vs. right brain people seems to be an important issue that may require additional thought and study.

For the working draft of ideas on levels of membership see VOLUME II, Chapter 1, "Levels of Membership in a Wisdom Group." [1] Currently it is recommended that there be an initial affiliative step followed by ten levels of membership with the core value of each level briefly described below. Of course these are reason-based and lack adequate empirical evidence to make them rules to be accepted without question. At best they are a starting place for discussion and study.

THE TEN LEVELS OF HUMAN DEVELOPMENT

0.a. <u>Initial</u>: Indicates a sincere interest in being associated with the group.

0.b. <u>Novice</u>: Participates in an activity comparable to studying Albert Ellis' "A GUIDE TO RATIONAL LIVING [2] to master the basic ideas of Rational Emotive Behavior Therapy in order to integrate this positive, effective process into their life.

1. <u>Alpha Value</u>: Exhibits compassion and concern for all other human beings. Understands the ideas of a *science of religion and ethics* including: A *sustainable feeling of well-being*, Human Beings Are the Ultimate Reference System, Ways of Wisdom, as well as their own personal philosophy. Also, has a general understanding of the major philosophical and religious systems including the strengths and weaknesses of each system. Accepts core ideas of a *science of religion and ethics* as a working hypothesis, or demonstrates why any should not be so accepted. Able to achieve intimacy at least with their spouse, or significant other.

2. <u>Beta Value</u>: Understands importance of physical affection and able to experience it at least in structured environments (massage, close friends, and the like.) (See *Body Pleasure And The Origins of Violence*, by Dr. James W. Prescott. [6]) <u>Attends Level One program of the Human Awareness Institute</u> [7] or something comparable.

Committed to becoming an Enlightened Person. Involved in the group in such a way as to experience full communion with the group, and a deep sense that all other human beings are comrades, and worthy of whatever a person can offer.

3. <u>Gamma Value</u>: Have taken and mastered the core ideas and experiences of a course such as the "Fire Walk" experience given by Anthony Robbins [8]: Importance of focus, How to change one's state, Taking charge of a their life, Achieving

personal power, and such. Have mastered first area of self-knowledge: (Confronting the traumas of their childhood and dealing with them sufficiently to be able to determine current motivations and obsessions. Have worked through these to the degree that self-defeating, negative behavior is not routinely followed, and/or does not unduly impair their over-all functioning.)

Experiences total openness and honesty with the group -- total trust and a feeling of freedom to be themselves.

4. Delta Value: Has a consistent and rationally based worldview that is not grossly inconsistent with the best knowledge currently available. Able to replace any of their beliefs when it becomes clear they would not be sustainable in an Enlightened Community; that is, do not provide a *sustainable feeling of well-being*.

5. Epsilon Value: Has achieved a sense of transcendence through identification with the goals of the group and the efforts of those involved in building a new foundation for civilization in order to work for the survival of the human species in such a way that each person is able to achieve a *sustainable feeling of well-being*.

6. Zeta Value: Lives consistent with their value system that in turn is consistent with the ideas and concepts of the Epsilon Level. Have mastered second area of self-knowledge. (Integrating all body functions and maintaining a positive, effective state so that their physical and mental functions are congruent.)

7. Eta Value: Demonstrates understanding of organizations, their value, and how they work; and how to be effective in them.

8. Theta Value: Focuses on development of their personal "bible," a collection of ideas and writings that express their own worldview. This project would vary tremendously from person to person depending on interest, ability, time available, and such. Have a clearly stated inspiring life goal that motivates

and directs their life, and are able to pursue this goal possibly within an Organization to Enhance the Quality of Human Life.

9. Iota Value: Possesses a healthy amount of humility. Ability to laugh particularly at themselves. Insight into their own motivations. Ability to see themself objectively. Have incorporated nurturing touch into every aspect of their life. Have mastered third area of self-knowledge. (Through biofeedback mechanisms or other means are able to control body functions to anesthetize any part of the body, and control heartbeat, body temperature, and mental state.)

10. Kappa Value: Exhibits the highest human attributes of friendship, physical affection, honesty, truthfulness, open-mindedness, and rational thinking.

It is unlikely that any person will be able to achieve the full dimensions of most of these levels of membership. But the core point should be able to be presented in a way that any person can achieve it.

As a Wisdom Group grows in knowledge and effectiveness, it needs to expand activities and develop a Center for the Practical Application of Wisdom. Membership also should be expanded as conditions allow. Special efforts need to be made to attract people of integrity. Except in the case of people who have already reached the higher levels of values and behavior it would be of questionable value to make vigorous attempts to recruit members before the structures are created to provide the support and guidance they need.

CHAPTER 20

OTHER SUPPORT ORGANIZATIONS (MORE DETAIL IN APPENDIX C)

As discussed throughout this book it seems clear to me that individuals can only become Enlightened Persons in an Enlightened Community. Obviously no one can accurately lay out the components of an Enlightened Community in advance since producing one is an empirical process and any plans or ideas for producing one must change as experience requires.

However, in the Appendix C I lay out some of my thoughts and suggestions about each of the below suggested organizations in the hope that it will be helpful in efforts to assist thinking in getting planning started. Of course any such ideas soon become outdated as societies change so what is needed and may look very different from the new perspective. So each of the below items must be viewed in that light.

OVERVIEW:

1. ORGANIZATION TO ENHANCE THE QUALITY OF HUMAN LIFE (OEQHL)
2. NEW IDEAS, REVOLUTIONARY INSIGHTS, AND/OR UNIQUE ANSWERS INSTITUTE (NIRIUA-I)
3. THE SCHOOL
4. CHOICES ARE US (CAU)
5. EMERGENCY SERVICES CENTER (ESC)
6. CENTER FOR MASTERING LIVING (CFML)
7. A PLACE FOR KIDS
8. THE COMPUTER CONNECTION
9. THE RADIO LINK

10. CORPORATION FOR UNIVERSAL EMPLOYMENT (CUE)
11. CENTER FOR THE PRACTICAL APPLICATION OF WISDOM NEWS GROUP (CPAW-NG)
12. HEALTH CARE CLINIC
13. REGIONAL PLANNING AND COORDINATING INSTITUTIONS
14. ORGANIZATION FOR THE PROTECTION OF LABOR

CHAPTER 21

SPREADING MEANING: A NEW FOUNDATION FOR CIVILIZATION

> *Old foundation* = *spirit causality (God/supernatural),*
> *or reason (assumptions the truth of which are taken to*
> *be self evident)*

> *New foundation* = **human nature (empirical study**
> **based on an understanding of human evolution)**

To the degree that the views I have expressed in this book are correct, they need to be universally welcomed – resulting in the formation of the organizations and techniques to ensure acceptance by everyone. If they are not one hundred percent satisfactory my hope is that they can be modified in that direction. If correct, they need to be able to replace or absorb all other worldviews. However, a religious/ethical system fails a person only when that system is found to be inadequate in some unacceptable way. This often takes years to come about if a person is enmeshed within a Pre-Enlightened Community that promotes beliefs and practices that appeal to their raw "tribal" genetic propensities. As a result most people die without ever discovering that their views were deficient. Also, if a person is stopped at some stage of development by adoption of an inadequate religious/ethical system they will have to be awakened to their potentialities before they can advance beyond that system. People who have been misguided from birth and are attached to certain beliefs supporting a Pre-Enlightened Community will undoubtedly have much difficulty escaping the web that holds them.

However, any inadequate religious/ethical system has practical, painful effects for the believer's life. Every worldview utilized by a group provides its followers a reason that attempts to justify their pain, and that calms their mind initially. But, at some times, in some areas the explanation doesn't fit and/or work. As a result there are always festering wounds that at certain times open the person to change so they can explore ways to reduce the pain, increase the joy, or both. The current extensive use of illegal mind-altering drugs, and legal such drugs for that matter -- alcohol, tobacco, Valium, Prozac, and such -- in America shows just how desperate many people are. If a Center for the Practical Application of Wisdom can provide ways to effectively deal with this pain, hope for a better life becomes possible. This step may help a person see how other areas of their life can be improved that had not even been recognized as deficient. To the degree that a Center for the Practical Application of Wisdom provides the right stuff these people can be helped and directed toward their own best self.

Since people's worldview is essentially shaped by their childhood experiences, examining one's childhood becomes crucial in overcoming this early conditioning, childhood trauma, and other effects that limit or distort brain development. But as stated before, a person can only discard core ideas if these ideas begin to seem wrong, inadequate, or the person finds something that looks better to them. Sometimes this happens as they begin to truly understand their core ideas – a rare state indeed. On some occasions these ideas are recognized as being discordant with reality and this becomes so obvious it cannot be ignored. If the ideas proposed in this book really approximate the necessary hypotheses for setting up an Enlightened Community, this needs to be able to replace any Pre-Enlightened Community. And, of course it needs to accomplish all the necessary functions that the original society performed. In addition it needs to eliminate the Pre-Enlightened Society's worthless, ineffective, or harmful parts, and improve any inadequate structures. A Pre-Enlightened Society can never be wholly adequate, not even for one of its members. Any system that is completely adequate obviously cannot, and need not be replaced since there is no reason to replace it. The ideas in this book need to help all people if they are correct. These ideas need to be able to displace every person's inadequate philosophy/religion (worldview) with a better and more rewarding one. However, the foregoing can only be achieved as the necessary organizations are developed. And here we are confronted with the problem that a person can only become an Enlightened Person if they are part of an Enlightened Community. And an Enlightened Community can only be produced by Enlightened Persons. Therefore, progress can only be made through successive approximations as it has been doing over the past 10,000 years.

The theories expressed in this book are supposed to discourage corruption and other self-destructive behaviors. Instead of establishing an authoritarian structure claiming absolute Truth, these ideas require an empirical process aiming to achieve congruency with each other and with objective reality. These ideas are only as binding as the evidence on which they are based can support. These ideas are believed to carry within themselves the mechanism for producing necessary changes. They include the claim that people can and need to be helped in terms that they accept as valid for them; that ideas that do not produce beneficial results are inadequate; and if such thoughts produce bad results they are wrong. The killer, sociopath, psychotic, and idiot cannot be written off, ignored, or sacrificed as defective merchandise, or part of God's plan. The goal for a *science of religion and ethics* is that the individual human being is seen as the focus for society's ultimate concern, and society's role in "failures" as well as "successes" needs to be acknowledged, understood, and then improved insofar as current circumstances permit.

A Center for the Practical Application of Wisdom focuses on individual human beings. Each of us depends solely on our fellow humans for a *sustainable feeling of well-being*. If other people seem inadequate, we need to search to learn how improvement is possible. And we cannot stop searching until every person has achieved a *sustainable feeling of well-being*.

The foregoing thesis may be difficult to accept (and of course even more difficult to actualize). It seems necessary for people to have a scapegoat or excuse to explain crime, and other antisocial, or ineffective behavior in general. Scapegoating appears to come more naturally than looking for an answer in the realm of cause and effect that can then lead to prevention or correction of such behavior. I take scapegoating to be part of the "us/ them" genetic propensity.

Universally, people who are financially successful tend to look upon the poor as being so because they are lazy or inferior in some way. The pseudo-intellectual says that the "average" person is too dumb to advance much in life and enjoy the "higher" things. The "average" person says that "too much" intelligence causes insanity, that money brings the wealthy more pain than happiness, that the simple things in life are what count. The athlete regards physical perfection as the highest value; the artist places aesthetic experiences above all other things. The aristocrat believes that a person's parentage is the measure of worth; the "low born" say that accomplishment is what counts. Orthodox Jews know that they are the chosen people; Muslims are sure that only their religion is right. The "skin head" prizes white skin; the Polynesian, brown. The religious fanatic condemns the "sinner"; the disillusioned say that humanity is a failed species and there is no hope for it, the skeptic smirks at the rest of humanity for believing in anything.

So currently each person's position is too narrow to embrace all, hence their worldview will have to fail all. Only a religious/ethical system of sufficient depth and breadth to include all people in the most basic and essential ways can prevent people from forsaking their fellow humans and therefore themselves.

Even the most despicable, hateful, ignorant person you know of need to be capable of becoming a productive, likeable, compassionate person; an Enlightened Person. This is the challenge! In a *science of religion and ethics* there is no support for "us vs. them" inside the human family. Every *Modern Human* is "us." We need to do whatever is necessary to achieve this state and maintain it.

Where Thomas Aquinas and most other religious philosophers were primarily concerned with supporting their system, that they adopted through blind faith, a *science of religion and ethics* is primarily concerned with creating a religious/ethical system that is grounded on science and open to change with new knowledge. Folk religions function so as to maintain the status quo to allow the perpetuation of the existing power structure. A *science of religion and ethics* needs to work to alter any system in which even one person unjustifiably suffers. But more specifically it would work to prevent the kind of suffering Steinbeck describes below.

FROM THE GRAPES OF WRATH

By John Steinbeck

"The decay spreads over the State, and the sweet smell is a great sorrow on the land. People who can graft the trees and make the seed fertile and big can find no way to let the hungry people eat their produce. People who have created new fruits in the world cannot create a system whereby their fruits may be eaten. And the failure hangs over the State like a great sorrow.

The works of the roots of the vines, of the trees, need to be destroyed to keep up the price, and this is the saddest, bitterest thing of all. Carloads of oranges dumped on the ground. The people came for miles to take the fruit, but this could not be.

How would they buy oranges at twenty cents a dozen if they could drive out and pick them up? And people with hoses squirt kerosene on the oranges, and they are angry at the crime, angry at the people who have come to take the fruit. A million people hungry, needing the fruit -- and kerosene sprayed over the golden mountains.

And the smell of rot fills the country.

Burn coffee for fuel in the ships. Burn corn to keep warm, it makes a hot fire. Dump potatoes in the rivers and place guards along the banks to keep the hungry people from fishing them out.

Slaughter the pigs and bury them, and let the putrescence drip down into the earth.

There is a crime here that goes beyond denunciation. There is a failure here that topples all our success. The fertile earth, the straight tree rows, the sturdy trunks, and the ripe fruit. And children dying of pellagra need to die because a profit cannot be taken from an orange. And coroners need to fill in the certificate -- died of malnutrition -- because the food needs to rot, needs to be forced to rot.

The people come with nets to fish for potatoes in the river, and the guards hold them back; they come in rattling cars to get the dumped oranges, but the kerosene is sprayed. And they stand still and watch the potatoes float by, listen to the screaming pigs being killed in a ditch and covered with quicklime, watch the mountains of oranges slop down to a putrefying ooze; and in the eyes of the people there is the failure; and in the eyes of the hungry there is a growing wrath, in the souls of the people the grapes of wrath are filling and growing heavy, growing heavy for the vintage."[1]

I believe that much of humanity's difficulty exists because "...while saints are engaged in introspection, burly sinners run the world." [2] Of course I only accept "saints" and "sinners" in a metaphorical sense. "Saints" are people working to develop the "wisdom" potential, and "sinners" are people who are functioning out of their raw "tribal" genetic propensities: those who are greedy, power seeking, deceitful, hypocritical, and the like. Corporate executives, labor leaders, religious fundamentalists, corrupt officials, and so on are not actually sinners because there is no sin. They primarily are misled and/or ignorant of the important facts. They are ruled primarily by their "us vs. them" and their "dominance/submission" propensities. The wise people of society who are attempting to rise above their raw "tribal" genetic propensities too often get caught in sophisticated aspects of the belief in magic and the power of wishing "tribal" genetic propensity, and end up being so removed from life and humanity that they do not understand the path necessary to develop their "wisdom" potential. As a result, essentially all people are forced to make decisions without sufficient knowledge and wisdom, or the support to allow them to work toward satisfying their own long-term self-interest; that is, understanding what is in their long-term best interests.

A *science of religion and ethics* is intended to promote change in people and thereby in societies. It is meant to reshape the world. It should, when properly developed, be available to all people, and aid them in making difficult decisions. A *science of religion and ethics* would allow all people to bond so firmly within our species that they could not feel alone in the darkest corner of the Cosmos. It would not be from a position of ignorance and blind faith that they attained the previously mentioned sense of well-being. They would gain peace of mind based on their life experience and knowledge, hence from a position of infinite strength. No search, no question would be forbidden (unless either caused physical harm to others). All knowledge or exploration would be open to every person. They would have not only the theoretical power to change inadequate structures, but also the actual power to do so.

If any person comes up with different answers from those usually accepted, they would be welcomed into the New Ideas, Revolutionary Insights, And/Or Unique Answers Institute. They would become a resource to stimulate the advance of society toward better answers, better ways to help humanity. To the degree that their answers were found to contain truth and wisdom, the bands would play and the crowds cheer for they are a great person and this is greatness. The goal would be to recognize and reward them in life rather than after death; to utilize their ideas rather than diverting them into a wasteland.

All of this is only possible in an Enlightened Community. Rapid improvements could be made because the members of an Enlightened Community are Enlightened Persons and do not have subconscious attachments to a tradition that prohibits thought and change. The foregoing should make it clear that the views in this book are expressed tentatively. These views are thought to avail themselves to the methods of scientific proof at least at key points; that is, in the Ways of Wisdom. But the bottom line is that nothing here can be accepted with any more conviction than the evidence merits. This means there will always be an openness to rejecting errors and accepting other approaches. Without the foregoing we would only be discarding one set of irrationalities for another. The primary hope in creating a *science of religion and ethics* is that an ever-increasing number of people will be helped to live at an ever-expanding level of mental development and well-being.

The only relevant way to test these ideas is by demonstrating their value in the rehabilitation of people using the proposed techniques as modified by experience. If these theories are correct, there is a mammoth task to be accomplished. There is a world to be won and consolidated. There are probably not more than a handful of people out of the billions on this planet not in need of rehabilitation, even though in many cases it would come easily, be little more than an awakening.

When these ideas are widely accepted and used to change societies, then our species will at last have reached the new stability (a dynamic equilibrium) congruent with our "wisdom" potential toward which we have been aimed for the past 30,000-60,000 years. At that time humanity will be able to take its true place in the cosmos. This can now happen because we have entered the first zone of utopia. There are now places in the world with freedom where we can speak openly and we have enough data to see the outline of that utopia. Science has given us an expanding personal wealth and machines to replace slaves. It is now possible to communicate with those willing to involve themselves in this seminal effort. It is within our grasp to make the world -- for now and for eternity -- a decent place for every person to live.

Our goal needs to be personal power for each person. It should not be considered enough to give a person food and shelter, and teach them how to endure pain until they are released by death. They need to be given their "soul" so they can understand and achieve the meaning of their life. They need to be helped to develop so they can see their opportunities and responsibilities. They need to be helped to see the path to tread and have their fellow humans ever available to support them in time of need. Humanity needs to be taught how to actualize love and compassion, and not mere hollow expressions of these concepts. Humanity needs to be shown that all we have to do to solve the "unsolvable problems due to the original human sin" is to discard the metaphysics and theology that perpetuate these "problems." Those difficulties resulting from "the human condition" <u>are</u> solvable. We can now see the light at the end of the tunnel. We can now understand the broad outline of how to integrate the needs of the person and the community in a way congruent with our language ability.

For all these reasons we can now begin to visualize utopia -- a perfect world. Yet in every direction we look we see people expressing the clear message: "Human beings are too dumb, too selfish, too short-sighted to work together in the way required to create a perfect world." As indicated before I propose that the perfect world is now almost within our grasp. Some will say, "absurd." Others will tighten their lips, and declare, "Impossible. Crazy. Wrong. The statement of a fool!" Perhaps all these comments are true. But consider the perfect world as this: One in which the ignorance of the day can be corrected by human thought and action; by peace, not bloodshed -- where it is recognized that there is no essential conflict between the crucial needs of the individual and of the society.

In any society that is controlled by fundamentalists of any folk religion, or other authoritarian rulers, peaceful changes will be difficult. So, these areas are part of the "almost" in "The perfect world is now almost within our grasp," in the preceding paragraph. Also ignorance is rampant in all parts of the world so this is part of the "almost." However, there now exists a wondrous opportunity. Many places in the world exist today where a *science of religion and ethics* could be introduced. In none of these places could we expect exponential growth and development. But much of this is due to the current formulation of a *science of religion and ethics*. As experience is gained, growth will increase in speed and size.

The technique recommended here for getting from the hope of today to the achievements of tomorrow is the thoughtful, planned steps of dynamic evolution. Each society needs to be helped to make careful steps as conditions allow. But our effort needs to be relentless in every possible sphere.

We need to lay the groundwork for change and not try to abolish or transform current social structures until we have something better to replace them. This process may take time, but it is the only process that is consistent with the principles of a *science of religion and ethics*. And, it is the only process that has any chance of being successful at least in the long run.

To destroy is easy. To build is difficult. Knowledge has given us the power to destroy civilization. Ignorance has given us the potential to destroy it.

It seems to me that the first goal for people interested in implementing a *science of religion and ethics* needs to be to set up a Wisdom Group. However under current circumstances that will not be easy. Therefore, the first step probably needs to be to establish a Study Group to examine this book and discuss it, and at some point it will become clear whether or not any members of the group see enough merit in these ideas to attempt to implement them to form a Wisdom Group.

If there is enough interest to do the foregoing, and meetings begin, a danger we need to prepare for is that one or several of the members will fall into the "dominance/ submission" model and attempt to run things in the traditional way -- jockeying for control. This won't work; that is, result in a successful Wisdom Group. Once it becomes clear that the person/ people cannot be reformed with the available resources then the next step would be to eject them from the group. If this can't be done then it will be necessary to drop out and start a new group.

Another serious problem the Wisdom Group will likely encounter is errors in the theory. Some of the ideas about how a Wisdom Group should function will turn out to be totally erroneous. Others will be insufficiently clear to be followed. Some will be good ideas, but difficult to implement with the resources of time, money, and knowledge currently available.

But whenever such a group becomes strong enough and sufficiently organized it should assemble a Center for the Practical Application of Wisdom (CPAW). Very likely many Wisdom Groups will encounter an overwhelming problem or problems before they are able to set up a CPAW. These problems may require some members to split off to try again. It is important that as many of these experiences be recorded and shared as possible to help others avoid the same mistakes. Hopefully, at some point some group will get all the necessary ingredients together and establish a Wisdom Group successful enough to organize a CPAW. Starting a CPAW will not be easy. It may not even be possible to do so. However, if it is possible, almost certainly it will take several attempts before an organization close enough to what is needed is established, and can begin to function along the lines of the theory (as revised with experience). At that point other groups should be able to follow the successful group's model.

There are two somewhat separate areas in which to pursue the *science of religion and ethics* message. One is the academic, and/or research domain. This is the realm of study, experimenting, and teaching. The other area that would draw from the first, and vice versa, is the implementation of our current understanding by starting with a Wisdom Group and building from there. A *science of religion and ethics* in its scientific/academic efforts can proceed somewhat independently from the implementation activities.

Of necessity teachers and researchers, as well as those forming Wisdom Groups will have to be people who have not yet achieved a *sustainable feeling of well-being*. As a result of the foregoing, Wisdom Groups should be slow and careful in proclaiming individual persons to be Enlightened Persons. This is a crucial point and a tricky point, one that could spell success or failure for a Wisdom Group. Can people refrain from setting themselves up as absolute tyrants when this is at least theoretically possible? Progress or failure rests on this point. The original founders of a Wisdom Group need to lean over backward to avoid mistakes in naming Enlightened Persons. The loss of not proclaiming someone an Enlightened Person will be minor compared to the potential for a major catastrophe in doing so wrongly.

A primary goal of a Wisdom Group after initial formation should be to determine how to produce Enlightened Persons and failsafe ways of determining when a person has reached this state. Perhaps, it would be wisest to proclaim those who start the work "Heroes of Humanity" and save the title "Enlightened Person" for those who come later.

Each Wisdom Group with its associated Center for the Practical Application of Wisdom, once developed, needs to initially exist independently from other [WG/CPAW] bodies. This initial separation of such groups is proposed in order to reduce the effect of a power grab by a Pre-Enlightened Person/Persons. Also, having Wisdom Groups and their associated Centers for the Practical Application of Wisdom exist independently of each other might encourage greater experimentation and variety during the initial stages when a working model is being developed. After the formation of at least two successful groups, a confederation might be established to exchange ideas and findings, share discussion of difficulties and concerns, lend support, and related activities. Conventions, either annually or less frequently, might be held to stimulate thinking and give recognition to effective people and what they are doing. Such a confederation would help in the dissemination of information.

Planning committees might be elected to set up structures and elect people to hold positions in them. They should plan and determine methods of communication such as publishing newspapers and magazines and setting up websites to distribute pertinent and useful ideas for relevant research and studies, facts, opinions, practical information and such. Of course with the growing power of the Internet most of this early work can be done with websites, e-mail, and such.

Membership would be expanded as much as possible with particular emphasis on people with high moral and ethical values. Centers for the Practical Application of Wisdom might spin off groups to take an active part in politics and assist those candidates, regardless of party, who support goals congruent with building Enlightened Communities. Such groups might point out waste, corruption, dishonesty, and anything else within the community that erodes trust and confidence in the Community. Then CPAWs need to initiate measures to eliminate those things that divert a person from being able to support the society.

As discussed in "Organizing for an Enlightened Community" (Chapter 19), a Center for the Practical Application of Wisdom might develop service groups to ensure that a voice of reason and compassion exists in every community. It is obvious that success will not take place overnight or come about automatically. These changes need to be introduced to alter social institutions as circumstances permit, as people are educated and prepared for their new role in society. A CPAW needs to constantly struggle to achieve worthwhile goals. If it is stopped from accomplishing one goal because of barriers, it needs to then focus energy on overcoming these obstacles possibly by making an end run around the obstacle in order to continue the forward motion. The thing of real necessity is that a CPAW sees the direction in which it desires to move and makes the necessary effort to proceed in that direction.

Enlightened Persons will not achieve mastery of economic and political policy by passive methods or use of violence. They need to create a world in which the illusion that oppressive power is a worthwhile instrument for producing change and that beneficial ends can be accomplished by use of autocratic force will be unable to gain support because these methods are recognized as coming from destructive memes that need to be replaced by better ones. Enlightened Persons will not be prevented from battling those who are so confused they claim to be the enemy. However, Enlightened Persons will work to achieve their goals by providing information and assistance to show the opposition a better way. No intimidation beyond peaceful confrontation, discussion, and resistance could be used since punishment, torture, bloodshed, or threat of force is exactly what is being opposed. The best method for producing change is to provide models showing how a *science of religion and ethics* affects all those who embrace it.

If history has taught us anything, surely it is the danger of violent revolution. When a violent civil revolution begins and sweeps away all that preceded it, the only thing that remains is a mechanism for using violence. The least compassionate, insightful, and visionary are almost always the ones left in control. (At least if the French and Russian revolutions are valid models.)

It is not the Enlightened Person's goal to destroy old ideas. Their goal is to build a useful structure on a solid scientific and ethical foundation. Enlightened Persons need to confront bigotry, graft, corruption, error, and bad ideas wherever they are found. But they should normally avoid attacking organizations of any kind, whether clubs, faiths, lodges, or nations. Any organization can change and become better with the right people working in it. Centers for the Practical Application of Wisdom need to confront always the ideas and actions of individual people. Only an individual person can be wrong. Who is the person misleading the organization, the club, the church, the nation? That is the person to focus on. But these people are not the enemies of Enlightened Persons. No individual person is an enemy to another in this system. A cruel, ignorant, selfish, corrupt, power monger is not an evil person. But they are misguided by erroneous and/or inadequate ideas, hurtful experiences, and/or physiological/psychological states. (All of which they may fight to the death to maintain.) It is not for an Enlightened Person to ridicule, look down on, or make light of these unhealthy people. It is the duty of all Enlightened Persons to hold a mirror up to unwholesome people so that they might better see themselves. It must be the goal to help them; to truly help them to be "reborn" as an Enlightened Person.

Steps need to be taken to aid all people in the community who need help, but in the form of real assistance, a loving support group. A Center for the Practical Application of Wisdom should strive to become not only a good agency, but also a force for good in the community and the world. Its primary purpose is to allow every person to feel connected, to be supported by every other person so their efforts can help maintain and develop the species. One way of doing this would be to set up the organizations discussed in Chapter 20. These include schools to provide alternatives that help young children understand values and how to live -- how to become an Enlightened Person.

In this regard, Enlightened Persons cannot use methods to extend their ideas and ethical system that are inconsistent with the ideas of a *science of religion and ethics*. The Enlightened Person needs to support the open search for information and understanding. Knowledge needs to be treated as an ally not an enemy.

Because all societies up to this time have lacked Wisdom (i.e., the knowledge to be able to properly use knowledge), they cannot be judged as failures for not having helped their members to become Enlightened Persons. Their efforts have made it possible for us to get where we are now. These societies based on erroneous ideas from the past were as incapable of discovering how to produce a *sustainable feeling of well-being* as were earlier cultures of discovering the mathematical formulations necessary to support work with quantum phenomena. However, the only people who can be used as positive role models are those who worked in a constructive manner toward the progress of humanity -- to move humanity toward cultivating the "wisdom" potential. These were the people who were tolerant, loved beauty, had compassion for all their fellow humans, sought truth, felt love, been true to themselves, used power constructively, labored to help other people, discovered, explored, created, searched, resisted tyranny and prejudice, struggled to overcome ignorance and error, and in every way possible attempted to avoid hurting others. There are few who have embodied all these attributes, but each person needs to be valued for their positive contributions while at the same time not overlooking their beliefs and behaviors that were based on their raw "tribal" genetic propensities. And these limiting beliefs and behaviors as demonstrated by the associated negative effects form part of the database to help us avoid similar mistakes.

Even today there are few societies that could explicitly adopt the goal of becoming an Enlightened Community made up of Enlightened Persons. Most societies lack the experience to recognize that they need to view the individual person rather than the group as primary if they are to function at their best.

The United States of America has many areas where these ideas might develop and grow. As a culture the U.S. is free of several disabling conditions: It is not fatalistic, so it believes one person can make a difference. It is not indifferent to the pain and suffering of others, so some of its members are willing to change things when they know how to. Such people think change can make things better. They do not prize sophistication above compassion. They have enough experience to value skepticism. They respect practical involvement. Soiled hands from honest labor are not demeaning. They appreciate learning, education, and research as tools to make a better life and a better world. They know that people are really what are important even though they sometimes lose sight of this vision. They do not see themselves as part of a monolithic culture, but rather participants in a diverse collection of cultures that to varying degrees respect this diversity. And, equally important they have gotten so far from fulfilling the needs people have for social bonding that there exists a vast reservoir of people longing for a better life. [3]

If our species is not only to endure but also to thrive we need a new paradigm. All human beings need to become capable of working together. All people need to realize that they are kin. If someone harms another person, they injure themselves more for they perpetuate their raw "tribal" genetic propensities and increase the difficulty of utilizing their "wisdom" potential. We need to find a way to achieve congruency between the person and society. When this is done each person will experience a joyful life. This is the result of understanding the meaning of human life based on human nature imposed on us by our evolutionary history. And we need to achieve this in a way congruent with our language ability and with objective reality. Humanity's salvation lies within our "wisdom" potential. Although any person's existence is finite, their unique contributions make it possible for their effects to be as infinite as humanity, and to extend humanity's existence toward infinity.

People who believe that they are demonstrating religious and philosophical sophistication when they proclaim life as a period of suffering after which personal immortality is attained are being seduced by childish fantasies from folk religions. They are being trapped by those genes that encourage them to believe in magic. These genes allowed humanity to survive after symbolic language provided us the capacity to question whether living was truly desirable. No other animal can consciously question whether or not to end their own life. Belief in magic and the power of wishing has allowed many people to choose life over death. Their success has now brought us to a new realm. Now we can understand our "wisdom" potential and see reasons to maintain our life for the proper reason: because it is worth living.

A *science of religion and ethics* makes clear that our one life on earth is all we have and that it is all we need. Our life is our true wealth (our only wealth, really). And how we spend it distinguishes the wise from the ignorant. We can throw our life away or we can use it well. Each person has two potentials. One is to become an Enlightened Person. The second is to help others achieve this state even though they do not achieve it for themself. Most frequently this is achieved by using their life to show others that beliefs to avoid because of the negative results. No one has yet been able to accomplish the first. But all of us are helping with the latter -- moving humanity to the place where every person will achieve a *sustainable feeling of well-being*. That will come about when we can produce a world where people do not believe that there is an essential conflict between people and their communities and our societies justify that belief.

Rather we must recognize that symbolic language provides us the possibility of living lives based on cooperation, and any conflict that would divert a person from achieving a *sustainable feeling of well-being* must be recognized as a sign of erroneous beliefs on the part of either the person, the society, or both. When *Homo sapiens sapiens* became *Modern Humans* some 30,000 to 60,000 years ago as a result of the evolution of the language ability they were cast into a time of confusion, although most of them have been only dimly aware of this confusion. Now we are ready to move beyond confusion and seriously apply ourselves to developing a whole different way of living. My hope is that this book will help focus our efforts to develop Enlightened Communities made up of Enlightened Persons. And this approach is now possible because we can clearly see the light at the end of the tunnel!

THE END?

APPENDIX A

HOW TO ACHIEVE THE GOOD LIFE - THE CORE OF THE MATTER

Following are the empirically based assumptions of a *Science of Religion and Ethics* to provide the basis for a user's guide for *Modern Humans* [1] to live the Good Life[2].

- Science is the approach that requires study of the natural world – the only world we can collectively know – and integrating this study into models that allow all data from this world to fit together in a congruent way.
- Religion's responsibility is to help us live the Good Life.
- The science of evolution places religion within the domain of science in the same way that physics, chemistry, and all the other realms of knowledge exist within the domain of science. (Some would call this scientism. I disagree.)
- The Good Life is an ethical life. Ethics deals with right and wrong behavior as measured in terms of human nature and human society.
- Behavior is judged to be right when it is in the person's long-term best interest in terms of maintaining and developing the human species.
- Behavior -- as well as feelings -- comes out of beliefs. And beliefs are the component of a person's being most readily within their personal control.

- A person's long-term best interests equate with achieving the closest approximation currently possible of a sustainable belief that a person's life has meaning thereby allowing them to become an Enlightened Person[3].
- The elements of a *sustainable belief that their life has meaning* can only be determined through empirical study measured in terms of science-based hypotheses.

The goal of this selection is to present the beliefs judged necessary to provide the basis for a naturalistic religion and ethics out of which achievement of a Good Life would flow. The basic details laying out a naturalistic-based religion/ethics are presented in this book.

Following are the introductory statements (The Eleven Ways of Wisdom) for the current working assumptions -- open to revision, clarification, or replacement with improved information -- judged to be essential in order to become an Enlightened Person and thereby live the Good Life.

1. Recognize that human beings are – for us – the ultimate reference system.
2. Endeavor to maintain and develop the human species. Support efforts to develop Enlightened Communities[4] -- communities promoting authentic happiness[5] for all their citizens.
3. Seek to understand. Pursue Wisdom.
4. Recognize that all knowledge rests on faith/beliefs and must always be open to questioning.
5. Strive to make the best choices possible.
6. Know and struggle to improve yourself; work to be physically and psychologically healthy.
7. Develop and adopt a perceptual framework in which pain does not prevent the achievement of a sustainable belief that your life has meaning.
8. Help and be helped by people. Recognize that all human beings are "us," everything else is "them."
9. Work to increase knowledge and all creative and artistic endeavors. Adopt an inspiring life goal.

10. Support efforts to ensure that every child is provided a loving, nurturing environment and all the things necessary to become an Enlightened Person.
11. Make of your life a spiritual quest[6]. Work to become an Enlightened Person. Use the fundamentalist genetic propensity to produce Enlightened Communities.

NOTES

1. **MODERN HUMANS** Discussed by Steven Mithen in *THE PREHISTORY OF THE MIND: The Cognitive Origins of Art and Science*. [Thames and Hudson, New York, 1996.] Modern Humans replaced *Homo sapiens sapiens* and appeared over a period of time from 30,000 to 60,000 years ago. Includes all current human beings.
2. Defining the Good Life = An Enlightened Person = Having a Sustainable Belief That a Person's Life Has Meaning = mastering the components necessary for such a belief.
3. An Enlightened Person is someone whose beliefs provide them the closest approximation currently possible of a sustainable feeling that their life has meaning; that is, they are living the Good Life. This is measured by the degree to which a person has achieved their full positive potential, and that the person is consciously involved in maintaining and developing the human species.
4. An Enlightened Community is one that promotes the belief and implements the idea that human beings are the source of meaning and value and that the individual person should be seen as the focus for society's ultimate concern.
5. Authentic happiness – Consists of three levels: the pleasant life (having as many positive emotions as possible), the good life (fulfilling a person's potential), and the meaningful life (being attached to something bigger than oneself) – collectively making up the Good Life. [See *Authentic Happiness* by Martin E.P. Seligman.]

6. The Spiritual Quest – The quest for wisdom: For a natural-based religion this involves accepting oneself as a natural being evolved in a natural world with the power of symbolic language that provides the ability to look beyond current knowledge and experience and draw inspiration from that vision of awe and the transcendent -- the eternal, the ultimate, the infinite, Truth.

APPENDIX B:

HUMANS AS THE ULTIMATE REFERENCE SYSTEM (CHAPTER 4 EXPANDED)

1. Why reality is not the ultimate reference system.

Reality is not the Ultimate Reference System for many reasons. One, discussed later, is that we can't directly access reality, but only know it through experience and thought; therefore, it cannot be our Ultimate Reference System. Another is that our knowledge of reality changes as we learn more and more. But we need to make all of our choices based on our current understanding. All of our motivations and knowledge are tied to what is known today. For these reasons Humanity itself is our ultimate reference system (HBAURS) -- because we live our full life making choices and plans with the Reference System current knowledge makes available to us. It doesn't matter to us that five generations in the future society's understanding of reality may totally change the way people live and the goals they pursue. Our life has limits. It exists only now. The future is just an unknown, and our only tie to it is our own individual life and our relatedness to humanity.

Because science allows us to better utilize our language ability we are getting better and better approximations to reality (at least insofar as it can be used to improve the quality of human living). But again, all of our interpretations are based on our current understanding of reality -- not on what reality truly is.

Some people have interpreted HBAURS such that they fear it would convince human beings to be satisfied with their current understanding of reality and overlook the need to compare all conclusions, ideas, assumptions, thoughts, and such to Reality As the Objective Reference System.

I take things to be just the opposite: HBAURS requires us to focus on quality of life that provides a driving need to learn more and more about everything that exists. Every aspect of our life depends on understanding reality including the reality of ignorance, disease, hunger, and how our bodies work. This would require that insofar as possible every person's ability would be as fully developed as possible and utilized in this process. Not just to learn, but also to apply our knowledge because for a *science of religion and ethics* that's what knowledge is for.

However, beyond the above issues I think there is another reason why some people exploring a *science of religion and ethics* are very uncomfortable with the HBAURS concept. I think the core of this resistance is that it reminds them of the dreaded anthropomorphism and anthropocentrism that their mothers warned them about!

With the foregoing ideas in mind, let us explore anthropomorphism and anthropocentric in more depth. *Webster's New Collegiate Dictionary* defines these terms as follows.

ANTHROPOCENTRIC: 1. Assuming human beings as the center or ultimate end. 2. Interpreting natural processes or phenomena such as animal instincts, in terms of humanity or the human mind.

ANTHROPOMORPHISM: Representation or conception of God, or of a god, with human attributes; also, ascription of human characteristics to things not human.

It seems to me that HBAURS is just the opposite of anthropocentric/anthropomorphism. Those concepts are based on the view that human beings have a special place in the universe deliberately assigned to them by the universe. HBAURS is based on the view that there are no privileged frames of reference in the universe. It is for this reason that humanity is limited by its own perspective from which it needs to stand as the ultimate interpreter of the universe. As indicated below this would not change even if we made contact with a more knowledgeable, wiser species from elsewhere in the universe. We would have to process their ideas and wisdom in order to apply it which would still leave Human Beings As the Ultimate Reference System.

Some people are bothered that my "ultimate" isn't the ULTIMATE they are used to thinking of: God as the supreme ruler, maker of humanity and the universe, definer of right and wrong, and such -- this is ULTIMATE. I have heard various religious people express the idea that without God there would be no reason to live. Science's model of objective reality – "Laws" of the universe as firmly fixed and infinite in time and space as the mind can conceive -- this is ULTIMATE. Some people are even willing to take the smooth functioning of Earth's ecosystem as an adequate ULTIMATE. But the individual human life! The perpetuation of our species! What kind of ULTIMATE is that?

The reality is that our individual life is as ULTIMATE as it gets! The idea that some people have to see their life as extending to infinity after death seems to me to come out of the human weakness to use symbolic language to take Platonic symbols as having objective rather than subjective existence.

My thesis is simple. The ideas we have been taught about ULTIMATE are as erroneous as most of the other basic ideas we have been taught. The "ultimate" we can reach is to develop ourselves as fully as possible (to achieve a Sustainable Feeling That Our Life Has Meaning) that includes using our accomplishments to help all other people attain a similar state now and into the future. And to do our best to ensure that humanity will prevail and maintain this vision. This vision would guide each person utilizing their "wisdom" potential. This is the step that is now possible for human beings to take. And any who are able to help make it happen would become the greatest heroes humanity has ever produced. Using Joseph Campbell's words, I take this as the "hero's journey." [1]

If Human Beings Are the Ultimate Reference System, what does "ultimate" mean in this context? Wouldn't "subjective" be more accurate?

I am using ultimate in the sense, "beyond which it is impossible to proceed [at this moment]." The reason it is impossible to proceed beyond human beings is not because we cannot learn more about the universe. History shows us that there is more to learn about the universe than we can even imagine at any given time.

It is impossible to proceed beyond human understanding because we are the observers. It is only what we can observe and interpret at this moment that defines our current limits. As we learn more -- were we to evolve and change -- the same principle would still be true. Until something impacts us we can't take it into account and be aware of it, understand how it affects our ideas about the universe, and how it might be used to improve the quality of human life. However, we can use what we now know to guide us to better understand the universe we live in.

It is not because the universe is affected by our observations, or depends in any way on them -- in spite of the contrary speculations of the Anthropic Principle and some who use the Copenhagen interpretation of quantum mechanics. Rather it is because we depend on our observations and inferences for whatever we know or believe about the universe. To think the universe is the reference system makes it easier to ignore the fact that every observation has more ignorance than information associated with it. The ignorance comes out of how we make observations, the knowledge and experience we bring to the observation, and so forth.

It doesn't matter that everything else -- all matter and all life -- would have its own reference system (i.e., be its own reference system). But, rather, because we are limited to our own reference system. We can learn, expand, correct, and improve our reference system so it may move closer to "objective reality." But regardless of the foregoing, we observe only from our frame of reference no matter how well or badly that frame of reference takes into account everything else in the universe. Even though our ignorance of what is unknown to us may kill us or otherwise affect us, until that happens we can't take it into account. Therefore, our reference system is ultimate for us. And, that is the most ultimate we can achieve. This is recognizing ultimate as an empirical term not a Platonist term.

I believe the ancient Greek sophist, Protagoras (c. 481 - 411 BCE), was making this point when he said, "Humanity is the measure of all things, of things that are that they are, and of things that are not that they are not." This position does not deny that there is a real world out there, nor that we are part of that natural world. It means that things do not have value in terms of some absolute reference system. The only value we can be aware of is the value we provide. It means that the well-being of human beings is the essential measure relative to everything. And of course value and well-being here as in all other elements of a *science of religion and ethics* means in terms of the most complete and long-term measures possible. However, human interpretations of necessity come out of a position of ignorance.

Our ways of understanding can only deal with discrete segments of the universe since we have no tools that allow us to understand it fully, and completely. In fact scientific study can only begin once we become aware of some part of the universe and find tools to subject that area to adequate study. But this study is always a work in progress and any conclusions are tentative, subject to change with more information.

Because we are and must always be ignorant of what the universe is really like, we need to stop thinking that our primary goal is to understand the universe. Our goal needs to be to use whatever information and knowledge we have to improve the quality of human living. Obviously, we need to learn everything we can about how the universe works in order to do this. But it is the application of this knowledge that gives it value. This doesn't mean that scientists should only work on "practical" problems. Essential information will surely continue to come from those striving to understand how things work, things that don't seem to have any possible useful benefit. Study of the history of science needs to lead us to believe that these efforts will provide bountiful dividends -- when their results are applied. However, thoughtful people should not miss the point that current human potential is only possible because scientists over at least the past 400 years have studied, pondered, and experimented based on questions that on the surface had no value to human life and well being. This situation can only become more true in the future as we enter realms that from the outside look almost like science fiction.

"Interpreter" as I am using it focuses on the point that human beings are affected by taste, touch, light, smell, and sound, but we have to process (interpret) those stimuli to "make sense" of them. Human beings need to interpret everything and regardless of whatever interpretation any other reference system makes we still have to make our own interpretation. If we become able to communicate with other intelligent beings, or when we develop conscious artificial life we will find that their reference systems are different from ours and we will still have to interpret all of our interactions with them.

Careful, open-minded analysis and study demonstrate that thinking is not promoted when we take an interpreter to have powers to see the ultimate. In addition it is not meaningful to propose reference systems more ultimate than human beings either in religion or in science. [2]

There can be no point outside of human beings themselves that can be used as an Ultimate Reference System. Any line of thought aimed at demonstrating an Ultimate Reference System outside of human beings fails. Any concept pursued to its essential implications inevitably leads a person to recognize the foregoing. Human beings are the observers, recorders, measurers, valuers, and such. Everything needs to be interpreted by human beings. Everything needs to be filtered through their sense organs and mental processes. People who claim a direct contact with reality (including Ultimate Reality) cannot be distinguished in any way from liars, psychotics, and/or people who are erroneously interpreting their mental processes. So these people like everyone else need to have their truth claims judged on the basis of standards that apply to faith arguments. See Fourth Way of Wisdom. [3]

All serious thought needs to at some point confront this issue. Philosophers have from early times attempted to get at the core of this issue through dividing studies into ontology and epistemology. In my mind the concept "human beings are the ultimate reference system" shows us that the distinction between ontology and epistemology is the distinction between conjecture and experience. Since ontology is supposed to be about the study of the fundamental nature of reality, and epistemology about our knowledge of that reality, we start by using our knowledge to examine our ignorance -- what we don't know (i.e., the fundamental nature of reality). The fundamental nature of the universe (reality) is unknowable -- hidden in ignorance -- so we can only make conjectures about it. What we take it to be at any given time depends on our knowledge. Therefore, we reflect that knowledge back to the universe and primarily see expanding versions of what we already know. Of course when science is working there is always some awareness of the deviation between what we think we know and what we observe.

As our knowledge grows we recognize the conflicts between our conjectures and observations and change what we take the fundamental nature of reality to be. But again we are looking at the interpretation of our knowledge that we have imposed on that unknown universe to see something about "the fundamental nature of reality."

But from a practical standpoint, what are we really discussing when we say Human Beings Are the Ultimate Reference System? How can we deal with the issue that each person is a unique reference system, yet when we discuss human beings as the ultimate reference system we are thinking about human beings in general? One way to approach this issue may be to use as a model some ideas Robert Plutchik discusses. He has a similar concern in naming emotions: "... [An] important point might be made about the problem of naming emotion compounds. This is a problem almost identical with that faced by the international conference that set out in 1931 to develop a system for the numerical specification of what a color looks like to the ordinary man or woman under a given set of conditions. Since there are certain differences in the reaction of individual observers, even after people with abnormal color vision have been eliminated, it was necessary to define a color match that would be acceptable to an average observer. This was done by defining how a 'standard observer' sees any particular color. The average data from a small number of selected observers provided an imaginary standard observer, and all results reported in the CIE [Commission Internationale De L'Eclairage; i.e., International Commission on Illumination] system are adjusted so as to satisfy the requirements of this standard observer. This is a system that has worked very well since 1931. Perhaps a similar system may be developed for the psychology of emotions." [4]

Perhaps the CIE system could also serve as a model for the concept, "Human Beings Are the Ultimate Reference System." With proper efforts it might be possible to define a "standard observer" as the reference system that projects, observes, interprets the universe, and serves as the reference system used by an Enlightened Person. This point of view is based on the assumption that in the ways that are most important, all human beings are the same. And, of course, this assumption conflicts with current beliefs about the nature of human beings.

2. A new paradigm for imagining the basic components of the Universe

If anyone desires to develop a new paradigm for solving the wave/particle "problem" I suggest a weeklong conference with a small group of quantum physicists and a similar number of artists. The physicists would present in as much detail as possible all of the experiments from which the dual nature of the quantum world is postulated. After each presentation there would be a significant period of time for questions and brainstorming. After the physicists discuss their data each person would have a chance to offer conjectures on what is really happening and lead a brainstorming effort focused on this particular discussion.

Papers would be written and exchanged. Each person (especially the artists) would make their best effort at describing what might actually be going on in these experiments. If no breakthroughs had occurred there would be a follow-up meeting after a year or so to either focus on the ideas generated or retrace their steps to see if something had been overlooked in the first go-around. And the conference would focus on all the ideas presented to see if any approach for imagining what was going on looked fruitful and if there were ideas for how to pursue them to see if they led to a working hypothesis.

3. Can we know when something is unpredictable?

Although many people believe that Heisenberg's Uncertainty Principle has pointed out a curtain beyond which humanity cannot look, this is not necessarily the case. The Uncertainty Principle, Second Law of Thermodynamics, Conservation of Mass-Energy, Einstein's speed of light do not necessarily represent the final word about how the Universe works. They represent humanity's best thinking and experience as of this time. But the future may present very different explanations. A hypothesis, theory, principle, "Law," or point of view is useful if it leads a person toward becoming an Enlightened Person with a *sustainable feeling of well-being*. We should on principle reject the idea that hypotheses, theories, or laws are totally accurate statements about reality, or define absolute barriers or limits. Any such barrier needs to contain a component of ignorance based on our unproven assumptions about the Universe, plus all the things we have not yet experienced. As David Hume's writings -- about human access to the ultimate nature of physical reality -- make clear, prediction is inherently risky. The foregoing applies to predictions about barriers to knowledge as well as about the future. In the spirit of John Dewey we should look at each prediction pragmatically as a tool to enhance thinking, not to prevent it.

To repeat myself a little it seems to me that Niels Bohr supports the foregoing position when he says, "It is wrong to think that the task of physics is to find out how Nature is. Physics concerns what we can say about Nature." [5] However, in my opinion Bohr violates his own principle in the process of attempting to apply it. It is my contention that the Copenhagen interpretation of quantum mechanics of which he was a primary author (but with the essential assistance of Werner Heisenberg) ends up demonstrating that physicists like everyone else can't avoid making assumptions about the nature of reality. In his effort to avoid ascribing attributes to quantum particles when they have not been observed, he ends up giving unobserved particles mystic attributes; that is, their wave or particle character depend on the observer, that they have no location until they are observed, and such. It is clear that what we can say about Nature to a large degree depends on our understanding at a given point in history. But regardless of this we need to make assumptions that go beyond our knowledge. And, although there may be absolute barriers, we need to forever remain in doubt as to just where those points lie.

Inherently Unpredictable: To demonstrate what is meant by inherently unpredictable consider the following example. What will be the exact path of a particular hurricane? We know the general direction in which all hurricanes move, but we do not have adequate tools to gather data and analyze it so as to predict the exact path of a specific hurricane. Chaos theory tells us hurricane paths are determined but impossible to predict except within certain time and geographical limits. Chaos theory says we can never know all the forces with sufficient accuracy to avoid the "butterfly effect" (a sensitive dependence on initial conditions). Also, errors must creep into our predictions unless all forces are considered because all things are interrelated in ways we don't fully understand. All things are not now known let alone being reducible to mathematical formulas and models. The ideas in this book will have been long superseded before the day arrives when most long-range predictions do not fail because they are overwhelmed by our lack of information and the subtlety of the effects of myriads of factors.

Of course the very act of using mathematics to understand or predict a physical force or event already misrepresents the physical reality. As Einstein said, "As far as the laws of mathematics refer to reality, they are not certain, as far as they are certain they do not refer to reality." Mathematics is a way of representing relationships within the realm of Platonic Ideals. There are points and lines without dimensions and myriads of other wondrous things. Reality is something quite different. Everything is messy and contingent. Although small segments of reality may sometimes resemble a given mathematical relationship, the conditions under which the correspondence will be maintained is always open to question. And even though mathematics has been almost a miraculous tool for studying reality it is in the final analysis a tool and must never be seen as more than that. In the absence of total knowledge some assumptions are always necessary and this makes most predictions problematical. Unless we are careful to correct these assumptions (such as the fact that mathematical points and lines lack dimension, while real points and lines have dimension, etc.) we will miss essential aspects of reality.

The more data we have and the more powerful our tools for processing it, the more accurate our predictions can be at least within some narrow range of space and time. Nevertheless, we cannot foretell what people of the future will be able to predict. It seems to me that they will be able to make predictions and use forces beyond our wildest imaginations. However, it is clear that totality is inherently unknowable to humanity due to the large number of individual factors. Also, these factors -- most of which are not even known at any given time -- even when known, interact in unpredictable ways, and others are not known with sufficient accuracy to permit long-term predictions. As a result totality must forever remain unknown and unpredictable.

4.   Levels of Feeling That A Person's Life Has Meaning

There are obviously different levels of a *feeling that a person's life has meaning*. At the highest level it equates with being an Enlightened Person such that the person is functioning in a state of happiness or even ecstasy much of the time. They are effective and competent, valued by their community and a contributing member at many different levels. They experience nurturing love and physical affection in all its forms. They are part of an Enlightened Community working to maintain and develop the human species. Their beliefs are supported by current knowledge, or at least not in conflict with it. They can change beliefs as knowledge grows so they can sustain this state as they develop and change over their lifetime and interact with an unpredictable universe. In this level the person is able to make choices deemed ethical by a *science of religion and ethics.*

At a more medium level people feel that they are a part of their society and participate in elections, have a job and/or other activities that contribute to the well-being of society, and a family that they love and that loves them. They feel good about themselves, what they are doing, and their community. However, they may feel no connection to humanity and may even feel it is flawed and the universe would be better off without it. They would say they are living a happy life. They hold beliefs clearly not supportable by existing knowledge, but these beliefs are necessary to support their good feelings; for example, that God loves them and hears their prayers.

At a lower level people may see themselves as part of a family, but there is no deep connection and sharing. They may be in a relationship but there are barriers to total trust and acceptance. They may have a job, but it very likely involves taking advantage of the public, or doing things that have little social value, or may actually be socially destructive. Off the job they spend their time watching TV, drinking beer at the beach, or in other habitual activities that sustain them, but do not develop their humanity. They have no life goal other than having as much fun as possible and doing as little work as they can get away with. There is little happiness in their life. They see their goals as inherently in conflict with the goals of society and other people in general. They may have a pet that is their closest friend. Or, possibly, their best friend is Jesus.

At still lower levels people may abuse drugs or alcohol, participate in criminal behavior, or take advantage of others to obtain money, and so forth. Their life is characterized by pain, misery, and other negative feelings. Happiness is a rare or nonexistent state. Most of their relationships are exploitative or superficial.

And at the bottom of the list are those who lack a *feeling that their life has meaning.* This is the person who engages in self-destructive behavior that eventually causes someone else to kill them, or else they take their own life -- either directly or through indifference and neglect -- abuse of drugs, frequent fist fights, ignoring medical problems, life-threatening behavior such as Russian Roulette, and such. However, normally before this state is reached they go through a period of despair and/or unbearable pain. Deep depression is their constant companion. Any happiness is too rare to be remembered. They have very bad health that may kill them at an early age.

APPENDIX C

OTHER SUPPORT ORGANIZATIONS (CHAPTER 20 EXPANDED)

This section develops the ideas about organizations presented briefly in Chapter 20. This is designied to initiate the process of thinking about this issue. These ideas are presented as working hypotheses. Obviously, no one can truly lay out all the structures needed to develop and maintain an Enlightened Community. Practical experience will be essential as steps are taken to reach necessary goals. However, we need a way to focus experiments and data gathering so that the process can begin. As in all aspects of a *science of religion and ethics* results are the criterion by which everything is measured. And results mean helping more and more people achieve a *sustainable feeling of well-being*.

OVERVIEW

1. ORGANIZATION TO ENHANCE THE QUALITY OF HUMAN LIFE (OEQHL)
2. NEW IDEAS, REVOLUTIONARY INSIGHTS, AND/OR UNIQUE ANSWERS INSTITUTE (NIRIUA-I)
3. THE SCHOOL
4. CHOICES ARE US (CAU)
5. EMERGENCY SERVICES CENTER (ESC)
6. CENTER FOR MASTERING LIVING (CFML)
7. A PLACE FOR KIDS
8. THE COMPUTER CONNECTION
9. THE RADIO LINK

10. CORPORATION FOR UNIVERSAL EMPLOYMENT (CUE)
11. CENTER FOR THE PRACTICAL APPLICATION OF WISDOM NEWS GROUP (CPAW-NG)
12. HEALTH CARE CLINIC
13. REGIONAL PLANNING AND COORDINATING INSTITUTIONS
14. ORGANIZATION FOR THE PROTECTION OF LABOR

DETAIL

1. ORGANIZATION TO ENHANCE THE QUALITY OF HUMAN LIFE (OEQHL) [1] (pronounced "equal")

An Organization to Enhance the Quality of Human Life (OEQHL) should be developed to function with a Center for the Practical Application of Wisdom (CPAW). Its goal would be to make sure that the frontiers of scientific discovery are being pushed in all areas of science to ensure that knowledge and understanding are developing as rapidly as desirable. An OEQHL would be particularly focused to help people achieve the Third, Second, and Ninth Ways of Wisdom. [2] It would work to disseminate and teach the latest scientific views to as many people as possible. It would also develop ways to put new information to work improving the quality of life. An OEQHL would also constantly review scientific laws and theories as to adequacy, focusing attention on their weaknesses and strengths. It would develop tests by which to assess the validity of theories. Then if no researcher had the interest or resources to work on the problems raised by an OEQHL, they would establish their own ways to do this.

The problem might be broken up and disseminated to local associations and organizations joined with an OEQHL. These could be groups established to allow everyone a chance to participate in new and useful research. The individual members of these local organizations would primarily be volunteers. They would work together as their time allowed to gather the data and do the research needed by an OEQHL. An OEQHL would assimilate, evaluate, and disseminate this data to assess its value. It would be through these local bodies that every person who wanted to would be able to achieve the <u>Ninth Way of Wisdom</u> (Work to increase knowledge and all creative and artistic endeavors. Adopt an inspiring life goal) and contribute to the advance of knowledge.

An OEQHL would have many projects waiting for those with the desire and talents to work on them. Also, people with particular areas of interest or concern would be able to submit them to an OEQHL for assistance in exploring the areas involving those interests. All people ready to develop this part of their psychological makeup would thus be able to fulfill the creative urge, and contribute to the advance of knowledge especially in areas where they might have a personal stake such as finding a cure for a disease or genetic defect, developing better tools to use in their business, and so forth.

See VOLUME II, Chapter 32, "Science for Everyone," for an excellent model to incorporate into an OEQHL. [3]

2. NEW IDEAS, REVOLUTIONARY INSIGHTS, AND/OR UNIQUE ANSWERS INSTITUTE (NIRIUA-I) [pronounced near-you-a Institute]

"A revolutionary insight disconnected from the current consensus is unlikely to be published." [4] It is easy to understand why this statement relative to scientific journal publishing policy is the case. Most ideas that have these characteristics turn out to be of little immediate value. Also, it's difficult to know what to do with such an idea, suggestion, or hypothesis. Because it is revolutionary much work is required to utilize it even if it is correct. But on the other hand the truly important ideas are revolutionary. Every currently accepted idea of true significance had to go through this barrier. All of them made it, or they wouldn't be discussed much today. But for every revolutionary insight that was able to reach the mainstream, probably 10 out of 100 got lost. They didn't get recorded anywhere. The discoverer lacked the skill, the clout, the contacts, the endurance, and the interest to put the idea out there in a way that would get attention and lead to discussion. This represents an irreplaceable loss to humanity. Although most revolutionary ideas when lost are rediscovered so eventually they receive the recognition they deserve, some do not. These ideas are so unique and require such an unusual experience and/or powers of observation to be recognized that they are totally lost to humanity. But even if they are eventually rediscovered, they were not available for use by all those in between the initial and the successful rediscovery. This problem needs to be addressed by an Enlightened Community and solved in a favorable way, since an Enlightened Community is very much here and now, not pie in the sky by and by.

All of the foregoing suggests that society is permanently losing really important observations, ideas, and ponderings because we have not yet developed and established a way to harvest these unique contributions. The methods of current scientific journal publication, not to mention all the other fields of study, do not allocate space for such purposes. However, an Enlightened Community cannot afford to depend only on current practices for mining ideas since such a community will be knowledge and idea-driven. Of course Internet adds a whole new dimension to this matter.

Nevertheless, a NIRIUA [5] Institute needs to be established to energize, support, coordinate, oversee and promote this approach. Its goal would be to provide a channel so anyone can get ideas into the society in such a way that those ideas can be used insofar as they have merit. One reason this resource is so necessary is that it should be able to alert the community to problems not detectable by mainstream thinking. Therefore, it is crucial that the merit of the input not be totally determined by mainstream thinkers. Otherwise, the most important ideas will be excluded, thereby defeating a key reason for the system.

This Institute needs to function as part of The Knowledge Bank [6]; that is, the primary resource of The Computer Connection (see below). It would aim to be the source for all the world's current knowledge. It would make available an expert system that would help anyone to input her or his contributions. People would be guided by an expert system in working through the necessary steps to describe their thinking. This would increase the likelihood that ideas could be presented so as to make their merit obvious. Wise ideas would then be processed for inclusion in related areas under public discussion. Some aspect of the Internet would fit naturally into this process.

Participants in the NIRIUA Institute would become a prized resource of an Enlightened Community. Participants would receive recognition, awards, rewards, and in all other ways be acknowledged for their value and worth. Only an Enlightened Community would have the flexibility and be able to provide the channels of communication necessary to make such a process work. A NIRIUA Institute would ensure that not only the alphas; that is, the people with loud voices and sharp elbows -- a willingness to keep hammering on closed doors -- would be able to be heard.

Also, the NIRIUA Institute would ensure that all areas where science impacts human life are kept under observation so that information is being used in the best way possible. In addition, potential problem areas effecting human well-being would be a topic of continuous consideration and concern. This group would ensure that the importance of any observations made, or concerns expressed in the community could be monitored and properly assessed. This is an essential factor if we are to build a society congruent with the needs of *Modern Humans* and ensure the perpetuation of the species -- the goal of a *science of religion and ethics*.

3. THE SCHOOL

Schools are another adjunct structure that Centers for the Practical Application of Wisdom (CPAW) should consider setting up soon after they are established. It is almost impossible for any current society to set up the kinds of schools necessary to produce Enlightened Persons. The primary goal of a CPAW's schools would be to make students aware of their full positive potential. These schools would provide, insofar as possible, all the resources to help students through the transition made possible by a *science of religion and ethics* and a CPAW: to work toward their own perfection and for the perfection of society. (Also see VOLUME II, Chapter 30, "Education in An Enlightened Community." [7])

Good teaching and good education are key issues in an Enlightened Community. Congruency is essential to good teaching and good education. And congruency is the weakness of current society's worldview. The binding religion of U.S. society (Christianity) shows us one image of the world (authority/tradition, miracles, souls, God, prayer, angels, heaven, hell, freewill, and such) -- and science shows us another; cause and effect, physical not mystical, mind not soul, atoms not God. This lack of congruency in society is a primary source of the chaos that undermines our well-being. Things will not get better until we reach a new congruency.

And it is the goal of a *science of religion and ethics* to provide the vision and plans to achieve that congruency. In this formulation meaning and ethics become part of a broadened vision of science. Also, good teaching affects a person's choices and how they interpret everything they encounter. It helps determine who a person is, and what they become. Teaching, experience, understanding are what make it possible to find and accept a congruent worldview. Only with superb teaching will any society be able to develop into an Enlightened Community made up of Enlightened Persons.

However, at the same time a CPAW needs to be concerned about improving in all ways possible the public school system and all private school systems. Our public educational system requires many changes if society is to move beyond the current chaos. Our present schools are based on the supernatural, as is much of society. They are designed to prepare a person for a brief "bondage" here on earth before going to a greater existence after death. Although the foregoing is not widely recognized, to me it is nevertheless clearly the case. This book presents the presupposition that supernatural concepts are products of our transition from ignorance (before the evolution of the language ability) toward knowledge (after the evolution of the language ability). Supernatural concepts came out of humanity's effort to symbolize the feelings and images that existed before words, thoughts, predictions could be shared with others and elaborated in our own brains. Most of them involve various aspects of our "belief in magic and the power of wishing" propensity. Supernatural thinking came out of our efforts to resolve the conflict between what we are and what we would like to be.

Before the evolution of symbolic communication, "meaning of life" (eat, reproduce, and die) was the natural birthright of all those people since it was the direct consequence of their genes as it is for the people of every other species evolved on this earth. After the evolution of the language ability we were able to ask the question, what is the meaning of life? At that point our history began. We set out on the journey that is discussed in more depth in Chapter 1. This journey has taken us along the many paths pursued over the past 10,000 - 15,000 years. All of these experiences and the resulting accumulation of knowledge have now made it possible to see the light at the end of the tunnel.

At the end of the tunnel lies an Enlightened Community made up of Enlightened Persons. This will provide a new stability based on our language ability, our "wisdom" potential.

How can a *science of religion and ethics* and a CPAW help society discard the old ways and adopt the new? To do this we need to decide on another goal for education. The vision of this book is that education needs to first and foremost permit discovery of people's full personhood, and simultaneously develop as a social being achieving congruency with all other human beings. Schools also need to provide ways to nurture curiosity and creativity as well as mastery of the facts and ideas on which to build a successful life.

A CPAW's schools should have as their goal the teaching of how the meaning of each student's life will be achieved as they master basic skills, especially the skill to find the answers to the questions that excite them. This might be combined with a deep, universal educational background, and a solid scientific/philosophical/religious/ethical foundation. The foregoing might be assisted by helping each student find their inspiring life goal; that is, an area where they have a consuming, overpowering curiosity or interest. This life goal would then serve as a reservoir of enthusiasm to draw from in tackling other school coursework. In addition, students would begin participating in the effort to expand human knowledge/ aesthetic creations as encouraged by the <u>Ninth Way of Wisdom</u> (Work to increase knowledge and all creative and artistic endeavors. Adopt an inspiring life goal.)

This curiosity and interest should also help students focus on where to direct their careers. After mastering the basic skills of learning they could begin employment in an area that involves their deep interest. They might then extend their education in various ways. In addition to regular college and university attendance, they might utilize correspondence courses, night courses, computer-programmed learning courses, and other part-time attendance in regular school courses mixing learning and application. But most of all they would have a mentor to help them through some of the chaos and confusion of choices.

Another area of concern should focus on the bigger issues of preparing our young people to take their place in society as effective, responsible participants. The problem area of the person's genetics has escaped consideration by current Western society. Also, those cultures that have developed writing have felt that they can ignore any genetic programming that exists within the person and treat youths in any way the culture desires without considering the effects of those inner forces. As a result puberty and possibly its deep meaning to the species is almost totally ignored -- although junior high schools were established in an effort to deal with some of these issues. For some thoughts on the issue of puberty and education see Chapter One. For other relevant educational concerns see VOLUME II, Chapter 30, "Education in an Enlightened Community." [7]

Through understanding and utilizing these considerations society should be able to provide alternatives to current educational approaches that cause people to be separated from their core needs by their schooling. This often develops the feeling in these students that they are removed from the mainstream of life and what they are doing is pointless. Educational institutions need to be intimately connected and integrated with all other social institutions. In addition they should be in harmony with the natural development of the person. People need to be able to move as easily as possible within the framework of the community. If a person has an aptitude for a certain subject or area of study an opportunity should be made available for them to explore that ability rather than diverting them in a thousand different directions and placing hundreds of obstacles in their path. When workers come to the place in their career where more knowledge and training are required, they need to be encouraged and supported to obtain that education.

Even more important is the dissemination of education: "... [W]e cannot afford to let the mass of humanity be uneducated." [8] For to do so removes these people from the path toward becoming Enlightened Persons. So, instead of helping to create an Enlightened Community they become obstacles and make the process even more difficult. Every attempt that is made to advance society is halted by the ignorance of inadequately educated people. Customs press on the society from every side. Tradition keeps the society from refocusing and revitalizing its efforts. Irrationalities become deciding factors in many people's decisions. Only through lifelong education and social support can the foregoing be prevented. This process needs to be of sufficient scope to enable people to know themselves and to feel their interconnectedness with all their fellow humans. It needs to help them avoid destructive bonding to hypothetical agencies such as God, angels, the environment, all life, and so forth. Also, such bonding to organizations -- whether nations, religions, families, or other aggregations -- that ask for total submission to unquestionable assumptions plus absolute loyalty and obedience needs to be discouraged.

At the present time people can be more successful and useful to themselves and society if they are specialists. Two things concerning this need to be kept in mind, however: 1) People need to have a broad enough general education to be aware of the important ideas of a *science of religion and ethics*. 2) People need not be confined to one specialty. If they are interested in more than one thing and are willing to expend the energy to become specialized in more than one area, they need to be encouraged to do so. These both will surely be rewarding, not only to the person but also to society. In an Enlightened Community "experts" need to be encouraged to function in the broader society, not just within their range of academic education and professional experience. They need to understand how the rest of knowledge impacts their field.

4. CHOICES ARE US (CAU)

Choices Are Us (CAU) would be established to help people achieve the Fifth Way of Wisdom (Strive to make the best choices possible). This service would initially be set up to help the members of Wisdom Groups in their efforts to move toward Tenth Level membership at which time they would be recognized as Enlightened Persons.

CAU might provide workshops and classes with training in making decisions. These classes could teach the procedures that lead to making the best choices. Also, such classes might include teachers who have advanced skills and training in choice making as well as appropriate tools such as expert systems and supercomputers with access to vast storehouses of information available to help in making a particularly difficult choice.

In addition each person's Computer, Tutor, Recorder, and Expert Systems (CTRES) could include a simpler "decision-making" expert system to help them grapple with normal day-to-day problems. Perhaps it would only be when the requirements of a given choice exceeded the capacity of their CTRES that they would be referred to Choices Are Us.

5. EMERGENCY SERVICES CENTER (ESC)

Emergency Services Centers (ESCs) need to be set up as part of CPAW. These would be facilities open at all times, always ready to help those who come to them. There would be procedures for extending aid to those requesting or needing it. People would also be channeled by all those working to build an Enlightened Community, or others working with people who need help. Some of these might be people who work where people needing aid gather: taverns, churches, social service organizations, skid-rows, employment offices, houses of prostitution, pornography outlets, free food distribution sites, homeless shelters, jails/prisons [9], and so forth.

Aid needs to start immediately when people make contact. This help needs to depend on the needs of the specific person. In situations where the person is in a state where they might commit murder or other violent or criminal acts, suicide, and such the highest level of support would be needed. ESCs' services should include crisis lines, suicide prevention, soup kitchens [10], emergency housing, and the like.

As our understanding of *Modern Humans* improves it becomes clear that each person needs continuing support. As we make the transition from existing ideas about the elements of human nature and the goals of society, we will encounter overwhelming problems. People improperly and inadequately educated and socialized will be difficult to help to become Enlightened Persons. It is essential to establish groups to help people not able to participate productively in society. Providing food and meals would be an obvious first step. Shelter and jobs are clear next steps. But most important, people need to have their personal power liberated so they can use their abilities to help society in ways that provide them the resources necessary to live at their ideal level. The goal is to develop a community in which each person can be a contributing part, and from this standpoint the possibilities are endless.

6. CENTER FOR MASTERING LIVING (CFML)

A Center for Mastering Living (CFML) needs to be established as part of a CPAW to work with all who are dissatisfied with themselves, or society. A CFML would have numerous activities aimed at helping a given person master every barrier to their becoming an Enlightened Person. It would be a resource to help interested people understand how the universe works. It would be focused especially toward those in the midst of dealing with a real problem such as earning a living, establishing or maintaining a love relationship, focusing their life in a constructive direction, achieving desired skills and education, and so forth. There is a great need for such an organization since we now have no social institution that is available to help people become their best selves and avoid those paths that move them in other directions. This is perhaps one of the greatest needs of our society. At one level or another most of us are lost sheep wandering around in the dark. This has been true since the evolution of the language ability. Sadly enough those who claim to be shepherds are more lost than almost anyone else. (They are not only on the wrong path; they are committed to their error in such a way that correcting it is almost impossible.)

The part of this organization working with law-breakers or potential law-breakers would work together with existing criminal justice institutions. However, its long-term goal would be to develop sufficient support to change existing laws and criminal justice institutions [9] to help them become congruent with the values and knowledge of a *science of religion and ethics*. (See VOLUME II, Chapter 22, "A Close Look at the Criminal Justice System.") [11]

The primary challenge would be to provide positive, effective alternatives to help the person deal more effectively with life. Because we currently have no organizations based on a *science of religion and ethics* it should not be surprising that effective, helpful organizations are so rare. There are few contemporary institutions that even come close to being able to cope with the problem of crime. Almost none recognize criminal behavior for what it is.

Crime is actually a symptom of either a person's own problems, a social problem, or both. For a person it might be rooted in having been raised in an abusive or exploitative family, or one providing insufficient bonding and/or support. It can come out of misdirected efforts to satisfy the alpha male/female drive. Or, it may be a self-destructive reaction to stress, or a biochemical imbalance. Once crime is recognized as being not only the problem of society, but also the problem of the very people who manifest it, then there is a chance for improvement. For a person, criminal behavior is almost never a solution to a problem. Rather, it creates bigger problems. Therefore, in most cases the need is not to protect society from people but rather to protect people from their own beliefs and behavior.

Any organization working with alienated people in an attempt to eliminate crime would need to have the type of reputation for help that would encourage people with problems to come for assistance voluntarily. To achieve this people would have to be convinced that the organization was trying to help them and that they were of intrinsic value to society as people, not just because of the problem caused by their behavior. Under the foregoing circumstances many people would seek help before they reached the ultimate in alienation and began to murder, steal, rape, commit suicide, abuse drugs, and such. One activity might incorporate the ideas and procedures invented by Hank Giarretto, PhD in Santa Clara County, California in the early '70s. (See VOLUME II, Chapter 23, "Child Sexual Abuse Treatment Program" [that evolved into the Giarretto Institute]). [12]

People who did not come of their own volition might be channeled by concerned citizens, or even through the criminal justice system.

7. A PLACE FOR KIDS (APFK)

A Place For Kids (APFK) would be a home set up to take care of orphans, as well as unwanted and abused children. [13] It would embody procedures designed to achieve the Tenth Way of Wisdom (Ensure that every child is provided a loving, nurturing environment and all the things necessary to become an Enlightened Person). These homes need to be open to experimentation in all directions. Current opinion, particularly among liberals, tends to hold the view that a child can receive the love and care they need only within a family. However, it is clear that the issue is not this simple. For an interesting look at some of the forces that drive our current opinions on orphanages and custodial childcare, see "Public Policy and the 'Wicked Stepmother'." [14]

8. THE COMPUTER CONNECTION

Individual people and families often move to a metropolitan area because they value the cultural opportunities there: sports, theaters, museums, libraries, universities, opera, and the hundreds of other resources possible when wealth and population come together.

However, up to this time this has been problematic. The very complexity that makes variety possible also forms a barrier. In every major city in the world, but particularly in the U.S., vast numbers of people sit alone and feel lonely because the mechanism for connecting with others who share their core values or important interests does not exist. Lack of adequate channels makes it difficult for people to meet and develop fulfilling relationships in spite of the large population living in the area who share similar core values, concerns, interests, dreams, and so forth. (See VOLUME II, Chapter 5.A, "Intimacy and a *Science of Religion and Ethics*.") [15]

The condition described here is one of the challenges faced by those who would work to build a better world, a place where people have the love and support necessary to live the good life. Today, fortunately, we have a resource that did not exist before -- the Internet with Facebook, YouTube, and such. With proper use of computers it is increasingly possible for people to connect with those who share key interests. The foregoing might allow people to spend the bulk of their time experiencing what we all need most -- nurturing, and learning/teaching interactions with others who value us and who we value in return.

Obviously, one of the needs we are most aware of is the desire for a mate, or a significant other. Almost everyone feels a longing for someone to intimately share his or her life and interests with. (See VOLUME II, Chapter 7, "Romantic Love and a *Science of Religion and Ethics*.") [16] This need is felt most intensely when a person lacks close friends. But most people experience a desire for many kinds of human contacts. Different people feel the need to share different areas of interest: intellectual and/or social conversations and thought; a particular interest such as playing cards or chess; physical activity such as jogging, golf, or other sports; dancing, poetry, star gazing, politics, and such.

With the proper effort each of these things should be available if not always, at least often enough to significantly enrich a person's life. Developing such networks should be a key goal of a CPAW.

The Knowledge Bank (see VOLUME II, Chapter 19, "The Knowledge Bank") would be a primary resource for helping people connect to fill social needs. [17] It would be a central tool of The Computer Connection, and possibly provide the motivating energy to establish it.

This organization would gather all the known information in the world and insofar as possible have it prepared, sorted, and available through the Internet or something comparable. This would ensure that all information necessary to develop an Enlightened Community and to become an Enlightened Person would be available in the best form circumstances permitted.

All of the organizations that would make up an Enlightened Community would be tied into the Knowledge Bank to gain assistance in doing the best that current knowledge permits. In addition this Knowledge Bank would provide much of the glue that would hold an Enlightened Community together. It might be one of the initial structures to start the growth of an Enlightened Community.

It would also be a primary tool in helping people deal with their practical problems and fundamental needs. One such need is the desire for a companion to love and be loved by. Because of the complexity of this problem in the modern world the Knowledge Bank might be very useful. Large cities attract many people not only because they offer a wide variety of jobs and professional activities but also because they offer recreational, cultural, and leisure activities. But best of all an urban area offers an almost infinite range of interesting people to meet, form friendships and partnerships with, and even marry. However, in spite of this potential many people live a lonely life because up to this time no way has existed to search through the potential richness available and make contact in a way that has a high probability to succeed.

And, each person's Computer, Tutor, Recorder, and Expert Systems (CTRES) would provide a powerful tool to tap into the larger computer system developed to deal with all matters related to being connected with other people.

As the "computer dating" project builds and develops experience and success it could, step-by-step, be expanded to bring in other needs and interests: sports, entertainment, special interests, and such. But the idea would be to also add the dimension of community so people would not only bond one-on-one, but also in groups so there is genuine social integration.

9. THE RADIO LINK

CPAWs need to do everything possible to help all human beings feel bonded to all other human beings. This bonding should be aimed at solving every problem people have. One such aid would be for each person to have a device for communicating (such as an implanted radio chip with GPS) that could be used in times of trouble. For instance, if their boat sank far from shore, if they were lost in the wilderness, or buried in a cave, rescuers could home in on the device and locate them. Such a device would be capable of saving many lives of those who are lost and die before they can be rescued. Perhaps its signal could be modified by brain waves so that if a person were "brain dead" rescue forces' efforts need not be pursued as frantically. Some might think nine billion radios linked to brains would be impossible. However, the future has more to promise than the past or present can even imagine!

10. CORPORATION FOR UNIVERSAL EMPLOYMENT (CUE)

Analyzing "employment and jobs" provides a powerful tool for getting to the core of what it means to be a *Modern Human*. With the evolution of the language ability, work like all the other elements of society lost its moral compass. Sorting out what was most important to the society from what was desired by someone with wealth and power became very difficult and was normally not done very well. (For more on this, see: **a.** Chapter 1; **b.** VOLUME II, Chapter 15, "The Hunter-Gatherer and a *Science of Religion and Ethics*," and **c.** Chapter 34, "Work and a *Science of Religion and Ethics*." [18]) The referenced chapters include important ideas about work. This not only provides a way to better understand the deeper elements of employment, it also provides a valuable tool to understand what this book is really about.

Chapter 1 shows how *Modern Humans* have been in a transitional mode since the language ability fundamentally changed the relationship between a person and their society, where before this change "meaning of life" was in the genes and the cultural element was very limited. Afterward "meaning of life" had a significant cultural component (because of memes) but there was no "user's guide" available showing how to utilize this cultural component. Moreover, it was not possible within the limitations of existing cultures to truly achieve a meaningful life in terms of a *sustainable feeling of well-being*. The hunter-gatherer lifestyle that worked for millions of years was no longer adequate. It is only now that enough knowledge and experience have been accumulated to make it possible to envision the image of a new "stability." Helping humanity achieve this new dynamic equilibrium is one goal of this book.

Part of the foregoing will require us to triumph over the devastating, smothering, staggering ignorance that characterizes so much of current human life. Contemporary social models are so misfocused they leave us clueless about what is really going on. Currently the majority of people are more interested in what happens after death than how to live a high-quality life on earth. Or, how our life can be enriched by our active involvement in enhancing the life -- now and in the future -- of all the members of our species. There is at this time no cultural vision or mechanism that can guide us toward properly utilizing our "wisdom" potential.

An essential part of such a vision would be to advance social and personal prosperity that would require creating a way to more satisfactorily harness the revolutionary possibilities of industry and manufacturing to enhance human living. Such a cultural vision would be a primary goal of Center for the Practical Application of Wisdom because one of their basic responsibilities would be to build Enlightened Communities made up of Enlightened Persons. The Corporation for Universal Employment (CUE) would provide a way for each person to transform their labor into wealth. This would be done in such a way that every person would be able to participate within the context of a sustainable human culture.

One part of a CUE would work with anyone having a problem of any kind related to employment. Part of this process would involve connecting people with a CFML (Center For Mastering Living) if there were any life problems keeping them from recognizing their potential and responsibilities. Their educational level, talents, experience, and such would be tested. And where these needed upgrading, necessary referrals would be made. All the help necessary to find satisfactory employment would be available.

If no satisfactory jobs were available or if the person wanted to explore new options, they would be able to join a Production and Planning Unit that would bring a wide assortment of people together. As a result the combined skills and interests would permit existing needs of society (even those not yet fully recognized) to be handled in a satisfying way for everyone. Some of these Production and Planning Units might consist of only one person. Others could consist of hundreds of people with the potential and plan to grow to include thousands of workers.

One part of a CUE needs to provide volunteer consulting services to help each Production and Planning Unit master the steps necessary to have a productive, profitable business.

Another section of CUE should work with Production and Planning Units to actually provide office space to help them get underway. This section might follow the model of the business incubator. (See VOLUME II, Chapter 34, "Work and a *Science of Religion and Ethics*," for more material on this point). [18 c] In spite of the hundreds of years of experience with corporations and thousands of years with urban industry we have not yet utilized the potential of industrial development to help construct a sustainable human culture, an Enlightened Community. The incredible idea of establishing such a process has not been explored at the essential level although socialism, communism, and communes have this goal in mind. However, socialism and communism have focused their effort too far from the core problem (achieving a *sustainable feeling of well-being*) and have been based on an erroneous analysis of social and industrial realities. Communes were set up on the hunter-gatherer model (not knowingly of course) and lacked the necessary structures to move members toward achieving their "wisdom" potential. But humanity now has the possibility of taking a critical step and utilizing the powerful social invention of corporate manufacturing and industrialization to allow an ever-increasing number of people to achieve a *sustainable feeling of well-being*. The foregoing resources are essential to create societies that are congruent with the needs of *Modern Humans*.

But (as discussed in more detail in Chapter 1) it is my firm conviction that the "tribal" genetic propensities, especially the "dominance/submission" and "us/them" drives, are primary road blocks that need to be overcome in order to allow all members of society to benefit from the fantastic potential of manufacturing and industrialization. In corporations as in all social institutions group politics coming out of "dominance/ submission" and "us/them" propensities lead to all kinds of distortions in human behavior that misuse, fail to develop, and misdirect human potential. A key goal of a *science of religion and ethics* is to avoid these stress-producing behaviors. When this is done it should be possible to utilize the human potential available in corporations in a way compatible with producing Enlightened Persons and Enlightened Communities.

11. CENTER FOR THE PRACTICAL APPLICATION OF WISDOM NEWS GROUP (CPAW-NG)

One of the first groups a Center for the Practical Application of Wisdom (CPAW) should establish is a news group. This group would work to promote the ideas of a *science of religion and ethics* by establishing its own magazines, newspapers, radio/TV components, and other media. It could thereby ensure that the CPAW activities and analysis of the news would be available in every community.

12. HEALTH CARE CLINIC (HCC)

When circumstances permit, a Center for the Practical Application of Wisdom (CPAW) should establish or support existing health care clinics so as to help members achieve the Sixth Way of Wisdom: Work to be physically and psychologically healthy. [19] This would allow them to achieve and maintain good physical health in order to live in congruency with the aims of an Enlightened Community and to become Enlightened Persons. (Also see VOLUME II, Chapter 20, "Health, Medicine, and a *Science of Religion and Ethics*") [20].

Important resources used by a Health Care Clinic would include the Knowledge Bank and each person's CTRES (Computer Tutor, Recorder, and Expert Systems).

13. REGIONAL PLANNING AND COORDINATING INSTITUTIONS (Rpcis)

There would be various Regional Planning and Coordinating Institutions set up to work on long-range plans for humanity in general but more specifically for a particular geographical or economic region. Its primary concerns would be related to the Second Way of Wisdom: Seek to maintain and develop humanity. It would deal with issues related to society's growth and development so that changes are not introduced until they have been thoroughly studied and it appears that their long-term benefits will outweigh any harmful effects. Obviously, this is a challenging task that cannot be done perfectly because there are no unmixed blessings, or unmitigated miseries. However, if we keep clearly in mind that the goal is to allow an ever-expanding percentage of the population to achieve a *sustainable feeling of well-being*, we at least have a way to measure our successes and failures and to make the changes that we are able to. (Also see VOLUME II, Chapter 28, "Managing Change in an Enlightened Community" [21]).

14. ORGANIZATION FOR THE PROTECTION OF LABOR

Fair treatment and opportunities for every person are a critical part of an Enlightened Community. Productive work is an essential part of this process. When such a community truly exists these issues will be dealt with directly. However, in the developing stages it will probably be useful to establish an organization to work with unions and other worker organizations to solve problems standing in the way of developing an Enlightened Community made up of Enlightened Persons. Part of the goal would be to help employees be as productive as possible while developing their humanity.

Appendix C has presented some ideas about organizations to initiate the process of thinking about this issue. These ideas are presented as working hypotheses. Obviously, no one can truly lay out all the structures needed to develop and maintain an Enlightened Community. Practical experience will be essential as steps are taken to reach necessary goals. However, we need a way to focus experiments and data gathering so that the process can begin. As in all aspects of a *science of religion and ethics* results are the criterion by which everything is measured. And results mean helping more and more people achieve a *sustainable feeling of well-being*.

APPENDIX D

BENEFIT CORPORATIONS, CO-OPS, ETC.

Today many insightful individuals work to promote <u>benefit corporations</u> as an alternative to traditional corporations (C corporations) because under traditional corporate law and practice, the purpose of the standard business corporation is to maximize profit so as to increase shareholder gains, and that, because of this purpose, such corporations have no inherent social and environmental conscience but only pursue social and environmental concerns if they are productive of, or at least not counterproductive to, maximizing profits,

Such a singular, profit orientation pursued above all other consideration is an impediment to the creation of a long-term, sustainable economic system because the pure profit motive can make it morally excusable for such corporations to externalize as many of the negative consequences of their behavior on society and the environment as is legally permissible,

A paradigm shift to a sustainable global economic system in which all corporations act as responsible global participants would be of great benefit to humanity as a whole, so in pursuit of a more globally-responsible corporate ethos, they support the concept of the benefit corporation which is structured to:

1. Expand the fiduciary obligations of its directors and officers to consider the effects of corporate behavior not only on shareholders but on stakeholders, such as employees, vendors and suppliers, the communities in which the corporation operates, and the natural environment, and

2. provide transparency and accountability to shareholders for meeting this broader purpose.*

---

* For the best on-line sources of information about benefit corporations see 1) John Montgomery's Forum for Humanist Community in Silicon Valley, 3/31/13 (https://www.youtube.com/watch?v=4djAObGZnmI), and 2) his article in the May/June 2014 issue of *The Humanist* magazine (https://thehumanist.com/magazine/may-june-2014/features/the-benefit-corporation). These references discuss benefit corporations in depth and make clear their value and why they are a growing corporate trend available in 34 states and deserve a little more push from the rest of us.

THE POWER OF STORIES: FROM EDEN TO UTOPIA – 3-18-19

Arthur Jackson (123arthurjackson@gmail.com)
Apology! This is a work in progress. I think it is very important. And, I regret having to bring it to you in its current condition. But the more I've worked on this the more it evolved. I'm realizing I need your questions, comments and criticisms to guide me further. So, when anything is not clear or you see it as wrong, etc. please let me know so I can work to make it all fit together better. Art

Here are some ideas that go beyond what I present in the rest of my book, "How to Live the Good Life: A User's Guide for *Modern Humans*."

I'll start by focusing on Christian, Jewish, Muslim stories. These of course lie in the realm of memes and symbolic language not simple genetics. They are a social construct that makes our species special and at the same time lie at the core of society's responsibility for its member's behavior since this is where memes exist.

Most people in the USA are familiar with the Jewish stories of Adam and Eve and their being expelled from Eden (God's paradise) for breaking God's command to not eat the fruit from the Tree of Knowledge. Some people take this to mean that human beings are innately bad, or at least can't be trusted to do the "right" thing.

These stories have memes (ideas) that influence human behavior. These memes are central to how their adherents and others influenced by them think about social behavior—particularly tribal behavior. These are religious stories; i.e., stories that help maintain a society over time by supporting moral behavior and a feeling that life has meaning. However, within the core of these stories lies an unrecognized effect that focuses our attention on punishment in a destructive way relative to responsibility (in my opinion).

These ideas of a punishing God provide the model for these societies: God (actually society) commands and the individual obeys. If an individual misbehaves punish them, don't look to see what God's (or society's) responsibility in the behavior might be. Therefore, using physical punishment of children, wife-beating, tough on crime, jails/prisons, etc. is presented as the proper path and this leads directly to providing a model for a society based on acts not causes. Trying to understand why a thing was done (it's cause) is taken to only encourage an individual to be thoughtless, lazy, irresponsible, etc.

I want to focus on the above issue and suggest that anyone would benefit by exploring how these ideas influence their everyday behavior and prevent them from considering that there might be better ways to deal with asocial/antisocial behavior (hereafter written as A/A behavior). I think of the foregoing as ways to produce a Utopia. Yet, it is widely accepted that any ideas about Utopia (which I think of as paradise) are fantasy thinking. I believe a key reason for this is because a substantial number of our citizens accept the idea that people are innately bad (or at least some people are) and therefore building a Utopia is not possible, and I agree that building a Utopia is not possible as long as many members of the group believe the society bears no responsibility for the A/A behavior of its citizens.

George Orwell's, "1984"; and Aldous Huxley's, "Brave New World," focus on what might happen if science gave us the keys to deeply understand the human brain. Their stories accept that understanding human behavior better would only permit A/A individuals to control their society using this knowledge to stifle societies in a totalitarian way. So instead of using this information to create a Utopia would use it to create a Dystopia (an anti-utopia), a society that is undesirable or nightmarish.

A more hopeful model is presented by Humanist Community in Silicon Valley member Dr. Masuma Ahmed detailed in a Forum, "Science Through the Power of Arts and Storytelling," (https://vimeo.com/293682894) that science by always looking for the causes underneath the effects provides us stories about the things important to human beings – the birth of the Universe, stars, and humanity, etc. I would like to build on one element of a story science explores– when humanity evolved symbolic language.

And it is my belief that a key event in producing Modern Humans (that arose when *Homo* evolved symbolic language) was related to the fusion of two chromosomes giving humans 23 chromosomes instead of the 24 our near ancestors (Orangutans, Gorillas and Chimps) have. [For background see, "23, How Humanity Came to Be," James Hunt, 2015/16.]

So rather than drawing from Adam & Eve I would like to propose a different approach and move discussion from the realm of spirit causality (the supernatural) to the realm of material causality (science). My suggestion is that when we judge behavior instead of focusing only on what was done, we also focus on the specifics of why the thing was done (that is working with cause and effect). For example, if someone tells a lie the "why" would involve studying the beliefs and the environmental influences that led the person to act as they did. Or, if a "monster" performs a cruel and hideous act and they are asked why they did it, they would be as unaware of the correct answer as you are.

This should force us to see the individual as a product of their society and how their A/A behavior comes out of their own pain and ignorance. When resources permit this effort might look a lot like psychoanalysis. Did they lie because they saw it as a matter of life and death or was it merely to provide more spending-money, or one of the hundreds of other possible reasons? This process by producing more stories digging as deeply as possible into the life of the "perpetrator" demonstrating the causes that led them to their A/A acts seems very important to me.

The biggest difficulty of current ideas about human behavior starts with the assumption that human beings are fundamentally bad (didn't follow God's command) and can only be "saved" by divine (supernatural) agency – and that punishment is the best way to deal with bad behavior (expelled from Eden/Noah's Ark). Once that assumption is accepted by a society, that society is hampered in how it can deal with asocial/antisocial behavior.

Though human beings are innately social animals we need to learn why some individuals, due to their genetics and experiences don't automatically recognize their social needs. (I call them the "conscience challenged") – i.e., the small part of a population (some of whom can become what have been called "psychopaths") who don't have a strong social concern with a deep inner "voice" telling them what is right, honest, compassionate. These individuals in the absence of necessary support often seek to take advantage of others and usually don't recognize why this is a mistake. Unfortunately, the stories about good and evil provide a model that supports these individual's behavior; i.e., the stories teach that people are innately bad so they can believe they are just doing what they have been taught all people want to do.

I think stories can turn a latent propensity humans have to physically assault others into a motivation for doing so.

Our stories over and over stress punishment as the obvious solution. Unfortunately, when the conscience challenged are apprehended and punished, they don't follow society's idea/thinking; i.e. expectation – to just stop the bad behavior and do the right thing. They follow a different rule – to win the confrontation whatever the price, especially in a hostile environment. And winning becomes the focus of their lives. (See Mendota Juvenile Treatment Center -- https://en.wikipedia.org/wiki/ Mendota_Juvenile_Treatment_Center_Program).

So, the conscience challenged often take guidance from the stories that people are innately bad. They accept that; therefore, they think what they are doing is just what everyone wants to do. They tend to be good actors and good liars so can take advantage of others who don't actually believe that everyone is innately bad since they aren't. And since we haven't developed tools and procedures to get deep enough into the thinking of the conscience challenged to find out why they are actually doing what they are doing, they live their lives unable to recognize the error of their ways.

It is my belief that our species has genes that produce a small percentage of individuals who are "conscience challenged." This may have come about because this attribute though problematic for the species may have importance to the long-term survival of a tribe. In difficult times the tribe can benefit by having someone who can ignore normal behavior and do things others would not think of doing and thereby get the tribe through a difficult situation. But letting them rule without oversight in normal times may not end up well.

In a violent, mis-focused society (like the USA) many of the <u>conscience challenged</u> will become so called psychopaths. (See, "Psychopath Whisperer: The Science of Those without Conscience," Kent A. Kiehl). In a loving society (like the Polynesians) probably almost none would become "psychopaths," because they have not been taught that people are innately bad, they are able to learn by example and see for themselves what works best for everyone including themselves. And in normal times that is not by lying, stealing, cruel behavior, etc.

Almost all the stories in the USA we see on TV and in movies, read in newspapers, novels, etc. take for granted that at least some people are innately bad, and that punishment is the answer to dealing with asocial/antisocial behavior. Our stories lead us to believe A/A behavior is part of essentially everyone's innate nature and without punishment essentially everyone would be a thief, liar, bully, etc. We are taught that essentially none would be good without punishment or the threat of punishment. And yet even in the USA essentially the whole population even without relevant teaching are good citizens!

So, if we ask, why could anyone believe that they would benefit from lying, stealing, abusing others, etc., I think that takes us back to our religious stories; i.e. that people are innately bad. We learn about these matters through the "Ten Commandments". "Do not lie" teaches us we can lie. "Do not steal" teaches us we can steal. "Do not kill" teaches us we can kill, etc., etc., etc.

A better approach would be to teach children about compassion, supporting each other, cooperation, etc. We have been taught by the conscience challenged that the foregoing is wrong, and this drives much of our politics. Which is "the individual is totally responsible for what they do, and the society bears no responsibility except to punish those who err."

The <u>conscience challenged</u> who lack the innate feeling of compassion tend to become the leaders and provide models for behavior. However, I believe change is possible as more and more people discard the belief that individuals are innately bad. This will allow us to see that most people are in fact socially responsible, even though they have been taught people are innately bad. (And in the USA only some .06% of the total population is in jail or prison, many of whom are not guilty as charged.) In addition, the foregoing allows us to recognize that, we all can learn to be responsible.

This can happen because we all can observe which behaviors work best for us in our society given time and support. But it would help to have stories that clarify why persons do what they did and fewer stories that only focus on what was done and leave us feeling good when "justice" triumphs and the so-called miscreant (as defined by the society in question) is punished. Hopefully, the foregoing might lead more and more individuals to recognize that any A/A act comes out of the individual's ignorance or pain (which of course is only a different way of saying the same thing).

So, if a society teaches that crime pays by its focus on what was done and fails to teach compassion when it ignores the why of the act, it shares the blame with the individual for the A/A acts of its citizens. It is my belief that the mass incarcerations in recent decades in the USA were done for racist reasons, but under the cover of our widespread belief that punishment changes behavior in a desirable way.

Basically, almost anyone raised in the USA would think it absurd to doubt that doing a "bad" act would not benefit the doer because we are taught that having things including one's own thoughtless selfishness is the goal of the day. They think they are behaving properly only because they don't want to be punished. They've been taught all their lives that people can benefit from being "bad" and this comes naturally from the idea that people are innately bad. Part of this includes the belief that having stuff is an important source of pleasure, and I view this as needing study and clarification. On the other side the pleasant feeling coming from being good/doing good and resisting "bad" acts such as being selfish is often dismissed as naïve, simple-minded, childish, provincial, etc.

And we are almost all vulnerable to the foregoing characterizations if done by individuals in power. The under-lying problem is the fundamental assumption upon which the three religions I mention is based. The immediate problem is that almost all our newspapers, magazines, novels, and visual media tell their stories in ways that ensure we won't look for the relevant facts, plus the widely held belief that searching to understand the underlying reasons someone did a bad thing would lead us to become "bleeding hearts" and pampering the guilty. And the foregoing is seen as a great danger to a society.

By focusing on what was done rather than why it was done – a much more difficult question to answer anyway – we prevent using humanist values to move things in a constructive direction. Instead we maintain a costly model that harms us all and promotes self-indulgent leadership by the conscience challenged. The foregoing provides the current model of innate sinfulness held in check by fear of punishment that is moving us toward the brink of disaster where our species is destroyed by global warming, over population, and/or nuclear/biological Armageddon.

It's only when we get to Humanism (or at least humanistic thinking) that we can question any society's core thinking. Are human beings fundamentally bad? Humanism would say no. We are fundamentally social beings. We must be taught to be bad, or at least not taught how to avoid these behaviors. I think it is critical that we give up the belief that anyone is innately bad.

It is my opinion that individuals have been led astray for centuries. A key idea in Jewish/Christian/ Muslim holy books is about punishment, and Christianity and Islam have moved into including a Hell where a loving god will burn you forever. These books were written by or for the conscience challenged leaders and the foregoing is an example of how beliefs have been tweaked over time to better empower the rulers.

It is easy to understand why these ideas on A/A behavior were adopted all those hundreds (even thousands) of years ago. This simplified maintaining the tribe, making it more manageable. I'm proposing an alternative that is only possible now using modern science and technological resources which fortunately are becoming available to us.

It's clear to me that the best place to start is to develop testable hypotheses leading to useful theories. First, we recognize that good and evil do not exist outside the brains of human beings. And since they exist in our brains, studies of how our bodies function can show what is really going on. Another first step would be to recognize that human beings are social animals. They are not born good or bad they learn their behavior from their interaction with the society in which they are raised - or are not taught and otherwise helped to avoid A/A behavior. For me this means studying A/A behavior and learning why it happens. So, a person who does A/A things must be studied to learn why those A/A things were done. Punishment would never be involved except in the sense that change of human behavior is rarely easy and sometimes very difficult. And for some this might feel like punishment.

The foregoing would be part of producing a Utopia – a place where every member is important. If any individual has mental quirks that lead to A/A behavior that should be seen as a gift to be studied and used to help the group better understand how brains and societies function while at the same time of course helping the individual as much as possible.

When we focus on an A/A act within the context that people are innately bad and must be guided by punishment to do the right thing, we can't ask why these acts were done – because that's already known – the things were done because the individual is innately bad and such behavior is to be expected. So labeling people "bad" ends up moving things in the wrong direction – toward punishment rather than rehabilitation and almost never solving the problem. Since there is no motivation for the society to study and search for the actual reasons that these A/A things happened, the society is stuck in a loop hampering its movement toward "the light at the end of the tunnel" (where material causality replaces spirit causality). The societies under discussion have been in that loop for many hundreds of years, even thousands of years. And this has taken humanity to a place where we might end our species.

And my guess is we got to this place because conscience challenged leaders have provided propaganda so we miss the real reasons why individuals do what they do. Introducing good and evil has allowed them to call the shots and manipulate the society, so we won't make the changes that would turn everything around to produce a society where everyone is involved in establishing the rules and all win and we could all live in a community of trust and fairness. This is what I call a Utopia. And, since human beings are not born good or bad, but are born as social animals we all need each other. Unfortunately, some persons have difficulty recognizing that fact.

Although an individual is totally responsible for everything they do or fail to do this shouldn't lead to punishment, but to education, and education at its core is the society's responsibility. Currently society's stories about A/A behavior automatically focus in the wrong place since they omit society's role in the member's behavior. When we ignore society's responsibility in its citizen's mis-behavior, we are critically misled since that missing component is an essential part of the real story necessary for finding solutions to prevent such behavior.

So, studying what a society is teaching and what is not being taught is essential because both influence everything else. For me it's clear that we must examine the tribal environment the society is providing as well as what individuals are doing, for us to get beyond the "what" and get to the "why "of bad behavior.

In my approach the bottom line would be, what would the society need to do so that an individual's A/A behavior wouldn't be repeated in the future? Here would be where the tools and processes of science would need to be used to gather and utilize information to explore changing the society so it would become a place where every person would be able to use their time and energy to make life better for everyone, and experience the joy of satisfying, challenging behavior such as improving society even if only in some very small way including satisfaction in a job well done, or behaviors beyond anything I can presently imagine. I define this as creating a Utopia.

The development of science has given humanity a power it's never had before – with both positive and negative possibilities. Positively used it could help us create a utopia, used negatively it can now actually wipe out our species along with most other complex organisms. More specifically on the positive side would be exploring effective ways to create a utopia where life is worth living; i.e., a setting where our differences are used to produce an environment where everyone joyfully works together for the good of all.

Since humanity lives in a cause and effect Universe (based on material causality, ruled by chaos theory) whenever we ignore the actual causes for behavior, we are stymied in truly understanding what's happening and thereby be able to prevent bad behavior. My proposal requires that we understand humanism (the belief that human beings are the source of meaning and value and that their morality comes naturally out of their evolutionary history) and what science and religion really are. My position is that humanism includes understanding humanity at the deepest level and that science is the search for congruency and religion is the search for meaning. And most importantly religion can be studied and understood using the methods science provides.

We need a new story where human beings are recognized as perfectible, where building a Utopia is seen as possible! So, this envisions seeing religion in a new way comparable to what happened when astrology moved out of the realm of spirit causality into the domain of science; i.e., material causality (becoming astronomy). This would be the way Baruch Spinoza discussed over 400 years ago, but no recognized thinker has followed that point since and which I'm committed to doing.

And who will be motivated to help create a utopia? I suspect I will be the conscience challenged persons who had the good fortune to grow up in an environment where they were able to recognize that building a better society is the best way for everyone to win and use their life energy to work toward that goal would define the meaning of their life.

What do you think?

GLOSSARY

Listed here are terms important to *How to Live the Good Life*. Some are included because they are not in common use, some are special words coined specifically for a *science of religion and ethics*, others are common words, but have special meanings here, not necessarily equivalent to how they are used elsewhere. If you find other words you think should be added to this glossary please contact me -- arthur@ arthurmjackson.com.

ABSOLUTE UNITARY BEING: Newberg and d'Aquili's term [in their book, *Mystical Mind: Probing the Biology of Religious Experience*." See Chapter 13] for the feeling of oneness achieved through meditation and similar experiences. Said to be a state of rapturous transcendence and absolute wholeness. In this state experiences feel "more real" than in their "normal state" ("baseline reality").

ALPHA MALE/ALPHA FEMALE: "Tribal" genetic propensity supporting dominance/submission.

ALPHA VALUE: Relates to the first level of membership in a Wisdom Group.

ALTRUISM: *Altruism* and *selfishness* are considered to be equivalent terms in a *science of religion and ethics*. They both are interpreted to mean acting in our long-term best interest.

AMERICAN HUMANIST ASSOCIATION:

A NEW FOUNDATION FOR CIVILIZATION: Based on the recognition that Human Beings Are the Ultimate Reference System, and that the meaning of human life – for the individual and for a society – is to maintain and develop the human species.

A PLACE FOR KIDS (APFK): Residential Group Homes set up to take care of orphans as well as unwanted and abused children. Functions so as to fulfill the Tenth Way of Wisdom: Ensure that every child is provided a loving, nurturing environment, and all the things necessary to become an *Enlightened Person*.

ARISTOTELIAN MODEL OF CAUSES: 1) the material cause, matter, the stuff of which a thing is made; 2) the efficient cause, the affecting, mobile operating force that produces changes; 3) the formal cause, the plan or structure inlaid into a thing; 4) the final cause, a goal, the end state toward which a thing is drawn.

AUTHENTIC HAPPINESS: Consists of three levels: the pleasant life (having as many positive emotions as we can), the good life (fulfilling our potential), and the meaningful life (being attached to something bigger than ourself) – collectively making up the Good Life. [See "Notes" for "How to Achieve the Good Life, *the short version*, or better, *Authentic Happiness*, by Martin E.P. Seligman.]

BASELINE REALITY: d'Aquili and Newberg's term [in their book, *Mystical Mind*. See Chapter 13] for what humans experience through their regular senses.

BELIEF: The neural structures over which a person has the most personal control that produce emotions and behavior.

BELIEF IN MAGIC AND THE POWER OF WISHING: "Tribal" genetic propensity underlying all folk religions.

BETA VALUE: Relates to the second level of membership in a Wisdom Group.

CAPITALISM: Economic system recommended by a *science of religion and ethics* when satisfactory regulatory guidance is provided by society to prevent alpha males/females from putting their short-term goals ahead of society's long-term needs.

CAUSE AND EFFECT: The model for explaining how things happen; that is, how the universe works used by a *science of religion and ethics*.

CENTER FOR THE PRACTICAL APPLICATION OF WISDOM (CPAW): Organization to develop, clarify, and apply the findings of a *science of religion and ethics*.

CENTER FOR THE PRACTICAL APPLICATION OF WISDOM NEWS GROUP (CPAW-NG): Works to ensure that the activities and analysis of the news essential to a *science of religion and ethics* would be available as widely as circumstances permit.

CENTER FOR MASTERING LIVING (CFML): Organization providing activities aimed at helping interested people overcome barriers keeping them from becoming Enlightened Persons.

CHAOS THEORY: Mathematical theory that the universe is deterministic, but that it is only predictable within varying limits of space and time due to the uncertainty of measurements of relevant factors and their initial conditions.

CHOICES ARE US (CAU): Organization established to help people achieve the Fifth Way of Wisdom: Strive to make the best choices possible.

CHRISTOPHER REEVE MODEL: Using our personal pain, disability, disease, and such to focus our energy to support finding a cure, or mitigating the condition suffered by all who share the condition.

CIE -- COMMISSION INTERNATIONALE DE L'ECLAIRAGE [INTERNATIONAL COMMISSION ON ILLUMINATION]: International conference of 1931 that developed the system for the numerical specification of what a color looks like to the ordinary man or woman under a given set of conditions. Might serve as a model for defining Human Beings as the Ultimate Reference System.

COMPUTER CONNECTION, THE: Organization utilizing computers to help people connect with those who share relevant interests.

COMPUTER, TUTOR, RECORDER, AND EXPERT SYSTEMS (CTRES): A specially configured portable computer system designed to help a person become and remain an Enlightened Person.

CONATUS: Term developed by Baruch Spinoza in the Fifteenth Century to propose a drive to maintain oneself with a feeling of well-being

CONGRUENT: A naturalistic system in which everything fits together and flows from one fact to another without artificial bridges or connections; that is the uniformity of nature.

COPENHAGEN INTERPRETATION OF QUANTUM MECHANICS: The nominal orthodox interpretation of physics, resting on the idea that the aim of quantum theory is merely to describe certain connections between human experiences, rather than to describe a physical world conceived to exist and have definite properties independently of our method of observing it. Statistical, noncausal.

COSMOS: I will use the term, cosmos to mean everything that exists, and universe as a subset of the cosmos that contains all of the galaxies and such in our part of the cosmos.

CTRES (Computer Tutor, Recorder, and Expert Systems): See earlier entry.

CORPORATION FOR UNIVERSAL EMPLOYMENT (CUE): Organization to provide a way for all people to transform their labor into wealth. (See **WEALTH.**)

CURRENTLY UNPREDICTABLE: Said of an event when: 1) Necessary predictive data cannot be gathered. 2) The ability to handle the necessary number of computations to predict the event exceeds the contemporary computation process and equipment, or it takes longer to predict the outcome than for the real-time change to take place. 3) No way presently exists to reduce the problem to mathematical, predictive form. (See **CHAOS THEORY.**)

DELTA VALUE: Relates to the fourth level of membership in a Wisdom Group.

DISCOVERY GAMES: Friends get together and use their time to process existing data that needs effort to interpret and make available to the scientists.

DOCTRINE OF FEAR: Assumption that punishment will change behavior in the desired way. Punish those who do not obey the leader.

DOMINANCE/SUBMISSION: In the context of "tribal" genetic propensities "dominance/submission" is seen as a genetic propensity for humans in social situations. Simplistically the dominant lead and the submissive follow. Propensity that inclines humans to function in a power hierarchy. Basis for kings/queens, generals, police, and so on

DEMOCRACY: System of group decision making to counter the "dominance/submission" genetic propensity.

EIGHTH WAY OF WISDOM: Help and be helped by people. Recognize that all human beings are "us;" everything else is "them."

ELEVENTH WAY OF WISDOM: Make of your life a spiritual quest. Work to become an Enlightened Person. Use the fundamentalist propensity to produce Enlightened Communities.

Eleven Ways of Wisdom: [Listed below as one component of a *science of religion and ethics*.]

1. Recognize that human beings are – for us – the ultimate reference system.
2. Endeavor to maintain and develop the human species. Support efforts to develop Enlightened Communities -- communities promoting authentic happiness for all their citizens.
3. Seek to understand. Pursue Wisdom.
4. Recognize that all knowledge rests on faith/beliefs and must always be open to questioning.
5. Strive to make the best choices possible.
6. Know and struggle to improve yourself; work to be physically and psychologically healthy.
7. Develop and adopt a perceptual framework in which pain does not prevent the achievement of a sustainable feeling of well-being.
8. Help and be helped by people. Recognize that all human beings are "us;" everything else is "them."
9. Work to increase knowledge and all creative and artistic endeavors. Adopt an inspiring life goal.
10. Support efforts to ensure that every child is provided a loving, nurturing environment and all the things necessary to become an Enlightened Person.
11. Make of your life a spiritual quest. Work to become an Enlightened Person. Use the fundamentalist genetic propensity to produce Enlightened Communities.

EMERGENCY SERVICES CENTER (ESC): Facilities in an Enlightened Community open at all times; always ready to help anyone who comes.

ENLIGHTENED: State in which one's *conatus* (i.e., drive to maintain oneself with a feeling of well-being) is in harmony with their beliefs supported by the best knowledge and scientific understanding currently available.

ENLIGHTENED BELIEFS: Those beliefs supported by the best knowledge and scientific understanding currently available that allow a person to maintain their life with a feeling of well-being.

ENLIGHTENED COMMUNITY: Formerly called Good, Moral, or Wise Community. One that promotes the belief and implements the idea that human beings are the source of meaning and value and that the individual person must be the focus for society's ultimate concern.

ENLIGHTENED PERSON: Formerly called Good, Moral, or Wise Person. Someone who has become Enlightened.

EPSILON VALUE: Relates to the fifth level of membership in a Wisdom Group.

ETA VALUE: Relates to the seventh level of membership in a Wisdom Group.

ETHICS: Ethical beliefs within the domain of a *science of religion and ethics* are defined as those beliefs concerned with maintaining and developing the human species. For individuals this means achieving a *sustainable feeling of well-being*.

FAITH;

EVIL PERSON: Concept rejected by a *science of religion and ethics* that recognizes that anyone can do things that can be considered "evil" as a result of their natural experiences and/or physiology, but that does not make the person "evil." Only the act is "evil."

FATALISM: An idea rejected by a *science of religion and ethics* as incorporating an erroneous model of how the universe works.

FEELING OF WELL-BEING: An emotion-state based on beliefs. Is defined as existing when a person who is able to end their life does not do so for the wrong reasons; that is, due to irrational beliefs and/or social isolation. (See *sustainable feeling of well-being*.)

FIFTH WAY OF WISDOM: Strive to make the best choices possible.

FIRST GOAL OF WISDOM: Escape the bondage produced by the accident of a person's birth.

FIRST ORDER GOOD: Something good of and for itself rather than because of its effects. For example, pain is not a first order good. It is good because it helps us to avoid serious injury and treat disease. Suffering can be good because it helps us avoid behavior that would be destructive to our well-being.

FIRST WAY OF WISDOM: Recognize that human beings are – for us – the ultimate reference system.

FOLK RELIGIONS: Faith-based/authority-based systems (e.g., Christianity, Islam, Judaism, Buddhism, Taoism, Scientology, Confucianism, and so on). They are not based on science – on falsifiable hypotheses – but like folk medicines, incorporate the wisdom of the culture. They have no mechanism to test that wisdom, except as the life process proceeds. Based on supernaturalism, mysticism, and obscurantism.

FORBIDDEN KNOWLEDGE: Information considered too dangerous for people to study.

FOURTH WAY OF WISDOM: Recognize that all knowledge rests on faith/beliefs and must always be open to questioning.

FULL POSITIVE POTENTIAL: A person's capabilities and possibilities. Developing this is a primary goal in becoming an Enlightened Person.

FUNDAMENTALISM (RELIGIOUS): Tendency to make the cognitive dimension of religion foundational and determinative. The religion then becomes a fixed body of truth of eternally valid propositions. Discussion therefore becomes apologetic rather than exploratory or critical.

FUNDAMENTALIST GENETIC PROPENSITY: Tendency to accept an idea as true in a way that it cannot be questioned. Normally this relates to matters deemed to be of ultimate value. When developed it is a source of tremendous energy, focus, and feeling of clarity. Relates to the Spiritual/Wisdom Quest but can get stalled before reaching these levels by accepting as true what is only relative.

FUZZY LOGIC: Area of mathematics that applies to the "excluded middle." Aristotle's "yes/no" logic only pertains accurately to the world of mathematics. Fuzzy logic pertains to the real world humans live in.

GAMMA VALUE: Relates to the third level of membership in a Wisdom Group.

GENE-BASED STABILITY: Condition that exists when the members of a species live in a stable state in their ecological niche due to their successful genetic adaptation. The normal state of all species except human beings. (See **MEME-BASED STABILITY.**)

GOOD LIFE: An ethical life aimed toward achieving a state of well-being for self and others. Living as an Enlightened person.

GOOD PERSON: Someone who strives to live the Good Life.

GOOD SOCIETY: A society made up of Good Persons with the goal of helping all citizens achieve this state.

HBAURS (Human beings are the ultimate reference system): See below.

HEALTH CARE CLINIC (HCC): Organization that supports existing health care clinics so as to help members achieve the Sixth Way of Wisdom: Know and endeavor to improve yourself; work to be physically and psychologically healthy.

HER/SHE: God. Used in this book to apply to God when a pronoun is used for God.

HERO'S JOURNEY: Concept proposed by Joseph Campbell. For a *science of religion and ethics* a person's effort to maintain and develop the species by helping others to achieve their full positive potential.

HOMO SAPIENS SAPIENS: Refers to the immediate predecessor of *Modern Humans.* They evolved some 100,000 to 200,000 years ago out of *Homo sapiens* and were a transitional stage to *Modern Humans. Modern Humans* evolved between 30,000 and 60,000 years ago as evidenced by the rapid transformation of tools and living patterns. I propose that modern language with all its elements had at that point finally come together and language lies at the core of these changes.

HOPE: The reward part of the flight or fight syndrome. Encourages survival behavior.

HUMAN BEINGS ARE THE ULTIMATE REFERENCE SYSTEM **(HBAURS):** Human beings themselves are the source of meaning and value, and this meaning and value derives from their existence as a biological species that naturally evolved in this universe with unique characteristics; that is, their human nature.

HUMANISM:: The belief that human beings are the source of meaning and value and that their morality comes naturally out of their evolutionary history.

HUMANIST: Person who practices Humanism.

INHERENTLY UNPREDICTABLE: Can never be predicted. We can never be sure if any given event falls into this class.

IHEU:

"I," OR "SELF": A person's feeling of selfhood. Result of our organic being, experiences, and the immediate circumstances in which they are functioning. Neither unitary nor permanent.

IOTA VALUE: Relates to the ninth level of membership in a Wisdom Group.

KAPPA VALUE: Relates to the tenth level of membership in a Wisdom Group.

KNOWLEDGE: information, data, understanding, prediction. Permits a person to manipulate and use the forces, attributes, and patterns of the natural world – utilizing what is known.

KNOWLEDGE BANK, THE: Organization acting as a primary resource to store and make available all information, data, ideas, and so on. It would be a central resource for the Computer Connection, that might possibly provide the motivating energy to establish it. The Internet provides a model, or first approximation of this organization. Google provides a good model though the idea proposed here is far different.

LAMARCKIAN EVOLUTION: Jean Baptiste Pierre Antoine de Monet de Lamarck [more commonly, Jean-Baptiste Lamarck] (1744-1829) suggested a mechanism for organic evolution prior to Charles Darwin's "evolution by natural selection." He proposed the theory that characteristics acquired by habits, use, disuse, or adaptations to changes in environment may be passed directly to progeny. Of course this isn't applicable in the bigger realm of evolution, but it works for epigenes and more relevantly to memes; that is, words, beliefs, concepts.

LIGHT AT THE END OF THE TUNNEL: For a *science of religion and ethics* the state in which human beings have reached dynamic stability based on memes. The tunnel is the metaphor for the path humanity has pursued since people lost their direct dependence on genes for their behavior.

LANGUAGE: A *science of religion and ethics* considers language to be the component of human nature that makes our species unique – at least on earth. Language provides a singularly powerful economy of reference through its ability to use sounds (or sight with sign language) to symbolically represent objects, events, and relationships. This tool permits us to fit into almost any environment on earth.

LONG-TERM INTEREST: Used to guide behavior for someone who desires to become an Enlightened Person.

MEANING OF LIFE: For any organism it is to perpetuate their species – "eat," reproduce, die. For human beings because they have symbolic language, this includes a feeling-state based on beliefs.

MEME: Term coined by Richard Dawkins in, *The Selfish Gene* (1976) to contrast with genes. It applies to ideas, thought patterns, actions, fashions, and so on that replicate themselves within a culture and are passed from mind to mind possibly over many generations and to many cultures. Dawkins defines the meme as a unit of intellectual or cultural information that survives long enough to be recognized as such, and that can be passed from person to person and changed dramatically at any point in its existence.

MEME-BASED DYNAMIC STABILITY: The goal towards which *Modern Humans* have been moving since losing gene-based stability. A state in which each person would develop their full positive potential, and thereby live the best life possible while also contributing toward maintaining and developing the species.

MODERN HUMANS: Discussed by Steven Mithen in *THE PREHISTORY OF THE MIND: The Cognitive Origins of Art and Science.* [Thames and Hudson, New York, 1996.] *Modern Humans* replaced *Homo sapiens sapiens* and appeared over a period of time from 30,000 to 60,000 years ago. Includes all current human beings.

MORALS/MORALITY: Ethical beliefs within the domain of a *science of religion and ethics* are defined as those beliefs concerned with maintaining and developing the human species. For individuals this means achieving a *sustainable feel of well-being.* Aimed toward achieving one's long term best interests.

MYSTICAL EXPERIENCES: Mind-state interpreted as coming from experiences outside the normal realm of the natural world.

MYSTICAL MINDS: Description of mental state achieved through deep meditation or similar experience, and interpreted as a "higher" realm.

NATURALISTIC ETHICAL SYSTEM: Based on components existing only in the natural world that guide religious/ethical behavior.

"NATURALISTIC FALLACY:" English philosopher G. E. Moore's term for any efforts attempting to get an "ought" from an "is." Considered to be a specious concept by a *science of religion and ethics* that works in terms of "if"... "then."

NEW FOUNDATION FOR CIVILIZATION: Based on the recognition that Human Beings Are the Ultimate Reference System, and that the meaning of human life – for the individual and for a society – is to maintain and develop the species. The old foundation was the supernatural; the new foundation depends on human nature as understood by a *science of religion and ethics.*

NEW IDEAS, REVOLUTIONARY INSIGHTS, AND/OR UNIQUE ANSWERS INSTITUTE (NIRIUA-I): An organization working to provide a channel so anyone can transmit ideas (memes) – insofar as they have merit – into society in a usable, or at least understandable form.

NINTH WAY OF WISDOM: Work to increase knowledge and all creative and artistic endeavors. Adopt an inspiring life goal.

NUDITY: Considered by a *science of religion and ethics* to be a relevant element of good mental health.

OBJECTIVE KNOWLEDGE: Belief that reality has certain characteristics that exist independent of human measurement and observation and that we can obtain certainty about what they are. Not accepted as true by a *science of religion and ethics*. For a *science of religion and ethics* all knowledge is interpreted because human beings are the ultimate reference system.

ORGANIZATION FOR THE PROTECTION OF LABOR: Group set up to help employees be as productive as possible while developing their humanity.

ORGANIZATION TO ENHANCE THE QUALITY OF HUMAN LIFE (OEQHL): Its goal would be to make sure that the frontiers of scientific discovery are being pushed in all areas of science to ensure that knowledge and understanding are developing as rapidly as desirable. Pronounced "equal."

PERFECT WORLD: One in which the ignorance of the day can be corrected by human thought and action; by peace, not bloodshed – where it is recognized that there is no essential conflict between the critical needs of the individual person and of the society.

POINCARE, HENRI: Widely known for his statement, "Scientists do not study nature because it is useful; they study it because they delight in it, and they delight in it because it is beautiful. If nature were not beautiful, it would not be worth knowing, and if nature were not worth knowing, life would not be worth living." See Chapter 4.

PREDESTINATION: An idea rejected by a *science of religion and ethics* as incorporating an erroneous model of how the universe works.

PRE-ENLIGHTENMENT: Condition of not yet being Enlightened as defined by a *science of religion and ethics*.

PRODUCTION AND PLANNING UNIT: Designed to ensure productive and useful employment for every citizen.

PSYCHOLOGICALLY UNIMPORTANT: Something that doesn't promote mental growth when it's done or later.

RATIONAL EMOTIVE BEHAVIOR THERAPY: Therapeutically utilizes the phenomenon that our feelings and behaviors are causally connected to the thoughts or beliefs that guide the way we respond to stimuli.

RADIO LINK, THE: A communication device (such as a an implanted radio chip with GPS) that the possessor could use anywhere in the world in case of need. Proposed as being worth developing to assist individual well-being.

REALITY AS THE OBJECTIVE REFERENCE SYSTEM (RAORS): Assumption that reality actually exists and can be studied, but must always be interpreted in terms of the knowledge and understanding of the day. Pronounced "roars."

REBT (RATIONAL EMOTIVE BEHAVIOR THERAPY): See above.

REGIONAL PLANNING AND COORDINATING INSTITUTIONS (RPCI): Organizations to deal with issues related to society's growth and development so that changes are not introduced until they have been adequately studied and it appears that their long-term benefits will outweigh the long-term harmful effects.

RELIGION: The social institution that provides a feeling of well-being for the members of that society. Based on human nature and therefore functions in the natural domain.

REQUIREMENT FOR CONSISTENCY: To be cogent any religious/ethical System must be comprehensive in scope, clearly stated, and internally consistent.

REQUIREMENT FOR OBJECTIVITY: To be cogent the premises of any religious/ethical System must be based on falsifiable concepts that are independently discoverable and available to all people.

REQUIREMENT FOR UNIVERSALITY: To be cogent any religious/ethical System needs to be of value to and able to be followed by all of humanity.

RAORS (REALITY AS THE OBJECTIVE REFERENCE SYSTEM): See above.

SCHOOL, THE: Would provide, insofar as conditions permitted, all the resources to help students work toward their own perfection and for the perfection of society as made possible by a *science of religion and ethics*.

SCIENCE: Defined by *science of religion and ethics* as the search for congruency, that is the uniformity of nature.

SCIENCE OF ETHICS: See *science of religion and ethics*.

SCIENCE OF RELIGION: See *science of religion and ethics*.

SCIENCE OF RELIGION AND ETHICS: Proposed in this book as a field of science that would study and deal with the naturalistic elements of religion and ethics. It would be theory-based, empirical, and experiment-driven. Specifically focused on issues of meaning of life and values, and meaning in general. Focused on helping individuals and societies use their "wisdom" potential to guide behavior to increase the likelihood of maintaining and developing the human species.

SECOND AREA OF SELF-KNOWLEDGE: Integrating body functions and maintaining a positive, effective state so that a person's physical and mental functions are congruent.

SECOND GOAL OF WISDOM: Avoid replacing restrictions imposed by birth with different ones that dictate equally irrational limits on one's ability to think and act.

SECOND WAY OF WISDOM: Endeavor to maintain and develop the human species. Support efforts to develop Enlightened Communities – communities promoting authentic happiness for all their citizens.

SELFISHNESS: *Altruism* and *selfishness* are considered to be equivalent terms in a *science of religion and ethics*. They both are interpreted to mean acting in one's long-term best interest. Since most choices come out of ignorance rather than wisdom they normally are based on short-term rather than long-term best interests. A *science of religion and ethics* would work to improve individual choices.

SEVENTH WAY OF WISDOM: Develop and adopt a perceptual framework in which pain does not prevent the achievement of a *sustainable feeling of well-being.*

SEXUALITY: That "tribal" propensity related to all elements of the drive involving sexual thoughts and behavior.

SFLIHM *(SUSTAINABLE FEELING THAT ONE'S LIFE HAS MEANING)*: See below.

SHORT-TERM INTEREST: Immediate gratification or satisfaction that gets in the way of long-term goals.

SIXTH WAY OF WISDOM: Know and struggle to improve yourself; work to be physically and psychologically healthy.

SOUL: Within a *science of religion and ethics* "soul" has no mystical attributes, but might be thought of as the "higher" elements of the self.

SPINOZA, BARUCH (BENEDICT): Born 1632 in Amsterdam of Jewish immigrants from Portugal forced to flee by the Inquisition. Because of his progressive religious ideas he was excommunicated from his Jewish religion and all family friends, and any member of the group was forbidden to communicate with him in any way. Worked to understand what the world was really about and in the process invented "conatus," an idea to tie all of human life together in the natural world. This had the potential to bring the naturalistic concerns of religion into the world of science -- but that hasn't happened up to this point!!

SPIRITUAL: In a *science of religion and ethics* no mystical connotations, rather the aspect of human desire to look beyond the mundane that often defines human life.

SPIRITUAL QUEST: Inner drive to find a meaning for a person's life. For a *science of religion and ethics* this involves accepting oneself as a natural being evolved in a natural world having the ability to use symbolic language that enables someone to look beyond their current knowledge and experiences and draw inspiration from that vision. Related to the fundamentalist propensity.

STANDARD OBSERVER: Related to the system established to deal numerically with the matter that colors are seen somewhat differently by each person. Proposed as a model that might be useful for dealing with this issue as it relates to Human Beings as the Ultimate Reference System.

SUBMISSION/SUBSERVIENCE: In the context of the "tribal" genetic propensity, "dominance/ submission" is recognized as a genetic propensity channeling human behaviors in social situations. Simplistically, the dominant lead and the submissive follow.

SUSTAINABLE BELIEFS THAT ONE'S LIFE HAS MEANING: Equivalent to a *sustainable feeling of well-being.* Said of those beliefs that can be sustained under intense scientific study to apply to all human beings at least within prescribable limits. Relates to the issue of the relationship between beliefs and feelings.

SUSTAINABLE FEELING OF WELL-BEING: Condition that exists when a person has a system of beliefs that are congruent with reality, or are able to be changed in order to maintain congruency as new knowledge is achieved. A major aspect of being Enlightened. (See SUSTAINABLE BELIEFS THAT ONE'S LIFE HAS MEANING.)

SYMBOLIC LANGUAGE: A form of communication utilizing words used as nouns, verbs, and other parts of speech making up sentences. Separates human language from the communication processes any other species currently uses.

SYSTEM: A cogent religious/ethical system.

TERRITORIALITY: "Tribal" genetic propensity to stake out some location as a person's own either individually or collectively.

TEN LEVELS OF HUMAN DEVELOPMENT: Proposed path for developing person's full positive potential.

TENTH WAY OF WISDOM: Support efforts to ensure that every child is provided a loving, nurturing environment and all the things necessary to become an Enlightened Person.

THE COMPUTER CONNECTION: Organization utilizing computers to help people connect with others who share relevant interests, needs, or values.

THE KNOWLEDGE BANK: Organization acting as a primary resource to store and make available all information, data, ideas, and so on.

It would be a central resource for the Computer Connection, that might possibly provide the motivating energy to establish it.

THE RADIO LINK: A communication device (such as an implanted radio chip with GPS) that the possessor could use in case of need. [Cell phone!]

THE SCHOOL: Would provide, insofar as conditions permitted, all the resources to help students work toward their own perfection and for the perfection of society as made possible by a *science of religion and ethics*.

THIRD WAY OF WISDOM: Seek to understand. Pursue Wisdom.

"TRIBAL" GENETIC PROPENSITIES: Current human genetic drives such as dominance/submission, us vs. them, territoriality, adolescent brain restructuring, hope, and so on These drives are interpreted as evolving out of those genetically controlled instincts that allowed proto-humans of some 2-4 million years ago to successfully fill their hunter-gatherer niche. These drives are now guided by symbolic language.

TRUTH: Ultimate reality, or objective reality. Not achievable by human beings even though both science and folk religions often propose or imply that it can be achieved.

Truth: Our best understanding of something at a particular time; provisional. Changes with more data. Realistically can only be said about statements, not about things in the Universe in general. Things in the Universe just are. A statement about something in the Universe may be true or false, and to varying degrees. But the thing itself is not a "TRUTH of the Universe." How the thing is understood may change completely, sometimes rapidly.

ULTIMATE: Human beings are as " **ULTIMATE**" as it gets. All other "**ULTIMATES**" are defined and experienced by human beings. They cannot be known to exist outside of humanity. See next entry.

ULTIMATE REFERENCE SYSTEM: That point used by human beings to compare to or to understand everything.

UNIVERSE: See **COSMOS**.

US VS. THEM: "Tribal" genetic propensity to divide all people into an in-group and an out-group.

UTOPIA: For a *science of religion and ethics* not a static, perfect state. Rather it is the state that exists for those working collectively to improve the human condition. A social environment in which people are free to work for change. And those involved would be seeking to improve circumstances for human living. Based on the idea that any conflict between what is best for the individual person and what is best for society exists because of erroneous beliefs. In such circumstances relevant beliefs need to be studied until it is determined what the actual source of the conflict is so these beliefs can be corrected.

WEALTH: Those things that make it possible to live the Good Life.

WAYS OF WISDOM: (See **ELEVEN WAYS OF WISDOM.**)

WISDOM: That aspect of Knowledge that when applied to someone's life increases the probability that they will achieve a *sustainable feeling of well-being*. The knowledge to be able to properly use knowledge.

WISDOM GROUP: Organization set up to help participants apply the ideas of a *science of religion and ethics* to their own lives.

WISDOM NETWORK: Informal connection among Wisdom Groups as they are set up and grow.

"WISDOM" POTENTIAL: The capability *Modern Humans* achieved with the evolution of symbolic language. This state guides human "tribal" genetic propensities (responsible for our chaotic social interactions since genetic instincts no longer control us) toward achieving meme-based dynamic stability.

WISDOM QUEST: See **SPIRITUAL QUEST.**

WISE COMMUNITY: Earlier term used for what is now called an Enlightened Community.

WISE PERSON: Earlier term used for what is now called an Enlightened Person.

NOTES

www.arthurmjackson.com/wpre.html

INTRODUCTION:

[1] *CONSILIENCE: The Unity of Knowledge*, Edward O. Wilson, p. 4, Knopf, New York, 1998.

[2] *GOOD NATURED: The Origins of Right and Wrong in Humans and Other Animals*, Frans De Waal, Harvard University Press, Cambridge, MA, 1996.

[3] VOLUME II, Chapter 18-A, "Ethics, Morality, and Science." (www.arthurmjackson.com/wchap18a.html)

[4] The Naturalistic Fallacy: English philosopher G. E. Moore's term in his 1903 book, *Principia Ethica*, for any effort attempting to get an "ought" from an "is." Considered to be a specious concept by *Science of Religion and Ethics* which works in terms of "if"..."then."

[5] Volume II: Provides additional supportive evidence, information, ideas, etc. for the ideas presented in this volume. (www.arthurmjackson.com/wii.html) To examine the content page of VOLUME II see the final section in this book.

PREFACE:

[1] I use the feminine pronoun to refer to God in order to demonstrate the hidden associations that exist when God is assigned a gender. I hope readers will utilize any feelings generated by this approach to better understand their own beliefs in order to change them if they desire.

[2] *A History Of God*, Karen Armstrong, Alfred A. Knopf, New York, 1993.

[3] Folk religions are faith-based/authority-based systems (e.g., Christianity, Islam, Judaism, Buddhism, Taoism, Scientology, Confucianism, etc.). They are not based on science -- on falsifiable hypotheses -- but like folk medicines incorporate the wisdom of the culture. They are based on supernaturalism, mysticism, and obscurantism; and, therefore, have no mechanism to test that wisdom, except as the life process proceeds.

[4] This term draws from the ideas presented in the book: *The Symbolic Species: The Co-Evolution of Language and the Brain*, Terrence W. Deacon, W.W. Norton, New York, 1997.

⁵   As discussed in *UNCOMMON SENSE: The Heretical Nature of Science*, Alan
    Cromer, p. 26, Oxford University Press, New York, 1993.
⁶   Deacon, op. cit., p. 458.

CHAPTER ONE: Humanity's Goal Now In Sight

¹   *FIRST BOOK OF EPPE*: An American Romance, Roderick MacLeisch, p. 99,
    Random House, New York, 1980.
²   Modern Humans is discussed by Steven Mithen [*THE PREHISTORY OF THE
    MIND: The Cognitive Origins of Art and Science*, Thames and Hudson, New
    York, 1996.] *Modern Humans* having symbolic language appeared over a period
    of time from 30,000 to 60,000 years ago. And in my mind this set us on our
    current path.
³   *Homo sapiens sapiens* refers to the immediate predecessor of *Modern Humans*.
    They evolved some 100,000 to 200,000 years ago out of *Homo sapiens* and were a
    transitional stage to *Modern Humans*, which evolved between 30,000 to 60,000
    years ago as indicated by the rapid transformation of tools and living patterns.
    I propose that modern language with all its elements had finally come together
    and this element lies at the core of these changes.
⁴   It is sometimes assumed that modern language evolved somewhere around
    100,000 to 200,000 years ago. This time-frame is used because that is the period
    when *Homo sapiens* are believed to have begun moving out of Africa. Since all
    human beings have modern language it appears that they must have had all the
    necessary physiological structures for modern language before leaving Africa.
    However, in my mind this seems too early since we don't see the consequences
    I would expect of that achievement at that time. But, another possibility is
    that the various components of the brain necessary for symbolic language were
    spread throughout the species and they were only concentrated through extreme
    selective pressures on a small isolated group of *Homo sapiens sapiens* in Asia some
    60,000 years ago and were then inserted into the rest of the *Homo sapiens sapiens*
    gene pool as alpha males wandered back to Africa from there.
⁵   The term meme was coined by Richard Dawkins in his book, *The Selfish Gene*
    (1976) to contrast with genes and apply to ideas, thought-patterns, actions,
    fashions, etc. that replicate themselves in a culture from generation to generation.
    Dawkins defines the meme as a unit of intellectual or cultural information that
    survives long enough to be recognized as such, and which can be passed from
    mind to mind, and they can change very rapidly.
⁶   LAMARCKIAN EVOLUTION: Jean Pierre Antoine de Monet de Lamarck
    [Jean de Lamarck to his friends] (1744-1829) suggested a mechanism for
    organic evolution prior to Charles Darwin's "evolution by natural selection."
    He proposed the theory that characteristics acquired by habits, use, disuse, or

adaptations to changes in environment may be passed on to progeny. Of course this can't work for genes, but it works for memes.

7 I was surprised and encouraged to find this idea also expressed in *SCIENCE AND RELIGION: A Critical Survey*, Holmes Rolston III, p. 93, Harcourt Brace, New York, 1997: "When natural selection moves into the cultural realm, what is selected is no longer merely genetic mutations, but, more importantly, selection is of acquired and learning-transmitted traits, a notion more Lamarckian than Darwinian." Another reference source more in tune with my efforts is *DARWIN'S DANGEROUS IDEA: Evolution and the Meanings of Life*, Daniel C. Dennett, p. 355, Touchstone, New York, 1996. "It [new memes produced by an individual by joining and altering other memes] is a sort of Lamarckian replication of acquired characteristics, as Gould and others have suggested." And, Dennett helps to clarify that I have reversed Dawkins's intent when he coined the term, meme. He focuses on the meme replicating itself and spreading. I am focusing on the role of the individual in creating and dispersing memes.

8 *THE LANGUAGE INSTINCT: How the Mind Creates Language*, Steven Pinker, William Morrow, New York, 1994.

9 *THE SYMBOLIC SPECIES: The Co-Evolution of Language and the Brain*, Terrence W. Deacon, W.W. Norton, New York, 1997.

10 *THE PREHISTORY OF THE MIND: The Cognitive Origins of Art and Science*, Steven Mithen, Thames and Hudson, New York, 1996.

11 These words were written in the 60s and have been maintained as evidence supporting the principle.

12 Deacon, op. cit., p. 395 ff.

13 See, *GOOD NATURED: The Origins of Right and Wrong in Humans and Other Animals*, Frans De Waal, p. 128, Harvard University Press, Cambridge, MA, 1996. This book helps clarify how these behaviors probably played out in early human societies.

14 Sociobiology has laid the foundation for exploring issues like this. Books like *Sex On The Brain* (Deborah Blum, Viking, New York, 1997) do an effective job of relating genetics and behaviors at a somewhat different level, and more importantly, *Genes, Mind and Culture* by Charles J. Lumsden and Edward Osborne Wilson.

15 Chapter 2, "The Science of Religion and Ethics: Defining Meaning of Human Life."

16 VOLUME II, Chapter 34, "Work and a Science of Religion and Ethics." (www. arthurmjackson.com/wchap34.html)

17 *THE FUTURE OF SUCCESS: Working and Living in the New Economy*, Robert B. Reich, Alfred A. Knopf, New York, 2001.

18 VOLUME II, Chapter 34-B, "The Future of Success." (www.arthurmjackson. com/wchap34b.html).

[19] *CORNERED: The New Monopoly Capitalism and the Economics of Destruction*, Barry C. Lynn, Wiley, Hoboken, NJ, 2010.

[20] *THE ALPHABET VERSUS THE GODDESS: The Conflict Between Word and Image*, Leonard Shlain, Viking, New York, 1998. Also see, (www.arthurmjackson. com/wchap17.html)

[21] I use the feminine pronoun to refer to God in order to demonstrate the hidden associations that exist when God is assigned a gender. I hope readers will utilize any feelings generated by this approach to better understand their own beliefs in order to change them if they desire.

[22] VOLUME II, Chapter 3, "The Enlightened Community." (www.arthurmjackson. com/wchap3a1.html)

CHAPTER TWO: The Science of Religion and Ethics

[1] *The Structure of Scientific Revolutions*, Thomas S. Kuhn, p. 169, University of Chicago Press, Chicago, 1996.

[2] The Naturalistic Fallacy: English philosopher G. E. Moore's term for any efforts attempting to get an "ought" from an "is." Considered to be a specious concept by *Science of Religion and Ethics* which works in terms of "if"… "then."

[3] See: *FUZZY THINKING: The New Science of Fuzzy Logic*, p. 256, Bart Kosko, Hyperion, New York, 1993. Also, VOLUME II, Chapter 17, "Fuzzy Logic and Science of Religion and Ethics." (www.arthurmjackson.com/wchap17.html)

[4] VOLUME II, Chapter 18-B, "What Fuzzy Logic Can Teach Us About Ethics, Morality, and a Science of Religion and Ethics." (www.arthurmjackson.com/ wchap18b.html)

[5] *The Culture of Pain*, David B. Morris, p. 186-187. University of California Press, Berkeley, 1991.

[6] FIFTH WAY OF WISDOM: Strive to make the best choices possible.

[7] CHAPTER ONE: "Humanity's Goal Can Now Be Seen."

[8] See, VOLUME II, Chapter 10, "Science and the Search for Truth." (www. arthurmjackson.com/wchap10.html)

[9] *Language, Truth and Logic*, Alfred Jules Ayer, p. 48, Dover Publications, New York, 1952.

[10] VOLUME II provides the supporting evidence for the positions presented by Science of Religion and Ethics. (www.arthurmjackson.com/wii.html)

CHAPTER THREE: How to Live the Good Life

[1] *COMMITMENT AND COMMUNITY: Communes and Utopias in Sociological Perspective*, Rosabeth Moss Kanter, p. 32, Harvard Univ. Press, Cambridge, 1972.

[2] *THE ASTONISHING HYPOTHESIS: The Scientific Search for the Soul*, Francis Crick, p. 215, Charles Scribner's Sons, New York, 1994.

[3] See: a) *Please Understand Me*, David Keirsey & Marilyn Bates, Prometheus, Del Mar, 1978. b) Also, VOLUME II, Chapter 26 for an analysis of *TYPE TALK: The 16 Personality Types That Determine How We Live, Love, and Work*; Otto Kroeger and Janet M. Thuesen, Bantam Doubleday Dell, New York, 1988. (www.arthurmjackson.com/wchap26.html)

[4] *WHAT YOU CAN CHANGE... & WHAT YOU CAN'T: The Complete Guide to Successful Self-Improvement: Learning to Accept Who You Are*, Martin P. Seligman, Martin E.P. Seligman, p. 95, Alfred A. Knopf, New York, 1994.

[5] *The Culture of Pain*, David B. Morris, p. 207, University of California Press, Berkeley, 1991

[6] *Science News*, "Hopelessness tied to heart, cancer death," B. Bower, p. 230, Vol 149, 13 April 1996.

[7] Ayer, op. cit.

[8] *FUZZY THINKING: The New Science of Fuzzy Logic*, Bart Kosko, Hyperion, New York, 1993.

CHAPTER FOUR: Human Beings Are the Ultimate Reference System

[1] *THE TRUTH OF SCIENCE: Physical Theories and Reality*, Roger G. Newton, p. 176, Harvard University Press, Cambridge, Mass., 1997.

[2] *MEANING: The Secret of Being Alive*, Cliff Havener, p. 173, Beaver Pond Press, Edina, MN, 1999.

[3] *New Bottles For New Wine*, Sir Julian Huxley, p. 287, Harper & Brothers, New York, 1957.

[4] *SCIENCE AND RELIGION: A Critical Survey*, Holmes Rolston, III, p. 34ff, Harcourt Brace, New York, 1997.

[5] *Mind, Matter, And Quantum Mechanics*, Henry P. Stapp, p. 117, Springer-Verlag, New York, 1993.

[6] Roger G. Newton, op. cit., p. 176.

[7] *A HISTORY OF GOD: The 4,000-Year Quest of Judaism, Christianity and Islam*, Karen Armstrong, Alfred A. Knopf, New York, 1993.

[8] *The Universe and Dr. Einstein*, Lincoln Kinnear Barnett, p. 112, Mentor Books, New York, 1950.

[9] *CHAOS: The Making of a New Science*, James Gleick, p. 201, Penguin Books, New York, 1987.

[10] Roger G. Newton, op. cit., p. 212.

[11] *The Structure of Scientific Revolutions*, Thomas S. Kuhn, University of Chicago Press, Chicago, 1996.

[12] Roger G. Newton, op. cit., p. 223.

13 *Looking For Spinoza*, Antonio Damasio, Harcourt, New York, 2003.

14 Antonio Damasio has done important neurological work to show the key role emotion plays in affecting reason. See, *THE FEELING OF WHAT HAPPENS: Body and Emotion in the Making of Consciousness*, Antonio Damasio, Heinemann, London, 1999. Also, http://www.hedweb.com/bgcharlton/damasioreview.html

15 *A Guide To Rational Living*, Albert Ellis and Robert A. Harper, Wilshire Book Co, North Hollywood, CA, 1997. Also, See VOLUME II, Chapter 38-A, "Rational Emotive Behavior Therapy. (www.arthurmjackson.com/wchap38a.html)

16 David B. Morris, op. cit., p. 169.

17 *Man's Search For Meaning*, Victor Frankl, Washington Square Press, New York, 1946

18 Morris, op. cit., p. 170.

19 *IN SEARCH OF INTIMACY: Surprising Conclusions from a Nationwide Survey of Loneliness and What to do About It*, Carin Rubenstein and Phillip Shaver, p. 91, Delacorte Press, New York, 1982

CHAPTER FIVE: Moral Behavior

1 *A Naturalistic Philosophy*, Robert W. Yohn, p. 11, 1450 Larkin Ave., Elgin, IL 60123, 1987.

2 VOLUME II, Chapter 11, "Victor Frankl and the Meaning of Live." (www.arthurmjackson.com/wchap11.html)

3 Victor Frankl, op. cit.

4 Seventh Way: Develop and adopt a perceptual framework in which pain does not prevent the achievement of a *sustainable feeling of well-being*.

5 Discussed in VOLUME II, Chapter 9, "How To Keep A Partner." (www.arthurmjackson.com/wchap9b1.html)

6 *Science News*, "Condition Critical: Is the Right-Heart Catheter Dangerous?" Kathleen Fackelmann, p. 376, Science Service, Washington, D.C., Vol. 150, 14 December 1996. In this example propensity scores have been used to study the value of right-heart catheter usage.

7 *PERSONAL DESTINIES: A Philosophy of Ethical Individualism*, David L. Norton, p. 158-215, Princeton University Press, Princeton, 1976.

8 VOLUME II, Chapter 24, "What We Can Learn From Studying Folk Religions." (www.arthurmjackson.com/wchap24a.html)

CHAPTER SIX: The Enlightened Person

1 Antonio Damasio: A neurobiologist doing research on understanding the neural systems that serve memory, language, emotion, and decision making. Has done

important neurological work to show the key role emotion plays in affecting reason. See *"DESCARTES' ERROR: Emotion, Reason, and the Human Brain.* Putnam, NY, 1994, 312 pages.

2   Sixth Way of Wisdom -- Know and endeavor to improve yourself; work to be physically and psychologically healthy.

3   *Nineteen Eighty-Four*, George Orwell, New American Library, New York, 1981. A science-fiction novel wherein Big Brother has every individual under constant observation and any sign of deviance, or independent thinking is overcome by re-programming the person.

4   *San Jose Mercury News*, "Iranian Cleric Reaffirms Death Decree," (for Salman Rushdie) p. 22A, San Jose, CA, 14 February 1998. Etc.

5   *Humanist In Canada*, "Active Humanism," Roy Brown, p. 19, Ottawa, Ontario, Canada, Summer 2001.

6   Fifth Way of Wisdom-- Strive to make the best choices possible.

7   Determinism accepts the idea that choices are caused. However, a common assumption attributed to determinism is that because choices are caused, they are predestined. There is nothing the individual can do to change their behavior; i.e., predestination/ fatalism describe human choice. *Science of religion and ethics* rejects this assumption for several reasons including the ideas of chaos theory.

8   See, *FOR YOUR OWN GOOD: Hidden Cruelty in Child-Rearing and the Roots of Violence*, Alice Miller, translated by Hildegarde and Hunter Hannum, Farrar-Straus-Giroux, New York, 1983.

9   *Cell 2455, Death Row*, Caryl Chessman, p. 353, Prentice-Hall, New York, 1954.

10   Alice Miller, *ibid.*

11   VOLUME II, Chapter 22, "A Close Look at the Criminal Justice System." (www.arthurmjackson.com/wchap22.html)

12   VOLUME II, Chapter 23, "Human Centered Treatment Programs." (www. arthurmjackson.com/wchap23.html)

13   *Healing And The Mind*, Bill Moyers, p. 121-122, Doubleday, New York, 1993.

14   For an in-depth presentation incorporating current research and thinking on this matter, see *The Astonishing Hypothesis*, Francis Crick, Charles Scribner's Sons, New York, 1994.

15   *The Universe And Dr. Einstein*, Lincoln Kinnear Barnett, p. 113, Mentor Books, New York, 1950.

16   Ibid., p. 113.

17   Ibid., p. 114.

18   *The Culture Of Pain*, David B. Morris, op. cit., p. 274, University of California Press, Berkeley, 1991.

19   *The Psychology Of Abnormal People With Educational Application*, John J.B. Morgan, p. 353, Longmans, New York, 1957.

[20] Crick, op. cit., examines some of the key issues relevant to understanding awareness. It is my assumption that future science will totally clarify this phenomenon.

[21] *ANIMAL MINDS: Beyond Cognition to Consciousness*, Donald R. Griffin, University of Chicago Press, Chicago, 1992.

[22] *NEUROPHILOSOPHY: Toward A Unified Science of the Mind-Brain*, Patricia Smith Churchland, The MIT Press, Cambridge, MA, 1986.

[23] Bill Moyers, op. cit., p. 122.

[24] WAYS OF WISDOM:

[25] 1. Recognize that human beings are for us the ultimate reference system.

[26] 2. Endeavor to maintain and develop the human species. Support efforts to develop Enlightened Communities.

[27] 3. Seek to understand. Pursue Wisdom.

[28] 4. Recognize that all knowledge rests on faith/beliefs and must always be open to questioning.

[29] 5. Strive to make the best choices possible.

[30] 6. Know and struggle to improve yourself; work to be physically and psychologically healthy.

[31] 7. Develop and adopt a perceptual framework in which pain does not prevent the achievement of a *sustainable belief that your life has meaning*.

[32] 8. Help and be helped by other people.

[33] 9. Work to increase knowledge and all creative and artistic endeavors. Adopt an inspiring life goal.

[34] 10. Support efforts to ensure that every child is provided a loving, nurturing environment and all the things necessary to become an Enlightened Person.

[35] 11. Make of your life a spiritual quest. Work to become an Enlightened Person. Use the fundamentalist propensity to produce Enlightened Communities.

[36] VOLUME II, Chapter 34-B, "The Future of Success." (www.arthurmjackson.com/wchap34b.html)

[37] Seventh Way: Develop and adopt a perceptual framework such that pain does not prevent the achievement of a *sustainable feeling that one's life has meaning*.

CHAPTER SEVEN: The Enlightened Community

[1] VOLUME II, Chapter 3-A, "The Enlightened Community." (www.arthurmjackson.com/wchap3a1.html)

[2] *The Good Society*, Walter Lippmann, Grosset & Dunlap, New York, 1943.

[3] *THE GOOD SOCIETY: The Human Agenda*, John Kenneth Galabraith, Houghton Mifflin Co., Boston, 1996.

[4] *COMMITMENT AND COMMUNITY: Communes and Utopias in Sociological Perspective*, Rosabeth Moss Kanter, Harvard University Press, Cambridge, 1972.

5   *DARWIN'S DANGEROUS IDEA: Evolution and the Meaning of Life,"* Daniel
    C. Dennett, p. 473, Touchstone, New York, 1995. Here Dennett refers to a
    useful article for understanding the Hutterites, by David Sloan Wilson and
    Elliot Sober. ("Re-introducing Group Selection to Human Behavior Sciences,"
    in *Behavioral, And Brain Sciences*, Vol. 17, pp 585-608).

6   *The Journal Of Individual Psychology*, "Social Interest, the Individual, and
    Society: Practical and Theoretical Considerations," Guy J. Manaster, Zeynep
    Cemalcilar, and Mary Knill; p. 110, Published by the University of Texas Press,
    Austin Texas, For the North American Society of Adlerian Psychology, Vol. 59,
    Number 2, Summer 2003.

7   Volume II, Chapter 1, "Levels of Membership in a Wisdom Group." (www.
    arthurmjackson.com/wchap1a.html)

CHAPTER NINE: SECOND WAY OF WISDOM: Endeavor to maintain and develop the human species. Support efforts to develop Enlightened Communities.

1   Superstar Christopher Reeves (Superman) became a paraplegic due to a horse
    riding accident. He thereafter focused his life, ability, and energy with the
    help of his loving wife, Dana, towards supporting efforts to find cures for
    this condition. (This issue is discussed in more detail in the Seventh Way of
    Wisdom.)

2   *Engines Of Creation*, K. Eric Drexler, Anchor Press/Doubleday, Garden City,
    NY, 1986. This book presents exciting ideas about nanotechnology and how
    science can make every person "rich," or misusing this power can make earth a
    barren desert or worse.

3   VOLUME II, Chapter 14.A, "Bionomics: Economics and the Enlightened
    Community." (www.arthurmjackson.com/wchap14a.html)

4   *Future Of Success*, Robert Reich, New York: Alfred A. Knopf, 2001

5   VOLUME II, Chapter 28, "Managing Change In an Enlightened Community."
    (www.arthurmjackson.com/wchap28.html)

6   See Chapter 20, Organization to Enhance the Quality of Human Life.

7   VOLUME II, Chapter 19, "The Knowledge Bank and an Enlightened
    Community." (www.arthurmjackson.com/wchap19.html)

8   VOLUME II, Chapter 32, "Science for Everyone." (www.arthurmjackson.com/
    wchap32.html)

9   *UNION NOW*, Clarence K. Streit, Harper & Brothers, New York, 1949.

10 *BIONOMICS: The Inevitability of Capitalism*, Michael Rothschild, Henry Holt,
    New York, 1990.

11 VOLUME II, Chapter 25.A, "A Universal Language and the Science of Religion
    and Ethics." (www.arthurmjackson.com/wchap25a.html)

CHAPTER ELEVEN: FOURTH WAY OF WISDOM: Recognize that all knowledge rests on faith/beliefs and must always be open to questioning.

1   URL for Bill Schultz: http://www.agnostic.org, c. 1999.
2   URL for Thomas Henry Huxley page: http://www.vbooks.org/free/THHuxley/coll_essays_5/Agnosticism.html
3   *Fundamentalisms Observed*, Edited by Martin E. Marty and R. Scott, University of Chicago Press, Chicago, 1991.
4   Martin E. Marty and R. Scott Appleby, ibid, p. 9.
5   VOLUME II, Chapter 10, "Science and the Search for Truth." (www.arthurmjackson.com/wchap10.html)
6   *The Structure Of Scientific Revolutions*, Thomas S. Kuhn, University of Chicago Press, Chicago, 1996.
7   Edward O. Wilson points out the importance of this idea in his book, *CONSILIENCE: The Unity of Knowledge*, Knopf, New York, 1998.
8   Kuhn, op.cit, p. 170.
9   *The Culture Of Pain*, David B. Morris, p. 112, University of California Press, Berkeley, 1991.
10 "Science is its own master and recognizes no authority beyond its confines." *The Rise Of Scientific Philosophy*, Hans Reichenbach, p. 214, University of California Press, Berkeley, 1951.
11 *THE UNIVERSE, THE ELEVENTH DIMENSION, AND EVERYTHING: What We Know and How We Know It*, Richard Morris, p. 164, Four Walls Eight Windows, New York, 1999.
12 Richard Morris, ibid, p. 184.
13 Richard Morris, ibid, p. 10.
14 *THE TRUTH OF SCIENCE: Physical Theories and Reality*, Roger G. Newton, p. 203, Harvard University Press Cambridge, MA, 1997.
15 Hans Reichenbach, op. cit., p. 203.
16 Hans Reichenbach, ibid, p. 326.
17 Reichenbach, ibid, p. 324.
18 *The Art And Practice Of Loving*, Frank Andrews, p. 208, G.P. Putnam's Sons, New York, 1991.

CHAPTER TWELVE: FIFTH WAY OF WISDOM: Strive to make the best choices possible.

1   Predestination/fatalism: everything we do is already known and determined by an all-knowing God, or the Laws of the Universe; there is nothing that can be done to change one's choices.

² *Culture Of Pain*, David B. Morris, op. cit., p. 185, University of California Press, Berkeley, 1991.

CHAPTER THIRTEEN: SIXTH WAY OF WISDOM: Know and struggle to improve yourself; work to be physically and psychologically healthy.

¹ *YOU'RE NOT WHAT I EXPECTED: Love After The Romance Has Ended*, Polly Young-Eisendrath, p. 135, Fromm, New York, 1997.
² *A Guide To Rational Living*, Albert Ellis and Robert A. Harper, Wilshire Book Co., No. Hollywood, 1997.
³ *THREE MINUTE THERAPY: Change Your Thinking Change Your Live*, Michael R. Edelstein with David Ramsay Steele, Glenbridge, Aurora, CO, 1997.
⁴ Antonio Damasio: A neurobiologist doing research on understanding the neural systems that serve memory, language, emotion, and decision making. Has done important neurological work to show the key role emotion plays in affecting reason. See *"DESCARTES' ERROR: Emotion, Reason, and the Human Brain*, Putnam, NY, 1994, 312 pages.
⁵ *San Jose Mercury News*, p. 9A, San Jose, California, Friday, 22 September, 1989.
⁶ VOLUME II, Chapter 20, "Health, Medicine, and a Science of Religion and Ethics." (www.arthurmjackson.com/wchap20.html)
⁷ VOLUME II, Chapter 19, "The Knowledge Bank and an Enlightened Community." (www.arthurmjackson.com/wchap19.html)
⁸ *THE PROMISE OF SLEEP: A Pioneer in Sleep Medicine Explores the Vital Connection Between Health, Happiness, and a Good Night's Sleep*, William C. Dement, Delacorte Press, New York, 1999.
⁹ VOLUME II, Chapter 36, "'The Promise of Sleep." (www.arthurmjackson.com/wchap36a.html)
¹⁰ *The Interpretation Of Dreams*, Sigmund Freud, translated from the German by James Strachey, Avon, New York, 1965.
¹¹ VOLUME II, Chapter 27, "'Will Power' and Free Choice." (www.arthurmjackson.com/wchap27.html)
¹² Fifth Way of Wisdom: Strive to make the best choices possible.
¹³ *Thou Shall Not Be Aware*, Alice Miller, translated from the German by Hildegarde and Hunter Hannum, Noonday Press, New York, 1998.
¹⁴ *The Journal Of Individual Psychology*, "Social Interest, the Individual, and Society: Practical and Theoretical Considerations," Guy J. Manaster, Zeynep Cemalcilar, and Mary Knill; p. 110, Published by the University of Texas Press, Austin Texas, for the North American Society of Adlerian Psychology, Vol. 59, Number 2, Summer 2003.

15 *A General Introduction To Psychoanalysis*, Sigmund Freud, p. 333, Garden City Publishing Co., Garden City, NY, 1943.

16 *Take Off Your Mask*, p. 47, Pyramid Books, New York, 1957.

17 VOLUME II, Chapter 1, "Levels of Membership in a Wisdom Group." (www.arthurmjackson.com/wchap1a.html)

18 Of course before good mental health can be achieved it will be necessary to define it. I would say that good mental health is equivalent to having a *sustainable belief that one's life has meaning.*

19 *A General Introduction To Psychoanalysis*, Sigmund Freud, p. 439, Garden City Publishing Co., Garden City, NY, 1943.

20 Freud, ibid, p. 467.

21 *Stop Forgetting*, Bruno Furst, Garden City Books, New York, 1949. Plus, the many other writings that are available on this topic.

22 *What To Listen For In Music*, Aaron Copland, p. 27, McGraw-Hill, New York, 1939.

23 *MUSIC, THE BRAIN, AND ECSTASY: How Music Captures Our Imagination,* Robert Jourdain, Avon Books, New York, 1997.

24 *ART & PHYSICS: Parallel Visions in Space, Time, and Light*; Leonard Shlain, William Morrow, New York, 1991.

25 VOLUME II, Chapter 31, "Art and a Science of Religion and Ethics." (www.arthurmjackson.com/wchap31.html)

26 *In Search Of Intimacy*, Carin Rubenstein and Phillip Shaver, Delacorte Press, New York, 1982. VOLUME II, Chapter 5-A (www.arthurmjackson.com/wchap5a.html) includes an in-depth analysis of this important book that provides a priceless resource on the importance of intimacy as it relates to the quality of life including physical health.

27 *Colour Of Love*, John Lee, New Press, Toronto, 1973. Provides the organizing structure for VOLUME II, Chapter 7, "Affiliative Love and a Science of Religion and Ethics." It's research and ideas are drawn on to develop a model for affiliative love. (www.arthurmjackson.com/wchap7.html)

28 Rubenstein & Shaver, op. cit., p. 3.

29 Dr. James Prescott's article "Body Pleasure and the Origins of Violence," examines the importance of nurturing touch. *The Bulletin Of The Atomic Scientists*, p. 10-20, Nov. 1975. Also, see VOLUME II, Chapter 4, "Nurturing Touch and a Sustainable Belief that one's Life Has Meaning" where this material is provided with accompanying analysis. (www.arthurmjackson.com/wchap4.html)

30 Chapter 19, "Organizing for an Enlightened Community Made up of Enlightened Persons -- It all starts with a single person."

31 VOLUME II, Chapter 34, "Work and a Science of Religion and Ethics." (www.arthurmjackson.com/wchap34.html)

³² VOLUME II, Chapter 24-A., "What We Can Learn from the Study of Folk Religions, and Other World-Views." (www.arthurmjackson.com/wchap24a. html)

³³ *The Culture Of Pain*, David B. Morris, p. 161, University of California Press, Berkeley, 1991.

³⁴ David B. Morris, ibid, p. 163.

³⁵ David B. Morris, ibid, p. 162.

³⁶ *Reconstruction In Philosophy*, John Dewey, p. 13, Beacon, Boston, 1948.

³⁷ *UNCOMMON SENSE: The Heretical Nature of Science*, Alan Cromer, Oxford University Press, New York, 1993.

³⁸ Dewey, op. cit., p. 17.

³⁹ *Nineteen Eighty-Four*, George Orwell, New American Library, New York, 1981.

⁴⁰ Chapter One, "Humanity's Goal Now In Sight."

CHAPTER FOURTEEN: SEVENTH WAY OF WISDOM: Develop and adopt a perceptual framework in which pain does not prevent the achievement of a *sustainable feeling that your life has meaning.*

¹ *A Guide To Rational Living*, Albert Ellis and Robert A. Harper, Wilshire Book Co, No. Hollywood, CA, 1997.

² *AN UNQUIET MIND: A Memoir of Moods and Madness*, Kay Redfield Jamison, Vintage Books, New York, 1995.

³ *San Jose Mercury News*, "Studies show rebound by victims of serious spinal injuries," p. 12E, San Jose, California, 20 June 1995.

⁴ VOLUME II, Chapter 29, "How Much Is a Human Life Worth?" (www. arthurmjackson.com/wchap29.html)

⁵ *ENTWINED LIVES: Twins and What They Tell Us About Human Behavior*, Nancy L. Segal, Dutton, New York, 1999.

⁶ Nancy L. Segal, p. 225 ff., ibid.

⁷ Nancy L. Segal, p. 303, ibid.

⁸ *The Culture Of Pain*, David B. Morris, p. 1, University of California Press, Berkeley, 1991.

⁹ VOLUME II, Chapter 12, "The Meaning of Pain." (www.arthurmjackson.com/ wchap12.html)

¹⁰ *Fuzzy Thinking*, Bart Kosko, p. 77, Hyperion, New York, 1993.

¹¹ VOLUME II, Chapter 24.A, "What We Can Learn from the Study of Folk Religions, and Other World Views." (www.arthurmjackson.com/wchap24a. html)

¹² A first order good is something good of and for itself rather than because of its effects. For example, pain is not a first order good. It is good because it helps us

to avoid serious injury and treat disease. Suffering can be good because it helps us avoid behavior that would be destructive to our well being.

CHAPTER FIFTEEN: EIGHTH WAY OF WISDOM: Help and be helped by other people.

1   VOLUME II, Chapter 4, "Nurturing Touch and a Sustainable Feeling That one's Life Has Meaning." (www.arthurmjackson.com/wchap4.html)
2   VOLUME II, Chapter 5.A, "Intimacy and a Science of Religion and Ethics." (www.arthurmjackson.com/wchap5a.html)
3   VOLUME II:
4   Chapter 6, "Love and a Science of Religion and Ethics." (www.arthurmjackson.com/wchap6.html) Chapter 7, "Romantic Love and a Science of Religion and Ethics." (www.arthurmjackson.com/wchap7.html)
5   Chapter 8, "Finding a Partner to Love." (www.arthurmjackson.com/wchap8.html)
6   Chapter 9, "How to Keep a Partner." (www.arthurmjackson.com/wchap9a.html)
7   VOLUME II, Chapter 21, "Living Space for the Enlightened Person." (www.arthurmjackson.com/wchap21.html
8   VOLUME II, Chapter 18.A, "What Other Animals Can Teach Us About Morality." (www.arthurmjackson.com/wchap18a.html)
9   VOLUME II, Chapter 18-B, "What Fuzzy Logic Can Teach us About Ethics, Morality, and Science of Religion and Ethics." (www.arthurmjackson.com/wchap18b.html)
10 *The Fifty-Minute Hour*, Robert Lindner, p. 48, Bantam, New York, 1956.
11 Which is not to say that Communism is always a psychological illness, only that it, like any other dogmatic religion, may function in such a way as to reinforce and build on the individual's psychological defects, or deficiencies.
12 Childrens Sexual Abuse Treatment Program of Santa Clara County. See VOLUME II, Chapter 23, "Child Sexual Abuse Treatment Program of Santa Clara County." (www.arthurmjackson.com/wchap23.html).
13 *COLLAPSE: How Societies Choose to Fail or Succeed*, Jared Diamond, Viking Press, NYC, 2005.
14 *CORNERED: The New Monopoly Capitalism and the Economics of Destruction*, Barry C. Lynn, Wiley, Hoboken, NJ, 2010.
15 VOLUME II, Chapter 34, "Work and a Science of Religion and Ethics." (www.arthurmjackson.com/wchap34.html)
16 *THE FUTURE OF SUCCESS: Working and Living in the New Economy*, Robert B. Reich, Alfred A. Knopf, New York, 2001.

[17] *Ideas Of The Great Economists*, George Soule, p. 207, Viking Press, New York, 1952.

[18] VOLUME II, Chapter 14, "Bionomics -- Economics and the Enlightened Community." (www.arthurmjackson.com/wchap14a.html)

[19] Evolution Institute, P.O. Box 7126, Wesley Chapel, FL 3354.

[20] *Florida Humanist Journal*, "Integrating Evolutionary Theory with Behavioral Economics," pg 26, Vol. 4, Spring 2012.

[21] *Mother Jones*, "Nothing Grows Forever: Why do we keep pretending the economy will?" Clive Thompson, p. 24, "The Last Taboo: What Unites the Vatican, Lefties, Conservatives, Environmentalists, and Scientists in a Conspiracy of Silence?" p. 48, San Francisco, May/June 2010.

[22] *MANAGING WITHOUT GROWTH: Slower by Design, Not Disaster*, Peter Victor; Elgar, Edward Publishing, Northampton, MA, 2008.

[23] *PROSPERITY WITHOUT GROWTH: Economics for a Finite Planet*, Tim Jackson, Earthscan Publications, Ltd, Sterling, VA, 2010.

[24] *STEADY-STATE ECONOMICS: Second Edition With New Essays*, Herman E. Daly, Island Press, Washington, DC, 1991.

[25] *HALF THE SKY: Turning Oppression Into Opportunity for Women Worldwide*, Sheryl WuDunn & Nicholas D. Kristof, Knoph Doubleday, NYC, 2010.

[26] *YOU'RE NOT WHAT I EXPECTED: Love After The Romance Has Ended*, Polly Young-Eisendrath, p. 9, Fromm International Publishing Corp., New York, 1997.

[27] VOLUME II, Chapter 7, "Romantic Love and a Science of Religion and Ethics." (www.arthurmjackson.com/wchap7.html)

[28] Polly Young-Eisendrath, op. cit., p. 109-110.

[29] VOLUME II, Chapter 8, "Finding a Partner to Love." (www.arthurmjackson.com/wchap8.html)

[30] VOLUME II, Chapter 9-A, "Beyond Romantic Love." (www.arthurmjackson.com/wchap9aintro.html)

[31] *Sexual Behavior In The Human Female*, Alfred C. Kinsey, et. al., p. 308, W.B. Saunders, Philadelphia, 1953.

[32] *THE SYMBOLIC SPECIES: The Co-Evolution of Language and the Brain*, Terrence W. Deacon, p. 406 ff, Norton, New York, 1997.

[33] *GOOD NATURED: The Origins of Right and Wrong in Humans and Other Animals*, Frans De Waal, p. 127, Harvard University Press, Cambridge, MA, 1996. Also, see VOLUME II, Chapter 18.A for an in-depth analysis of this book. (www.arthurmjackson.com/wchap18a.html)

[34] VOLUME II, Chapter 6, "Love and a Science of Religion and Ethics." (www.arthurmjackson.com/wchap6.html)

[35] *Peace Of Mind*, Joshua Loth Liebman, p. 72, Simon and Schuster, New York, 1946.

36   Reaction formation: An ego defense mechanism in which dangerous desires and impulses (such as wanting to hurt and abuse others) are prevented from entering consciousness or being carried out in action by the fostering of opposed types of behavior and attitudes.

37   Liebman, op. cit., p. 79.

CHAPTER SIXTEEN: NINTH WAY OF WISDOM: Work to increase knowledge and all creative and artistic endeavors. Adopt an inspiring life goal.

1   VOLUME II, Chapter 31, "Art and a Science of Religion and Ethics." (www. arthurmjackson.com/wchap31.html)

2   *San Jose Mercury News*, Chris Woolston, p. 1F, San Jose, CA, 18 July 1995. This article deals with an experiment in which several tons of very small iron particles were spread over hundreds of square miles of ocean to examine its effects on increasing plant life in the oceans which some believe is limited by the amount of iron available.

3   VOLUME II, Chapter 28, "Managing Change in an Enlightened Community." (www.arthurmjackson.com/wchap28.html)

CHAPTER SEVENTEEN: TENTH WAY OF WISDOM: Support efforts to ensure that every child is provided a loving, nurturing environment and all the things necessary to become an Enlightened Person.

1   *THE UNTOUCHED KEY: Tracing Childhood Trauma in Creativity and Destructiveness*, Alice Miller, p. 25, Anchor Books-Doubleday, New York, 1990.

2   SEE: *The Bulletin Of The Atomic Scientists*, "Body Pleasure and the Origins of Violence," James W. Prescott, p. 10-20, Nov. 1975. Also, see VOLUME II, Chapter 4, "Nurturing Touch and a Sustainable Belief that one's Life Has Meaning" where this material is provided with accompanying analysis. (www. arthurmjackson.com/wchap4.html)

CHAPTER EIGHTEEN: ELEVENTH WAY OF WISDOM: Make of your life a spiritual quest. Work to become an Enlightened Person.

1   The focus of this recognition would be formulated mainly within the Fifth Way: Seek to advance humanity.

2   *THE MYSTICAL MIND: Probing the Biology of Religious Experience*, Eugene d'Aquili and Andrew B. Newberg, Fortress Press, Minneapolis, 1999. (See

VOLUME II, Chapter 37, "Mysticism and a Science of Religion and Ethics.")
(www.arthurmjackson.com/wchap37.html)

3   VOLUME II, Chapter 37, "Mysticism and a Science of Religion and Ethics."
     (www.arthurmjackson.com/wchap37.html)
4   d'Aquili and Newberg, op. cit, p. 112-113.
5   *ROCKS OF AGES: Science and Religion in the Fullness of Life*, Stephen Jay Gould,
     Valentine Publishing Group, New York, 1999.
6   *THE MYSTICAL MIND*, op. cit, p. 205-206.

CHAPTER NINETEEN: ORGANIZING FOR AN ENLIGHTENED COMMUNITY:

1   VOLUME II, Chapter 1, "Levels of Membership in a Wisdom Group." (www.
     arthurmjackson.com/wchap1a.html)
2   *"A Guide To Rational Living,"* Albert Ellis and Robert A. Harper, Wilshire Book
     Co., No. Hollywood, 1997. Also, *THREE MINUTE THERAPY: Change Your
     Thinking Change Your Life*, Michael R. Edelstein with David Ramsay Steele,
     Glen bridge Publishing, Aurora, CO, 1997.
3   "Truth" is the individual person's subjective conceptualization of how the
     Universe works, what is most important, how one should live their life, one's
     life goals, etc. The foregoing is differentiated from TRUTH: A concept based
     on the presupposition that human beings can directly experience God, or
     understand reality (achieve Objective/Certain Knowledge), rather than only
     interpret perceptions.
4   *TYPE TALK: The 16 Personality Types that Determine How We Live, Love and
     Work*, Otto Krueger and Janet M. These, P.286, Bantam Doubleday Dell, New
     York, 1988.
5   VOLUME II, Chapter 26, "Type Talk." (www.arthurmjackson.com/wchap26.
     html)
6   *The Bulletin Of The Atomic Scientists*, "Body Pleasure and the Origins of
     Violence," James W. Prescott, pp. 10-20, Nov. 1975.
7   HUMAN AWARENESS INSTITUTE: Started by Stan Dale. www.hai.org.
8   See, *Unlimited Power*, Anthony Robbins, Fawcett Columbine, New York, 1986.

CHAPTER TWENTY: OTHER SUPPORT ORGANIZATIONS:

1   OEQHL (Organization to Enhance the Quality of Human Living) is pronounced
     "equal." Its goal would be to ensure that the frontiers of scientific discovery are
     being pushed in all areas of science to ensure that knowledge and understanding
     are developed as rapidly as desirable.

2 Ninth Way of Wisdom: Work to increase knowledge and all creative and artistic endeavors. Adopt an inspiring life goal. Second Way of Wisdom: Seek to maintain and develop humanity. Third Way of Wisdom: Seek to understand. Pursue knowledge and Wisdom.

3 VOLUME II, Chapter 32, "Science for Everyone." (www.arthurmjackson.com/wchap32.html)

4 Uncommon Sense, Alan Cromer, p. 148, Oxford University Press, New York, 1993.

5 NIRIUA-I (New Ideas, Revolutionary Insights, and/or Unique Answers - Institute) is pronounced, "near you, eye." Its goal is to provide a channel so anyone can get ideas into the society in such a way that they can be used in so far as they have merit.

6 Knowledge Bank, a resource of the Computer Connection, having the goal to provide all the world's current knowledge, literature, ideas, speculations, history, cultural information, etc.

7 VOLUME II, Chapter 30, "Education in an Enlightened Community." (www.arthurmjackson.com/wchap30.html)

8 Mathematics For The Millions, Lancelot Hagen, p. 273, W.W. Norton, New York, 1951.

9 In an Enlightened Community what would be considered a "criminal act" would be very different from what is now so defined. See Ain't Nobody's Business If You Do, Peter McWilliams, Prelude Press, Los Angeles, 1996 for some ideas that would help focus these changes. In-depth work with prisoners/inmates would lay the basis for beginning the process to make necessary changes in society.

10 Modeled on the lines of Sisters of the Road Cafe, Portland Oregon. See their how-to book, Dining With Dignity, A Manual For Non-Profit Cafes, $30, 133 N.W. Sixth Ave., Portland, OR 97209, (503) 222-5694, 1994.

11 VOLUME II, Chapter 22, "A Close Look at the Criminal Justice System." (www.arthurmjackson.com/wchap22.html)

12 VOLUME II, Chapter 23, "Children's Sexual Abuse Treatment Program of Santa Clara County (CA)." (www.arthurmjackson.com/wchap23.html)

13 See VOLUME II, Chapter 4, ("Nurturing Touch and a Sustainable Feeling that one's Life Has Meaning") for an essential component of life required by every child. (www.arthurmjackson.com/wchap4.html)

14 The Humanist, Michael A. Pawel, M.D., p. 16-21, American Humanist Association, Amherst, NY, January/February 1995. (Washington, D.C., as of 2001.)

15 VOLUME II, Chapter 5.A, "Intimacy and a Science of Religion and Ethics." (www.arthurmjackson.com/wchap5a.html)

16 VOLUME II, Chapter 7, "Romantic Love and a Science of Religion and Ethics." (www.arthurmjackson.com/wchap7.html)

[17] VOLUME II, Chapter 19, "The Knowledge Bank and An Enlightened Community." (www.arthurmjackson.com/wchap19.html)

[18] a. Chapter 1, "Humanity's Goal Can Now Be Seen." VOLUME II, b. Chapter 15, "The Hunter-Gatherer and a Science of Religion and Ethics." (www.arthurmjackson.com/wchap15a.html) c. Chapter 34, "Work and a Science of Religion and Ethics." (www.arthurmjackson.com/wchap34.html)

[19] Sixth Way of Wisdom: Know and endeavor to improve yourself; work to be physically and psychologically healthy.

[20] VOLUME II, Chapter 20, "Health, Medicine, and a Science of Religion and Ethics." (www.arthurmjackson.com/wchap20.html)

[21] VOLUME II, Chapter 28, "Managing Change in an Enlightened Community." (www.arthurmjackson.com/wchap28.html)

CHAPTER TWENTY-ONE: Spreading Meaning – A New Foundation for Civilization

[1] *The Grapes Of Wrath*, John Steinbeck, p. 476, Viking, New York, 1939.

[2] *Reconstruction In Philosophy*, John Dewey, p. 196, Beacon, Boston, 1948.

[3] *In Search Of Intimacy*, Carin Rubenstein and Phillip Shaver, p. 205-206, Delacorte Press, New York, 1982. Or, VOLUME II, Chapter 5-A, "Intimacy and a Science of Religion and Ethics," where this important book is analyzed.) (www.arthurmjackson.com/wchap5a.html)

APPENDIX

[1] *MEANING: The Secret of Being Alive*, Cliff Havener, p. 173, Beaver Pond Press, Edina, MN, 1999.

[2] VOLUME II, Chapter 10, "Science and the Search for Truth." (www.arthurmjackson.com/wchap10.html)

[3] FOURTH WAY: Recognize the importance and necessity of faith/belief.

[4] *EMOTION: A Psychoevolutionary Synthesis*, Robert Plutchik, p. 161, Harper & Row, New York, 1980. The CIE is an organization devoted to international cooperation and exchange of information among its member countries on all matters related to the science and art of lighting.

[5] *THE COSMIC CODE: Quantum Physics as the Language of Nature*, Heinz R. Pagels, p. 92, Simon and Schuster, New York, 1982.

ACKNOWLEDGMENTS

Grateful acknowledgment is made to the many authors quoted herein – where credit is given – without whom this book would not have been possible.

VOLUME II: PREFACE

A NEW FOUNDATION
FOR CIVILIZATION

By Arthur M. Jackson (arthur@arthurmjackson.com
Copyright 2001, 2002, 2003, 2010

If I had been able to consummate my vision, an infinite amount of empirical study would be included, or at least referenced here in Volume II of *A NEW FOUNDATION FOR CIVILIZATION*. This material would have supported every speculation, idea, theory, or suggestion included in VOLUME I (formerly titled: *SCIENCE OF ETHICS: Guide for Modern Humans*). However, for obvious reasons this was not possible. I can only hope that enough material has been presented so that the merit of this project is clear and that others will be willing to tackle whatever area captures their imagination and carry out the study, analysis, research, and integration of the data and its dissemination to the world to make known whether their efforts support, refute, or indicate that some totally different approach is needed.

VOLUME II, by and large, is a first effort to look as deeply as time, ability, and available data allow to determine how congruent all the ideas in VOLUME I are. Congruency supported by empirical evidence is the criterion of success in my mind.

Part of the process for achieving the foregoing goal is to examine seminal books with important ideas deemed essential to a Science of Religion and Ethics, and initiate a "conversation" with the author. Key thoughts from that valuable source are presented and then responded to as if this were a dialogue. This technique has been very useful for me because examining a challenging concept -- over an extended period of time, from various perspectives, repeatedly -- provides a tool for focusing thought more deeply than would otherwise be possible. Most chapters in VOLUME II use this structure though they are in various stages of assimilation.

But in some cases the seminal resources cannot be provided at this time. In these instances the reader will be referred to the seminal document and some general introductory remarks provided. However, the reader would do well to go to the original source in all cases to better understand what is being discussed. At least in some cases what I'm saying may be misleading without the original material.

In an ideal world my responses would then be answered by the author so conflicts could either be resolved or their causes made more clear. At the same time readers' comments, criticisms, suggestions, offers to help are warmly solicited. This kind of back and forth is necessary in order to move discussion significantly forward.

Material is still in the process of being edited, prepared, and transferred to VOLUME II. If you have a particular interest in anything not yet available, let me know and I will give it special attention. Originally this project was focused on creating a Science of Religion, then as a Science of Ethics, and now as a Science of Religion and Ethics.

VOLUME II: CONTENTS

INDEX

The naturalistic desire to experience well-being, intellectual fulfillment, reach the highest of which one is capable. I use *spiritual* not in the sense of the mystical or the supernatural, but rather as looking beneath those realms to understand the yearning that our life have meaning for us.

A

G

N

Printed in the United States
by Bookmasters

Printed in the United States
By Bookmasters